MW01224712

My Journey Through Wonderlands

"... you'll spread your wings and you'll take to the sky"

For Vladimir

With Best Wishes,

Joe & Brenda Rodrigues

Mumbai, 5 Sept-2017

Brenda Rodrigues

Goa 1556

Joe & Brenda Rodrigues

"Osprey", Chorao Island Resort, Belbhat, Chorao, Tiswadi, Goa 403 102 INDIA
jbrodrigues@gmail.com; brendarodrigs@gmail.com;
+91-832-2239898 / +91-83082-50080 / +91-93246-09797

Title: My Journey Through Wonderlands

Author: Brenda Rodrigues

Copyright © Brenda Rodrigues 2012

ISBN: 978-93-80739-37-3

Published by
Goa 1556
784 Saligao 403511 Goa India
Phone: + 91-832-2409490
Email: goa1556@gmail.com
Website: http://goa1556.goa-india.org

Printed by Breakthrough Communication Services, Bandra, Mumbai 400050
at Studio Bahar, Chowpatty, Mumbai 400 007, Maharashtra

THIS BOOK IS FOR
all the friends and relatives who hosted us
during our many travels abroad and in India

Clare & Johnny Arago, Barcelona, Spain

Asha & Dr. 'Bash' Bhasker, Southampton, UK

Sharmila & Sudhir Bhatia, Walnut Creek, California, USA

Yucca & Len Bocarro, Montreal, Canada

Shahnaaz & Farhad Cama, Pittsburgh, USA

Olga & Ivan Caspersz, Toronto, Canada

Vivian & Ariosto Coelho, San Bruno, California, USA

The late Fr. K.V. Devasia sdb, Mon, Nagaland, India

Melissa & Joslyn D'Silva, Perth, Australia

The late Tony D'Souza, Penge, UK

Fr. Wilfred D'Souza sdb, Dodoma, Tanzania

Yolande & Emilio Fernandes, Scarborough, Canada

Nadja & Gianni Fontana, Lugano, Switzerland

Lynn & Jim Fraser, Pencaitland, Scotland

Andrea & Michael Hancock, Perth, Australia

Anne-Marie Hascher, Paris, France

The late Hedy Hausch, East Aurora, USA ...

Rita & Mario Jellici and Family, Tesero, Italy
Mabel & Aubrey Jiggins, Wallington, UK
Fr. Tom Kunnel sdb, Nairobi, Kenya,
Livia Lobo, The Hague, The Netherlands
Debra & David Pereira, Toronto, Canada
Frederick Pitter, Southall, UK
The late Fr. Gerard Prior, Edinburgh, Scotland
Fr. Mathew Pulingathil sdb, Mirik, West Bengal, India
Audry & Bel Rodericks, Girona, Spain
Allyson & Neil Sequeira, Toronto, Canada
Jen & Rod Serrell, Langkawi, Malaysia
Nola & Dr. Sandi Syiem, Shillong, Meghalaya, India
Fr. Joseph Thelekkatt sdb, Guwahati, Assam, India
Fr. M.P. Thomas, sdb, Nagaland, India
Fr. Anthony Valluran sdb, Silchar, Assam, India

And very specially for our children
Melissa, Kerman and Kerissa
Vanessa, Sanjay and Gaia

CONTENTS

ix

FOREWORD

Brenda Rodrigues is a lady of exceptional talent. I got to know her fairly well through her lovely daughters Melissa and Vanessa who were my students at St. Andrew's College. Her husband Joe has been closely associated with our college and our students have benefited from his rich experience in leadership training.

Brenda and Joe are a remarkable couple who have travelled widely both in India and abroad. An account of their travels started with the yearly Christmas Newsletter that Brenda so meticulously wrote and sent us. I was quick to notice that she had a wonderful way with language and painted beautiful word pictures of all the exotic places she visited with her family and friends.

The extent of her travel is indeed breath-taking. She has travelled to about twenty different countries, these include, besides India, USA, UK, Canada, Italy, France, Portugal, Germany, Netherlands, Spain, Gibraltar, Tanzania, Kenya, The Holy Land, Egypt, Dubai, Malaysia, Thailand, China and Australia. There is harmony and beauty in each of the accounts and we are made to see, each place clearly, with our mind's eye.

In the words of Kylie Minogue, I invite you to
'Please fasten your seat belts…

Take a breath and take the plunge my dear
Maybe things you don't know are better
I'll take you in my capsule out of here.'

Dr. Marie Fernandes
Principal, St. Andrew's College
19 August 2011

AUTHOR'S NOTE

"Without a song or a dance what are we?
So I say thank you for the music, the songs I'm singing ..."

This book has taken shape because of the constant encouragement and coaxing of several friends and especially that of my husband, Joe. What clinched matters was the response I received from Dr. Marie Fernandes, Principal of St. Andrew's College, Bandra, to my 2006 Christmas newsletter. She wrote saying that she had enjoyed reading about my travels during the year and suggested that I publish this, and accounts of my earlier travels, in a book, with photographs. She added, 'Travelogues are considered an important part of literature. We will all be proud of you. You must go ahead and do it. Don't forget to invite me for the book release.' This encouragement from a person, who is a Ph.D. in Literature, meant something special to me.

'You must write a Travelogue!' came from Professor Sudhakar Solomon Raj of Wilson College, Mumbai's landmark at Chowpatty. 'It really is a very good idea. You write very well and you have the ability to make the place come alive on the page. Please work on the idea as the project for 2007. I am eagerly looking forward to your book and will be among the first to buy a copy.'

With so much encouragement I took the plunge and began this project early in 2007. By the end of 2008 it was completed, together with another book, which was intertwined with the family trees I had been compiling. However, both books were shelved for the whole of 2009 which found us caught up in household matters that required full time attention. At the start of the following year, both my books were edged out by a frantic rush to bring out the volume on 'Lydia Brides' to commemorate the 92nd birthday of Joe's mum in March 2010. We had taken a decision to make 2010 a 'no-travel' year when we would stay put in India and complete the editing and publishing of both my books, but like many of our plans, this too changed abruptly. Our daughter Melissa's stint at the Corporate Office of Jet Airways in New Jersey had entitled her to a set of complimentary tickets which had to be availed of during 2010. So it was off to New York in May, and to London in July. We scarcely returned before leaving for Goa to attend to house renovations, and then we packed our bags for our first visit to Australia (which had been planned before the New York and London visits came up).

Our priority in 2011 was the Travelogue, and for most of the year we worked on the fine tuning between and during the many trips to Goa. Despite a hundred other tasks clamouring for attention, we managed to get a lot done, but then we left in November to visit both daughters in Dublin and New York, to spend our first Christmas together as a family after years; so of course, one more chapter was added on! In fact, the final manuscript went to over 700 pages. I had the option of going for two volumes, which my publisher was urging me to do. However, I chose to keep to a single book and hence decided to edit and cut down the content by almost 40 per cent. In the process many interesting incidents and descriptions have had to be left out.

As for why I chose to have a song line under for each section: From the time I was a little girl I've always had a song on my lips, often singing to myself in front of a mirror, imagining how great a singer I would be some day. And while in the last year at school, I one day pointed to an announcement of the Christmas and New Year dances that year and told my friends that next year they would see my name there as the singer. That is exactly what happened in 1963! However, my stint as a professional singer with a full 12-piece orchestra lasted for just a little over a year. I stopped when I realised that it was not the life for me. But I continued to sing at parties, weddings, in the office, while working at home and sometimes even when walking out with my friends. So it was only natural that I thought of starting every section with a song on my lips. Most of the songs I've chosen belong to the old era of music and may not be recognised by the younger generation, but then, those were the days when the lyrics could be heard and understood unlike the screaming and repetition of a single line in many modern-day songs.

Before I end, I have to confess that all my writing is done only after invoking the Holy Spirit. If, as I have been doing, I could turn out a one-act play in a single day even when my mind is a blank at the start, I have to credit this to a higher power. Few can believe that even my annual Christmas Bulletins have been written in single sittings, with another week spent pulling it into shape. I truly thank the Lord for this gift together with my photographic memory and also for the privilege of being allowed so much of travel, not forgetting the many wonderful and generous friends and relatives who hosted us on most of our visits.

So taking Dr. Marie's and Prof. Sudhakar's advice, and encouraged by so many others, here then are the accounts of our various travels as far back as I can remember. From 2001, some of these have been taken from my annual Christmas bulletins. This book is not meant to be a treatise on the geography or history of the places we have visited, nor even just a sharing of interesting or exotic information. In exploring new places, I discovered more of myself, often validating many of my personal beliefs and values.

I do hope you enjoy the journeys with us.

Brenda Rodrigues

ACKNOWLEDGEMENTS

"I can fly higher than an eagle,
but you are the wind beneath my wings"

My Grateful and Sincere Thanks to

My husband, Joe
for his invaluable editing, creative inputs,
encouragement and support throughout

Mr. Ramakant V. Pawar
for the cover design, the book layout, but especially
for coming out of his 'retirement' to make time for our family

Mr. Dinkar Salian
who willingly extended his professional expertise at a crucial juncture

Mr. Ankur Gupta
for his infectious cheerful enthusiasm backed by practical assistance

Dr. Marie Fernandes
for giving me the push to get started and for writing the Foreword

Mr. Frederick F.N. Noronha of 'Goa 1556'
for undertaking to publish this book and his
uncompromising insistence on excellence

Mr. Dexter Valles
for sparing time to do part editing in the early days

Durga Arts
not only for their efficiency and speed of execution for the final
formatting but also for the cheerful manner in which this was done

Studio Bahar
for the very personal interest in every aspect of the
print-production of my very first book

Chapter One

1970
MY FIRST VISIT ABROAD – LONDON
*"Yeh patloon Englishtani ... Phir bhi dil hai Hindustani"**

I first saw England in the far distance, from the top of a hill in the village of Dongri, located in a suburb of Greater Bombay. At least, that was what we youngsters were told by an older cousin who had taken us for a ramble. I was just about 8 years old, and we children believed him implicitly. Even as the others turned and continued their walk, I stayed back, staring with awe into the distance, just wondering and wondering.

On the hilltop from where I first 'saw' England, I am in the centre, front row

My friend, Mida

Later, as a young schoolgirl, I would read repeated forecasts in the newspapers predicting that I would travel the world. Living in a family that struggled to make ends meet, we could not afford to think of a simple holiday, leave alone a journey abroad – that was definitely in the realm of the Impossible. It was only after I started working that I went on short excursions to neighbouring Pune and Matheran, and made one trip to Bangalore in 1968. For some strange reason though, one of my school friends, Mida, was quite convinced that I would indeed travel to many parts of the world, and she kept telling me so. Maybe my subconscious mind registered that implanted thought, accepted it unquestioningly, translated it into belief ... and eventually I 'created' a reality which manifested itself in

* ***"These trousers are English ... but even so, my heart is Indian"***

1

my later years. Never had I consciously dared to imagine that I would one day traverse not only the length and breadth of our own country but also journey to exotic lands overseas.

'The journey of a thousand miles begins with a single step.' For me, it all began with a single thought. It was just after my birthday in June 1970, that I suddenly got it into my head that I would like to go to England. Considering how rooted I had been in Bombay, it was a most audacious thought. Though I had been working for six years, I had not saved much, and I recall that my bank account held just a little more than I would need. In those days, the return fare to England on Air India cost me the princely sum of Rs.5,756. (I still have the receipt.) Of course, with two elder sisters, Lily and Mabel, living in England, I did not bother to think beyond the cost of my airfare.

We took off from Bombay on 2 October 1970. It was my first ever flight. I can still vividly recall that long torturous route – Bombay to Delhi to Cairo to Frankfurt and finally London.   Interestingly, my travelling companion in Economy class was none other than the legendary actor Raj Kapoor, who was going to London to collect the prints of his film *'Mera Naam Joker'* (My name is Joker). We got to chatting and he was most impressed by the fact that I could solve crossword puzzles, which I had carried with me to pass the time. He attempted one clue but soon gave up. Instead, he spent the best part of the journey checking out how much whisky he could hold until he reached London.   At some time during the night, he gave up

My fiance, Joe, seeing me off at the airport

this pursuit and generously handed over to me half a bottle of Scotch, though I told him I did not want it. Much later, one of the cabin attendants came to me and said that Raj had enquired if he could have it back for a session with the crew.

As we were getting ready to touch down at Cairo, I experienced an agonizing pain in my ears. Nobody had warned me about this side effect of air travel and it was a relief when the pain subsided after we landed. At the airport, several of us disembarked to use the washroom, and once again, nobody had warned me about the dangers of going to an airport toilet alone, late at night. Of course, they were deserted but I did not think anything of going in by myself. When I came out, there was a local guy (possibly an airport menial) pretending to wash his hands at a basin. What the heck was a man doing in a ladies' toilet?! He had an odd gleam in his eye and a leery smile on his face, neither of which was reassuring. Alarm bells began clanging in my head. I almost froze. I still believe it must have been my guardian angel who grabbed my hand and made me run out without a backward glance. Thereafter I was more careful.

Arriving in Frankfurt, Germany, we learnt that there was a red alert ('highjack' was just entering the lexicon of air travel) at the airport, and no passengers were allowed to alight. Instead, a uniformed official came on board, gave us a disarming smile and wished us a polite 'Good morning'. The next instant, his smile evaporated; his eyes narrowed and his voice had a steely edge as he ordered: 'Your passports, please.' A chill ran through me and I immediately thought of all those books I had read on the Third Reich. The moment passed and I settled back to reflect on the journey thus far.

On the last leg of the flight, Raj, as down to earth as ever, had gone around asking who was not availing of their liquor quota (read 'Scotch'). I do not think he found too many but at Heathrow he was waiting anxiously for a tall, lanky Sikh gentleman who was returning to London with his young bride from India. He was a long time in getting out and Raj breathed a sigh of relief when he finally did, and handed over the precious liquid. My sister, Mabel, and her family were at the airport to meet me. I introduced them to Raj Kapoor who invited us to visit him at Twickenham Studios. We never did get round to going there, but I phoned Raj once and chatted with him and he renewed his invitation to visit the Studios. I had promised to keep in touch when back in India, but did not. I was saddened to hear of his death in June 1988. I still have the card (found by chance in 2008) on which he had written out 'Tel: 892-1621' for me under his name.

At journey's end, I was extremely tired and just needed to sleep, so I dozed off on the drive to West Croydon in Surrey. Even so, we had barely stowed my luggage at Mabel's before we all trooped out on a shopping expedition. London in October was already cold – for me. I still remember on that very first day I bought a lovely red quilted dressing gown for 17 shillings from a shop called Lyons at the Whitgift Centre. Believe me, though I used that dressing gown for over 35 years, it still was in good condition. Because of sentimental reasons, I found it hard to part with, but eventually I did pass it on to my granddaughter in New York – and it fit her perfectly though she was just 10 years old! After she outgrew it, she returned it to me and it is now back in my possession, just a little the worse for wear – which is not at all bad for 40 years of use. In those days clothes were made to last!

It is strange how the first sights and smells of a new land remain imprinted in one's mind and senses forever. Even today, certain things instantly recall my first trip to England, like the smell of hair spray (which was widely used at the time) some of the popular songs like 'No Milk Today', 'Yesterday', and others, which were played regularly on the radio station, flavoured 'crisps' which were quite a novelty for me, to name a few. (Soon enough I learned I had to say 'crisps', not 'wafers', which were used in ice cream, nor even 'chips', which were fried potatoes.)

After relaxing at home for several days doing nothing except listening to the radio and watching TV (during the day my sister and her husband were at work and my niece was at school) I started to make enquiries about getting a job so that I could earn some cash for shopping before returning to India. I hoped I could also make up the money I had used for my trip.

Although I was not familiar with the place and bus routes, I discovered it was quite simple to find one's way around London on one's own, and it was practically impossible to get lost on the streets, unless one were very stupid. There were signs at every corner. So I walked about, explored the neighbourhood, found the Labour Office where I got a card permitting me to work, went to several employment bureaus and registered myself. I cannot remember exactly where I worked for the first time, but there were a series of 'Temp' jobs, some for a week, others for two days, some longer ... I collected my pay cheque from the agency each week and it felt good to be earning something, however little. During lunch hour, I would dash off to the shopping malls, pick up a sandwich and crisps, which I would eat quickly, and spend the rest of the time checking out bargains at all the stores. For the occasional hot meal, I would go to the café at British Home Stores and, to save money, I often stuck to baked beans and chips, the cheapest available 'hot' meal. Sometimes I would treat myself to a pork pie or Shepherd's Bush (simply mashed potatoes and mince). How I did not bloat to double my size with that kind of diet is still a wonder, but I credited that to the accelerated metabolism of youth.

How quickly I learnt the ropes! I discovered that many stores put out tempting deals on a Thursday (when most customers were near broke) but would pull them off the shelves on a Friday, which was payday. Accordingly, I saved my money and scheduled my buying for Thursdays. That is how, with a really tight budget, I did some marvellous shopping. On this my first time in England, the sum-total of my 'travel' was a few trips to London city and a one-day excursion to Brighton. Hence, this account is not so much about places visited as about my personal experiences during the six months I spent there.

After the thrill of being in England wore off, I began to feel very homesick and kept thinking of going home. What held me back was my determination to make up the money I had spent on my fare and have something to show for it on my return. Still, I could not shake off the homesick feeling. One day, while walking through the Croydon Shopping Centre, I chanced upon someone from India whom I vaguely remembered as 'George'. Seeing a fellow countryman, I was so happy that I wanted to hug him, but of course, I didn't. However, he was politely distant, and that was the only meeting with him. Then I saw another girl I knew from Bandra; I thought she would be as happy to meet up as I was, but to my surprise, she pretended she did not know me all that well. Why, I pondered, did some Indians develop ethnic amnesia at the sight of another Indian abroad? Is it any wonder then, that I was thrilled when our friend from Bombay, Cosmas Rosario, landed up in London on assignment from Lintas? We met as often as our work allowed and it was thanks to him that I saw the Oxford Zoo and Madame Tussaud's.

I really enjoyed the visit to the zoo where, for the first time in my life I saw a gorilla. I was awed by his size – he was so huge that his cage seemed to have been built around him! I felt sorry that he was confined in such a small enclosure, but that may have been a temporary arrangement. As the antics of monkeys always fascinate me, I spent a lot of time watching a particularly naughty (and intelligent) chimpanzee. He would clap his hands and get onlookers outside his cage to also clap in sync with him. Then he would nonchalantly stoop down for a long drink – and before one realized what was happening, he would spray everyone around with a stream of water from his mouth. Oxford Zoo was truly amazing – the snake section housed very many different species worth observing, but even an entire day was not enough to make a full round of the zoo.

Had I gone to Madame Tussaud's on my own, I would have baulked at the high entrance fee but as I had not really spent money on any outings so far, and with Cosmas already paying for his ticket, I too laid my cash on the counter. I am glad I did. Madame Tussaud's was absolutely fascinating. As I admired each stunning lifelike likeness I could not help recalling the tale of Michelangelo striking his marble creation of David with a hammer and commanding the statue, 'Speak!' (Thirty-four years later, I discovered that the price of an entry ticket to Madame Tussaud's had taken a quantum leap.)

Two things made an indelible impression on me in England. One was the vast network of trains, all run with clockwork precision. My first sight at Victoria Terminus, of those huge boards announcing Arrivals and Departures astounded me. To a newcomer they seemed complicated and intimidating, but they eliminated the need to ask anyone for information. Moreover, once on the train, there were announcements at every station telling you where you were and when and where to change trains for a particular destination. What made an even 'deeper' impression on me was the London Underground. At times one had to take two or three escalators almost into the bowels of the earth, in order to get to the Tube. I could not believe how deep underground some stations were located – three or even five storeys below road level. No wonder they proved such secure shelters during the War.

My first experience of an English winter (without central heating) was just awful. Every night as I shivered in bed, I would vow that the following morning I would finalize plans to go home, but when morning came, I invariably told myself I would wait another day. Then in December that year, my sister delivered her second daughter, Sharon, at home and I felt quite useless not being able to help much

7

around the house since I had never done housework at home. (As the youngest in a family of seven girls, I became expert in dodging household chores.)

On Christmas Eve, I was looking out of the silent window of my room and thinking of all the fun and excitement back home, when suddenly, for the first time in my life, I saw snow begin to fall. Yes, it was a White Christmas and everything looked beautiful. I went to morning mass that Christmas day. Back home in Bandra, a new dress was a must, but here it made no difference because no matter what you wore, it was covered under a long coat. And, in the strange mixed-up mood I was in, to prove the point, I wore an old short green

With my sister, Mabel, and her family outside their home in Croydon

dress with a long white slip showing at least 15 cms below it. The streets were deserted and there was not even a dead cat in sight. I talked to myself and kicked snow as I walked to and from Church. When I got home and took off my coat, everyone screamed and I could not understand why. Well, with all the static, my dress and my slip had ridden up and had bunched up around my waist!

In Bombay, Christmas evening meant dressing up for a dance, usually at the Bandra Gym, but here, for want of anything better to do, I ended up accompanying Tony D'Souza, who wanted to visit his 'girlfriend' who worked as a nurse and could not wangle a Christmas 'off'. Tony was a friend of Mabel's family, and like me, a godparent to Mabel's second daughter, Sharon. What Tony had not told me was that his friend was working in a mental asylum! Well, watching some of the inmates proved a diversion, but it was also a bit scary, especially because one of them kept following us around and insisted on patting my head at every opportunity. After walking through several corridors and making many enquiries, we finally found the room of Tony's friend, Mary. We knocked and entered to find her in front of the TV in a darkened room – all 'wrapped up' in another guy. That was one present Santa could not have brought Tony! So leaving them to it we returned home with thoughts as unsettling as the heavy snowstorm through which we were driving.

Much could be written about the interesting experiences and incidents in the offices where I worked, but I will mention just a few. When I first started working in England, I confess I had a bit of an inferiority complex, not because of the colour difference but because I thought the locals just had to be smarter. Most often, I was the only Indian among all those whites so I kept to myself and did not mix much, in stark contrast to my livewire presence wherever I had worked in Bombay.

During my six months' stay in Britain, there was a postal strike, which lasted quite a while; one of the fallouts of the strike was a shortage of jobs. My forte, secretarial work, was difficult to find. The only jobs going were for 'audio typists', and I had no idea how to operate a dictaphone. Revealing this fact cost me several job opportunities. Finally I decided on a daring gamble and said 'Yes' when asked at the agency if I could do audio typing. When I went to work – it was in a law firm – I innocently told them that I did not know how to operate that particular make of machine. I asked for instructions and from then on it was easy. In fact, as I secured temp jobs in different offices, which had dictaphones of different makes, I soon graduated from novice to expert.

Wherever I worked, I kept pretty much to myself, concentrating on my typing rather than on the constant chatter of the others in the pool. One day, when I was working at an insurance company, the girls were noisily consulting each other about the spelling of a word and I was not sure I was hearing right. One of them finally looked up the dictionary and said aloud, 'Here it is, w-a-r-n, warn'. Another time they were foxed about a particularly difficult word, and this time, all the girls in the pool replayed the dictaphone tape several times, but they could not figure out where to look for the word in the dictionary – under 'C' or under 'K'. Seeing their distress, I finally piped up and said, 'The word you are looking for is a liqueur and is spelt C-o-i-n-t-r-e-a-u'. They looked shocked that I had spoken and perhaps even more because I knew the word – and the spelling proved to be correct. Then one of them said, 'How did you know? Do you drink?' My response was brief: 'You don't have to drink to know how to spell!' That was the day I shed my complexes once for all.

In fact, it was a reverse culture shock for me to find out that many of the office girls could not spell simple four-letter words – and I do not mean the wrong kind! A further boost came when I overheard a few girls discussing my output. My typing speed was around 150 words per minute and I spent no time in the inane office chitchat which is why, as it transpired, I was turning out ten times more than they were. I guess this did not escape the attention of the bosses who offered me a permanent job with the firm, but I declined.

My last job before I left England was with a company called Beckman Riic, dealing in surgical instruments. I was assigned to work for a pleasant Scotsman named Tony Lodge. When he dictated letters to me, he would spell out every word that contained more than four letters. At first, I thought he was being condescending because I was an Indian and because he presumed I might not know English well enough. Then I realized he was trying to be genuinely helpful, so one day I asked, 'Do you need to spell out all these words?' He stopped and said, 'You mean you know how to spell them?' My response, 'Am I not supposed to know how to spell if I am a secretary?' seemed to stupefy him. What he said after a pause stupefied me instead. Mr. Lodge explained that if he did not spell out the words for the other girls, they would just walk out of the job and he and the other executives would be left high and dry. Hence, all the girls were pampered and treated with velvet gloves – a far cry from the situation back home! Apparently, not many would complete their schooling or qualify themselves for the job before they started working as secretaries. I told Mr. Lodge to just dictate and if I had a problem, I would interrupt him. He could not get over this, especially as one day when he was dictating a letter addressed to a man with a long complicated Polish surname, he started to spell it out for me and I completed it before he could finish. This was too much for him and he wanted to know how I did that. I told him it was simple – one, I went by the pronunciation, and two, I just happened to be good at spelling!

Now even more than before, Mr. Lodge and the other executives would keep trying to convince me to stay on and accept a permanent job with the firm. They offered to take care of everything, from work permit, to even getting my fiancé residency in England – not to forget my

Mr. Lodge, my last boss in the U K pet Dachshund, Kruger, who was pining f o r me back in Bombay! (I still have the letter of the Employment Agency I dealt with giving me a reference and adding that if ever I returned to England they would get me employment immediately.) This is what I told Mr. Lodge: 'I thank you for your offer and I have enjoyed working with you, but it has taken a visit to your country to learn to appreciate my own. I'm going home.' Even this response did not stop him from repeating his offer to me daily.

Chapter Two

1971
PARIS EN PASSANT
"Oh what I'd give for a moment or two ..."

One of my first jobs in Bombay was with Franco Indian Pharmaceuticals Pvt. Ltd., where I worked for five years in the second half of the 1960s. My work involved typing, also in French, on a French typewriter where the placement of some keys was different from that of a regular English typewriter, so one had to be constantly alert. I also did small translations occasionally, so to hone my skills in the language, I enrolled for classes in Alliance Francaise de Bombay. I soon found out that my teacher, Mme. Anne-Marie Hascher, was the wife of M. Antoine Hascher, who was on assignment to Franco-Indian. In the course of my work and my studies, I developed more than a nodding acquaintance with both. In fact, they invited me to their farewell party, and also to see them off on the evening they boarded ship to leave India with their three sons. Mme. Hascher and I continued to exchange letters and when I asked if I could make a stopover in Paris on my way back to Bombay from London, she generously agreed. As I left England (wearing, just for the fun of it, a brown-blonde wig I had recently bought at a sale) I was really looking forward to spending five days in Paris with the Haschers.

From Orly airport, I found my way to the Gare de Lyons where Mme. Hascher was to meet me. She was late in arriving and when she did, I had to tell her how uneasy I became with the far from subtle approaches I had to endure while waiting for her. Mme. Hascher was quite amused and told me that this was Paris, where, rather than getting annoyed, I should consider such marks of attention as compliments. I had to admit that no one actually pestered me, but quite a few were not bashful in signalling their amorous intentions.

We moved to the taxi stand and were entering the first cab in the queue when there was quite a commotion with another driver, way behind, calling to us and gesticulating wildly. I could not follow the rapid-fire French. Mme. Hascher finally alighted and went to speak to the agitated man. She returned calling him an 'imbecile' and other words that could not have been complimentary, before she told me what it was all about. The driver was insisting, nay begging, that we shift to his cab, offering to take us anywhere we wanted, for free. The reason: by my looks, he could tell that I was Spanish and he was so homesick that he just wanted to speak to someone from his country. She could not convince him that I was Indian so she just left him still pleading pitifully. I guess that wig caused a lot of mischief so I left it behind for Mme. Hascher who was happy to have it.

All I had time for during the few days in Paris was a coach tour of the city on a Citirama bus, a visit to the Eiffel Tower, a ride in the metro and shopping – strictly window shopping. Everything was much too expensive and I later told friends who asked what I brought back from Paris, that you could not take even a step without paying '*dix francs*' – and I had scarcely more than that in my pocket!

Something I did bring back – and it did not cost me a sou – was the fascinating story of the Eiffel Tower, named after its designer Gustave Eiffel. He had offered to erect the tower in Barcelona, Spain, for the Universal Exhibition, but those responsible for taking a decision thought it was too strange and expensive a construction which would not blend with their city. Instead, the design won approval as the entrance arch for the centennial celebrations of the French Revolution held in Paris in 1889. The tower met with much criticism, with many calling it an eyesore. Newspapers were filled with angry letters from eminent people, including Alexandre Dumas. Guy de Maupassant claimed he hated the tower, but he lunched there daily, saying it was the one spot from which he could not see the structure!

The Eiffel Tower, made entirely of iron, soars 300 mts into the Parisian skies on the Champ de Mars by the River Seine. At the time of its construction, it was the world's tallest tower but now I think it has slid into fifth place. Maintenance involves applying 50,000 to 60,000 kg of paint every seven years to protect it from rust. I was surprised to learn that three different shades are used to paint the structure – the darkest at the bottom and the lightest at the top! This is to present a uniform appearance to an observer on the ground. Gustave Eiffel had a permit for the tower to stand for 20 years. The contest rules required that the structure could be easily dismantled, and the city planned to tear it down in 1909, but it was left standing as it proved useful for wireless communication; a 24-metre antenna was mounted at the top of the 300-metre high structure. That, in short, is the story of how Paris acquired and retained its famous landmark, considered to be a most riveting piece of engineering art, and still ranked as one of the most-visited monuments in the world.

Now for the last bit of my narrative which I hesitated about adding, but since I've limited myself to just a few incidents I felt I should not omit this one, especially as everyone I recounted it to on my return found it hilarious. I had told Mme. Hascher that I was keen to buy a particular type of bra so she took me to Galleries La Fayette, one of the biggest stores in Paris. The lingerie department alone must have been the length of Boran Road where I lived, and the variety in shapes, sizes, styles and designs had to be seen to be believed. One can imagine how awed I was by this sight alone, because in 1971, Bombay offered very limited choices in a few select stores. While we waited patiently for the saleswoman to attend to us, I ran my eyes over the fascinating display – bras from a size to accommodate a rupee coin to others with the capacity to hold watermelons and larger. Suddenly I noticed the saleswoman bending over the counter and feeling around a woman's breasts. I was just too shocked for words and asked Mme. Hascher what was going on. Mme. Hascher was most cool and matter-of-factly said she was fitting the customer for a bra. I persisted in asking why she was touching her and was told, 'How else will she know the exact fit and style she needs?' That is when I decided I could do without the bra – from Galleries La Fayette. So it was about face and out, much to my host's puzzlement and amusement. However, I could not help thinking how delighted our salesmen back home would be with the perks of such a job. I returned to India on 1 April 1971, cleared Customs and walked out to be hit full on by a blast of hot air. Joe was there to meet me with his new second hand Honda motorcycle, and we wobbled our way to Bandra with a friend following in a taxi with my luggage. I reached home to a rapturous welcome by my pet Kruger, who scarcely let me out of his sight for months after that.

****

More than a fortnight after my return, one of Joe's office colleagues expressed his surprise and hurt that we had not bothered to thank him or send even a token of appreciation to his friend for all his valuable help. It took quite some sorting out: 'office colleague' had requested 'friend' who was a customs officer to 'help' young lady of short stature coming in on Air India flight from Paris on 1 April. Friend claimed he went out of his way to do so. It was then that I recalled, that while questions were being fired at me and my suitcases were being rummaged, I noticed another lady being deferentially escorted out, no duty paid, with lots of luggage that she had brought in! Oh well, it was April Fools' Day!

Chapter Three

1972 ...
GOING, GOING, GOA-N
"Underneath the mango tree ... "

Over the years, people have written numerous articles about Goa, that glorious land of sand, sun and *feni,* fabulous beaches and laid-back lifestyle. It is no wonder then that Goa has become one of the most popular tourist locales today and will continue to be so for decades to come.

I often envied our Goan friends who owned large rambling houses in their *'vaddos'* or villages. Why so many of them still chose to live in the concrete jungle of Bombay I will never fully understand, but I guess the lure of big city life and bigger pay packets was the main attraction. I am reminded here of that oft-told story about a farmer who lived a life of unhurried ease on his sprawling farm. A big city slicker observing him lazing around treated him to a lecture on how he could develop his property and get better returns on it. He went on to advise how he could then invest in more property, develop that in the same way, and thus become a really rich man with lots and lots of money. The villager listened to him respectfully and then asked what he should do with all that money. The educated urbanite told the unschooled farmer that he would then be able to retire and live a life of comfort, doing almost nothing. The villager, with irrefutable logic, pointed out that he was already doing exactly that! Most of us, unfortunately, do not know when we have a good thing going because the grass is invariably greener on the other side.

On my very first visit to Goa in 1972, I was hardly enchanted with the place despite the fact that we were there on our honeymoon. It was the month of May and miserably hot, and we were not used to calling it a day by 7 pm. If we missed the last bus, we would have had a long walk back home. 'Home' was an apartment in the little village of Caranzalem, offered to us by Joe's sister, to save on hotels (we had just about covered the expenses of the wedding and had a little left over for this trip to Goa). Not knowing our way about or any local people either, we soon decided to cut short the honeymoon and return to Bombay and more familiar territory.

Four years later, in 1976, with our 3-year old daughter, Melissa, in tow, and a group of other friends, we had our first real taste of Goa and its native charms. We had discovered that the Fernandes family, keen to cash in on the incipient tourist trickle, was offering rooms in their rambling old bungalow. This was located in Cobravaddo (yes, village of cobras) on the way to Baga, the extension of the already famous Calangute Beach. Lunch, in this holiday home, was a feast we all looked forward to – always a lavish spread of eight to 10 typically Goan dishes in typical Goan tradition. That, I think, accounts for how the afternoon siesta got established in the land of *sussegad*! Joe, who is a small eater, would take portions of just three or four dishes, which did not escape the eye of the materfamilias. One day she took me aside and asked what dishes Joe liked so she could prepare them, as she could not bear to see him starving. My assurances that Joe was more than satisfied with the helpings he took scarcely seemed to convince her. Fortunately, dinner was a less sumptuous affair. In those days, this luxurious holiday cost us – hold your breath – an unbelievable Rs.25 per head per day: Rs.5 for the room and Rs.20 for our meals! The evening bonus was the sit out in the sprawling *balcao* as we listened to the talented Fernandes family playing the guitar and singing their Goan *mandos* and other popular English songs in which we joined lustily for hours. It was a delightful holiday and we made many friends on this trip.

For some, the charm of Goa lies not just in its beaches but also in its historical monuments and relics, but travelling from one place to another could pose a big problem without your own transport. Yet, you can never really get the full flavour of Goa if you have never travelled in an overcrowded bus or in a taxi shared by many. The number of people the driver can succeed in squeezing into his vehicle has to be seen, or rather, experienced, to be believed. I was the victim of one such cabbie who had been paid for 'full taxi' by Joe to take Melissa and me back to Cobravaddo while he was having our car serviced at neighbouring Mapusa. After pocketing the full fare from Joe, he proceeded to collect paying passengers along the way and he continued to keep squeezing in more and more, directing newcomers to sit on the others' laps. Finally, he even accommodated one between himself and the door, while Melissa and I were shoved into a tiny corner with scarcely room to breathe. I am not sure now, but I think we totalled at least 15 people in that Ambassador taxi. Incredible? True!

My introduction to *feni* was a bit unusual. *Feni* is the local brew, made from palm or the cashew fruit. The aroma of cashew *feni* is overpowering, and it is virtually the first odour to assail your nostrils when you enter Goa. For years, I had been plagued with allergic colds and hay fever and would wake up each morning with a running nose and itchy eyes that made life miserable. While in Goa, the lady of the house where we were staying in Cobravaddo suggested that I should try cashew *feni* to cure my colds. And the way to have this was to pour it into a saucer, add a little sugar and set it alight while stirring the mixture to melt the sugar. After putting out the flame, one had to drink the liquid at a gulp. This, I was told, would alleviate my suffering. As I could not bear the smell of the liquor, I declined to try that remedy. There was no way I was going to touch that awful-smelling stuff and I couldn't even stand being near someone who had imbibed it, as the unmistakable smell seemed to exude from every pore of the body. Besides, imagine swigging the stuff at that time of the morning! However, after several mornings of my holiday spent in this suffering, I finally gathered my courage and decided to at least give it a try. Pinching my nose shut, I took a few tentative sips. Lo and behold, after some time my allergic cold actually stopped and I was relieved of that constant sniffling. Now that I had found a remedy, I had only to overcome my revulsion to the smell when putting a glass to my lips – but as with most people who discover *feni,* that did not take long either!

Let me clarify that I am not recommending that all cold-sufferers should try this remedy, because it probably will not work for everyone (not to mention the risk of getting addicted). As for me, I did not get habituated to *feni,* nor did I need a daily dose, because Vitamin C taken regularly can work as well, and my daily allergic colds fortunately stopped. But for those who would like to sample the local brew for non-medicinal purposes, topping it up with chilled fresh coconut water makes for an excellent cocktail.

The ideal months to visit Goa are from November to February. However, if you want to savour the best *feni* and fruits of the land, then the summer months will offer you all this and a chance to meet many people (especially from Bombay), who return to Goa to keep their homes in good repair and let their children imbibe some of their culture.

I have continued to take every opportunity to return to Goa whenever I can, even though I am not a Goan who owns a large family house in one of the many rustic villages. I am happy to have had opportunities to live in Goan villages on three occasions. I know now, that if ever I get rich enough to buy a house there, it will be in a village, with at least one *garafon* of *feni* buried in my garden (to mature).

****

Since writing this piece, we did manage to buy a home in Goa. This is in the village of Belbhat, on the exotic-sounding Island of Chorao, which is a veritable oasis of greenery and peaceful solitude. When the birds (of which there is a great variety, as the island is a bird sanctuary) are not singing their heads off, you can almost hear the silence! And while we do have our garden, that garafon of feni has yet to find a place in it! More about our Goa retreat later.

Chapter Four

1985-1986
NAGALAND NUGGETS
"The Hills are alive with ... "

It seemed like such a rash decision to say 'Yes' in such an impulsive manner to Fr. K.V. Devasia, when he invited us to the Northeast. He was in Bombay for a brief visit, and when Joe told him he was booked to conduct a seminar in Calcutta, he immediately invited him to hop across to Nagaland. Joe's 'No, it won't be possible' was scarcely uttered before I blurted out, 'Yes, and I'm coming too!' There and then Fr. Devasia drew up travel plans, instructing us to take the flight from Calcutta to Jorhat, where he would be waiting to meet us on the day after Joe's seminar – whether we turned up or not! Of course, Joe thought we were both mad, but then he gallantly gave in and made the necessary air bookings.

In 1985 it was not easy to make phone contact with Nagaland, and even letters took ages to reach. We then tried sending a telegram to Mon, which is a small village at the north-eastern tip of India, but the post office in Bandra had no idea where the place was! Well, we just had to trust Fr. Devasia to be waiting for us in Jorhat on the appointed day as he had promised. When we stepped out of the airport arrival hall at Jorhat, our hearts sank because there was no sign of him and because we were in a strange place and did not know what to do next. However, within minutes he came bounding in with his usual exuberance to tell us that his jeep had had a breakdown.

We began the long road journey to Mon with several halts on the way for meals and refreshments and because Fr. Devasia had to complete several errands. From Jorhat to Mon was quite a distance and the ride was not always over smooth terrain! Fr. Devasia kept us entertained throughout with interesting and entertaining stories about the people

20

and their customs. Though he drove fast, he was unable to make it to the border check-post at Sonari before the 7 pm closing time. The barrier was already across the road when we reached and no one was to be seen in the tiny guard's cabin. Fr. Devasia halted the vehicle, pulled the hand brake, switched off the lights but left the engine running. In the darkening silence, the sound was magnified. We impatient Bombay folk were used to honking to wake up the night watchmen and I was wondering why Fr. Devasia was not doing just that. When I said as much he told us to be patient and I was intrigued because there was no sign of life for at least five minutes. Then a sleepy head peeped out of the little cabin. After peering at our jeep, the guard lifted the barricade and let us through with a wave of his hand. Fr. Devasia then explained that anyone reaching the border crossing after it was shut for the night just had to remain waiting till the next morning. However, the 'Don Bosco' emblem on the front of the jeep was the 'Open Sesame' for us. How thankful we were that we did not have to spend the night out in the open because by the time we reached Mon it had become pitch dark and it was freezing cold.

Our first glimpse of the hills of Nagaland in the morning light took our breath away. I remember telling friends who asked us what it was like, 'It's as if God created those beautiful mountains dressed in immaculate foliage and then forbade man to alter any part of it.' I was truly awed by the natural splendour and the greenery all around and I was humbled by my insignificance amidst those undulating and unending foothills of the Himalayas. Fr. Devasia showed us round the simple setup in which he lived and worked and later took us on a tour of Mon and also the neighbouring villages. It was gratifying to interact with the locals who were so guileless and sincere.

The people of Nagaland are far from rich but they are a proud race and will not accept charity or beg, yet there are only two things that they will not hesitate to ask for – education for their children and medicines. Fr. Devasia often mentioned that his small box of medicines was his most precious possession, and I made a mental note of this, because we were keen to do something not just to repay his hospitality and kindness, but also for the people of Nagaland. So when we got back to Bombay, I wrote to every pharmaceutical company I could think of and started a personal campaign to collect medicines to be sent to those remote tribal villages, most of which did not have a doctor or a even a place to buy medicines. The response I got was tremendous, and medicines I had requested began to flow into Nagaland in a steady trickle.

When our visit in Mon ended, Fr. Devasia drove us back to Dimapur for our onward journey to Kohima.   Keeping in mind that Joe was conducting seminars for companies, Fr. Devasia suggested that he also do something for the Salesians while we were there.   Joe willingly agreed and so a one-day seminar was organised for the young students of philosophy and novices at the Salesian College in Dimapur. This was the first time we met Fr. M.P. Thomas, who was Rector of the College.

Joe had been conducting seminars since 1980 but till date I had never attended a single one of them. Listening to all he had to say, I realized what a powerful speaker my husband was. He had indeed made a great impact on those who listened to him and also on me. As we were nearing the end, he came to something of a block in making the group of over 60 participants understand a certain concept he was speaking about: 'Working Miracles' and 'Creating what you want'. I had sat still for the entire day without opening my mouth – till then. I think Joe was as surprised as all the others when I interrupted to ask if I could help clear that point. I started to speak and the discussion went on for some time till we reminded them that we were already late for dinner. As the interaction had gathered momentum, Fr. Thomas asked the group if they would like to postpone dinner (in religious houses, timetables are sacrosanct) for about an hour, rather than break the flow. They all agreed. I ended up speaking for almost that entire hour!

It was this first talk in Dimapur that led to all our subsequent frequent visits to the Northeast.

We left the next morning for Kohima. The name derives from 'Kew Hi Ma', which means 'men of the land where the Kew Hi flower grows' (some say the original name was 'Thigoma', meaning 'the land where all travellers are eaten'!). It is the capital of the state of Nagaland and was once the site of the largest village in the world. In Kohima we visited the War Memorial and the museum briefly.

Due to pressure of work back in Mon, Fr. Devasia had to regretfully leave us in Kohima, from where we took the local bus to Imphal (in Manipur) to catch our flight to Calcutta. The drive took us five hours and the scenery kept changing as our bus, which had seen better days, slowly wound its way down from a height of over 1525 mts above sea level into the plains of Imphal. Joe and I were both wary of spending even one night in any hotel in Imphal after the frightful stories we had heard of tourists having their throats slit for even a paltry sum of money. This was one of the problems related to widespread drug abuse in that city. Especially, and because of this, Fr. Devasia had given us letters of introduction to the Bishop of Imphal.

The Rt. Rev. Bishop Joseph Mittathany, Bishop of Imphal, was in his garden reciting the rosary with the community when we reached, and we joined in. After introductions and a little small talk, we went in for dinner. Joe and I were both tired after our long journey so we were glad when we were being shown to a room soon after the meal. However, only my bags were brought in and we were told that Joe's bags had been taken to another room upstairs. 'My' room was big enough for both of us so we said that it was quite okay and we would share the same room, but they insisted that Joe occupy the separate room upstairs. As we were sharing the toothpaste, soap, etc., we kept telling them that we would be most comfortable together in the same room. Finally, one of the priests addressed Joe saying, 'No, father, we have kept a room for you upstairs'. We were a little disconcerted at first but later amused; we both laughed and assured them that Joe was not a priest and that we had been married for 13 years! It is surprising how often Joe is taken for a 'padre'.

NO HOLDING BACK
"Give me a hand when I've lost the way
Give me your shoulder to cry on"

When we were invited to Nagaland a second time in 1986, we unhesitatingly said 'Yes' once again. Fr. M.P. Thomas, who was to become a close friend of ours in the years to come, invited us to conduct a three-day seminar at the Salesian College in Dimapur. After my 'speaking debut' in 1985, Fr. Thomas insisted that I also be there and of course I was happy to oblige because I loved the thought of visiting Nagaland again. Joe had already agreed to conduct two other seminars in Bandel, Calcutta, and this time he insisted that I too play an active part. After Calcutta, we would be travelling to Nagaland and then to Shillong, so we routed our tickets Bombay-Calcutta-Dimapur-Guwahati-Shillong-Guwahati-Mumbai.

After two very fulfilling seminars at Bandel, Joe and I took the flight to Dimapur where Fr. M.P. Thomas was waiting for us. The seminar was meant only for the third-year students of philosophy, but the others too were keen to take advantage of the opportunity. Joe would limit the group size to 24, which was to ensure that each participant could receive individual attention. However Fr. Thomas persuaded Joe to relax his rule so that all could benefit – and we ended up with over 100 participants! It was quite a feat coping with that big group, especially for the special meditation exercises. At the conclusion of three days of intensive working, with the last session stretching till dinner, we had planned to go to bed quickly as we had to get up before dawn to catch the early morning flight out. This was not to be as there was something else in store for us.

But lest I forget, let me add that on one of our evenings in Dimapur we were happy to see Fr. Devasia. He had driven all the way from Mon to meet us and also to collect the measles vaccine which we had brought for the children of Mon, generously donated by one of Joe's clients, Serum Institute of India. This vaccine, specially packed to maintain the 'cold chain' had been delivered to us by a distributor in Calcutta. Later, Fr. Devasia wrote to tell us that he had all his school children vaccinated, and that year, for the first time, there were no deaths in the area from complications after measles. I believe that when the process was repeated the following year, government officials sat up and took note and initiated a vaccination programme in Mon district ever since. They were happy to report that death from measles complications is now a thing of the past in Mon.

On our last night in Dimapur, whilst we were packing in our room we were told there were some participants who wanted to meet Joe or me for one-on-ones. The queues were unending, and since the nature of the discussions was generally delicate, each took his time coming to the point and we couldn't hurry any of them. Still, we were getting conscious of the lateness of the hour and our drooping eyelids. One of the students had insisted on waiting and being the last to see us both together. You can guess our state by then, especially when he spent the first 10 minutes making 'idle' talk. However, something in his manner told us that this was different. We both realized he had something of vital importance to say, but he could not bring himself to speak about it. By now, Joe and I were wide-awake again though we had spent the entire night without a wink of sleep, and it was already close to dawn. This person, we'll call him 'Denis' for reasons of privacy, sat with clenched jaws in an almost defiant attitude. Though he had a sort of fixed smile when he talked, one didn't need to be an authority on body or face language to see the suffering and hurt he was concealing under this mask. With a lot of patience and gentle leads we were finally able to get him to open up.

The previous morning we had taken one session on Interpersonal Relationships, and Joe had narrated the heart-wrenching story of a near-violent break up between a father and son and how, against all odds, this relationship was not merely repaired, but strengthened. In response to the follow-on question whether anyone present had gone through a worse experience, not a single hand was raised. It became evident that though Denis had not raised his hand during the session, he did have a relationship problem, and had come to share his experience with us privately. He told us about his life as a tribal in Assam, the miseries of his childhood days, and how, because of the inhuman way his father had treated him, he deliberately set out to kill him. Though still a child then, Denis was an expert marksman. The arrow he shot narrowly missed his father's eye. He never repeated the attempt and he never again communicated with his father.

This was the first time we had come across someone with an experience worse than the one Joe had related. All through the telling of it, we sensed the pain, the guilt and the deep hurt he was carrying for so many years, which showed in his face and his eyes, in the way he was sitting and speaking. There was an exhausted silence. My immediate impulse was to reach out and embrace him. Then 'Reason' intervened – here was a person studying to dedicate his life to a higher purpose; he was a male; from a totally different culture – how might he react to a strange woman holding him, even with her husband present? I stupidly allowed myself to be held back. Only words trickled out, but they served their purpose. Denis made a commitment to bridge the broken relationship with his father the next time he went home. He left, comforted but dry-eyed. I left, regretting that I had not followed my impulse which, I realize, would have allowed Denis to let go and let his tears wash away the past in a torrent of healing renewal. It was almost five in the morning. We packed in a daze, and still in a daze, said our goodbyes to Fr. MP who dropped us at the airport and we slept through the flight to Guwahati.

****

For years I was haunted by Denis' pain and the ache of my own holding back. Then I made a firm promise to myself that if ever I was confronted with a similar situation I would act spontaneously. This opportunity was given to me in March 2001 during an Inner Healing meditation when I heard someone sobbing inconsolably. I hesitated for just a second before I went and embraced him and held him close while he continued to weep, and my tears fell freely too in empathy. No words of comfort were necessary as we both communicated in the outpouring of cathartic release. Later I learnt that this person had just emerged from a very traumatic event in his life. After the meditation, participants were greeting each other and I suddenly found him standing in front of me. From the long, shuddering and heartfelt embrace he gave me I knew he had found peace. And the haunting memory of Denis was at last laid to rest.

THE SCOTLAND OF THE EAST
"Let's fly way up to the clouds, away from the maddening crowds"

Had it not been for the resolve I had made, and followed through, to collect medicines for the underprivileged of Nagaland after we returned from there in 1985, we might never have reached Shillong. I was co-ordinating dispatches with spiritual and social worker, Brother Bimal Lakra, and as our correspondence became more personal, he insisted that (as we were going to be in Nagaland anyway) we make a 'small' detour and meet him in Shillong. Besides, we would be there in time for his Diaconate Ordination. Joe and I acceded to his request although it meant three extra days away from home. This spontaneous acceptance of an invitation to visit Shillong brought us in touch with one of the most beautiful places we have in India. One could not but fall in love with it. Shillong struck some chord deep within my being and I remember remarking to Joe that this was one place where I would like to live.

The early morning flight from Dimapur brought us to Guwahati in good time for our onward journey to Shillong, which is located in the East Khasi Hills at an altitude of 1496 metres. Shillong is the capital of the State of Meghalaya, one of the smallest states in India. It has only one tiny airstrip located at Umroi, 30 kms from Shillong, near the Barapani Lake. Only small planes can land and take off from this airport which is controlled by the Air Force. Flight cancellations are a regular feature, because of weather conditions – we must not forget that Meghalaya means 'the abode of the clouds'. I have heard that there are plans to extend the runway and efforts are also on to ensure that the airport will be functional in all weathers, but I would not venture to travel there by air again.

The crisp and bracing air of Shillong, the Tudor-style houses perched prettily on various levels of this city in the clouds, and the absence of our Bombay crowds in this picturesque story-book type of setting does a lot to make you feel that you could be in England. One of the largest golf courses in Asia called 'Gleneagles of the East', is located in an undulating valley covered with pine and rhododendron trees. No wonder the British referred to it as 'The Scotland of the East'! How many of us know that India offers practically the entire spectrum of climatic conditions one may encounter across the globe? My thought then was, 'Why make long and expensive journeys abroad when we had Shillong in our very own country?'

I became fascinated when I saw an unusual costume which the local women were wearing which I found very becoming. It was not a sari but it looked charmingly feminine and graceful. I learnt it was called a *jainsem,* the traditional dress of *Khasi* women. It was basically just two lengths of material, worn over a blouse and half petticoat, each draped loosely on the body, taken under one armpit and over the opposite shoulder where it was secured with a decorative safety pin. I could not wait to go to the crowded market and buy one for myself; I proudly wore it to dinner the same evening, much to the delight of all in the Institute where we were staying. A touch of dark red lipstick gave me the trademark red-lipped look of the betel-chewing belles of Meghalaya. (I realised just how fond the *Khasis* are of chewing this nut, when I heard of the phrase they use when speaking of a person's death, 'He/she has gone to have betel nut in God's parlour'.) I was told that my height and features added to the 'look' and I could easily pass for an authentic *Khasi*. In fact, when we had walked down the street, my husband Joe, to his great surprise, got distinctly dirty looks from the local males who, we were later told, do not like their women being 'stolen' by outsiders – and one can understand why!

Unfortunately, we had kept only three days for Shillong, but not wanting to miss the opportunity of our being there, one of our priest friends in the Northeast had organized a seminar at the Christ King College for two days. And it was here at Christ King College that we first met Fr. Joseph Thelekkatt, who, like Fr. M.P. Thomas, was also to become a close friend of ours. Besides the seminar, and except for that one trip to the market, we did little else, because we had not kept time for any excursions.

We had come to Shillong mainly to meet Bro. Bimal Lakra but we had not yet done so. That was because he was attending a week-long retreat in preparation for his ordination. However, on our last morning there, we were to attend his Diaconate Ordination at the Sacred Heart Church in Mawlai, and were looking forward to meeting him before the ceremony. But by the time we reached the Church it was too late as he had already taken his place for the service in the sanctuary with the other *ordinandi* (those who were to be ordained). The ceremony was solemn, and very long. Midway we realized that if we were to catch our flight, we would have to leave for the airport without delay. As we exited our pew to leave, a priest friend went up and whispered to Bimal. Bro. Bimal in turn spoke to the person in charge, and then leaving the sanctuary, as the congregation looked on in surprise, he walked down the aisle right to the entrance of the church to meet and greet us. The joy on his face was evident even though our meeting was so brief. Nor was our joy any less, and we remain ever grateful to him for cajoling us to take that happy detour that made us inadvertently 'discover' Shillong!

Chapter Five

1986
LONDON – AFTER FIFTEEN YEARS
"The truth is I never left you"

For years after I returned in 1971 from my first visit to England, I kept having recurring dreams of being transported back there, shopping in unfamiliar markets, eating crisps, getting lost and so on. Yes, the call to travel was strong but the finances were low and so we (Joe and I got married in 1972) contented ourselves by taking advantage of every opportunity that presented itself to travel to many regions of our own country, India.

It was 15 years and two children later, before wishful thinking could be translated into serious planning for another foreign trip. Mabel (my sister in England) and Aubrey were celebrating their Silver Wedding Anniversary in August 1986 and we decided to accept their invitation for the event. Early on the morning of 13 August Joe and I found ourselves roaring down the runway in an Air Canada plane, gathering speed for takeoff. Suddenly there was a heart-stopping explosion and in a while, the aircraft came to a standstill. We sat on the tarmac for about 45 minutes with no explanations from the staff, and only conjectures as to what could have happened. Then the plane taxied back and we were asked to disembark amid whispered talk about a faulty engine. I could not help thinking that it was nothing short of a miracle that the engine had played up while there was still time to abort the take-off. I also knew whom we had to thank: Vanessa, our 8-year old daughter! Earlier that night, in the flurry of packing, giving instructions, completing last minute chores and dressing, she had insisted that we all stop and pray the rosary together before leaving. And thankfully, we had done just that.

After an interminably long wait at the airport, with no reassuring information, I grew increasingly cheesed off and upset to the point that I just wanted to go back home. But Joe knew that once home, I would most likely cancel the entire trip, so he convinced me to hang on. I had a paid ticket on Air Canada, while Joe was travelling on an interline ticket (he had a free ticket on Air India, courtesy of his sister who worked for that airline). Air Canada offered to put me on the first available flight out, but I refused to leave without Joe. Our friend, Melissa Hancock, who worked for Air Canada, finally arranged for both of us to travel on Alitalia up to Rome. By then we had been stuck at Bombay airport for more than eight gruelling hours!

We reached Rome exhausted, wanting more than anything else, to sleep. We were handed two meal coupons so we stumbled along to the cafeteria but found ourselves so drowsy that we decided to eat later. In fact, we rested our heads on the tables and promptly fell asleep but shortly after we were rudely awakened and almost chased out. It took us some time to realize that a flash strike had been called and the staff refused to serve any meals, so our coupons went to waste – while we went hungry. The wait at Rome stretched to eight hours, and sharpened our appetites considerably, but just glancing at the prices of eatables in the airport served as a most effective gastric clamp. By the time we thought of the smoked salmon we were carrying in our hand luggage for a friend in England, we discovered it had gone bad, thanks to the interminably long waits at both the airports.

When finally on board a British Airways flight to London we thought the worst was behind us, but at Heathrow, none of the personnel could tell by which airline our luggage would be arriving: Air Canada, Alitalia or British Airways. We checked every conveyor belt, but there was no sign of our two suitcases. Most of the passengers had already left, so we registered a complaint and then went back for a final cursory look. What we saw made us livid with rage. One of our suitcases had been dragged to a corner and seemed to have split open or had been forced open. A middle-Eastern family group was busy taking out items and stuffing them into plastic bags. When we confronted them, asking what they thought they were doing, one of them hurriedly explained that they were just helping to put back whatever had spilled out of the suitcase! By the time we called Airport Security they had made themselves scarce. Fortunately, we got back all our stuff and later even found the second suitcase. The drive to Croydon was a happy ending to that sequence of harrowing experiences.

I was delighted to find that even after 15 years, I could still recognize places and roads, and knew I would be able to find my way around just as easily. I have little recollection now of the Anniversary celebrations except that I did sing 'Congratulations' with the band, and that Aubrey's brother, Donald, drove us all to Brighton after the function, just for a lark. Since it was an unearthly hour of the morning, there was little to see or do so we drove back all half asleep (except the driver!) During the days that followed, we made several excursions on our own to museums, and other must-see tourist spots, of which I shall single out only the Tower of London, which fascinated me because of its rich historic associations. I confess I was upset to learn that the entry fee to the Tower was £8 each! At that time £16 was definitely a lot for us, but we had taken a decision that we would spend our money on seeing places rather than on shopping and I am glad we did just that.

Thirty-five Yeomen Warders (known as Beefeaters) man the Tower. Originally, they provided security for the Crown Jewels, and also acted as prison guards but later (since the time of Queen Victoria) they took over as tour guides, and their colourful uniforms never fail to attract the attention and admiration of tourists. The Tower is actually a complex of several buildings within two concentric rings of protecting walls, which in turn are surrounded by a moat. Some of the many who were imprisoned, tortured or buried here, were Sir Thomas More (who refused to give his assent to Henry VIII's second marriage to Anne Boleyn while his first wife was still alive) Queen Anne Boleyn herself (who was accused of adultery, treason and incest) Queen Elizabeth I, daughter of Anne Boleyn (for her alleged involvement in Wyatt's Rebellion), and even Sir Walter Raleigh, a one-time favourite of Elizabeth I, whom she had imprisoned for 13 years together with his wife and two children. It will be seen that being in a position of power did not offer life-long immunity from a fall from grace. With so many beheadings having taken place there, could it be any wonder that the Tower of London is reputed to be the most haunted building in England? Many ghosts keep wandering about and one such is Anne Boleyn who has been seen walking around carrying her head under her arm and haunting the chapel where she was buried.

The undoubted 'big' attraction in the Tower of London is the Jewel House, in which the British Crown Jewels and coronation regalia are kept. These were formerly housed in Westminster Abbey from where they were stolen in 1303, but fortunately, most of the precious items were recovered soon after. From then on, the jewels were kept in the Tower for safety. We entered the Jewel House to find it dimly lit with only the jewel displays picked out by spot lights, all surrounded by multiple high security devices. The items on display were mainly the regalia worn by the monarchs at their coronations. The most impressive crown on display was the one fashioned for the late Queen Mother (when George VI was King, and she was Queen) in which is set the famous Kohinoor diamond, whose origin can be traced back to the 13th century. In 1850, the British East India Company took the Kohinoor away from India and presented it to Queen Victoria. This priceless diamond is said to bring good luck to any woman who wears it, but it spells doom for a man.

August was ending and so was our holiday in England. Joe needed to return to India as he had seminar bookings so he took an Air India flight back to Bombay. Looking back, I was happy to have seen so much more of London on this my second visit to England. And I was happy that my first to America was about to begin.

MY FIRST EVER VISIT TO THE USA
"And the dreams that you dare to dream really do come true"

When I wrote to Hedy Hausch, our friend in the USA, about our travel plans, she coaxed me to think of making an intercontinental leap in order to visit her. Very considerately, Hedy also told me not to bother about any expenses, but just to get there and leave the rest to her. On 1 September I boarded an Air Canada flight to Toronto. Hedy Hausch lived in a place called East Aurora, near Buffalo, in the North of the State of New York. She had advised me to book my ticket to Toronto which happens to be closer to East Aurora than New York's JFK airport. She had her friends, Hella and Ed Morgan, drive her across the border to pick me up.

Hedy had recently lost her husband, Harold, to cancer, and now lived alone in a sprawling house situated on a vast property. For my first meal there, Hedy had set a beautiful table laid out with the most elegant appointments, and we lunched in grand style. Several tactful enquiries later, I found that she normally supped in the kitchen except when there were visitors. I finally convinced her that if we both wanted to be comfortable, that is where we would eat in future. I also made a bargain with her that I would do the daily washing up; she resisted at first – as I was a 'guest' – but then happily agreed, when she saw that I really meant it.

In East Aurora, I experimented with Indian cooking for the first time and, fortunately, everything I cooked turned out to be not just edible but tasty too. I surprised myself – I had not dared to tell Hedy that I had never cooked before, but she was longing to eat Indian food and presumed I was a good cook. You see, before getting married I did not make the effort to learn how to cook, and after marriage, meals were always on the table without me lifting a finger. I had carried some recipes along with me just in case I wanted to indulge my fantasy of cooking, and my powers of observation as a young child watching my mother cook, had stood me in good stead. Hedy not only enjoyed what I dished up but also saved some meals in her freezer to savour later. This gave me the confidence to know that with a little more effort, I could become a good cook, and that is what I concentrated on doing when I went back home.

In the one month I spent in the States, I met Hedy's wide circle of friends. We went to parties, lunches, dinners, and on many outings, one of which took us across the border to Canada, to Niagara Falls, the second largest in the world after the Victoria Falls in Africa. Of the many Falls, including those on the American side, the most spectacular of all are the 'Canadian' Horseshoe Falls, spanning 793mts with a drop of 51mts. What a stupendous sight it was to see tons of water cascading down endlessly. I was too faint-hearted at the time to think of boarding the 'Maid of the Mist' boat that took one right to the foot of those thunderous Falls.

Later, while wandering round the Maple Leaf Village shopping mall, we noticed a 'Sing Like a Star' sign outside a soundproofed booth. Karaoke was a novelty at the time. There were some going in to sing to pre-recorded sound tracks and having themselves taped, but I was too nervous. Hedy insisted I record some songs, and as she refused to take 'No' for an answer, I sang just one, 'For the Good Times,' which was the first song I ever had recorded, and it sounded quite professional. The original cassette is still with me, and many of my friends in Canada and America made copies for themselves.

On another occasion, we went to the German Club for the Lorelei Dance, which is held annually in October. I was thrilled to meet and be introduced to a real live Sheriff, Tom Higgins. I asked if he carried a gun (like in the movies!) and he responded by graciously showing me his badge and his gun, and then posed for a photo with me, and gave me a kiss and a big hug.

Hedy wanted me to prolong my stay with her, but after almost a month of a laid-back lifestyle, I had begun to miss my own home and family. Though Hedy was kindness itself and did everything to keep me entertained, I knew it was time to go. I left East Aurora with a promise from Hedy that she would visit us in Bombay soon.

CANADA CAPERS
"Who knows where the road will lead us ..."

Loaded with gifts from Hedy, I took the Greyhound bus to Toronto where I was met by Olga Caspersz and her son, Hans, who struggled to lift my suitcases, which were stuffed to overflowing. Olga's brother was married to my sister, Beryl, so that made her almost family; Olga's husband, Ivan, was from Colombo, and as a teenager, I remember thinking at their wedding how tall and handsome he looked. In the few days I spent with them, in the beautiful large home they had built in Agincourt, I saw the Science Museum and several other interesting sights. Time was now blurring though I had not yet reached the end-point of my long trip.

While in Canada, I also had a sleepover at Yolande and Emilio Fernandes' house in Scarborough. These were relatives of my friends, the Hancocks, but they welcomed me as one of their own and I was touched by their kindness and generosity. To crown it all, Yolande heaped beautiful gifts on me and I still have some of them. It was at their house that I met up with Marise Pereira, whom I knew from her days in Bombay. Marise took me to the CN Tower, which is located in downtown Toronto. This communications and observation tower stands 553.33mts high and held the record of being the tallest building in the world – till it was surpassed by the Burj in Dubai. The glass-walled lift that took us right to the top of the tower allowed us to look out as we ascended but I found that pretty scary. My stay in Canada – another first for me – was short, but I enjoyed it immensely.

With suitcases stuffed to bursting point I was ready to return to Bombay. The elderly gentleman at the Air Canada counter was very kind and sympathetic, but glancing at the scales, he said that much as he would like to, he could not accept any bag weighing more than the stipulated limit, as the loaders would refuse to handle it. Evidently there was no way round this one and I wondered how I was going to be able to discard any of my stuff. I was glad that Olga's son, Gary, and his girlfriend, Noella, had come to see me off, so I could offload the excess on to them. My dismay turned to heartfelt relief and thankfulness when this Air Canada gentleman gave me a large carton in which to put my 'excess' stuff – all at no charge. At that moment, I could have hugged him. I really could. Instead I hugged Gary and Noella for helping me, and dashed off to board my flight.

As I entered the aircraft, I was greeted with dazzling smiles and bows from several of the crew. I had no idea what was happening; some asked in a conspiratorial whisper, if it was my birthday, and I truthfully answered in the negative. Even so, after the dinner service had been cleared and passengers were settling down to sleep, the crew gathered round me and brought out a cake for me to cut, to 'celebrate my birthday'. In fact, not just one, but two cakes were cut and distributed and the remaining portion was handed to me in a neat parcel. My first thought was that it must have been my Air Canada Guardian Angel who was responsible for this, but there was no reason for his kindness to extend that far.   It took me some time to figure out the mastermind who had plotted this charade and who also had the pull to ensure it was executed. Evidently our friend, Melissa Hancock (who worked for Air Canada in Bombay) had been upset over the miserable time we had on our way out of Bombay, so to compensate, she stage-managed that special treat for me. It was the only year in my life when my birthday was celebrated twice – once in June and again in September!

HEDY HAUSCH - A VERY SPECIAL PERSON
"Let's just be glad we had some time to spend together"

We were looking forward to Hedy being with us in February 1987, but she wrote to say that she was not too well and her doctor had advised her not to make any long journeys. Hence, she put her visit on hold. Later on, she said she would come to see us in December of the same year. For this special guest, we had our entire flat painted and spruced up.

However, our enthusiasm was dampened and we could not hide our disappointment when Hella Morgan called to tell us that Hedy had taken very ill and could not possibly travel. Months passed and we still waited, hoping for news that the doctor had given Hedy the go-ahead to travel.   Instead, Hella called again in April 1988 with shocking news: Hedy was suffering from a form of galloping cancer and was deteriorating rapidly.   Hella gave me Hedy's telephone number in the hospital but I did not have the courage to speak to her for fear of breaking down. I wrote one last heartfelt letter to her, which she received while still in hospital. Later, Hella told me that Hedy was extremely touched when she read it, but I cannot quite remember what I wrote. Hedy passed away in May 1988.   In spite of the physical distance separating us, I was devastated by the news. I was glad now that I had not deferred my visit to her.

I was touched to find Hedy had remembered me in her Will with a small bequest, and on her deathbed, had orally directed that her very expensive gold Rolex wristwatch also be given to me. It serves (even today) as yet another reminder of her generosity. Hedy had been stunningly beautiful (this was confirmed by those who knew her, and by her photographs, which I chanced to see while I was living with her). She had lived a good part of her life in Macau and in India, and was a close family friend (Joe's family) whom I had met for the first time in January 1980 when she was in India on holiday with her husband, Harold. She remarked how isolated she felt with no news of family happenings. We got to talking, found we were both fond of writing letters, and before leaving, she made me promise that I would keep in touch with her. I frankly thought she was just making conversation so I did not write – until one day I received a letter from her. Thereafter, we kept up a steady stream of correspondence and our friendship grew. She was also very impressed with my writing style and would compliment me often. Hedy was one person who would constantly urge me to take up writing seriously, and though I always made light of it, she continued to encourage me to do so.

Soon after Hedy's death, I had a complex and very frightening dream and even now, so many years later, it is still vivid in my mind. I saw this incredibly huge mansion which I knew, deep within, belonged to me. Yet for no reason at all, I was filled with a paralyzing dread of entering it. This became worse when I saw that the first room was filled with fierce dogs, which snarled and snapped at me, making me too scared to think of setting foot inside. However I felt that I just had to enter and get past that terrifying pack in order to take possession of what was mine, and explore the entire house. I finally plucked up courage and ventured into the room. To my relief I found that the dogs were chained and could not touch me though they strained at their chains. And to my utter surprise thereafter, once I was actually in the room, the dogs settled down into a corner and ignored me. I need not have had any worry after all! However, I was still afraid when walking from one room to the other. Sometimes I came up against a blank wall and had to retrace my steps. In one room I finally found Joe and was happy that I had him to rely on but then he suddenly jumped out of a window and left me again on my own saying he would return (but he didn't) and I had to journey on alone for the time being. Joe's interpretation of my dream put it into a context which made sense. It was up to me to claim what was mine just for the taking (huge mansion) by facing my needless fears of inadequacy and failure (fierce dogs) which in any case would not have been able to reach me and drag me down (my articles were later published in national newspapers). I needed to explore further (writing a book?) on my own … I'm sure any reader could work out the symbolism in the remaining portions. For me, the message came through loud and clear: I should just plunge into writing and in the process I would discover my true potential.

I could not help associating this dream with Hedy who had constantly encouraged me to write. When my articles on Shillong, Nagaland and the King of Chui were accepted for publication in the Travel Section of various newspapers, I finally knew there would no turning back. Thank you, Hedy!

Chapter Six

1987-1991
DETOURS AND ADVENTURES IN NAGALAND
"On my own, would I wander through this WONDERLAND alone?"

Our flight from Bombay to Calcutta on the morning of 11 July passed off without incident. We had no inkling, when we boarded the onward flight to Dimapur that detours and adventures lay ahead. This would be our third visit to the Northeast, in response to a request from Fr. M.P. Thomas to conduct a seminar for their people. This time, instead of the Philosophate in Dimapur, the venue would be the Mount Tabor Retreat House in Kohima. Fr. MP (as we now called him) would be waiting at the Dimapur airport to drive us to Kohima. I forget why, but our plane was diverted to Imphal (in Manipur). This was the first time something like this had happened to us – and to think it was to Imphal, a place we were afraid to visit! It was not just our fear of staying overnight there. We really were concerned about reaching Kohima that very evening so that we could start the seminar the next morning as scheduled. Seeing our determination, Indian Airlines' staff organized a car for us to drive to Kohima; two other passengers who were also keen to reach Dimapur that same night joined us and we were grateful for their company. I was the only lady in the group. Many warned us against the road journey, especially as it was already getting too late to travel.

At any time of the year, it is dangerous to travel in these regions at night. During those particular days of July 1987, it was even worse because the Naga underground militants had recently killed several army personnel, and revenge killings were rampant all round. For this reason, security had been tightened throughout. The army had set up check posts manned by tense and grim-faced jawans all along the route, and we were stopped by the army at least 12 times. On each occasion we were questioned about our identities and the purpose of our journey, and our baggage was opened and examined.

While travelling in the Northeast, we found it amusing at first to be stopped at airports, on our way in and out, and interrogated about our nationality. When asked where we came from, and we said we were from Bombay, the officials wanted to know from which country we had come to Bombay. Sometimes an official would summon me aside to question me further about Joe, and ask whether he was from London, New York, or elsewhere. I would stress that we were both Indians and had lived in Bombay all our lives. Very reluctantly, they would let us go but often we found our host also being grilled again about our origins by some official. Whenever this happened, we just exchanged smiles.

The possible reason for this was the colour of Joe's hair (and beard). It was a bright flaming red, which earned him the nickname of 'Ginger' from childhood. (The red hair in his family has come down from his father's side. This intrigued me so much that in 2008 I actually set out to trace the origins of the red hair in the family, which resulted in my working on several interconnected family trees.) Hence, on our subsequent visits to Nagaland, in order to save ourselves trouble with the authorities, we decided to carry our Indian passports to show that we were truly Indian. Who thought this would lead to even more complications?

So there we were travelling from Imphal to Kohima and late in the evening we were stopped yet again at another security check post. As we were having more than the normally-encountered difficulty in convincing them about our nationality, Joe finally took out his passport to show to the jawan. Holding it upside down, he studied it for a while and then put it away saying we could leave. When we asked him to return the passport, he said he would be keeping it to hand over to his superior officer! After much haranguing, Joe asked to meet his superior and was led to a bunker on the hillside. After due explanations, we were all allowed to leave – with the passport. Thereafter, the two gentlemen with us told Joe to leave all interactions with officials to them. We had one more hiccup. One section of road in the hilly terrain had caved in, so the menfolk had to get out of the car and push it through thick sludge.

Only later we were told that the Nagas, who, as a race, lack any facial hair, are suspicious of, and intensely dislike people with beards. They associated this extra foliage with the military, and members of the underground would not hesitate to slit a jawan's throat! If Joe had been spared this fate, it was undoubtedly thanks to the Salesians of Don Bosco who always accompanied us in the Northeast. But on that journey from Imphal to Dimapur there were no Salesian priests with us, which made it even more dangerous; nor did we have in hand our permits to travel in Nagaland, which our hosts normally arranged and kept ready for us on arrival. Security in border territories is understandably strict. Special permits are required even for Indians going beyond Dimapur, while foreigners are not allowed beyond the city limits.

Fortunately, we reached Kohima safe and sound but it was already dark and the streets were deserted. Our taxi had dropped us just outside one of the Don Bosco Institutions and sped off, and there was not a soul in sight. Luggage in tow, we struggled up the steps of the building till we reached the entrance door, which was locked. We could hear voices inside so we shouted to draw their attention. Eventually someone heard us and came to the door. We were relieved to see a familiar face. It was Fr. Felix Vernal whom we had met briefly in Kohima in 1985. He offered us dinner and a place to stay but we explained the urgency to get to Mount Tabor that very night. Fr. Felix said he would drive us there immediately. I don't know how he could find his way on those winding roads through the thick mist that had enveloped the area but we reached Mount Tabor safely. Fr. MP was most delighted to see us and said that he knew we would somehow succeed in finding our way there.

Though the Mount Tabor Retreat House was located at a level below the town, it was still very cold there. Only the next morning could we appreciate what a beautiful and serene place it was. After the three-day seminar, Fr. MP accompanied us on the drive back to Dimapur airport, and once again we, including Fr. MP, went through the routine of being quizzed by police and army personnel. Fortunately there were no hassles or delays as we boarded the flight to Guwahati.

THE TARRED BEANSTALK
"There's a new world somewhere they call the Promised Land"

Fr. Joseph Thelekkatt, with whom we had kept in touch after our first meeting at Christ King College in Shillong, was waiting to welcome us at Guwahati airport. After reaching Guwahati we left that same evening for Shillong, this time by road. Many had told us that the drive from Guwahati to Shillong was something not to be missed and they were right. The distance of 120 kms could be covered in three hours. Once you left Guwahati city, the drive was charming, with every turn and curve presenting beautifully landscaped vistas. The pineapple plantations covered every free slope, and the variety of summer blossoms made it look as if coloured lights were lovingly placed by Nature all along the route especially for us. As we kept climbing, we wondered, would we find a fairy tale castle at the end of our tarred beanstalk?

Shillong's terrain does not make a railroad feasible and the maze of roads winding up and down over the hill slopes, typical of all hill towns, seemed quite complicated at first. We were put up at the Pastoral Centre, on Tripura Castle Road. A charming old Tudor-style bungalow on the property was retained in its original avatar while a large modern building to house many had been constructed next to it. We were happy to meet Bro. Castellino (whom Joe knew from earlier days) and his pet monkey, Rani. No sooner did she come to sit on my shoulder than she began to inspect my head hoping for juicy titbits.

Fr. Thelekkatt had organized a seminar for young priests at Pastoral Centre. Knowing how much I admired the *Khasi* dress, he made sure that I was presented with a beautiful yellow-gold silk *jainsem* after the seminar, while Joe was draped with a classic Naga shawl of the Lotha tribe. We conducted another seminar for the nuns at St. Margaret's Convent, Peachlands, and their superior, Mother Rose, presented us with a lovely bone china tea set.

On all our 'seminar' visits to the Northeast thus far, Joe was always in a hurry to get back home and declined invitations to visit neighbouring places. However, after this last trip, I gave him an ultimatum: I would not accompany him or help out with the seminars unless he made time to venture further afield on sight-seeing excursions. Thank God this arm-twisting tactic worked – as will be seen from the subsequent chapters.

THE MYSTIQUE OF THE MOUNTAINS
"High on a hill, it called to me"

I was intrigued when we received a letter from a Fr. Mathew Pulingathil, asking us if we could conduct a seminar in October 1989 for his young seminarians and priests at the Salesian College, Sonada (West Bengal). I had never heard of any place called Sonada nor were we acquainted with Fr. Mathew. In his letter he did mention that he was referred to us by another priest. It did not take time for me to find out that Sonada was in the vicinity of Darjeeling, and I had always wanted to visit Darjeeling. Besides, we were ever willing to work with young people, so of course we accepted.

We booked a flight from Bombay to Calcutta and from there to Bagdogra. After lunch in Bagdogra, we drove through Siliguri, in the plains, and up Hill Cart Road to Sonada, in the mountains. We had a mini-adventure when we reached *'pagla jhora'* (meaning 'mad torrent' or 'waterfall') which is a major source of worry to all, especially during the rainy season. As ill-luck would have it, what we had been warned about had actually happened – due to incessant rain, the road near *pagla jhora* had caved in to a depth of nearly 2 mts. Unable to proceed further, we found ourselves at the tail end of a long pile-up of vehicles. Nothing was moving and it looked like nothing would, till next morning at the earliest. After a painfully long delay, with all of us praying, our driver decided to take a daring risk. He manoeuvred the jeep out of the 'queue', and reversed as far back as space permitted. Then revving up, he picked up speed, swung down into the depression behind and shot up the other side at full throttle. I don't know how, but he made it!

Besides several tea estates, a couple of large Buddhist temples, Tiger Hill, Observatory Hill and the Bengal Natural History Museum, there was little else to see in Sonada, which is a small market town, located about 7 kms south of Darjeeling. I remember well how cold it was in Sonada and how I spent every minute trying to keep warm. I did not think twice about refusing the invitation to see the sunrise at Tiger Hill and catch the spectacular view of the Kanchenjunga. I am definitely not a 'morning' person and going to Tiger Hill meant leaving at 4 am. Sonada has also had snowfalls occasionally, which will tell you how cold it could get. Though I took care to wear warm socks and closed shoes during the day, my feet would freeze and feel so uncomfortable that I had to rush out of the seminar hall several times just to soak them in hot water and get my circulation back. And the damp was perpetual.

We met and made many new friends in Sonada, among them Fr. Luigi Jellici, who was generally seated next to me at table so we chatted a lot. The moment meals were over he would be off on his trusty cycle pedalling his way to various villages and we rarely saw him in between meals as we were busy with the seminar. Later, thanks to our continued correspondence, and also meeting up again in Bombay, we came to know each other better and realized how irrepressible, humorous and mischievous he could be. Through him we also met his family later and developed a close friendship with them too.

Our only free day after the seminar was kept for Darjeeling and I was looking forward to finally seeing the place we had heard so much about from our friends, the Gilders. The name is said to have been derived from 'Dorje-ling', meaning 'place of the thunderbolt' perhaps because of the awesome pre-monsoon storms in that area. As Fr. Mathew took us round the town, which still had traces of the old British Raj, I was quite disenchanted to find that the 'Queen of Hill Stations', spread over many levels with houses crowded together, was not as spruce as I thought it would be. Some people had actually built the bathing and toilet areas of their shanties over running streams that continued to flow down the mountains and the water was probably being used by those lower down the slopes. In fact, when we got home and mentioned our views on Darjeeling to the late Dr. Jal and the late Jeroo Gilder, they were up in arms to defend not only Darjeeling but also Calcutta which they had not re-visited after returning to Bombay years ago and so had no idea of how much these places had deteriorated. We hated to be the ones to disillusion these two wonderful people with whom we had more than a doctor-patient relationship, but I don't think they ever believed our version, God rest their good souls.

The Darjeeling Toy Train was one of the charming features of the place. Powered by a steam engine, this little train runs alongside the road for the most part, sometimes on the inner, safer, side of the road and then criss-crossing it to chug along the outer edge overlooking sheer drops to the valley below. This is probably what provoked Mark Twain, who travelled on this train in 1895, to remark, 'The most enjoyable day I've spent on earth is of mixed ecstasy, of deadly fright and unimaginable joy!'

The train climbs from Siliguri to Ghoom, at a height of about 2259 mts above sea level (which makes it the highest railway station, not in the world as some think, but only in India; the highest in the world is the Chinese Tanggula Pass at 5072 mts). From Ghoom it starts descending, completing the double loop at Batasia and going on to Darjeeling. We did not have the luxury of time to travel on that historic train which takes almost seven hours to cover the 80 kms from Siliguri to Darjeeling; the journey by car takes half that time.

In spite of some of the negative aspects I've mentioned, let me hasten to say that we still liked Sonada and the fabulous mountain views. About Darjeeling, I will reserve my judgement for now. Though we had never met before, the week we had spent in the company of Fr. Mathew helped us develop a good understanding of each other and our later associations with him cemented this into a wonderful friendship that continues to this day.

ENDLESS ENCHANTMENT
"We are family ... Living life is fun and we've just begun
To get our share of the world's delights"

Both our daughters, Melissa and Vanessa, were thrilled when we told them about plans for all four of us to travel to the Northeast in May 1991. This was to be the fourth visit for Joe and me and the very first for the children, and we were all excited about the hectic three-week schedule we had chalked out.

Our friend, Fr. Joseph Thelekkatt, was now the Provincial of the Guwahati province, and we had asked for his help in arranging our stay in Guwahati and Shillong. On the very day we landed in Guwahati, Fr. Paul Kootala drove us up to Shillong and kept us entertained throughout the journey. The children were particularly happy as he made them laugh a lot. It was also interesting to know that for part of the way, from Khannapara to Burnihat Bridge, we were driving between two states, with Assam (where there was prohibition of alcohol) on our left and free-spirited Meghalaya on our right. So wine shops were located on the Meghalaya side only – all one had to do was cross the road to get one's preferred poison/tipple! However, as tax revenue was going to Meghalaya from the Assam revellers' pockets, the Government of Assam wised up and relaxed prohibition in the border districts. Although there are wine shops on both sides of the road now, there are many more in Meghalaya, which had an early start. When we passed a bar named 'Stagger Inn' we were inclined to stop and suggest they change the name to 'Stagger Out' instead!

One of the first visitors we received while we stayed at the Mathias Institute in Mawlai, Shillong, were Dr. Sandi Syiem and his two small children, Gideon and Ila. His wife, Nola, was home with the youngest, baby Ezra. Dr. Syiem first drove us to his San-Ker Nursing Home and Rehab Centre (now known only as SAN-KER). This was 'tucked away in a wooded lane on the edge of town that only jeeps can negotiate.' These words are from an article written about Dr. Syiem and SAN-KER by Sanjoy Hazarika in the Express Magazine dated 29 July 1990. It recounted how Dr. Sandi Syiem had had the choice of following up a brilliant academic record with a lucrative career abroad, but he chose to return to his native state and work tirelessly for his own people. After purchasing the land for SAN-KER, he started with just a couple of small converted cowsheds and a few in-patients. As the trickle of patients swelled to a stream, SAN-KER struggled on with the donations he received occasionally and with what the families of patients could pay him. In fact, many could not afford to pay anything at all, so it was extremely difficult to cope, but I guess the good Lord was taking care of their needs.

I was very impressed to learn of the work he was doing and this prompted me to write directly to him in August 1990. Our correspondence resulted in my collecting as many medicines as I could for SAN-KER, and we were all happy to see for ourselves how greatly his own *Khasi* people had benefitted from his dedication. We were told that some of the patients had come there voluntarily and seemed happy to remain there. A few sometimes had outbursts and threatened to leave but never actually did. Unfortunately for some, their families did not want them back even after they were cured.

After doing the rounds of SAN-KER, Dr. Sandi took us to the beautiful home he had built and we were happy to meet Nola for the first time. Joe was particularly thrilled to see Dr. Sandi's bonsai plants all around the large garden; it was evident that he enjoyed gardening and had developed an exceptional skill with bonsai. This first meeting with Dr. Sandi and his family was the start of a long friendship.

We were fascinated to learn of some *Khasi* customs. They follow a matrilineal system where descent is traced through the mother, and the children take her name. According to *Khasi* laws, a woman cannot be forced into marriage and the ownership of property vests in her. The youngest daughter – the '*khadduh*' – carries the family name and inherits the property. (I too am the youngest daughter in my family of seven sisters and one brother, but unfortunately, not in a *Khasi* family!) A woman is also allowed to end a marriage at will and her husband cannot object. Is this women's lib or what?!

Fr. Paul Kootala was our constant companion on most of the days we were in Shillong and he accompanied us to the Lady Hydari Park. The park, spread over four hectares, was an oasis of greenery and colourful blooms, with a lake and a mini zoo as added attractions. We strolled around the zoo feeling really sorry for the black panther that kept pacing his cage in aimless frustration. It was obviously miserable at being confined in such a tiny space. The pelicans were soaking up the sun, lazily stretching out their huge wings and flapping them to wave to us from time to time. We took some lovely photographs amidst all those beautiful flowers in full bloom, and also of the bougainvillea that had climbed up and draped itself gracefully from a huge tree.

Our 19th wedding anniversary was made memorable with eight priests concelebrating mass in the chapel of Mathias Institute. I wore my *jainsem* again and remained in it all day. It was our second day in Shillong and an excursion to Cherrapunjee with Bro. Castellino was on the agenda. On the way, near the Shillong View Point, we saw a sign that read, 'Wear helmets to avoid death'. We wondered if this was a new prescription for immortality! Compared to the distances we were used to covering in the Northeast, the 56 kms to Cherrapunjee was not all that much, yet the drive along winding paths, often through thick mist, somehow seemed much longer than the two hours it took to get there. We had been warned that the weather and the temperature could change quite suddenly, and had we not experienced this for ourselves I would have thought it an exaggeration. Yet, on our drive to and from Cherrapunjee, it was alternately dull, then bright with sunshine, then thick with mist round the next turn and past yet another curve we drove into heavy rain. We kept donning and discarding our warm shawls as the weather dictated. In some places, there were sheer drops to the valleys thousands of metres below. The continuous climb gave the impression that the road ahead disappeared into the clouds and ended abruptly, so that when we suddenly came upon a village we were surprised to discover that human beings existed so far away, and wondered how they got there and how they survived in the back of beyond.

In school, we had learnt that Cherrapunjee had the heaviest rainfall in the world, and that's about all I knew of the place. Now we were learning that it had only one season, the monsoon, as there was not a single month without rain. The average annual rainfall was around 10,870 mm. This was one place where the clouds are known to bring joy to the people and the entire town comes alive from May till September when they have maximum rain. Surprisingly, it rains mostly at night and so it does not disrupt normal daily activities. A little known fact is that Cherrapunjee no longer holds the world record for rainfall. This credit now goes to the village of Mawsynram, which is about 10 kms from Cherrapunjee, and has an average of 12,163 mm of rain. This 'shift' occurred because of climatic changes in the region.

We stopped at the St. John Bosco Shrine, a very old Church in Cherra Bazaar, before driving on through kilometres of eye-straining mist to Shella. From those heights, we saw Bangladesh in the plains below. It was truly a sorry sight to see almost all the land inundated because of the tidal waves and cyclones in early May that year. Further on we stopped at a scenic spot to enjoy our lunch of chicken and chow, but after driving a little further, we decided to turn back as we kept encountering thick mist at practically every turn. Bro. Castellino took over from the driver, while the rest of us dozed fitfully in the back seats.

That evening we went across from the main building to the Tudor-style bungalow which housed a small chapel, a sound recording studio and Fr. Juan Larrea's office. What followed was a delightful combination of good food, good conversation and good fellowship with Frs. Thelekkatt and Larrea, and Bro. Castellino, who joined us later. It was the most wonderful anniversary we celebrated. The following day, Joe's 50th birthday, we once again began the day with a concelebrated mass in the chapel. For lunch Fr. Thelekkatt took us to a Chinese restaurant called "Abba's", after which we went boating on Ward Lake, which was partially covered with a carpet of red lotus blooms. That evening we went to St. Margaret's Convent at Peachlands where Joe had been asked to speak to the nuns. When we entered, a group of melodious voices greeted Joe with a birthday song. After the talk they gifted him with a *Karbi Anglong* shawl in vivid red/black/white stripes and treated us to a great dinner, before we went back to Mathias Institute for our last night in Shillong.

I cannot close my chapter on Shillong without touching on the outrageously original names some *Khasis* choose for their children. Here is a sampling of names given to living persons: Curfew, Skylab, Bus Stop, Hitler, Mussolini, Dirty Face, Birth Control, Full Moon, Ms. Ice Cream, Firstly, Reading, Full Back, Half Back, First Gear, Second Gear, Third Gear, Gear Box (all in one family, with three boys and one, the last-named, a girl), Evening, Twilight, Moonlight, Rivulet, Omelette, Cutlet, Toilet (the last three in one family), Provincial, Bishop, Superior Mary, First Born (we met him when we were at the cathedral), Pass Class IV ... the list goes on. We got to thinking of what would happen if Bishop married Superior Mary, if Omelette ended up a bad egg, if Toilet was introduced to Dirty Face, if Pass Class IV reached college, and what the truck driver (running out of gears) would name his other children!

When we woke up on the 22nd morning, we were stunned to be told the tragic news of Rajiv Gandhi's assassination the previous night, and took some time to get over it. We were also sad to be leaving Shillong that morning. The children had enjoyed themselves so much that they felt they would not have as much fun elsewhere. I told them to wait and see how the holiday unfolded and to enjoy each experience.

NAGALAND SAGALAND
"In my heart it will remain"

It is a pity that photography is not allowed at airports in India because we would have loved to take pictures of the new impressive single storey Naga structure that greeted us on our arrival at Dimapur airport. In the novel airport lounge, virtually open to the elements, passengers wait in cool natural comfort for their luggage to be offloaded from the plane and everyone sits around as if at a picnic, unmindful of the dusty city outside. There were no conveyor belts for the luggage, which you simply collected as they are brought to the lounge. While we waited for our baggage, Fr. M.P. Thomas arrived to welcome us. He was now Vice Provincial and it was good to see him again.

Of the eight Administrative Districts of Nagaland, only Dimapur and Kohima are cities, and Dimapur is the only city linked by train to the rest of India. Known as 'The Gateway of Nagaland', Dimapur means 'City of River People'. Once it was the capital of the ancient Cachari Kingdom whose flourishing civilization existed here before the Ahom invasion in the 13th century. Huge menhirs (stone megaliths) from that era were found all over Dimapur, and these are now placed together in a fenced off area, but it was not well protected and could easily be vandalised. Today, Dimapur bears little resemblance to the beautiful valley it once was. I suppose being the commercial capital of the state with increased industrial activity, this was bound to happen. Unfortunately, it was not the best introduction to Nagaland that we could give our children.

After lunch and freshening up at the Don Bosco Provincial House, we set off for Kohima in the company of Fr. MP. We were happy we were going to show our daughters this place we had spoken so much about. The drive from Dimapur to Kohima by jeep took about two and a half hours. It was raining and gloomy when we arrived. The gloom had more reason to do with the death of Rajiv Gandhi the previous day. The Northeast mourned his passing for three days – all shops were shut and life was virtually at a standstill.

The Kohima War Memorial too was closed on that day. We were keen for our children to see it, and with some string-pulling, we managed to gain entry. The area was once known as Garrison Hill and formed part of the tennis courts of the British Deputy Commissioner.   It unexpectedly turned into a battlefield during the Second World War, when the Japanese invaded India from Burma. Concealed in the branches of a cherry tree on the premises, a lone Japanese sniper used that post to inflict much damage. The British could not locate from where the fatal shots were being fired, but it was a Naga who managed to spot the sniper and stealthily led the British to him. In the battle that followed, the cherry tree was burnt down but from its stump another grew in its place. It is this tree that marked the limit of the Japanese advance into India.

The Kohima War cemetery remains a dedicated tribute to the 10,000 and more soldiers who lost their lives there.   Even today the Commonwealth War Graves Commission maintains this cemetery, which has immaculate lawns and is extremely well preserved.   Small stone markers with bronze plaques on them commemorate the British, Indian and Japanese soldiers buried there.   It is not so much the touching epitaphs on the stone slabs, as the ages of the soldiers, many in their early 20s, that pull at your heartstrings. British and Japanese delegations continue to visit the memorial from time to time. A monolithic slab at the foot of this terraced and landscaped cemetery bears these words:

> 'When you go home,
> Tell them of us and say
> For your tomorrow,
> We gave our today.'

We were touched by these words but very upset to see this monument desecrated by a 'Vote for ...' political poster callously pasted directly beneath the inscription.

We were also shown a modern *pucca* Naga home, which looked like any flat in Bombay, but we saw that they still had the traditional old-style kitchen detached from the main house. Our daughters thought the girls looked very pretty with lovely long jet-black hair, so it was funny to hear them say that they envied the Bombay girls for their looks! Marina, the eldest young lady of the house showed us the traditional jewellery her parents were collecting for their five daughters. We could not help admiring the unusual orange, black and white beads, all laboriously hand-carved. Each girl had to have about seven elaborate long strands to make up one good necklace for her marriage. We had no idea how costly each strand could be, until a few days later, when we tried to buy one ourselves.

Kohima by night is a spectacular sight, like a star-spangled night sky turned upside down. It had become quite cold and I was shivering despite my shawl and fur hat. We spent the night at the same Mount Tabor Retreat House we had been to in 1987. We actually needed a room heater – and this, in the heart of their summer! In the morning we were fascinated watching the clouds drifting in and out of our windows and also at the sight of so many clouds far below us. It was like being on Cloud Nine!

We made our way to the museum and while waiting for it to open, we wandered around taking photographs, including one of a replica of the massive war drum carved out of a single large tree. The Director of the museum described the tribal ritual involved in the making of a war drum, starting with the selection, blessing and chopping down of the tree. For the ceremonial 'consecration', human blood was required. Without batting an eyelid he told us that when the hollowing out of the bark was nearing completion, the warriors of that particular village were sent to hunt out enemies whose blood could be used for the ceremony. No wonder the youth of neighbouring villages went underground on such occasions – this in our 'enlightened' 20th century!

From Kohima we went back to Dimapur, and though we were on holiday, we could not refuse the request to conduct a three-day seminar at the Salesian College from 25-27 May. This time too we had a large group of 60 since the Rector was keen that all of them benefit. During those three days our children were kept entertained by others, with excursions to nearby places. After another fulfilling seminar, we left for Mon, accompanied by Fr. MP. As we would have to make a few stops along the way, we decided to leave at 4 am in order to reach Mon before nightfall.

Armed with bananas and cameras we were all charged up with excitement as we headed for the Nambar forest. We were told that wild elephants regularly halted traffic on the highway, which cut through the forest, and demanded a 'toll'. If the expected bananas or sugarcane were not forthcoming there was no saying what would happen – you might have to wait a few hours till the elephants decided to move away or your vehicle might be moved off the road by them. It became an established practice for people passing through the forest to carry their toll of ripe bananas. The children and I were very keen to see the elephants but were doomed to disappointment. I remembered how on our previous drive through the same forest, the intrepid Fr. Devasia was thankful that we did not have an encounter with them. We were told they invariably came out around 8 am (for breakfast?) and we were an hour too early. We thought it uncanny when our Salesian hosts informed us that on several occasions, though the elephants were blocking the road, they stepped back for the Don Bosco jeeps to pass and did not even accept the proffered bananas. It looks like the Don Bosco name carried a lot of weight in that region, even with those 'weighty' creatures.

It was raining when we reached Mon, but our wonderful Fr. Devasia welcomed us in right royal style and it felt good to be back there a second time. As in all the other places we had been to, we made sure (by the power of our intentions) that perfect weather greeted us the next day. The school had expanded and the number of classes increased since our last visit. We had to bid farewell to our quiet, self-effacing Fr. MP who had spent a lot of his precious time escorting us to Kohima and to Mon, and now he had to return to Dimapur to catch up with his numerous duties.

Fr. Devasia then took us to the marketplace, which was simply fascinating and transported one back in time. Casually ambling around, we would come face-to-face with some colourfully attired Nagas with tattooed faces and earrings made from spent cartridges in which they stored their opium. Some, however, were scantily clad with just narrow strips of loincloth, not in the least perturbed when those not very effective coverings flapped open in the wind. I was particularly fascinated by a very old grandma with a baby at her breast, obviously substituting for its mother. How we longed to photograph each individual toting their '*daus*' (a type of axe, some decorated with dyed goat's hair), or guns or both, but as we were unsure of the reaction this would provoke, we decided to play safe and walked on.

The people of Mon belong mainly to the Konyak tribe. Each tribe has its own dialect, dress and customs and some have a rich oral tradition which has been handed down through generations, similar to tribal cultures in Africa. The Konyaks are considered the fiercest of all Naga tribes who, even as recently as the 19th century, were head hunters. They also believe that they are the direct descendants of Noah. Some of them even have biblical names like Moses and Aaron.

There are 16 major tribes in Nagaland but I can recall only 15: Konyak, Lotha, Rengma, Chang, Sema, Ao, Angami, Mao, Phuchori, Zeliang, Chakasang, Sangtam, Yimchunger, Phom and Rongmai. The shawls of each tribe have their own distinctive patterns and colours, and one can recognize to which tribe a person belongs from the shawl he/she is using. The hand-woven ones can cost quite a lot and are not easily available. However, we did not have to buy any as we were presented with so many. Of course we have been sharing this bounty with friends, especially those living abroad, as they keep a person very warm in winter.

When Joe and I were in Mon in 1985, we had heard about the King of Chui, a Konyak village in Mon district, but had no chance of meeting him. To mitigate our disappointment, our ever thoughtful Fr. Devasia sent us not only a picture postcard of the king, but also his '*dau*'. The King of Chui had presented this *dau* to him as a special mark of esteem and affection, and he in turn presented this precious gift to us. I often wondered how many heads had been lopped off with that particular *dau* which came into our possession!

THE KING OF CHUI VILLAGE
"Somewhere over the rainbow, way up high, there's ..."

It was such a thrill when, on our second day in Mon, Fr. Devasia told us that he was taking us to Chui village to see the king. As we piled into the rugged jeep, with Fr. Devasia at the wheel, we did not know what to expect, but there was a general feeling of excitement and adventure. As we drove along the 8-kilometre stretch to the village, we kept marvelling at Fr. Devasia's skill in dodging the potholes and rocky outcrops on the 'road' to Chui. Government officials had seen to the laying of paving stones to ensure that there was a smoother ride leading to the village on the occasion of Rajiv Gandhi's visit to Chui, after which they had the stones removed and taken away!

As we neared the village, we began to spot the cluster of thatched roofs with wispy threads of smoke spiralling from chimney-like devices jutting through the roofs. Chui village nestles deep in the Naga Hills and cannot be seen easily from outside, so you are taken quite by surprise when you suddenly come upon it. But would we be welcomed now or would we have to face hostile stares? Would the King be at home and would he condescend to meet us? We were about to find out, because we had finally reached the imposing thatched-roof 'palace', approximately 45 mts long and about 12 mts wide, situated on a slight rise dominating the village. Among those who came swarming out and surrounded the jeep to give Fr. Devasia a boisterous welcome, were Ah Ching, the king's son, and Throton, both former students of the Don Bosco School at Mon. They accompanied us, translating, giving explanations and answering our questions.

In front of the king's palace was a huge stone slab about 3 mts by 1.2mts where animals killed in the hunt were brought and laid out. They were then ceremonially cut up. The heads would be given to the king and the other portions distributed to the families in the village, each according to their status. The outer wall of the palace was decorated with a profusion of animal skulls. We could identify mithun, deer, monkeys and hornbills, and near the entrance, two mouldy elephant skulls. We were lucky to find the king at home, sitting near a fire in the main room with two bodyguards crouched beside him. There was no mistaking his commanding presence. His tattooed body was wiry and muscular, with a flat, toned abdomen. All he was wearing was a pair of shabby black shorts, and three cane hoops round his slim waist. He graciously agreed to let us photograph him, but only on condition we send him some of the photographs. For his 65 years, he looked amazingly fit, and I noticed that whereas in the picture postcard we had of him, he had been wearing four brass skulls, he was now adorned with five! The number of skulls round a warrior's neck indicated how many men he had killed. We were told that in days gone by, unless a man had killed at least one person, he was not considered virile enough or worth marrying!

In the main hall where the king was ensconced, we saw three large circular bronze gongs surmounted by three hefty ivory tusks, each at least 1.5 mts in length, and blackened with years of exposure to smoky fires. Also, hanging from the ceiling was a tatty, moth-eaten stuffed tiger, which seemed to be disintegrating. The Naga belief is that the kings turned into tigers when they died. We walked through the entire palace as though on a tourist sightseeing trip. Sadly, the weather and the passing years had taken their toll and left gaping holes in some places. To stem the damage, some parts of the palace had been sealed off from the rest of the living quarters. Leakages were destroying priceless objects and it was tragic to see such an irreplaceable heritage being slowly eroded due to neglect. The 'furniture' included huge bedsteads carved out of a single tree – legs and all. A grain-threshing plank (also carved out of a single tree), which was about 4.5 – 6 mts long, was also beginning to rot on one side where the rainwater had soaked into it. The palace roof was supported by a central row of pillars made from the Nahor trees. These were rock-solid and felt like metal to the touch, which is why they are called 'ironwood'. The government had promised to repair and restore the roof and the palace, but until the date of our visit in 1991, nothing had been done. I do not think the villagers were aware of the treasures the palace contained nor, I think, would it have mattered to them if they knew.

In one of the inner rooms, we came upon the king's chief wife (who looked much older than her royal spouse). She was sitting on her haunches next to the central fire in the kitchen with a grey cat purring next to her. The two of them seemed to have a close affinity and looked as though they had not moved from their position in years. When we asked if we could photograph her, she promptly covered her face, turned her head away and spat into the fire. Older Naga women believe that if anyone took their picture, their soul would take its departure from the body. This reaction was evident in the market place too when we tried to capture some of the beautifully wrinkled faces on film. In fact, when we passed tribals on the road, some would turn their heads away and spit, which I translated to mean they were warding off the evil eye of us 'foreigners'!

By the time we completed our tour of the palace, the king was ready – he came out sporting the same black shorts but topped by a red felt jacket, wearing his necklace of five skulls, with long hollowed goat horns through his earlobes, and a hat embellished with monkey fur, a wild boar tusk and a feather of the hornbill. (I should mention here that the hornbill was looked upon as an object of beauty by the Nagas in the old days. In fact, one of the best blessings you could receive from them was 'May fertility be upon you as the mother spider and may your children grow up to be as handsome as the male hornbill.') In his own way, the king looked imposing, and though on the slight side, he stood erect with chest out and a practised fierce look on his face. He was a ruler of 36 villages, each village with its own '*angh*' or king, and his word is law. In all Nagaland, Mon is the only district to have this unique institution of '*Anghship*', and succession is hereditary.

We were told the king had a wife from each village, but Ah Ching, the son of his first wife was the Crown Prince who would inherit after him, and the king loved him dearly. Ah Ching was married to the granddaughter of the King of Tang, whose skull we saw displayed in a special cone-shaped basket attached to a pole. It appeared the King of Chui had not spared his son's grandfather-in-law who was his erstwhile enemy. (Could that have explained the additional brass skull round the king's neck?) The enemy skulls, numbering about 250 were arranged on shelves in a 'pucca' shed, constructed by the government. This was located directly opposite the king's palace. It was gruesome looking at all those human skulls; Fr. Devasia informed us some years later that they were given a burial and the shed demolished. Behind the shed of skulls was a mound with upright stone slabs. A warrior was entitled to plant a stone there for every enemy killed. Beyond this was a 'morung', which used to be a common dormitory for the youth of the village. They had to live there for three years while they were taught about life and trained to be warriors. Chui had three such 'morungs', but none were in use – they were overgrown with weeds, with goats and pigs scavenging around in them. Another sure sign of the changing times!

As we were leaving I presented both Ah Ching and Throton with some colourful picture books; the king materialized once more, sans his regalia, and made signs that he too wanted a book for himself. Fortunately, I had one bigger than the others to give him. He then asked for reading glasses. Joe gave him his own to check whether he could see better so that we could send him a pair with the same number from Bombay. However, we could not tell whether the glasses made any difference, whether he could understand anything from the pages he was looking at, or whether he just wanted them as a status symbol. On our return to Bombay, we sent him a gift parcel through Fr. Devasia. The king was delighted and wryly remarked that many who came to see him had promised to send him the photos they had taken, but we were the only ones who had ever done so. Our parcel contained reading glasses, colourful sunglasses, several photographs we had taken of him – some enlarged and laminated – and a new pair of black shorts, which, I presume, he will treasure until our next visit to that almost make-believe village called Chui.

Truly we had had the most delightful and wonderful holiday together. Melissa and Vanessa had been thrilled with everything. On our return to Bombay, still flush with the excitement of experiences which few others could have enjoyed, I decided to write one common newsletter to all our friends. It was exceptionally well received. The positive feedback that poured in spurred me to take another look at it, and so I broke the piece up into three separate articles. All three were accepted for publication, two in the Indian Express and the third in the Delhi Economic Times Travel Section – and I even got paid for them! I know for a fact that saying 'Yes' can often land us in difficulties, but from my experience, I have found that even landing up with more than I could chew brought me much gain in unexpected ways. Not only have I discovered the beautiful places we have in our own country, not only have we made a host of wonderful warm friends, not only have our children discovered that priests are not 'boring' people, but I discovered my potential to write. And it all began with a simple 'Yes'.

****

On the very day (in March 2011) I was editing this chapter for publication, we chanced to see on TV a documentary on the King of Chui and the village in Mon.   I was happy to see the king looking fairly fit and spry and that the government had finally re-constructed his palace which now had concrete walls and imposing pillars at the entrance, and a roof of asbestos sheeting.   Some of the ornamental animal skulls still adorned the outside walls in neat rows but quite a few were just piled up haphazardly in one heap.   The inside of the palace too was greatly improved and I was happy to see the three gongs and the ivory tusks still in place.   And yes, I almost forgot to mention that the king was still sporting his black shorts.   Not sure to which era they belonged! We felt quite nostalgic watching the film and we were actually contemplating going back to Mon a third time and Chui a second time, but when we wrote to Fr. M.P. Thomas in Nagaland to tell him of our intention, he informed us that the king had recently passed away.

As for our beloved Fr. Devasia, although we kept in touch and wrote to him often (he never was a great letter-writer) we did not meet again. We were so very sorry to hear that he had passed away on 20 September 2004 in Imphal. We know he could have written volumes on his adventures in Nagaland – not all of them funny or amusing. He also went through some traumatic moments living as he did in a land of tribal rivalries and influenced by underground movements, but he came smilingly through them all.

Chapter Seven

1993
DAY ONE OF THE FAMILY FEST
"People who need people are the luckiest ..."

On my very first day in Rome I felt what I had felt only once before, when we visited Shillong for the first time in 1986. Nor have I, in the seven years since then, ever had the same feeling – till I came to Rome: here was a place where I would not mind living the rest of my life. We were in Rome in June 1993 as delegates to the International Family Fest organized by the Focolare Movement. It was my first, and Joe's second visit to Rome. Our group was put up at a place called 'Oasi' (oasis) located on one of the seven hills of Rome. Oasi sat on the edge of the scenic Lago Albano, directly opposite Castelgandolfo, the Pope's summer residence. Villas belonging to the rich and the famous dotted the slopes surrounding the lake. From our terrace balcony, we had a clear and uninterrupted view of the city of Rome in the distance. We could see planes landing and taking off, and also Rocca di Papa, another part of the city built on one of the seven hills. It was indeed a breathtaking panorama. The entire Castelgandolfo area has an old world charm that keeps growing on you the longer you stay there. That first day as we circled part of the lake and traversed the Via Appia Antica to connect with the Via Cristoforo Colombo, I sent up a silent prayer of thanks for the privilege of actually being there, because, till the very last moment, Joe and I had both been unsure of joining the group.

The Family Fest we were attending was a multi-congress for families of every country, culture, tradition, race and religion, which focused specifically on family life and was promoted by the New Families branch of the Focolare Movement. The Movement itself was founded in 1945 by a young girl, Chiara Lubich, when, with a group of companions, she began living the Gospel in a literal hands-on manner.

The main aim of the Movement is to foster unity – in the family, in the working environment, between generations, among social categories and among nations. Chiara advocated that we should first LIVE the Gospel and only then preach it. While this is easier said than done, those who are actually putting this way of life into practice will tell you that the results are certainly worth the effort. Chiara, a Catholic, received encouragement in her work from Pope Paul VI and later, from Pope John Paul II. Yet, the beauty of this Movement is that living its spirituality is not restricted to Catholics alone. From the very start, this ideal of unity has attracted people of other ideologies too. The fact that Chiara was once invited to share her Christian experience with an audience of 10,000 Japanese Buddhists, speaks for itself, as they are very conservative in matters of religion. The ongoing dialogue has extended to various countries, involving people from all faiths like Jews, Muslims, Taoists, Sikhs, Hindus and even animists and atheists.

For almost everyone in our group from India, this was the first experience of attending a Family Fest so we were not sure what to expect. On Day One of the Fest, we breakfasted, got ready and boarded a bus to take us all to the venue. The moment we stepped off the bus at the Piazza Marconi and saw so many people of so many different nationalities alighting from the buses that kept pulling up at the Piazza, we felt electrified with the excitement in the air. Not one of us was prepared for what happened next. One minute our group was posing for photographs among ourselves and the next we were bombarded from every direction – not by bombs, but by camera and video buffs! We Indians did present a colourful and exotic spectacle. The ladies had a range of pretty saris and a variety of salwar-kameez outfits. The men in our group had chosen to wear western suits. Joe and I had decided to represent other parts of India, so instead of the traditional sari, I wore the *Khasi jainsem* of Meghalaya, while Joe wore a striking black Pathan suit with gold embroidery around the neckband.

It began with a lady from Argentina, named Beatrice, who ran up to me, held me round the waist, and asked her friend to take a photograph. Thereafter, until we reached the stadium we were stopped innumerable times either to be photographed by ourselves or along with others. As we made our slow progress through the crowds to find our allotted entrance we were spontaneously applauded by several other groups. When people are happy or like something, they clap their hands and applaud you. On our part, we too were as entranced with the colourful costumes of people from distant lands. There was nothing to stop us from also asking other delegates to pose with us or take their photographs. Those coming from Africa, Mexico, Guatemala, Korea and India wore the most colourful ethnic outfits that day. A few from north Italy, dressed in traditional Tirolean outfits also stood out. It was almost like a fancy dress party.

The Palaeur stadium, or the Palazzo dello Sporto as it is officially known, is located on the outskirts of Rome, south of the city. This fully enclosed stadium can seat over 15,000 people. As we entered, we were all given dockets containing a brochure giving the day's programme and different coloured flags. All except the Italians had headphones for simultaneous translations into English, Urdu, Arabic, Chinese, Korean, Cantonese, Russian, Polish, Pyck, French, German, Spanish, Portuguese, Magyar, and Creole. The purpose of those different coloured flags became evident when they were unfurled and we all waved them at the same time – it looked like an undulating rainbow, and even that was a moving sight. Representatives from each section of the audience were seated on the main stage in the well of the stadium. Two gigantic TV screens relayed the happenings on the main stage, in front of which sat the VIPs who were honouring the Fest with their patronage and presence.

The aim of the Family Fest was to give a message of hope for the future of the Family. As the basic unit of society in the natural order, each family could carry the seeds of unity to every part of the globe.

The six-hour programme encompassed a gamut of fantastic presentations ranging from personal experiences and group sharing to live interviews of eminent persons. These were interspersed with cross-continental link-ups and cultural interludes. The experiences being shared were all very touching and powerful, but what made a particular impact on me was the poignant sharing of a boy from Bosnia who, because of his mother's influence, learned in time to forgive the neighbour whom he had witnessed killing his father.

When we broke for lunch, we witnessed another minor miracle – the feeding of so many thousands. Several huge vans had brought hot meals to us in insulated boxes. The groups then spread themselves out on every available grassy patch around the stadium to eat their lunches, and but for the modern garb it could have been a scene from the bible – the Sermon on the Mount, or the Miracle of the Loaves and Fishes. Many chose to sit where they could soak up the sun while we Indians chose a shady spot, which happened to flank a busy traffic intersection. I don't know who was more entertained – the people in the cars looking at the motley groups and wondering if there was a costume convention nearby, or we, catching the expressions on their faces. Some made bold enough to stop and ask what in heck was going on, while others smiled, waved and seemed to enjoy the spectacle. Yet other motorists were stony faced and looked indifferent, but I am sure those could not have been Italians!

Strolling back to the stadium after lunch we stopped to talk to several different people from different countries. It was interesting to note that though many of us could not communicate in a common language, we somehow managed to understand each other. For instance, we met a young Czech couple who could speak neither English nor Italian (of which we had a passable knowledge), and while we were in the middle of our exchanges I suddenly noticed that the young lady was smiling in a self-conscious way and was looking a little awed. On turning around, we saw that the four of us had become the focus of a team with a huge video camera and sound equipment. As there were several video crews going around they no longer attracted any particular attention. It therefore took us some time to realize what our new friends were trying to tell us – this particular crew was from the Czech National TV and they signed to us to carry on our 'dialogue' with each other and to say something about India while their cameras rolled. That was one of several interviews in which we featured, and which Joe and I had no opportunity to view!

The carabinieri, the Italian police, in their smart crisp uniforms were out in full strength to provide high security for the President of Italy, Dr. Scalfaro, who attended part of the programme in the afternoon. The speech he made that day had not the slightest hint of any political agenda. It came from the heart of a family man. Other eminent personalities present were Dr. Sokalski, co-ordinator at the U.N. for the International Year of the Family, Mrs. Jomo Kenyatta, wife of the founder and President of Kenya, Christina Asong, Mafua (Queen) of the Bangwa tribe in the Cameroons, and Egon Klepsch, President of the European Parliament, among several others. The audience at the Palaeur was linked via 13 satellites to about 600 million viewers worldwide, with many networks broadcasting the event live. We were also linked via satellite to Patriarch Bartolomeo I in Constantinople, Imam Barkat in Algeria, the Venerable Etai Yamada in Japan, Cory Aquino in the Philippines and Pope John Paul II in the Vatican.

Family gatherings simultaneously in progress in Melbourne, Hong Kong, Yaoundé (Africa), Sao Paolo (Brazil), Buenos Aires (Argentina) and New York were brought live to the gigantic TV screens in the Palaeur for a two-way dialogue. An international hotline (15 lines) made available free of cost by Italcable for the entire duration of the Family Fest resulted in more than 1000 calls coming through to the Palaeur with offers of adoptions and accommodation and shelter to the homeless people of Bosnia.

As one can imagine, the entire day had generated a mixture of emotions. It was a feat in itself to have created an event that could retain the involvement of such a large crowd for so many hours. Still, as the day's programme came to a close I guess we were all more than a little tired. We followed the same routine for dinner though it felt a little odd to be eating so 'early', with the sun still shining high up in the Italian summer sky; and even when we returned to Oasi at around 9 pm it was not yet dark.

DAY TWO OF THE FAMILY FEST
"And I think to myself, what a wonderful world"

On Sunday, 6 June, our bus arrived punctually at the appointed time, and once again, we all piled in, decked up in our Indian finery. This was the day the Holy Father would meet the New Families and conclude the Fest with mass in St. Peter's Square. As our streamlined, luxurious bus wound its way down the old Appian Way, we passed remarkable old buildings, the remains and ruins of amazing aqueducts, the historic catacombs and centuries-old monuments. We felt ourselves almost transported back in time to the days of the Roman Empire. Our bus drove up the Via della Conciliazione and parked near the other buses also bringing people for the special mass. It is one thing to look at pictures and quite another to be actually standing in front of the world-famous St. Peter's Basilica in Rome. I was overawed. As we neared the Piazza San Pietro we noticed there was high security for that day.

We had been issued special passes for the enclosure where rows of chairs were arranged, and our group had to enter from the Colonnato Di Destra, Portone di Bronzo. That is easily translated as the Bronze

Gate on the right colonnade. Designed by Bernini to hold half a million people, St. Peter's Square gradually began to fill up and once everyone was settled in their seats, the flurry of photographing began again. We Indians found still and video cameras trained on us from all directions. Joe had worn a white silk kurta with a white raw silk bandhgala jacket, while I had a black ensemble set off by a magenta silk jacket embroidered with gold zari paisleys, which Joe had bought me from Lucknow. We chatted with more Czechs, Germans, Argentinians and Brazilians and they all loved Joe's outfit. Some even asked the other Indians in our group if Joe was some sort of religious leader back in India!

There was a long wait before Mass began at 10 am. We were all a little fidgety as the sun climbed higher to focus more intently on us. The Westerners were a good example for us. If they, who were used to cooler climes could tolerate the heat, so could we all. At 10 am sharp, the bells of St. Peter's chimed and a solemn procession of cardinals, bishops and priests preceded the Holy Father as they emerged from the Church. Despite the fact that he did not look very well and was slightly bent over (with age or tiredness), the Pope still had a very strong presence. As the solemn two-hour Mass progressed, I confess I was more than a little distracted with the heat and the sun's rays (to which I am allergic) on my back and neck. The distribution of Holy Communion was a bit chaotic, and both Joe and I felt that St. Peter's, Rome, could pick up a tip or two from the orderly way this is done in St. Peter's, Bandra! But I guess it would take quite some doing to have orderly queues and to control those thousands of devotees in Rome.

After Mass, all of us joined in sustained applause for the Holy Father. He then came down the steps of St. Peter's to meet and bless the people. I was very eager to touch his hand and miraculously managed to make my way through the crowd till I was at the railings in front. My intention must have been very strong because the Pope, though far to my left, suddenly swerved and made straight towards me. I kept willing him to come closer, and when he was just a few metres away, I broke my concentration to get my camera ready. As suddenly as he had veered towards me, he turned once again and went back up the steps. It all goes to prove that you cannot really concentrate on two things at the same time!

After a reasonably relaxed lunch in the Piazza del S. Uffizio, Joe and I were among several other Indians interviewed by the Italian Raisat TV crew. We were asked for our experience of the Family Fest event, and also other questions about life in India. The square had cleared by now and the doors of St. Peter's were opened to the public. We had some time on our own so Joe and I decided to make this our first sightseeing stop. I have already used so many adjectives and superlatives thus far that I do not know if I can find any more or adequate enough to describe St. Peter's, but I will try. First of all, just stepping through the portals and knowing that you are on hallowed ground brings out the goose pimples even as the size and vastness of the monument astounds you.

We learnt that the Basilica of St. Peter's, which has come to be considered the symbol of Christendom, was built by the emperor Constantine on the spot where St. Peter was buried. The artist Carlo Maderno conceptualized the present façade, while the cupola was designed by Michelangelo. Besides the Papal altar in the centre under the main dome, and the Tribuna with Bernini's imposing and famous canopy at the centre and at the head of the Basilica, there are 12 chapels, six on each side, with the Chapel of the Pieta being the first on your right as you enter. Each of these chapels is the size of a small Church. It is impossible to describe every detail: the treasures, the sculptures, the paintings, etc. Visiting the underground tombs of all the Popes was like going backwards in time and I could scarcely believe I was there seeing it all first hand. This lower level maze was as fascinating as the Basilica and I could almost feel the spirits of those holy and pious men around me. I stopped to pray specially at the tombs of St. Peter and of each of the Popes of my lifetime, from Pius XII onwards.

After all that walking, we were quite tired by the time we were back in the basilica. We rested briefly in the Square and then decided to visit Castel San Angelo. As we walked down the Via della Conciliazione, we stopped at all the souvenir shops lining one side of the road. I had been abroad before and I knew that if you stop to convert prices to Indian rupees, you end up buying nothing. Yet, it is not easy for the Indian mind to stop doing spot calculations. After some time I refused to even enter shops because the prices depressed me. How was I ever going to be able to take back a few gifts and souvenirs for family and friends? The best rosaries in India are cheaper than the most ordinary ones in Rome. I did not need Joe to remind me that unless I could overcome my constant lire-rupee cost-comparison habit, I was going to be miserable throughout my holiday.

With the unwonted exertion of the day, my feet had almost given up, but time was precious and the thought that I might not get another chance to return to Castel San Angelo made me push beyond my usual bounds. Somehow, we trudged the few yards up to its imposing portals, only to discover that on Sundays, it closed at midday! I stopped to pose for a photo with the Castle in the background, and while Joe was focusing, a youth on a motorbike stopped and started to speak to him in halting, broken English, but could not make himself understood in spite of repetitions. By the time Joe switched to Italian, and '*capisced*' that the young man was offering to click a photo of Joe standing beside me, and that Joe should pass him the camera, he became aware of strange throaty noises. He turned to see that these sounds came from some vendors (mostly Indians and Pakistanis). It was clearly a warning. As suddenly as he had appeared, the young man sped away. The vendors then explained that if Joe had handed him the camera, he would have zoomed off with it. Apparently, this was a favourite haunt of snatch thieves who must have conned many gullible and trusting tourists at that very spot. We thanked our 'saviours' and exchanged a few words of Hindi with them, to their great joy.

Another very good thing about Rome is its many fountains with cool drinking water, which we found in some unlikely places. We were told that private individuals often bribed the authorities to divert water from the aqueducts and give them illegal water connections, and some pipes could be seen sticking out of walls in old houses – and till today they still bring cool, clean and refreshing water. Apparently bribery and corruption in Italy too go back a long way.

THE 'ECONOMY OF SHARING'
"There'll be Pennies from Heaven for you and me"

After the Family Fest, we attended the Family School, which was conducted at Centro Mariapolis, in Castelgandolfo. This is the headquarters of the Focolare Movement in Rome. Just near the Reception area is a beautiful chapel that invites one to prayer; and we found the Reception desk so efficiently manned (by women) that five-star hotels could well take a few tips from them! At the Centro, we had our first sit-down meal, with generous helpings of wine, without which no meal in Italy could be considered complete.

The large sprawling grounds surrounding the building are tastefully landscaped with beautiful plants, well-manicured and inviting lawns, long promenades where one could walk off those delicious meals, and tall hedges that separated us from the Pope's private summer residence.

At the Family School, we were exposed to several programmes that were instructive, impressive and inspirational. One afternoon, a cardinal from South America gave us a very long talk during which I noticed that several in the audience were prolonging their afternoon siesta. When we all clapped for the cardinal after one hour, the good man was so delighted and enthused with the applause that he prolonged his discourse for another 30 minutes! In all, there were about 1,400 people from 66 countries at the School, so every day we met more people and made more friends. On the second day, different couples from various countries shared their experiences. Mrs. Kenyatta also spoke briefly but movingly that afternoon. When talking about the importance of the role of a family in today's world, she quoted her husband as saying 'Unless a man can govern his own family he cannot govern a nation'. She had given vast tracts of her land to the Movement so that people from all over the world could meet there and spread the message of love and unity.

Queen Christina of Fontem (Cameroons) also attended all the days and was much in demand to be photographed by and with everyone. She was a well-educated, well-spoken and simple person who did not put on any royal airs, and was always well dressed in exotic long gowns with matching turbans. In fact, she made sure she had no special privileges and even waited her turn in the long queues for meals. She also shared her experiences with us, dressed in full regalia and holding a carved ivory staff, evidently an insignia of her position.

At the Family Fest, we also had occasion to experience at first hand the power of the 'Economy of Sharing' advocated by Chiara Lubich. Essentially, this is the 'give and it shall be given unto you' principle. During the breaks, a mini-bazaar would open with handicrafts from different countries being offered for sale. While some delegates hoped to recover part of the expenses they had incurred for the trip, others aimed at getting funds to 'share' with those who were not so well off. There was an eye-catching variety of ethnic artefacts on display and sale. I realized this was a chance for us also to pitch in and help. We had taken along a suitcase full of Indian handicrafts, many of which were meant as gifts for our friends, and we had packed in certainly more than enough and to spare. So we too set up shop, with a spread of our desi stuff; apart from people admiring our display of goods we also netted rapid sales, all at good prices. In fact, some showed interest even in the clothes we were wearing. That's how I came to sell (with his permission) even the two heavy silver necklaces Joe had brought along as my birthday gift. I was delighted at the high price these fetched and the buyers were ecstatic with the workmanship and also to get them so cheap! At the end of it all, we found we had collected quite a tidy sum. After keeping a part of this to cover an uncalculated major expense involving our stay, we contributed the rest to the common pool of the 'Economy of Sharing'. Soon after this, I found I had lost my fear of spending! Not only did I allow Joe to buy me a snack and cold drink from those vending machines which fascinated me but I also splurged when we went shopping in the square outside Castelgandolfo. I chose for myself one of those beautiful and expensive handbags that Italy is so famous for (after all, it was to be my birthday present in lieu of the silver necklaces!).

Skeptics might argue that my change in attitude was because of the 'extra' money that came in. I can say that it certainly did help to relieve part of our burden, but this alone was not responsible for the dramatic change in my attitude. I know for a fact that by a true 'giving' you automatically attract providence and bounty. How this works I do not know. I only know it does. Even Nature follows this fine art, and whoever coined the phrase, 'Give to the world the best you have, and the best will return to you' apparently knew what he was talking about. Thereafter, through all our remaining stay in Italy, while we were not foolishly extravagant in our shopping, we bought gifts without hesitation, and really had a splendid holiday with our very generous friends. Not only did we return home with a suitcase full of gifts but, unbelievably, with money to spare as well. Talk about the proverbial jar of oil that never ran dry!

My birthday passed off uneventfully except towards the evening when, after the last session, there was an announcement over the system for 'Joe e Brenda Rodrigues da India' to go to the Reception. What a joy it was to see there our Salesian friend, Fr. Cyril DeSouza, who was doing his doctorate in Rome. Together with two other priest companions, he insisted on taking us for dinner, more so after he heard it was my birthday. And so we had our first meal in an Italian restaurant. We chose a nearby restaurant in the Castelgandolfo area and the view from the balcony, overlooking Lake Albano would have sent a poet into raptures. Needless to say, the meal was great and the company even better. It was a good thing we had very generous hosts and did not have to pay for that meal or we would have had to cut short our stay in Italy by a few days. After dinner, we returned to Oasi for another celebration with our group. However, it seemed that everyone was dog-tired and in no mood to celebrate. It had been the turn of the Indian group to do kitchen duty and clean up that evening. What had appeared like child's play when others did it, turned out to be a lot of hard work.

TOO-GOOD-TO-MISS TESERO
"Let me wander over yonder till I see the mountains rise"

Our next stop was Loppiano, where we intended to spend a few days. However, after only one day there, we received a call from our friends in Tesero, which made us change our plans. So on the morning of 14 June 1993, we took a train to Florence from Filigne, the nearest railway station, and changed to another line, going north to Trent. Shortly after we had boarded the train at Florence, two sedate and serious nuns entered our compartment, which was empty save for us. There was no attempt at conversation from either side – we, because we were tired, and they because they had probably been schooled to maintain a contemplative silence. The only signs of animation they exhibited occurred when the train stopped at Bologna and they spotted a man who was gesticulating wildly and talking to himself. The nuns seemed a little alarmed or afraid that he might board and enter our compartment, but that entertainment was eliminated when the train left without him.

We slept for a good part of our six-hour journey but were wide-awake as we chugged into Verona (the hometown of Romeo and Juliet) where the nuns got off and a couple who were returning home to Austria after a holiday entered. They spoke German but the wife knew a little English and so we could communicate haltingly. They were very friendly and wanted to chat and ask us more about India, but our common vocabulary was too limited to allow a stimulating exchange of ideas or information. Our train was now climbing into higher regions and we were moving between awesome white-faced mountains, which at first I thought were the Dolomites. We were glued to the window, as every turn of the train brought us to new, breathtaking sights. I did not know what our destination, Tesero, was going to be like, but I loved what I had seen thus far. Our Austrian travelling companions helped us with our luggage when we alighted at Trent and we said our goodbyes.

On the platform, Mario and Rita Jellici ('J' is pronounced as 'Y'), gave us an arms-open-wide welcome that is the trademark of the warm-hearted Italians. Had it not been for the insistent invitation of the Jellicis we would never have reached this far north, and Rome would have been all that we would have seen of Italy. I feel most reassured if I can find a friendly or known face when in a strange place, and Mario and Rita proved to be such affectionate and generous hosts;

they showered us with such lavish hospitality that made all the difference to our holiday.

Mario drove smoothly up the mountain in his Alfa Romeo that zoomed along the winding road effortlessly. On the way, he halted to give us a breathtaking view of the Val d'Adige in the South Tirol region. This valley is the largest fruit orchard in Europe, extending from Trent right up to the Bolzano valley. Bolzano, the main city of the bilingual Alto Adige, which we visited days later, is more Germanic and very different from most of Italy. We learned that this whole area once formed part of the Austro-Hungarian Empire, and it was only in 1919 that Italy acquired South Tirol from Austria. Driving through the many villages we passed on our way to Tesero was fascinating. We finally reached the Jellici's beautiful multi-storied home which was perched on a slight rise almost at the end of the village, with the mountains as a backdrop. If the outside looked so charming, the inside was even more impressive, and Mario, who is a carpenter by profession, had built it virtually all on his own, with a little local help I guess. Inside, we were greeted by Fabio, the Jellici's younger son, whom we had met the previous year in Bombay, but we seemed destined to keep missing the older boy, Claudio, who was completing his stint in the army.

It was only when we sat down to a coffee in the cozy dining room, that we realized how much inconvenience we must have caused Mario and Rita. The drive from Trent to Tesero had taken two and a half hours. Imagine someone driving from Pune to Bombay and back just to welcome their guests to India! Bolzano would have been a closer pick-up point but we had not thought of checking this out with our hosts before buying our train tickets. Of course, Mario was not a bit fazed when I remarked this and coolly offered to drive us down to Trent again if we wanted to go sightseeing.

Joe and I were given a self-contained suite, which had all the creature comforts of a five-star hotel and yet the warmth of a home. In typical

Italian style, we had our meals with the family in the kitchen, where Rita served us delicious new confections daily. In Italy, any meal without wine and pasta is almost a sacrilege, so it is truly surprising that we managed to keep our weight down after three weeks of this diet. Below the floor on which the family lived, Mario had his workshop which occupied two floors and from these there were further mezzanine offshoots into the wine cellar, the boiler room, the lumber room and more ... I lost track. Looking at all the modern equipment and massive machinery that Mario had, we realized how hopelessly outdated our poor carpenters in India are. The topmost floor, which had several suites, was let out to tourists during the season.

The little village of Tesero is charming and picturesque, and home to approximately 2,500 people. It is one of the 15 villages that dot the Fiemme valley, which is surrounded by two impressive mountain chains. On our first evening there, Mario took us for a walk round the village and we landed up at the little cemetery, which has to be seen to be believed. The gravestones are of granite or marble and each bears the photograph of the deceased. Some graves are adorned with beautiful statues, or elaborate vases and lamps. Once a week, and sometimes twice, family members troop to the cemetery, wash the graves, replace the faded flowers with fresh ones, put a candle into the lamp stand and then pray for their loved ones. Nowhere have I ever seen people lavish so much care and time on the memorials to their dear departed. This cemetery was no mournful abode of the dead – it was alive with colour and drenched with the love of the living.

A huge, awesome sculpture dominates the cemetery. It was designed to commemorate the terrible tragedy that struck the neighbouring village of Stava on 19 July 1985. Mud from mining excavations on the mountain had been piled up, eventually forming a solid wall; in the large trough behind the compacted 'wall', water had been accumulating. After a spell of incessant heavy rain, this sort of dam could not withstand the increasing volume and pressure of the water, and without any warning, gave way. With a loud roar, water and slush rushed down the mountain and wiped out almost the whole village of Stava that lay in its path. Every vestige of human life was swept away, save for a few miraculous escapes. Not a single body of those who perished was ever recovered despite extensive searches right down into the valley below. The sculpture is a chilling depiction of a huge sort of monster (which is what the flood waters turned out to be) crouching with outstretched arms over young and old, all cringing and struggling in helpless agony while they gaze in terror at the flood waters about to engulf them. It captures the horror of the tragedy so powerfully that a viewer tends to shiver even if he does not know the story that inspired it. To think that this terrible and horrific event happened right here in the bosom of such tranquil beauty!

We moved to a dedicated section of the cemetery, sacred to the memory of all the flood victims. Here each family that had lost one or more members in the tragedy was assigned a grave for a memorial. I was drawn to look at the sculpture again and this time when I retraced my steps, I met the artist, Felix Deflorian, who had designed the masterpiece. Someone who had seen us taking photos of the monument had probably relayed the news to him. We were able to congratulate him and posed for a photo with him. He told us that after he designed the monument, it was then cast in bronze and iron in Verona, from where it was transported all the way to the beautiful little cemetery in Tesero. Sig. Deflorian is a well-known and talented artist who has his own art outlet in Tesero.

On a subsequent visit to Tesero several years after this, we met an actual survivor of the Stava tragedy. She had been standing on her doorstep waiting to greet her child and husband when the flood hit. By some miracle, she was carried right across the valley and by a strange coincidence, landed virtually on her brother's doorstep, though under a pile of mud. Her life was spared but her husband and child were washed away with the house. When we met her, she had remarried and had borne another child but her face, though smiling a welcome to us, seemed to be marked with the shadow of a sadness that would never die.

Attached to the cemetery in Tesero is the small Church of St. Leonardo, which was consecrated on 18 May 1136. As we pushed open the huge ancient door to enter, a nun suddenly appeared, waving her arms and shouting, and shut the door on us. Mario, Joe and I were all taken aback. While we stood there, puzzling over such strange behaviour and wondering what to do, the door opened and the same nun smilingly welcomed us in. She explained that she was about to lock the church up for the night, and had just switched on the alarms, when we pushed the door open. Had she not shut it immediately, the alarms would have gone off, summoning the entire village to deal with the intruders. This tiny church had retained every vestige of its antiquity and still had the original pews, doors and belfry. There were many paintings and sculptures, and even the walls were covered in frescoes, some of which date way back to the 16th century. Time seems to have stood still inside that little church, with the exception of the modern electronic alarm system. In fact, we noticed that even the tiniest chapels we visited in isolated places had such security systems. With the centuries-old treasures they contain, this has become a necessity.

To return to the nun, after her welcome and explanations about the Church, her natural curiosity about us was aroused. While Joe and Mario were busy studying the altar, she pointed to Joe and asked me who he was. When I said he was '*mio marito*' she seemed surprised, but when I told her we had two children and the oldest was 20, she said, 'Ma, non. Sembra che tu abbia solo venti-cinque anni!' Poor Joe, his white beard always makes him look older, but I could have hugged the nun for thinking I looked just 25!

One morning Mario drove us to Bolzano, which is on the border of Austria. We found everything most orderly, clean and beautiful – and very expensive – so we indulged in a lot of window-shopping only and stopped for coffee at a sidewalk café. When we were back in Tesero, we chalked out plans for our 'must-see' places because Mario wanted to show us all round the countryside and take us up his beloved Dolomites. We were keen to go to Padua, Venice and Vienna, and knowing how quickly time passes when enjoying ourselves, Mario suggested we should first complete our visits to the more distant spots, and we thought so too.

PADUA'S SAINT AND CITY OF MIRACLES
"Then I know why, I believe"

Padua, better known as the city of St. Anthony, was one of the places we planned to visit, mainly to pray at the famous shrine of this popular and powerful saint. So, early on the morning of 16 June, Joe and I piled into the car with Mario, Rita and Fabio. It was a long drive from Tesero in the Italian Alps to Padua, which we reached by mid-morning. Padua is also an important art city, with a very long history. Our first stop was the Scrovegni Chapel, which is one of the city's oldest monuments. From there we moved on to the Town Museum, which adjoins the Chapel and was once an Augustinian Hermits' Monastery. Studying some of the works of art from the 14th century was so absorbing that I tended to lag behind the others. I scarcely noticed the intent stares of a museum guard who appeared to have found me suspicious – or fascinating, as I preferred to think! We were practically alone in one of those huge, rambling high-ceilinged halls, and wherever I went, he followed with a fixed smile and footsteps that echoed strangely on the parquet flooring. It was all so evocative of a quintessential murder mystery, but I did not want to fantasize about its denouement, so I hurriedly moved on to catch up with the others.

We then did a round of the Chiesa degli Eremitani to admire the wonderful wooden ceiling built at the turn of the 13th century. There was much, much more to see in Padua, but we decided to conserve our energies for the Basilica di San Antonio, which was the main reason we were in Padua. Hotel San Antonio on the Via San Fermo seemed welcoming, and the tariff suited our moderate budget so we checked in there, had a bite to eat and rested till the afternoon sun went down. Then we set out for the Basilica.

As we walked towards the Piazza Garibaldi, we saw a large crowd – large by Italian standards, but nothing compared to what you can muster in India, more particularly in Bombay, by just standing in one spot and gazing fixedly at the sky! There were police cars sealing off the entrance to the square and carabinieri swarming around, with police helicopters hovering overhead. Curiosity got the better of us. We too stopped to enquire and learned that a bank robbery had just taken place. One of the robbers had been shot dead, and when someone lifted the sheet covering his body, we noticed that it was a dark-skinned person. For a moment, I felt a flush of shame tinge my cheeks because I thought he was an Indian. Mercifully, it turned out that he was not; the robbers were Neapolitans from the South who are quite dark complexioned. The other four of the gang had been arrested. It was terrible and also very exciting to be witnessing a real live heist, but we did not stop there long.

After walking down the Via degli Zabarella which continues onwards as the Via del Santo, we found ourselves in the Piazza del Santo, The Basilica San Antonio is an imposing construction and quite original in appearance, with a blend of different architectural styles. I was curious about this and later found out that its eight large domes revealed Venetian and Byzantine influences, the two towers at the rear had minarets like Oriental mosques, the apse, with its chapels, was Gothic, while the façade of the Basilica was Romanesque. We all made to enter, but Mario was stopped, because he was wearing shorts. After a brief sotto voce conference, Mario told us to go ahead and instructed his son Fabio to complete his round of the shrine quickly and meet him outside. Later, Mario joined us inside the basilica and we were amused to see that he was wearing Fabio's jeans; fortunately, both were the same size making the switch possible. I was surprised to see how vast this Basilica appeared – it was almost as grand as St. Peter's in Rome, but nowhere as large. Mass was in progress when we arrived, so we had to wait until it was over before we could visit the tomb of the Saint. When I stopped to say a prayer, I was startled to find several grown people around me weeping openly and unashamedly, and I was touched by their devotion.

We moved on to admire the rest of the shrine, particularly the main altar and the beautiful chapels of the apse. Walking around these big churches is very tiring and I needed to stop and rest my feet. While Joe and the Jellicis wandered off elsewhere I sat down in one of the Gothic choir stalls in the Chapel of St. James, directly opposite the Chapel of St. Anthony. I also decided to attend mass which was in progress, and take the opportunity to pray in a special manner for everyone back home, and just in case I had forgotten anyone, I opened my little book to check the names I had written of people who had asked for special prayers at the Shrine. That's when I discovered that I had totally forgotten one person and I felt ashamed because my daughter, Melissa, had specifically asked me to pray for her friend, Alison. Alison, a pretty and talented girl, was a member of the Sangeet Abhinay Academy, a dance group to which my daughter also belonged. In April 1993, Alison met with an accident, which landed her in hospital and worse, in a coma from which she had still not recovered; the doctors were not optimistic about her chances either. Having forgotten to pray for her at all the shrines we had visited thus far, I now prayed most fervently for her and asked St. Anthony, the worker of miracles, to make Alison open her eyes and speak again. After buying a few souvenirs at the shop, I felt I could not leave without first touching them to the tomb of the saint. So it was all the way back to the tomb. Something strange happened as I prayed there, and I knew not how or why, but tears came unbidden to my eyes. Nor was I was embarrassed by the flow. Was it a sign?

From the basilica, we strolled down charming old cobble-stoned streets under ancient arches, and revelled in the sight of the alluring goods displayed in the shop windows. Then we lounged, placidly sipping bitters, at the open-air café on Piazza dei Signori. The place seemed almost deserted, as it was still too early for the evening crowds to venture out. From where we sat, we could look across to the Palazzo del Capitanio, which housed the old Clock Tower with the great astronomical clock that was conceived by Jacopo Dondi in 1344. Even six and a half centuries later, it was still working! To its left was the Loggia della Gran Guardia with a few people sprawled idly on its steps. What a transformation of the scene when we retraced our steps along the same way after having dinner! For one thing, the square was packed with people and there was not a single free table at any of the many bustling cafes lining it. Recorded music from one café competed with someone singing to the accompaniment of a piano at another. A variety of aromas, dialects, cultures and colours assailed our senses, and we were surprised to see so many Africans and Indians among the throngs. This was Padovan nightlife at its vibrant best. We did not stop to savour it as we had to make an early start for Venice the next morning. So it was off to Hotel San Antonio for a good night's rest.

Short though it was, our visit to Padua was very fulfilling and the moving experience at the tomb of the saint still made me tingle. More than the city he made famous, it was St. Anthony who made a lasting impression on me.

****

Many in Bombay had heard about Alison, and several had been praying for her recovery. Some time after we returned from Italy,

Rayna, one of the girls in my office, casually mentioned that Alison had regained consciousness and had begun to speak a little. Surprised to hear this, I phoned my daughter and told her to check the exact date when Alison came out of her coma. It turned out to be 17 June, the very day after I implored the Saint's help. Several days later, on 3 July, St. Anthony, so gentle and so obliging, answered another plea of mine in really desperate circumstances at Dubai airport while I was on my way back to Bombay. I did not belong to the category of those who professed special devotion to St. Anthony. Like most, only when something was lost, I invoked his assistance with the childish but popular couplet, 'Saint Anthony, Saint Anthony, please look around, something is lost and it must be found.' But with the Dubai deliverance and the Alison episode, this most beloved of saints had won himself a fan for life.

ROMANTIC VENICE – LA SERENISSIMA
"We'll take the boat to the land of dreams"

"Venice!" The merest whisper of the name would conjure up vistas of Romance and Adventure and recall scenes from Barbara Cartland novels, set in the 18th century. Joe had often said that besides Rome (The Eternal City) and Turin (the city of Don Bosco) he wanted someday to also see Venice, which was unique as cities go – it was ancient, an engineering marvel, a repository of priceless art, and it promised to be a traveller's delight. As for me, I scarcely dared to dream of Venice. It always seemed an unreachable destination. Yet now it was just a 40-minute drive away. It was the morning of 17 June 1993 and we were en route from Padua to Venice in Mario's Alfa Romeo. Hotels in Venice are known to be frightfully expensive, so an overnight stay was out of the question, which made us determined to cram as much as possible into the single day we had planned to remain there.

My knowledge of Venice was gleaned mainly from romantic novels, which I had lapped up in my teen years, and so I was prepared to be awed by everything I saw. Yet strangely, my pulse did not race as we floated in a waterbus along the winding waterway of the Grand Canal. Under bridges we went, past ancient buildings and gay gondolas, but the excitement somehow seemed to be missing. What was it? Why wasn't my blood racing at the thought of being in Venice? Would the feeling come later? As we approached the famous Rialto Bridge where there was a buzz of activity and many animated tourists, I 'forced' myself to feel a little excited. I mean, who could imagine actually being there, at the locale of so many famous movies, and not feeling even the teeniest thrill?! Wouldn't people say I was dumb if I returned home and told them I had not been enthused to the marrow of my bones by Venice? I know I will shock many fans of this city, but the fact remains that I was not impressed, so I do not intend to pretend that I was. Perhaps the moment was too big for me, considering my primed up expectations of this undeniably very special city.

Along the way, our waterbus stopped to let off and take on passengers until we ourselves alighted at San Marco, which was the last stop. St. Mark's Square was filled with tourists and pigeons in equal numbers and I gasped at the welcoming array of Venetian masks which greeted us. The Basilica of St. Mark the Evangelist stood out in regal splendour. The present Basilica is the third church to be built on the site. The first one was commissioned to commemorate the arrival of the body of St. Mark in Venice in 828, and was rebuilt after a fire in the year 976. In the second half of the 11th century, the church was entirely remodelled and reconstructed on a much larger scale, using the same foundations and masonry work. Above the central arch stands the statue of St. Mark with angels on either side, and below him a gilded lion, the symbol of the evangelist and also of the Republic of Venice.

We were sad to see some sections of the basilica floor resembled undulating waves, doubtless due to the pressure of the water from below. Where this was very pronounced, rugs had been placed over the buckled surface to prevent tripping.

The entrance fee to the Doge's Palace was steep, but worth every lira. All the great monuments and works of art we had seen thus far in Italy had impressed us a great deal and the Doge's Palace too contained some priceless art treasures. Every step of the way was fascinating, right from the larger-than-life marble statues at the entrance, to the huge salons and audience rooms enriched with magnificent paintings covering all the walls and the ceilings (mainly by Tintoretto and his son). The size of these paintings was awesome and we saw some that covered an entire wall. We did see part of the dungeons but did not venture over to the other side of the Bridge of Sighs – so called because the prisoners who walked across it in the days of the Republic, never returned.

Venice is one of the most expensive cities in Italy, but I found it, to word it as mildly as I am able, not too clean. Thinking back, I realized it must have been this subconscious observation that had dampened the euphoria I was so keen to feel when I first set foot in Venice. I had heard that it was a dying city; now I could see why. It was gradually sinking. We were told that the water had flooded many cellars of the old buildings and ruined priceless art treasures. As we wound our way along the Grand Canal, I had noticed that the massive ancient doors through which the gondolas entered the old palaces and buildings had rotted at their bases due to centuries of water logging, and the paint on most of the buildings was peeling off in strips. If this was their faded glory, what must have been the pomp and opulence those same structures exuded in centuries past! I realized that the cost of maintenance would be prohibitive, yet a sense of heavy sadness filled me on seeing how the majestic structures had fallen prey to the elements and had been reduced to such a shabby state.

As for some of the smaller canals and internal waterways, they resembled dirty back alleys – with a stench to match. It is considered a must for visitors to take a trip in a gondola under the Bridge of Sighs to ensure that one returns to the famous city which has been romanticized and immortalized on the silver screen. All I could think of when I saw many tourists following this routine was that they must have strong stomachs!

It was drizzling when we arrived in Venice that morning, but the sun had come out for us and stayed with us all through the day. After lunch in a typical Venetian café, we attempted entry to a couple of other places but found them closed for the afternoon siesta, so we strolled around at random. I got one plump gondolier to pose for me on one of the small bridges, and another very vocal one we passed, took one look at Joe with his beard and cap, waved heartily and shouted out to him, 'Eh, Garibaldi!' which made us all laugh.

Towards evening, without any warning, it suddenly turned quite dark and the sky became overcast. It threatened to be a heavy downpour, and since we had not so cleverly left our umbrellas in the car back at the car park, we decided to leave at once, but not before we bought some of those beautiful hand-painted masks on sale. Then the rain started, and we dodged from one shelter to the next until we reached the waterbus, mercifully without getting fully drenched. As we retraced our route down the Grand Canal amidst grey and angry sheets of rain, I recall telling Joe that I was not sad to be leaving. La Serenissima (the most serene) was weeping for herself.

MAGNIFICENT MARMOLADA
"I'm on the top of the world, looking down on …"

It was nearing the end of our holiday in Italy. Our hosts, the Jellicis, had shown us all they could of their beautiful and beloved little Alpine village of Tesero and its surroundings. We had gone as close as we could to the majestic Dolomite Mountains, wandered around the picturesque countryside and walked amid a variety of mountain flowers that dotted entire hillsides like yellow or red-speckled carpets. We took innumerable photographs against breathtaking backdrops, from snow-capped mountains to undulating landscapes of verdant green valleys in which nestled cosy little villages. We had been welcomed in homes with open-arm affection, partaken of local delicacies, engaged in stimulating discussions with some who spoke English, and slept deep restful slumbers. Yet we still had another treat awaiting us.

The Jellicis arranged a picnic to Marmolada di Rocca, which, at a height of 3265 mts (around 10,000 ft above sea level) is the highest mountain peak of the Dolomites. The Marmolada is snowbound all through the year, so Mario and Rita took plenty of warm clothing for all of us. They also packed a picnic lunch and, of course, enough wine to wash it down. Our friend, Lucia Doliana, her father, Tarcisio, and brother, Marcello, joined us.

The ticket for the cable cars and lifts to the top of the peak was a steep L32,000 (about Rs.1600) but it turned out to be well worth the expense. As we stood at the base of the magnificent mountain and looked up its steep slopes, I was awed by its size. I confess I was also a little bit scared as we entered the large cable car with several others, some of whom were carrying skis. As we ascended smoothly and quickly, I held my breath because it felt as though we were suspended from the sky looking down at the world below that was getting more miniscule by the minute. The view was fascinating, indescribable.

Just as we neared the station, it seemed as if we were going to slam right into the side of the mountain. When we disembarked, I thought we had reached our destination, but soon realized all were making their way to a second cable car that took us further up. Joe and I had been handed heaps of thermal wear with the advice to don additional layers as we kept ascending. The third lift took us to the highest station on top of the Marmolada, and at that point it was hard to believe that we were not actually on top of the world!

There, enthroned in an alcove, was a beautiful statue of the Madonna cast in bronze, known as the Marmolada Madonna. Our efforts to get closer to the statue were defeated by the compacted ice-covered floor on which we kept slipping, so we offered our prayers standing at the entrance of this very amazing grotto. Mario then took advantage of the slippery ice and gave a comic demonstration of skating on it in his boots while we held our breath, expecting him to land on his derriere at any moment. However, his skating and balancing antics could rival Charlie Chaplin's any day! In fact, Mario's passion was climbing his beloved mountains and he had developed exceptional mountaineering skills; he was also a member of the helicopter rescue team, which demanded a high degree of expertise and physical fitness.

We then went out into the glare of bright sunlight that reflected very strongly off the white snow, and even my sunglasses seemed inadequate to block it. By now, we were all clad more warmly, Joe and I more than the others, looking like bloated furry animals and still shivering a bit. There were many besides us at the peak; unbelievably, some of them were sunbathing in scanty clothing, while others were excitedly preparing to ski down the slopes. I was too scared to go anywhere near the edge, afraid that I would roll off. The snow beneath our feet was not soft like freshly fallen snow, but crunchy like crushed ice. However in other spots, our feet sank in up to our calves. Our footwear was out of place and impractical in the snow, and in no time my socks and walking shoes were soaked through. My feet began to feel like two blocks of ice, but that did not stop us from romping about like children.

I was truly amazed at all the planning and detail that went into making the Marmolada Peak such a great tourist attraction throughout the year. From our spectacular viewpoint, we could look across the Alpine range to the mountains in Austria, and Mario pointed out to us the place where the Iceman, Otzi, was discovered. (Several years after this, we were in Bolzano and actually saw Otzi from close up, in the museum). Just being on the Marmolada was exhilarating. This was truly the experience of a lifetime and we were thrilled beyond words.

On our return journey, we were the sole occupants in the cable cars as many had opted to ski their way down. Taking advantage of the situation, we sang a lot of mountaineering songs that sounded even nicer in that empty silence and did not cause any avalanches! As we descended, we each grew several kilos lighter, as we kept peeling off our outer warm clothing layer by layer. If only we could do the same with our body weight! When we were 'down to earth' again, we stowed our warm clothing in the car and found a beautiful spot in the sun, at a place called Malga Ciapela, with the rugged base of the Marmolada in the background. The first thing I did was to remove my snow-soaked socks and shoes and they dried out very quickly in the hot sun. We then got down to devouring all the goodies brought along for our picnic lunch, for which we had built up a great appetite. The two bottles of red wine we downed probably accounted for the long and lusty singing that followed. Since we knew many common tunes, we sang on, often alternating stanzas in English and in Italian.

On our drive back, we stopped to have steaming cups of coffee at Passo Valle, located at a height of 2033 metres. The family-run café claimed to have shown hospitality to tourists and travellers for almost a century. Two huge St. Bernard dogs were sprawled out in the sun making the best of their idle months. Apart from raising a lazy eyebrow when we tried to wake them, they did not display any sign of life or any interest in us. Mario, our very own stand-up comedian, entertained us by climbing into an empty *brenzo* (a hollowed tree trunk into which fresh water from a mountain spring is channelled) and mimed having a bath, vigorously scrubbing his back with an imaginary brush. We thought he looked so comic and laughed hilariously – and so did some other travellers who had driven up unnoticed by Mario.

Our next stop was the Paneveggio Forest Station where we viewed specimens of the flora and fauna of the region neatly displayed for visitors. This was once a part of the Austro-Hungarian Empire. In fact, during World War I, the front line of battle was right within this forest where, as can be imagined, a great deal of damage and devastation was caused. Mario later informed us that Antonio Stradivari (1644 to 1737) would come to the Paneveggio Forest to select the wood to fashion his legendary instruments. He was undoubtedly the greatest artisan in his field, and the violins, cellos, guitars, violas and harps he produced have kept his name alive. Of over 1000 instruments that he crafted, only about 650 survive to this day. These are valued as the finest bowed stringed instruments ever created; today a 'Stradivarius' violin could fetch untold millions. In June 2011, one was auctioned for $15,932,115. The bidder was anonymous and the proceeds were donated to help victims of the earthquake in Japan. The wood from the Paneveggio Forest has found its way to distant corners of the world in the form of artifacts exquisitely carved by the talented artists of that region. The shops stock vast arrays of these, ranging from miniature to life-size, from realistic to whimsy; and we have many specimens of these with us, some bought and others gifted.

In Bombay, we would have been exhausted with just one simple outing. Here we had had such a full day and yet, when we touched base in Tesero later that evening, we were as fresh as ever and went out visiting again. The mountain had certainly invigorated us; or rather, cast a mystic spell on us. Even if time dims some of these memories, we are unlikely ever to forget this jolly, fun-filled and memorable day, or the magic of Marmolada, The Magnificent.

TRANQUIL TIROL AND ITS MADONNA
"Hail Queen of Heav'n"

Joe had never forgotten his disappointment at having to forgo his visit to Vienna on his first trip abroad in 1981. For me too, the waltz capital beckoned with irresistible force. So, though it involved extra running around and great expense, when planning our trip, we had taken care to obtain visas for Austria. We had contemplated an overland journey from Bolzano to Salzburg, then on to Vienna, and back to Tesoro after a couple of days. It all seemed so simple on paper but when we studied distances and likely expenses, it was quite another matter. Mario had heard us talking of Vienna very animatedly and was all set to drive us there. However, when we toted up all the trips we had made from our mountain base in Tesero to Venice, to Padua and the surrounding regions, not to mention the day excursions to so many places of interest, we just couldn't think of putting our kind hosts to any more trouble and expense. They had insisted on accompanying and driving us everywhere, and anyone who has travelled abroad will know that the costs involved could not have been little. This was the main reason we decided to give Vienna a miss. Of course, Mario and Rita would brush aside such considerations, and it took quite some persuasion to convince them that the journey would tire us too much. We pointed out that for us plains-folk, the long drives along winding roads through mountainous territory took some getting used to – your body moved one way and the insides of your tummy the other!

Mario and Rita then came up with the suggestion that the next best would be a visit to the Tirol region, which had the full flavour of Austria. So on Sunday, 20 June, dressed in our Sunday best we left to attend mass at the famous shrine of the Sanctuario Madonna Addolorata Di Pietralba (Sanctuary of the Sorrowful Mother of White Rock). The Church is located in the middle of a green meadow at 1530 mts above sea level. After finding parking place in a field near the Shrine, we ascended the rather steep (for me) flight of steps leading up to the Church, which was on a plateau atop a small hill. I was embarrassed to be puffing and panting as I climbed – so much for our sedentary city life! The church was filled with pilgrims and devotees, but we managed to find standing room at the rear while mass was being said in German, the language of that region. Being the only Indians there (and I feel sure Indians are rarely seen in those parts) we must have evoked a lot of curiosity, but the natural reserve of the people prevented them from showing any overt interest either in our outfits or in us. In their code of conduct, it would have been impolite to do so.

The sanctuary traced its origins to the discovery in 1553, of an alabaster statuette representing the Pieta, which was found by a farmer while he was digging his fields. The fame of this spread far and wide after it was credited with having miraculous powers, and even today, it continues to attract thousands of pilgrims and tourists from all over. Pope John Paul II also made a first-time papal visit to this renowned sanctuary on 17 June 1988. The statuette was installed in a primitive, very tiny chapel, which today is inside the baroque church, which was built in 1638, around and above the original shrine. It reminded me of a fireplace or hearth, and we had to stoop a bit to enter and light our votive candle. I must record that while standing and praying devoutly in that confined space, a sense of peace, warmth and love enveloped us.

After mass, we stopped to read some of the hundreds of framed testimonies hung on the walls, documenting escapes from death, recovery from disease and relief from a variety of other problems, all attributed to the miraculous powers of this statuette. Many had put up newspaper cuttings and photographs as proof of the gravity of their problems. We also made a fervent request for help in the life-threatening situation we were facing. Not only was our problem solved within the year, but we also unexpectedly got the opportunity to return to the shrine in 2000 to thank this beautiful Mother of Sorrows.

After buying a few rosaries, souvenirs and post cards, we drove on to the Lago di Carezza. As its name implies, the lake truly looked like it was made of marble and its still waters were a most unusual shade of blue. The lake was fringed all around with tall, shady pine and spruce trees that were perfectly reflected in its placid surface; it was an ideal picnic and camping ground. However, camping and fishing were strictly prohibited in the area. All you were permitted to do was to walk or sit around and enjoy the natural beauty and palpable serenity of the place. Mario told us that Austria was very similar to the Tirol region we were in, so any regrets which may have lingered for change of plans, evaporated – though if someday we do have a chance to visit and savour all the beauty and cultural riches Austria has to offer, we would jump at it.

After driving around lazily on that Sunday afternoon, enjoying the alpine scenery and the neat and picturesque cottages and chalets, we stopped for lunch at a typical German/Austrian restaurant and opted to eat outdoors on huge wooden trestle tables. A few inquisitive deer wandered out from the nearby forest to peek at us and scampered back in a hurry before Joe could get out his camera. While tranquillity reigned as far as eye could see, our immediate vicinity was slightly chaotic as hungry, vocal humans competed for the attention of busy, bustling waiters to place their orders for lunch.

On our return journey, Joe and I predictably fell asleep in the car. We used to tell Mario that his car seemed to cast a spell on us. I think it was the continuous swaying, as we took the sharp curves up and down the mountain slopes, that would invariably rock us to sleep – much to our embarrassment and to their amusement. When we returned to Tesero – this time by another route – we were greeted by a sky that was dark and overcast. Mario told us how lucky we had been with the weather thus far. The Bishop of Darjeeling had visited him twice but never once experienced the nice weather we enjoyed. Our knack of 'arranging' for good weather wherever we go had never failed us so far! Now it seemed as if our imminent departure was being mourned as the heavens opened and wept amidst thunderous protests. It felt so good to be so loved even by Nature.

LAST SUPPERS AND FAREWELLS
"Now is the hour when we must say goodbye"

With just two days to go before leaving the tiny village of Tesero to return to Rome, Joe and I spent the morning strolling around on our own (unescorted for the first time). Despite the different street levels and many tiny side lanes that passed through and under some ancient houses, we found our way back to the Jellicis' house easily after doing a little shopping. That evening we were invited to the Dolianas' home for dinner. We had met Lucia Doliana and her father, Tarcisio, when they came to India with Mario and Fabio Jellici in 1991/92. One brother, Marcello, joined the group going up the Marmolada, and now we met the other two handsome lads, Claudio and Ciro, as well.

Lucia served us a lavish meal, which she had taken great pains to prepare. After dinner, the piano was opened and Ciro entertained us with his mastery of the ivory keys. While all of us joined in the singing and were enjoying ourselves, I noticed Lucia had slipped away; I found she was doing the clearing up all alone, so I joined her, seeing there were no maids or helpers around. Italian men naturally expect their women to handle certain jobs, so all of them, including Lucia, were appalled when I insisted on attacking the mountain of crockery and cutlery piled up around the sink. Lucia must have been exhausted preparing that enormous dinner single-handedly for all of us and I could not bear to think of her being confronted with all that washing the next morning. Brushing aside all protests, Rita and I helped Lucia clear up. We worked systematically scrubbing, rinsing, drying and putting away dishes – three pairs of hands certainly made short shrift of the work. Then we were all free to enjoy the delicious desserts and liqueur – and better, the bonhomie that followed. We were all very happy and so relaxed that Joe even ventured to tell some jokes in Italian. Later he confided that he did not know whether they were cracking up because of his punch lines or because of his cracked Italian. Whatever the truth of the matter, we were all having a laughingly great time.

On the morning of 22 June, Joe and I woke up late and took another lazy ramble around the village, and in the afternoon, Mario drove us up another mountain. On our many jaunts around the place, we had noticed the great numbers of ski lifts all over. The Fiemme Valley is known as the paradise of cross-country skiing and rightly so, because it provides some of the best facilities for tourists who flock there for various sporting activities in winter. In the late afternoon, we drove to a nearby town, Predazzo, to see how pasta was made in a factory owned by one of Mario's cousins. It was fascinating to see that the entire process from start to finish was computerized and mechanized, down to the packaging, labelling, storing and despatch. Even the farina used for preparing pasta, brought in by large trucks, was unloaded mechanically. In that huge, spacious factory with so many different processes going on simultaneously, there was barely a handful of skilled people to work the machines and supervise the production. And what a variety of pasta the factory turned out!

Finally our last day in Tesero dawned. From the time we had left Bombay on 3 June, so much had happened that it felt like we had been away from home for months. We had enjoyed every moment of our stay, and the ten glorious days we had spent in Tesero were incredibly relaxing and refreshing – just the break Joe and I needed, away from the life-threatening problems at home, which we had unbelievably managed to put out of our minds for all that while. We were not unduly sad to be leaving because we definitely intended to return and also because we knew that we would be seeing Mario and family in India before long. After a sumptuous last supper, we drove down to Bolzano to catch our night train to Rome.

When we reached the Bolzano railway station, I was contemplating whether to phone Karen Laimer, a girl who had studied Italian with me in Bombay, now married to a German and settled in Italy. I had not contacted her during our stay in Tesero as I thought she lived at a great distance from any place we would be likely to visit. After taking one look at her address Mario told me that Merano (where she lived) was just an hour's drive from Bolzano. We had an hour and more to spare while waiting for our train so I rang up and told Karen I had called to say hello-and-goodbye, and also mentioned from where I was phoning. Karen's reaction revealed how homesick she must have been; she got her husband to drive her to the railway station, though it was very late at night, just to be able to meet and talk to us face-to-face even if for a few minutes! It was just great to have those unexpected precious moments with Karen and Gunther Laimer before our train arrived and we found our berths.

The time had come to say our final goodbyes to Mario and Rita Jellici. My usual spontaneity of breaking into song at every turn had deserted me. For all our talk about not feeling too sad to leave, that moment was quite heart wrenching for all of us, and amidst all the kissing, hugs and embraces, there were also a few silent tears. The ten days spent in each other's close company had cemented our friendship. With hearts filled to overflowing, we were leaving behind friends with sad faces, but we were taking back with us beautiful memories.

ARRIVEDERCI ROMA
"City of a Million Warm Embraces"

We had decided to take the night train from Bolzano to Rome in order to catch as many precious daylight hours as possible in the Eternal City. The contrast in train facilities abroad and in India was too striking to miss. Sad to say, even the second-class compartment in Italy was several notches better than the first class in India. On reaching Rome early the next morning, we took a taxi to Via Poliziana to the house of Mrs. Judith Daniels, an Indian lady who let out rooms and who immediately made us feel at home. We had just a day and a half in Rome so we did not want to waste a minute of it.

After a refreshing shower and a perky cup of coffee, we left to visit the Vatican Museum. Those who go to Rome and leave without seeing this museum and the Sistine Chapel deprive themselves of one of the finest feasts of exquisite art, and spiritual and political history that Italy has to offer. The entrance fee was L12,000 each, but from the moment you step in until you leave, you are overwhelmed by the magnificence and splendour of every exhibit. We walked almost in a daze down endless corridors and halls filled with priceless ancient treasures. Yet if you ask me to describe any one in detail I would be at a loss. It is humanly impossible to take in such marvels within just a few hours; you would need to return daily for a month (with a pile of lire notes!) before you could begin to get the flavour of such a panorama of grandeur, and even begin to appreciate Michelangelo's famed masterpieces in the Sistine Chapel. How we longed to lie on the floor and gaze at the ceiling at leisure, but we had to be content with craning our sore necks backwards and practically rushing through every display before closing time.

We then dashed back to the city to catch a guided tour of Rome. Having become attuned to higher price levels by now, we were skeptical about the kind of tour we had been recommended, and had booked, at just L6,000 a head, especially when we noted the itinerary promised to cover about 43 landmarks in the space of a few hours. Well, it would be next best to legging it to a few adjacent monuments or not being able to see anything worthwhile of Rome before we left. Our first impression of the tour guide was reassuring; he was Italian, very outgoing and spoke fairly good English quite fluently. In fact, Alessandrini Annito proved to be a very informative and entertaining guide and everyone on the tour was very pleased with him, though I do not know how he kept up that constant commentary, first in Italian, then in English, and also managed to spike it with his terrific sense of humour till the end.

Italy has preserved its cultural heritage so meticulously that practically every step you take brings you to a centuries-old monument or heritage site. There are hundreds of churches and chapels, all full of antiques, some dating back a thousand years and more. And each has its own interesting story. I do not intend recounting all the stories of all the places we visited on this tour so I'll touch on just the ones that particularly interested me.

The Basilica of St. Peter's was, naturally, one of our very first stops, with 20 minutes allotted to look around. As we had already been to the basilica, Joe went off to make a few phone calls, but I thought I'd go back for one more look. I was tempted to just walk around admiring the church again, but was drawn to the chapel of the Blessed Sacrament on the right. I intended to say a short prayer and move on, but a benediction service was in progress so I stayed till the end, after which I had to rush and rejoin the group immediately, as our guide had thrown out enough warnings about returning punctually. Some might feel that I could have used those 20 minutes more fruitfully instead of kneeling in one place, but I felt a tremendous sense of peace and satisfaction from that unexpected benediction.

On the Campidoglio, one of the Seven Hills of Rome, stands the Church of S. Maria d'Ara Coeli, built around the 6th century on the ruins of Juno Moneta's temple (which are still visible at road level). We climbed up the long flight of stone steps with much puffing and panting, while our guide continued his non-stop patter almost without pausing to draw breath. The church, which was under renovation when we were visiting, contained many works of art from the 13th and 14th centuries, but its fame lay not so much in its vintage as in the famous statue it houses: the Holy Bambino of Ara Coeli. This statue is said to have been carved in the 15th century by a pious Franciscan friar, from the wood of an olive tree in the Garden of Gethsemane (Garden of the Agony of Jesus). Legend has it that the friar had no paints to complete his handiwork, but an angel miraculously performed that task. While returning to Rome, the friar was caught in a raging storm at sea and was forced to throw overboard his small case containing all his belongings and his carving. Even so, the statue of the Bambino arrived at the port of Livorno all by itself, in the wake of the ship. Soon, unusual miracles were attributed to it, and the holy image was installed with great joy in the Eternal City where it receives special veneration.

Next stop: Circo Massimo. True, it could not hold a candle to today's super-stadia, but even in ruins, it still inspired a feeling of awe. As we gazed round, it was not hard to imagine that at any moment chariots would come thundering round the curve, covering another lap in a fierce competition reminiscent of the one we saw in the movie Ben Hur. This arena, located between the Aventine and Palatine hills, has remained virtually untouched since the times of Romulus when the first horse races were run. Parts of the structure and the tiered seating had fallen into ruin, as also the stables. Yet if the stones in those ruins could speak, how many tales of heroism and victory would we hear, while the walls resounded with shouts of acclaim!

Announcing the next point of interest, our guide reinforced his commentary with dramatic demonstrations of what could happen (if legends were to be believed) at the Bocca Della Verita. What we heard sparked our interest; Joe and I were keen to see it first hand and up close, so we were the first to get up and out of the bus. It was totally unexpected to find this pagan sculpture in the portico of a catholic place of worship. We were given the explanation that the Church of Santa Maria in Cosmedin had been constructed on the site of the Temple of Ceres, and that as a matter of policy ancient artefacts were preserved and maintained as near as feasible to their original location. We crowded excitedly round the dark alcove to the left of the entrance to the church, gaping at 'The Mouth of Truth'. What stared back at us was an open mouth from the face of a longhaired, bearded deity, carved on a large marble medallion which measured roughly 1.6 mts in diameter (about as much as the span of your arms outstretched) mounted on a stubby pedestal. A large fissure sliced through the left eye, ran down the left nostril to the gaping mouth, widening further as it cut through the lower lip. This added to its fearsome aspect.

The name Bocca Della Verita, given to this sculpture, derived from the legend that a person suspected of bearing false witness or of lying was asked to put his hand into the mouth. The 'Bocca', it was said, would spare the innocent, but bite the hand of the guilty. Our voluble guide was now defying us to insert our hands into the 'Mouth' if we dared. Remember the scene in 'Roman Holiday' with Gregory Peck and Audrey Hepburn? It did not need any streak of daredevilry for many of us to attempt this, though we did notice that some were unusually quick to withdraw their hands! Did the 'Bocca' really bite? Perhaps it did. This sculpture goes back over 2200 years, and is considered one of the earliest pieces of religious art. Conceivably then, a concealed mechanism could have been cleverly installed and operated behind the scenes, making the divinity 'bite' some and not others, which would create wonder and awe in the populace.

Still discussing the Truth about the Mouth, we drove along the Via dei Fori Imperiali, a beautiful boulevard flanked with trees and archaeological ruins. At the end of this road, we came directly to the famous Coliseum. This incredible amphitheatre was the largest ever constructed in the Roman Empire and was considered one of the greatest works of Roman architecture and engineering. It was built in a valley which previously held an artificial lake around which were porticos and baths. Standing in the city centre, the Coliseum is symbolically and literally in the heart of Rome and continues to remain its iconic symbol. To our great disappointment, we were firmly refused entry as we had reached after closing time. We could admire the gigantic historic stadium only from the outside, marvelling at its size and the massive walls, and the heavy metal links to which prisoners would be chained. I had a sneaking suspicion that our arrival at the Coliseum had been timed to ensure we could not explore the inside, as this would have proved so absorbing that to shepherd everyone back to the bus would have been a difficult task for our guide, whose spirits were beginning to flag. This was another regret I carried back with me.

We had packed a lot into the day, which had been most interesting but also tiring, and our energy levels had started to dip. True, we had missed out on seeing some important landmarks, but it would have been physically impossible to do any more in the time available to us. Our guide was touched that we had taken up a collection in appreciation of his excellent and entertaining services, and he spontaneously invited us to have a beer with him. Alessandrini Annito was surprised to hear that we were catholics. He said he had observed me make the sign of the cross and watched me praying in the churches, which puzzled him because he thought that only Hindus and Moslems lived in India (the incidents of racial violence had made big news all over the world). It was amazing to discover, time and again, how little most people know about our country or, in fact, anything outside of their own small worlds.

The next day, 23 June, was our last in Rome. The taxi to the airport set us back L65,000! Joe and I parted there, as we had to report at different terminals, he to return to Bombay on Air India while I took the Emirates flight to Dubai to visit with my niece, Debra Pereira, and her family.

At the Immigration counter I innocently mentioned that my husband was also travelling but on a different airline. That set alarm bells ringing and I had quite a bit of explaining to do after this. I was grilled for at least 45 minutes about our purpose in visiting Rome and why we were departing by different airlines. Eventually I managed to convince them that we had participated in the Family Fest (which most people in Rome had heard about) and I had various papers from the event to back us up. I also explained that while Joe had a free ticket on Air India with a Rome-Bombay-Dubai-Bombay routing, I had opted to travel by Emirates, which had a direct flight from Rome to Dubai where Joe would join me after a day. It was disconcerting for a passenger to feel she was being viewed with suspicion, but in hindsight and with all the hijackings and bombings on aircrafts, I could appreciate the need for the airline people to be extra cautious – and passengers to be extra co-operative.

I was sad to be alone and sad to say Arrivederci to Roma, but not too sad to know that come what may, I would return to the land that had stolen my heart. I do not think there is anyone who could resist falling in love with Italy. Our love affair too had begun and it promised to be as passionate as the natives are.

MY DUBAI SHAKES
"Then I shall bow in humble adoration, and there proclaim my God how great Thou art"

All alone on my way from Rome to Dubai, I went into a cocoon of inaction. Travel, whether by plane or train, seems to have this strange effect on me: I just clam up, talk as little as possible and rarely move out of my seat. When I'm travelling by myself, it's even more pronounced. This behaviour in one who is usually talkative may seem out of character, but perhaps I absorb many more details about my surroundings in this way. Who is it who said, 'You cannot listen if your mouth is open?'

At the immigration counter in Dubai the official riffled through the pages of my passport and asked for my visa; I told him that my niece had assured me that she had obtained one and, according to accepted procedure, it was awaiting my arrival. He made no comment, but went on to ask a series of questions: the precise address of the place where I would be staying, with whom, for how long, and how well was I acquainted with my hosts. Questions answered, I held my hand out for my passport, but evidently he had other thoughts; he carried on 'talking' to me, asking if I were alone, how and why I was travelling unaccompanied, and then said I should give him my telephone number! By now, I was acutely aware that this form of screening went beyond the bounds of legitimate information gathering but I remained polite and managed to keep the smile on my face. I had a vague recollection of having heard that single women were interrogated more thoroughly than others; being married, I certainly did not expect such treatment. By then it was late at night and I could not help noticing that most of the passengers had departed; I still managed to keep my cool and patiently continued giving him the same answers in flat measured tones. My niece, Debra, and her husband, David, were waiting patiently at the exit. In fact I could see them through the glass wall, using sign language to ask what the matter was; I pointed them out to the official who then grudgingly permitted me to make my escape. Debra and David were greatly relieved when I finally stumbled out, and were very surprised to hear what I had to tell them about my welcome to Dubai.

To counterbalance this, I must mention that on my first stop at Dubai airport on my way to Rome, though I was apprehensive being on my own, I was very pleasantly surprised to find that the local personnel at the Duty Free outlets and Immigration were courteous and polite. In fact they were helpful beyond the call of duty and I was very impressed.

Joe was scheduled to join me in Dubai a day later; instead he phoned to tell me that some nasty developments had taken place during our absence from Bombay, and the upshot was he had to stay back and handle that crisis. This news upset me greatly and I was very dejected for the first couple of days. Then I realized I could either continue being miserable and make my hosts miserable too, (in any case I could do nothing about the situation in Bombay) or I could put the matter aside and go on to make the best of my stay – which is just what I did. I also met up with many friends I knew from Bandra, strolled on the beach and of course indulged in a bit of shopping. Considering one had heard so much about Dubai being dubbed the Shoppers' Mecca, I didn't really do much, but I do remember buying a beautiful large lacy tablecloth for our eight-seater dining table.

'Incredible' was my word for the gold souks. It was dazzle dazzle all the way, with shoppers buying and buying like mad. It surprised me to see many women in burkhas who, I was told, were adorned with loads of gold which were all covered up under their flowing robes and could not be seen. The gold was of genuine 24 ct. and very soft, and the prices were much lower than the Bombay rates. Gold still held some attraction for me then, so after bargaining for four bangles for my daughter Melissa who was to be married that year, I could not resist picking up a simple necklace and two bangles for myself. Like most women, I too could not resist buying gold ornaments. Today I have passed that phase and, in fact, I rarely use any of the gold I have.

Debra and David were good hosts who took care of me well, and their three energetic children kept me entertained. The week with them passed quickly and soon I found myself back at Dubai airport on 3 July 1993 to catch my flight to Bombay. Ticket formalities completed, I said goodbye to Debra and David who had come to see me off, and went on to Immigration. I handed over my passport and was asked for my Dubai visa. I fished in my handbag but could not find it. The official was insistent that I should produce this. Another frantic search of my handbag and cabin baggage drew a blank. I was told that there was no way I could get onto the flight unless I produced this visa, so there was no alternative but to check the rest of my luggage; I was sure that I had the visa whilst packing. Now I was really glad that my niece and her husband had insisted on waiting till I cleared immigration before they left. I called them in to help me and once again we sifted through my handbags – no visa!

With some difficulty, we recalled my checked in luggage though it meant I would have to go through the whole process of checking and security clearance once more. More than anything, it was embarrassing to have to open up my suitcase with so many people milling around. I am very methodical and well-organized and so could not understand how all my travel papers were not in one place together with my passport and ticket. After more frantic rummaging, we still couldn't trace the errant visa. While the three of us looked at each other blankly and helplessly, I remembered St. Anthony, whom we pray to when we lose something. I desperately pleaded with him and kept silently repeating, 'Help me Jesus, help me St. Anthony,' even as I began to repack my suitcase with a heavy heart. I knew that if I did not leave by that flight I might be stuck in Dubai till the end of July, as all outgoing flights were fully booked till then. Just before shutting my suitcase, I pressed down lightly on my dressing gown, which was right on top, when a paper seemed to float out ... Yes, it was the visa, though how it got there was a mystery I had no time to reflect on at that moment. I only gave praise to God and thanks to that wonderful saint who acts so promptly, before once again thanking my niece and her husband profusely and rushing off to catch my flight.

Finally settled in the aircraft, I had time to reflect about the visa and how it came to be where we found it. What had happened was this: when I had completed my packing, I realized I was well over the 20-kg limit allowed by Emirates Airlines and would have to pay a tidy sum for my excess baggage. Accordingly, I re-distributed heavier items in such a way that I would be carrying more in my hand baggage – another foolish thing we Indians do! However, at the last moment, a friend of a friend promised to have a word with a friend working in Emirates to overlook the excess weight. Other friends who had come to say goodbye then helped me repack and, in the scramble of moving items from one bag to another, the visa, which I had kept right on top in my hand baggage, was somehow pulled into the suitcase with my dressing gown, which was one of the last items to be packed. The dressing gown would have been the last article I would have thought of checking. Even so, I seemed to recall that the visa slipped out virtually on its own, which also amazed me at the time. If that wasn't a miracle, I don't know what is!

Chapter Eight

1995-1996
CHURCH OF 'MIRIK-CALS'
"Now I shout it from the highest hills …"

In November 1995, we found ourselves once more winging our way to Bagdogra via Calcutta and then motoring up to Sonada. Once you leave the plains the drive is pleasant with mile after mile of eye-soothing tea plantations and scenic vistas along the winding mountainous route. We were back again after six years, and again, during the cold season which I dreaded! Actually, the main purpose of our trip was to visit Mirik, not Sonada, but since we were going to be in the region anyway, our friend, Fr. Mathew Pulingathil, had requested us to conduct a seminar at their College of Philosophy, so that was our first stop.

After the three-day course, we were off to Mirik which was a place we had never been to before. Mirik is a very small and typical hill town located in the Sing-lila Hills region at a height of 1767 mts above sea level. The town's main attraction is Lake Sumendu, which offers boating facilities and has a 3.5-km walkway around its perimeter. There are some decent, inexpensive hotels in the area, with tourist cottages and a few landscaped gardens. Some time-share companies have already acquired properties here. But we were always guests at the various Don Bosco institutions and it was the same in Mirik. That November, we were not the only visitors to converge on Don Bosco, Mirik. Parishioners from nearby and also from far-flung villages kept pouring in for the great celebration: the solemn ceremony of the blessing of the new Don Bosco Church. This had been built mainly with funds received from the relatives and benefactors of Fr. Luigi Jellici. And since by now we had established close ties with his family in Italy, he and Fr. Mathew (who had both been transferred to Mirik) were keen for us to be part of the festivities.

113

The Salesian house stood on a rise on a hill in Deosidara district and the new church had been constructed facing it. Joe and I were given the special guest room at the rear of the church, which commanded a sweeping view of the surrounding landscape. We realized that it had been allotted to us with every good intention, but the recently plastered walls were still damp, and because of its elevated location, it was fully exposed to the cold air coming up from the valley. For us, it was like living in a refrigerator! At the first opportunity we shifted to a room in the main house, but even there it was pretty cold. Although temperatures can drop very low during winter, in summer the maximum in Mirik reaches 30°C.

The blessing of the church was well attended; it was truly 'church full' and we ended up in the gallery from where we had a bird's eye view of the entire long, solemn ceremony. The devotion of the people was remarkable, many of them having come from quite far away, mostly on foot. After the service, we mingled with the many guests while a simple lunch was served to all.

As our air travel from Mumbai to Calcutta to Guwahati and onward to Bagdogra or Dimapur cost as much as a cheap return ticket to New York, we decided that whenever we were bound for one place in the Northeast, we should try to visit at least one other in the vicinity. Hence, on this our first visit to Mirik we planned a trip to Sikkim as well. So the day after the celebrations we set off in the school jeep accompanied by both Frs. Luigi and Mathew, with a very pleasant driver who could negotiate mountain roads skilfully.

IN THE SHADOW OF KANCHEN-DZONGA
"There are mountains we need to climb, but the mountains standing in our way are only in our minds"

Sikkim chose to remain an independent monarchy when India gained independence from the British in 1947. However, through a set of diplomatic exchanges and negotiations Sikkim acceded to India in 1975, becoming its twenty-second state. We had planned to visit Gangtok, the capital and the largest town in Sikkim. This popular tourist destination is located in the Shivalik Hills of the eastern Himalayan range at an altitude of 1437 mts above sea level. Gangtok means 'High Hill', and the name is most apt as the city sits on a ridge that overlooks the Ranipool River. The main communities living there are the Nepalis, Lepchas and Bhutias.

We checked into Hotel Tibet in the heart of the shopping district and were pleased with the clean and comfortable rooms. As we left the hotel to go sightseeing I noticed a shop right next to the hotel that was selling some interesting fabrics and, woman that I am, I could not resist checking this out. I ended up buying some nice Chinese satin silk material for a dress which I later had made up in a typical Chinese pattern. We visited some of the many monasteries dotting Gangtok and later drove up to the top of Menam Hill, which is at an altitude of 3140 mts above sea level. From there we got a clear and uninterrupted view of the Kanchenjunga (or Kanchen-dzonga as it is known in Sikkim), the world's third highest peak. It looked so much closer from here than it did from Darjeeling or Mirik. One could also see the Kalimpong and Darjeeling Hills which stretched from the south right across to the Indo-China border in the north. It was spectacular.

Though it was such a short stay, I did enjoy those two days in that beautiful hill state very much. Before leaving we bought some of the Sikkim liqueurs which were extremely cheap compared to their prices in Mumbai. ('Bombay' was officially changed to 'Mumbai' in November 1995.) I remember also buying a whisky in a flat bottle shaped like a kukri, the typical knife that Gurkhas carry. We bought this only to add to our collection of unusual bottles and miniatures which Joe had been collecting from his trips abroad. Frankly, I had the feeling that the whisky might be quite harsh and there was no way we even thought of sampling it. Most probably we gave this away when we disposed of our collection years later.

Hearing of the proximity of Pashupati to Mirik, we made time for a foray there. Pashupati is on the border of Nepal; it takes about half an hour to cover the 11-km-drive from Mirik. We went via Sukhiapokhri (I remember being very amused by the name, which stuck in my head) to the Pashupati-Simana border along a route that had Nepal on one side of the road and West Bengal on the other. Only Indians are allowed to pass through this border outpost and we were quite thrilled that we were able to enter Nepal without our passports. Of course, there were checkpoints and guards, but this was a tiny village that had small shops selling 'foreign' goods that we Indians craved at one time. We bought several items, including some crystal cut-glass tumblers which I packed carefully to carry back home – only to discover later that these were available at Crawford Market in Mumbai for much less than what we had paid in faraway Pashupati via Sukhiapokhri!

SILIGURI, PHUNTSHOLING, KALIMPONG
"Those faraway places, with strange-sounding names"

In the course of our correspondence, I made the 'mistake' of informing Fr. Mathew that Joe had been booked for a seminar for Maersk Shipping in Calcutta in May 1996. The next we knew, he had convinced us that their new batch of philosophy students would benefit greatly by a three-day seminar. Another reason for acceding to Fr. Mathew's request was the lure of a visit to Bhutan. He was now posted in Nazareth Bhavan, Sevoke Road, Siliguri, as novice master. So after Joe completed his programme in Calcutta, I joined him there and we travelled to Bagdogra together. Fr. Mathew met us at the airport and drove us to Nazareth Bhavan.

What made the Northeast so strikingly different for us was the fresh simplicity and openness of the people we interacted with there, which you did not often come across elsewhere. We could observe time and again the phenomenon about which Joe often remarks in his programmes: the deepest truths and paradoxes are most readily grasped and accepted by the truly simple of heart. In fact, he confesses that initially he himself had this major block: he would get inextricably entangled in analyzing and striving to 'understand' with reasoning and logic – and fail miserably. To overcome the intellectualizing habit was not at all easy for him.

The evening after the seminar Fr. Mathew took us to the market and I remember we bought a black hard-backed suitcase which, after 15 years of regular and rough use for local and international travel, is still going strong, while other more expensive luggage we bought needed to be scrapped after just a few trips.

The climate and topography in the plains is so very different from that of the hill areas and it can get uncomfortably hot, so we were happy when we took off for Bhutan the following day. Fr. Mathew had made arrangements for a vehicle and a driver. Though we landed up in the border town of Phuntsholing at a decent hour of the working day we found that the Tourist Information Office, located in the Bhutan Post Building, had shut for the day. We had wrongly presumed that we would get entry permits on the spot. On checking further we learnt that the formalities for getting these permits entailed more than filling and signing forms at the counter. My great excitement at actually being inside the Kingdom of Bhutan turned to disappointment. After stopping to have lunch at one of the restaurants in Phuntsholing, we started on our journey back. To make up for our disappointment, Fr. Mathew made a diversion to Kalimpong.

All I knew about Kalimpong was that it was famous for its cheese! All hill towns have a similar look and Kalimpong was no different. We went to visit a very special church known as the Relli Road Church. This was built in the Buddhist style and looked impressive; it had a distinctly spacious feel, as there were no pillars and the ceiling rested on the four outer walls. Looks and feel apart, there was some inbuilt flaw as the walls had started to slope inwards and seemed likely to cave in. I've often wondered if it is still standing. After wandering around the town, we stopped to buy some of the cheeses and were surprised to find that they did not come cheap at all.

Although this had been a short and comparatively uneventful visit capped by the disappointment of an aborted trip to Bhutan, we had no regrets. Rather, even today, the thoughts of those faraway places, like the sirens' call, find us powerless to resist. So we keep echoing Arnold Schwarzenegger's, 'We'll be back'!

Chapter Nine

1996
C'EST MAGNIFIQUE
"Ooh la la la ..."

The years 1989 to 1995 were perhaps the most stressful and expensive of our lives. Though we did travel during that period, it was with constant apprehension of what could be happening back home, and what fresh troubles we would have to face when we returned. On more than one occasion our fears proved true. In 1995 we finally came to a 'settlement' over the issue and we all moved out of our ancestral property to a new location. By 1996, having settled down in our new home, our thoughts once again were on travel. We planned on visiting Anne-Marie Hascher in Paris, friends in the UK and Fr. Gerry Prior in Scotland, and we booked return tickets on Kuwait Airways for Rs.26,735 each.

Landing in Paris on 4 July, we found our way from the airport to Boulevard St. Michel, where Anne-Marie lived. I was going to meet her after a quarter of a century! It would be Joe's second meeting with her – she had put him up in 1980 when he had been to Europe alone. This time she was more eager to meet him after all I had written about the seminars he had been conducting since 1981, and she was looking forward to many stimulating discussions. After the death of her husband, Anne-Marie lived alone. Her three handsome sons had left to make their own homes – Dominique in Paris, Thierry in Germany, and Xavier, the youngest, in England, and she now had only her two beloved cats for company. During the ten days we were in Paris, we had many interesting discussions and we also did quite a bit of sightseeing on our own, with armchair guidance from Anne-Marie.

Our first outing was to the Palace of Versailles which I had always associated with Marie Antoinette. The train journey from Paris took about half an hour; we had no problem about where we had to alight, as loads of tourists were also making a beeline for the same place. All we had to do was go with the flow. Passing through the entrance, with its towering gold and black gates, we paused before the resplendent statue of Louis XIV on his horse, which dominated the scene. Stretching out beyond this was a spacious expanse leading to the Palace proper. The gardens were beautifully laid out, the hedges perfectly manicured and symmetrical, the pathways spotless – it felt as if nothing had changed through the passing centuries, and we may not have been too startled if the clatter of horse hooves announced the arrival of Royalty in gilded carriages. As we walked on, it was inevitable that I should begin to bombard Joe with snatches of what I had read, in fact and fiction, about this simple hunting lodge that expanded into a royal chateau and then into a palace famed as the epicentre of style and elegant living. It is inevitable again, that I should set out some details of this fascinating palace.

It was Louis XIV, better known as the Sun King, who took the greatest interest in Versailles, and over the years transformed it into the mother of all palaces. In 1678 he constructed the famous Hall of Mirrors. This was at a time when the Venetian Republic held the 'monopoly' on the manufacture of mirrors, and mirrors were among the most expensive items one could possess. In order to ensure that the items used in the ornamentation of the Palace were all of French provenance, several workers from Venice were enticed to France, where all the 357 mirrors used to adorn the 17 arches of the Salon were manufactured. The Galerie des Glaces became the venue for official receptions, prestigious marriage celebrations and gala balls. On 25 February 1745, at one such extravaganza, the Ball of the Yew Trees, Louis XIV, who came dressed as a Yew Tree, met Jeanne-Antoinette Poisson d'Etiolles who was dressed as Diana, goddess of the hunt. She was to become the king's mistress and known to the world as the Marquise de Pompadour.

When Louis XIV lived at Versailles, he had one room reserved just for his wigs – and he had over 500 of them. Another room housed the rarest and most valuable treasures, and access to these rooms was only by personal invitation of the king. Life at court was closely regulated by etiquette, which became the linch-pin of one's status and acceptance in society. Some amusing rules of etiquette were: Someone wanting to speak to the king could not knock on his door. Instead he had to use the little finger of the left hand to gently scratch on the door; as a result, many courtiers grew this finger nail longer than the others. A lady was never to hold hands or link arms with a gentleman. This was considered bad taste, but the fact was that the hooped skirts women wore were so wide, that the gentlemen could not get close enough to do either. The procedure for a gentleman to seat himself was to slide his left foot in front of the right, place his hands on the sides of the chair and gently lower himself into sitting position. There was a very practical reason for this – if a gentleman sat too hastily, his fashionably tight trousers might split.

A gentleman was to do no work except write letters, give speeches, practise fencing or dancing. For pleasure (like he needed more!) he engaged in hawking, archery, indoor tennis or hunting. Life for the 'beautiful people' at Versailles was one round of pleasure and wasteful pursuits and it's a wonder that the French Revolution which it triggered did not erupt much earlier! Yet for all that, the overwhelming grandeur of the palace ignited a passion for imitation among the powerful and the elite of Europe. Many sought to build similar palaces, complete with their own hall of mirrors and formal gardens. Replications of this palace can be found in Germany, Russia, England, Sweden, Austria, Hungary, Italy, Spain and even in India. The last Maharaja of Kapurthala in Punjab built the famous Jagatjit Palace which was designed by a French architect on the same lines.

The palace tour was most gratifying for me. I was very interested in Queen Marie Antoinette and also in her grandfather-in-law, the colourful Sun King, Louis XIV, as I had read a lot about them in novels by Jean Plaidy and other authors. Every hall, every corridor, every chamber was a picture of ornate elegance. The young queen's bedroom in particular, was opulent, with a lot of gold in the décor. Despite all her follies that eventually led to her beheading, Marie Antoinette has retained an undeniably romantic image through the ages. For me, it was soul-satisfying to finally see the famous Palace of Versailles I had read so much about, and to actually tread the paths so many historic personages had trod in an era of bygone glory.

The Louvre was next on our agenda. In the courtyard, we saw a large glass pyramid. This structure was not there in 1971, when I could at least say that I 'saw' the Louvre, though I did not go in! The entrance to the Museum proper was through this pyramid, descending to a lower level to the ticket counters. We were faced with a choice of viewing different sections housing Oriental, Egyptian, Greek, Etruscan or Roman antiquities, Objets d'art from the Middle Ages and Renaissance onwards, Sculptures, Paintings, Prints and Drawings, etc. We decided to stick to the Paintings, Antiquities and Sculptures.

I was keen to see Da Vinci's celebrated Mona Lisa; with the fame and lore surrounding this particular work of Art, I was led to expect an impressively large painting. So for me it came as an anti-climax to find that the portrait of the lady was so small. That too was encased in a special glass-protected case which made taking photographs difficult and it was also some distance away from the viewing public. Well, the enigmatic lady succeeded in keeping her mystic aloofness intact. Though we spent the whole day at the Louvre, we did not manage to cover very much and, by the end of the day, we were quite exhausted with all that walking. We spent the next day at the Musee d'Orsay and though it was not as extensive and as famous as the Louvre, this museum too offered much to admire and enjoy. It had three levels – ground, middle and upper, and contained a wealth of paintings by famous artists like Gaugin, Degas, Renoir, Manet, Seurat,

Monet, Toulouse-Lautrecand others. We stopped to specially admire 'Whistler's Mother.' And that was the end of another day with very sore feet and dancing eyes!

LOURDES – THE ENDURING MIRACLE
"Mary Our Mother, Hail Full of Grace"

We had always wanted to visit Lourdes and were told it would be a long train journey from Paris, as Lourdes was almost on the border of Spain. When we went to buy our tickets we enquired for the most economical fares. There were discounts for students, for senior citizens, and a few other categories for which we did not qualify. We continued asking anyway, till eventually we were told that there was a special 'couple fare'. To claim this we had to fill out some forms and affix our photos. We grabbed the forms, rushed to a photo booth and got ugly mug shots, but we also got our tickets – at a considerable discount. You see, if you persevere and ask around, you can save on practically everything! Then it was back to Boulevard St. Michel, for a hurried supper after which we left on the night train. Our compartment was filled with boy scouts in good spirits, but even so we managed to grab some sleep.

Dawn had just broken when we reached the small town of Lourdes early on the morning of 9 July. It was cold, and there was no one around at that hour to enquire in which direction we should head. We ambled along till we found one café that was open and went in to have breakfast and ask the way to the Shrine. From the many souvenir shops lining the road it should have been apparent that we were going in the right direction. Eventually we crossed the Pont St. Michel and entered the Shrine complex where you were greeted first by a beautiful statue of our Lady on a high pedestal. A circular grille railing around this was festooned with bouquets of flowers brought by devotees.

The church is located on a low hill that rises directly above the grotto and we were lucky to reach in time for an a mass in English. I was happy that the hymns were familiar and I could join in the singing. In fact, I belted out 'How Great Thou Art' with such feeling, that the lady next to me turned to me and whispered that I should continue to glorify God with my voice. After mass we climbed down the steps and walked towards the grotto. By then the place was swarming with pilgrims and tourists, yet it had an air of serenity and peace. We bought a large two-foot candle which I lit at the grotto while I prayed for our family and friends back home. The miraculous spring of water from the Rock of Massabielle was located below and to the left of the grotto, now covered by a protective glass. From here it flowed to taps that supply water to the baths and also to a long row of faucets where people could collect water freely. We filled bottles we had brought with us to take back home and I splashed some on my face – it felt cool and very invigorating.

The baths are on the left bank of the placidly flowing river Gave. Pilgrims had to take their place in long winding queues. The men's queue was considerably shorter and more distracted than the women's, where the rosary was being continuously recited aloud. When I saw the long queue for the women's baths, I was put off because I felt I would have to wait for hours, so I decided to come back later. Big mistake! Because of the short time we had to spend in Lourdes, we wanted to see and do as much as we could, so we left to see the house of Bernadette Soubirous soon after Joe finished having a dip in the holy water. He described the procedure for me but I am not repeating it here as I have recounted my own experience in another chapter.

Bernadette was the first to see Our Lady when she went to gather firewood at the cave of Massabielle. This occurred on 11 February 1858. She was born in 1844, exactly one hundred years before me, in the small town of Lourdes which had just 4,000 inhabitants. We saw the Boly Mill where the Soubirous family lived for ten years till misfortune struck with the failure and ruin of the Mill. The family then moved to the Cachot which was a small one-room cramped and squalid refuge for the parents and their four children. One can only guess at the hardships the family endured living there, especially during the bitter cold of winter.

When we returned to the baths to see if I could finally get the opportunity for an immersion it was too late as they had stopped taking in people. To make up for that, I went back to the taps and splashed water all over myself. I'm sure Our Lady blessed me in full measure even with this mini-ablution. In the evening we joined the torchlight procession with thousands walking along reciting the rosary. The sick and disabled were in the forefront in wheelchairs or being carried by special volunteer nurses. It was an inspiring sight which touched one at a deep inner level.

We retraced our steps by the same route we had come and stopped for a bite to eat at Hotel Beausejour, which was just outside the railway station. We were in good time for our train and found an empty coupe which we had all to ourselves so we could stretch out and sleep very comfortably for the entire journey till dawn lit up the Parisian skies. For me, being in Lourdes was a miracle. The whole day was a miracle. One more of my dreams had been fulfilled.

THE FLAVOURS OF PARIS
"Stranger beware there's love in the air under Paris skies"

You cannot leave Paris without seeing the Eiffel Tower so that was where we spent another full day. Looking at the Eiffel Tower from the outside, one would never imagine what a skilful and intricate piece of engineering it is, or how massive it is. I recall being struck by this when I first stood before it in 1971. A very simple-minded office colleague had once asked me if the Eiffel Tower was bigger than our TV tower in Mumbai! I couldn't help laughing as I remarked that it was like comparing a small mosque to the Taj Mahal. In pictures, the Eiffel Tower doesn't look all that big, but standing under its shadow you realize how puny and insignificant a human appears. Entry to the Tower is through any of its four legs, each of which covers a large area and houses huge lifts. Tickets are priced according to the ascending levels; the higher you wish to go, the higher the price. Every level has shops and eating places and, on a clear day, you can see the whole of Paris from the topmost station.

The next day we walked the short distance from the place where we were staying in Boulevard St. Michel to the Notre Dame Cathedral. As usual, there were tourists milling around, literally rubbing shoulders as they squeezed in at the entrance; we got caught up and practically carried forward in a large group of Japanese sightseers. In the midst of that surging mass, a young urchin began tugging at Joe's shirt sleeves, pestering him for money while his sister (so we presumed) swayed in front of Joe, chanting something like, 'Baba, paisa, paisa, baba, baba, you give, you give,' as she thrust a thick cardboard tray not merely at him, but right into his midriff. Joe twisted and turned, to no avail. I shouted at the girl to leave us alone, but she just carried on; however the boy then directed his attention to me and coming between me and Joe, started waving his hands in front of my face. In the confusion I became aware of a Japanese gentleman agitatedly saying something to Joe and pointing to the cardboard. Seeing that we did not understand, he suddenly brought his open palm down on the cardboard, slapping it away. We still did not understand till he said, 'Look'. We looked and saw that the waist pouch Joe was wearing had been unzipped, all under cover of the cardboard tray. The pouch contained not only our money, but also our passports! We could only babble our stunned thanks to our saviour.

As for those gypsy urchins, far from being scared or ashamed at being caught out, they just glared at us and uttered a few emphatic words in their language (from the look in their eyes I gathered they were far from complimentary) before moving out to target more unsuspecting tourists. Needless to say, Joe was badly shaken and went cold for quite some time. We were even a little nervous about exiting the church later in case the gang of pickpockets was still lurking around. Despite this incident, we managed to regain our composure and complete our tour of this famous Shrine. Both of us loved the ancient decorative hinges on some of the doors and also the circular stained glass windows high up in the church. The one non-religious association that did intrude was: would we see Quasimodo swinging down from one of the galleries? But there was no sign of the famous hunchback anywhere!

We took Anne-Marie out to dinner that evening. The Latin Quarter near her house served practically every type of cuisine, from classic French to Lebanese, Turkish, Spanish, Chinese, Italian, you name it. She said she liked sushi so we went to a sushi restaurant where she relished the meal, while I could only pick politely at the elaborately dressed fare. On another evening we were invited to her son's house for dinner. Dominique, her eldest son, was a judge in the High Court of Judicature in Paris and married to a beautiful girl named Laurence. Their angelic daughter, Louise, was supposed to be in bed at the hour we arrived, but she couldn't resist peeking out – and then charming her *grand mere* to allow her to stay around with us for most of the evening.

One morning we walked towards the Pantheon and then found ourselves near the City Hall where a wedding party was gathering. Keen to see a Parisian bridal couple, we moved closer to watch. Looking around us, we saw a gentleman in a car who kept beckoning from across the road. We couldn't think why, but out of politeness Joe went to meet him. Then he called to me and I joined them. The man asked where we were from and told us how he had always wanted to meet someone from India; he was delighted and wanted to know more about our country. He also offered to drive us to any place we wanted. Today I can't believe that we actually accepted this invitation from a total stranger in a foreign country.

I don't remember where we said we wanted to go, but we found ourselves in his car and this is the story he told us … He was from Milan and had come to Paris representing Valentino for a trade show-cum-exhibition. He had two calf leather jackets left, one for a gent and another full length one for a lady. Since he liked us, he said he wanted to give these to us, and of course we refused to accept, but he kept insisting that we take them as he did not want to carry them back. As there were obviously no strings attached, we finally thanked him and said we would take them, though we had no idea what we would do with them. Still, they were very beautiful jackets, genuine Valentino, and we knew we'd find someone to give them to.

Then came the spiel of how terribly embarrassed he was to confess that he had been in a gambling-drinking session with friends the previous night. His luck had been rotten, he was out of cash, but had to drive back to Milan that day. So, could we kindly lend him a few hundred francs to buy petrol? My antennae were up immediately and I tried to signal Joe who was not looking my way. Fortunately, Joe told him that we did not have so much money with us. Our 'friend,' still in a very apologetic manner, said we could stop to exchange some traveller's cheques but I quickly said we had not carried these with us. He finally agreed to take whatever we had. I was willing to leave the coats behind and walk away, but before I could say anything, Joe consented and gave what francs we had with us, which was over 700, I think. (And people say women are gullible!) It was still far short of what the jackets were worth, so once again we told him that we could not accept them, but he just smiled a bit regretfully and drove off.

We were in a tizzy about what to believe and discussed it till we got back to the apartment. We showed Anne-Marie the jackets. She examined them, and was impressed saying they must have been very expensive. Then we told her the story! By then we had realized that we had met a very clever con artiste, only this time we had unwittingly got the better of him. We wondered if he had stolen the coats and needed to get rid of them quickly. There could be no other explanation. Anyway, we gave the long jacket to Anne-Marie since she could make better use of it than we ever would, and also because we did not have room to carry both. We kept the other one but can't remember to whom we gave it later. That was a good lesson for us and we have to admit that we must have looked like ready-made suckers!

Fourteenth July was Bastille Day and a big day in France. We were excited to be in Paris for the celebrations. Anne-Marie said she preferred to stay home and watch the show on TV but we were keen to be where the action was and took the metro to the Arc de Triumph. Thousands of people were already there but apart from some military tanks and trucks filled with soldiers going past in procession and a few aircraft flying overhead, there was nothing spectacular enough to justify our expectations of a stunning show. Only later did we discover that we had been at the wrong place and the real action was elsewhere! And Anne-Marie had seen it all from the comfort of her own cozy home. Oh well, it was still fun to be among the crowds where the excitement was palpable. As the crowds began dispersing we decided to walk slowly down the Champs Elysee. When we became a bit footsore, we found a bench in a quiet siding and had our sandwich lunch. Some pigeons joined us uninvited, but we willingly shared what we had with them. We later walked along the Seine and also took breaks sitting on benches to observe the world passing by. In the evening we took Anne-Marie with us to the Place de la Bastille where there were live bands playing and people dancing with abandon in the streets. We too joined in all the fun till we got tired and went home to bed.

The day before we left Paris, we bought day passes for citywide bus rides; we went to Montmarte where several artists had exhibited their paintings, then climbed up the long flight of steps to the Sacre Coeur Church. What a spectacular view of the city from up there and what lovely shots I got on my ordinary camera! With time on our hands in the evening, we just rode the bus from one terminus to another for the heck of it, and to drink in at leisure the sights along the way. We were happy we could do so much during the 10 days we were in Paris. Anne-Marie had invited us to also see her summer home on the exotic-sounding Ile d'Yeu on the west coast of France. Tempted though we were, we had to decline – perhaps another time, another dream.

A 'TONY' NEIGHBOURHOOD
"Memories, light the corners of my mind"

While absorbing the joie-de-vivre of Paris we had toyed with the idea of 'Chunnelling' our way to London. But the fares on the Euro Star train were quite high, so we had to deny ourselves the joy of a unique under-the-sea experience. Besides, we had already paid for our flights from Paris to London.

Our friend, Tony D'Souza, had insisted that we stay with him at his house in Penge on this trip, especially as he wanted us to be there for his Silver Wedding Anniversary. He also insisted on coming to Heathrow airport to pick us up, but when we arrived there on 15 July, we found no sign of him. So, instead of standing around with our luggage, we found a place to sit and await his arrival patiently. As the minutes ticked by I felt it was unlike Tony to keep us waiting for such a long time and only then did it register that one particular individual had passed us several times as he walked up and down, frantically scanning faces and it finally dawned on me that this was none other than Tony. I got up and walked towards him and said, 'Tony?' I could see the instant relief and recognition on his face when he finally 'found' us, and we greeted each other affectionately. The truth was that 11 years had robbed Tony of his youthful appearance, and he had also grown very thin – and when Tony gallantly assured me that I looked the same as I did when we last met, I took it with the mandatory pinch of salt. It was a happy reunion. Tony was one of the few persons we had come across who was utterly simple, with no pretensions whatsoever. He used to write to us regularly and had absolutely no inhibitions about the fact that he was not educated and could not spell even simple words, and I just loved those letters which were so full of mistakes and so brimful of affection and sincerity.

We trundled over to the parking lot to find that Tony had brought along Ray Fitzgerald, another old friend I had met in 1970. He was to 'chauffeur' us, as Tony confessed he was not authorized to drive in Greater London. Tony's Irish wife, Breda, gave us a warm welcome and we stayed up for quite a bit of the night chatting about the old days and all the fun we had, especially on Sundays when Tony would drop in at Mabel's with a container of biryani or *pullao* wrapped in a cloth, along with a bottle of sherry. More often than not, one bottle of sherry was not enough, but with the Off License just round the corner, it was easy enough for one of us to slip out and replenish our stock. Since then, I have always associated Harvey's Bristol Cream Sherry with those Sunday get-togethers.

Joe and I left for Southampton on 18 July to spend a weekend with Dr. Basker, his wife Asha, and their two boys, Nandu and Karthik. I had been corresponding with them for many years but, unbelievably, we had never met in all that time. This was going to be my first meeting with them and Joe's second. His first encounter has a story worth telling and I'm saving it for another time. When Bash (as he is fondly called by friends) and Asha heard that we would be coming to England, they insisted that we visit them in Southampton. We hesitated, knowing the costs of travel in England, but in the end we decided to accept their invitation. And we're so glad we did because we had a really great time. We were given a warm welcome and showered with hospitality that really touched us. Between the two of them they showed us quite a bit of the surrounding countryside. Asha took us to see the old Roman ruins at Fishbourne, which I found fascinating, and Bash drove us to Stonehenge and later, to Salisbury Cathedral.

We had always wanted to see the famous Stonehenge monument which dates back to prehistoric times and was erected by a culture that left no written records. Some say it was used as a burial ground from as early as 3000 BC. Archaeologists have other theories. So too astronomers – might it not be a primitive observatory designed to predict eclipses and track other celestial phenomena? And as the many colourful theories about its origins and purpose continue to hover over the rough hewn megaliths, Stonehenge retains its air of brooding mystery.

When it was time to leave, Asha, with Karthik in tow, dropped us off at the railway station. It seemed to be little Karthik's first time there and he was so entranced with the trains that he wanted to come with us! Long after we left, he continued to talk about the trains.

We were back at Tony's place in Penge on 20 July, in time to celebrate their Silver Wedding Anniversary. The actual date was 24 July, but the celebrations were kept for 20 July, since it was the weekend. It was a simple affair but we had a lot of fun. On 21 July, the day after the celebrations, Joe and I left for Edinburgh, Scotland. This was going to be another first for us.

IN SCENIC SCOTLAND
"O Ye'll take the High Road and I'll take the Low Road"

My great interest in history (English history included) was sparked off in school and then again when I began reading historical novels. It led me to also read much about the Scots whose monarchy was intertwined with that of the British. Many of A.J. Cronin's books, of which I was an avid reader, had also evoked an interest in Scotland. Hence, Scotland was definitely on our radar when I had written letters to our friends abroad telling them of our proposed travel plans. (I'm talking of pre-e-mail days here!) While I received welcoming replies from London and Paris, there was a deafening silence from Scotland. Accordingly, I finalized our itinerary to go first to Paris and to Lourdes, then to London and finally to Southampton.

Just a week before we were to leave, out of the blue, Fr. Gerry Prior called from Scotland. He said he had been so busy with his parish work that he had had no time to write (which he hated doing anyway), so here he was phoning to apologize and say how 'verrrrra' happy he was that we were actually coming to meet him in Scotland. It took time to tune in to his Scottish accent, and longer to interrupt his rich rolling words of welcome, to say that we had already finalized our travel plans and dates and Scotland was out of the question. Gerry insisted that we visit him, saying he had kept himself free for an entire month just to be with us and show us around. With the suffusing warmth of such an invitation, we could not but make changes to include Scotland in our itinerary.

Buying return tickets works out a little cheaper than single fares, so we bought our return train tickets for £22 each and travelled on the Flying Scotsman from King's Cross to Edinburgh. Fr. Gerry was at the station waiting to greet us and take us to his parish of St. Peter's in West Lothian. He had vacated his own room for us and moved to a smaller one, and our protests did not have any effect on him. Besides, he had taken care to stock every kind of liquor and goodies for us not only downstairs but also in the private sitting room attached to his bedroom. As if that were not enough he kept asking if there was anything more we needed!

At mass the following Sunday Gerry announced to his congregation that if they didn't like having him as their parish priest they had to blame us, because we were the people who had saved his life in India. Trust Gerry to be dramatic! He also told them that he would not be available for some days as he was going to be taking us around the countryside. True to his word, he took us all round Edinburgh and Glasgow. We spent the first day at the ruins of St. Andrew's Castle and St. Andrew's Cathedral. There was really nothing much to see from the outside and I wondered why he had brought us there or why an entry fee was charged. Only when we went in to explore did we realize how well they had preserved these ancient ruins; it was like leafing through a history book.

St. Andrew's Castle was located on a rocky promontory overlooking the North Sea. There was a castle standing on this site from 1189. This was destroyed and rebuilt several times as it changed hands between the Scots and the English. On entering, we first viewed a display tracing the history of the castle, which included some well preserved fragments. The castle had also served as a notorious prison – we saw the 'bottle dungeon', which was a musty, damp and airless pit in the shape of a bottle, hewn out of solid rock, from where prisoners had no chance of escape. Besides the dungeons we also saw several underground passages, which gave one a sense of the horrors of medieval siege warfare. By 1656 the Castle had fallen into such disrepair that masonry material was removed from it and used to repair the pier. Fortunately, the authorities managed to later preserve and maintain a sizeable portion of the Castle and its history for future generations.

A short walk away from the castle stood the Cathedral of St. Andrew's, dating back to the year 1158. The relics of the Apostle Andrew were said to have been brought to Scotland from Patras, where the Saint was buried, and they came to rest in this cathedral, but were later moved to Rome. St. Andrew is honoured as the Patron Saint of Scotland and he is also the patron saint of the parish I belong to in Mumbai.

From there we drove to Fife, which was a truly charming place. It was the birthplace of Alexander Selkirk, on whose real-life adventure the story of Robinson Crusoe was based. The people there were proud of their celebrity townsman and, predictably, there was a Crusoe Hotel where we stopped for a break before going to Dunfermline Abbey.

For me, the highlight of this visit to Scotland was the tour of the Edinburgh Castle, the symbol of Scotland, which sits atop Castle Rock. I was fascinated with all I learnt. In the 11th century, a medieval castle was first built on this rock which is so hard that four centuries later, during the Long Siege by the English, an agent reported, 'There is no mining that can prevail in this rock but only battery with ordnance to beat down the walls.' A regular royal residence was established in this castle around the 12th century but control of the castle changed hands time and again because of the several bloody battles with the British over many years. What was, till the middle of the 18th century, only a narrow rocky ridge outside the Edinburgh Castle, was expanded into a broad esplanade and a large platform was created as a parade ground. In recent years, this has been used as the venue for the Military Tattoo which is organized every August. It is a spectacular show which has become a huge tourist attraction. Conducted in the late evening hours, with the castle forming a dramatic twilight backdrop, the festival ends with the appearance of a lone piper on the battlements of the castle ... I can just hear the skirling of those haunting bagpipes!

The Crown Jewels, also known as the Honours of Scotland, were kept in the Crown Room on the first floor of the Palace. They were said to be the oldest surviving regalia and consist of a gold Crown, a Sceptre, and a Sword. All these were used together for the first time at the coronation of the infant Mary, Queen of Scots. And now for the interesting story attached to these jewels ...

King Charles II was the last to use the Crown Jewels for his coronation on New Year's Day 1651. Soon after this, to avoid discovery by Cromwell's army, they were buried beneath the floor of a nearby church where they lay from 1651 to 1660. Then, after the Treaty of Union between Scotland and England was signed in 1707, the Scots did not want their Honours falling into the hands of the English, so they were hidden once more. The English looked high and low for them, but they were never found.

In 1818, 111 years later, the Scottish poet, Sir Walter Scott, asked permission of the Prince Regent, the future King George IV, to break open a particular wall in the Crown Room. Behind it was a chest which they forced open, and lo and behold, the Honours which were 'lost' for over a century, were rediscovered. These were immediately put on display for the public, except during the Second World War when they were buried once again, this time in David's Tower, the highest point of the castle. How happy we were to have a chance to see this precious regalia that had such a long, romantic history.

We completed our tour of Castle Rock and stepped out on to Edinburgh's Royal Mile Road: 'The largest, longest and finest street for Buildings and Number of Inhabitants, not only in Britain, but in the World ...' Looking down the road that connected Edinburgh Castle to the Palace of Holyrood House, we had no doubt it merited such rich praise as Daniel Defoe bestowed on it in 1723. Even two and three quarters of a century later, its charm had not faded. The Royal Mile is a tourist's delight with diverse interesting buildings, institutions and establishments like the Camera Obscura, which we were told, was an absolute 'must-see'.

This optical wonder has been in operation since the 1850s and was located on the sixth and topmost floor of the Outlook Tower. Fortunately we did not turn back on learning that we had to rely solely on leg-power to reach there. As we ascended the spiral stairway we paused on intervening floors to take in the exhibits of old photographs, pin-hole camera images and even holograms. The top deck was a darkened chamber with a large circular white table around which visitors positioned themselves. On this, via a clever series of mirror, pinhole camera and lenses, views of the city of Edinburgh were projected. By tilting and controlling the mirror, the operator gave us a panoramic 360-degree visual tour of the entire city. The accompanying commentary, spiced with wit, added to the pure magic of the 15-minute presentation.

The Palace of Holyrood House, the official residence of the monarchs, marked the end point of the Royal Mile. This palace too has a history going back several centuries and we were fascinated with what we saw of the older Historical Apartments and the State Apartments, full of beautiful paintings, decorations and plasterwork going back to the 1600s. The guide took great pleasure in pointing out to us the spot where Rizzio, the secretary and confidant of Mary Queen of Scots was stabbed to death. This was done at the behest of Mary's second husband, the effeminate Lord Darnley. A blood stain on the wooden floor of the room marked the spot, but I wonder whether it is the original stain or whether it is now artfully refreshed for the sake of giving tourists an extra thrill.

Back in Edinburgh we went to meet Gerry's parents, Agnes and Owen Prior and his sister Lynn. They were warm, loving and welcoming, and Owen thanked us a countless number of times for looking after their son in India. Who knew that the small service we had rendered

Gerry would go such a long way! July 22 was Gerry's birthday and we were happy to be celebrating it with him. We were also invited to dinner with Lynn and her boyfriend, Jim Fraser, and spent a lovely evening with them. The night before we returned to England, Gerry took us and a few friends to a fabulous dinner which he paid for from what he called his 'onions and potatoes' money. He had very wisely left the church collection money and every aspect of the finances of his parish to the parishioners themselves, and he defrayed his expenses from the funds they allocated to him.

Our week in Scotland soon came to an end. We had the most enjoyable time and we left grateful to Fr. Gerry for his warmth and generous hospitality, and with a gift of the famous Scottish haggis. We had indeed travelled the High Roads and the Low Roads of Scotland and both were on the level!

SAMOSAS AND SOUTHALL
"For all we know we may never meet again"

We returned to England from Scotland on 26 July. After two more days in Penge with the D'Souzas, Tony drove us to Freddy Pitter's house in Southall and we bid him a last fond farewell. It was literally our last farewell, because Tony passed away not long after that. Maybe it was providential that we had fallen in with Tony's wishes that we stay with him that time. On our next trip to England we did meet Breda for a condolence visit, and she took us to Tony's grave so we could pay our respects to that simple soul. However, we lost touch with Breda after that.

As Freddy Pitter lived alone, he was always glad to have company so we decided to spend five days with him. Freddy's house was located in a clean, well-maintained neighbourhood, far removed from the main thoroughfare, and from there we soon learned to get about on our own. Southall was a veritable Little India. It was almost completely peopled by Indians, predominantly Punjabis, and the aroma of delicious samosas and *chole-bhature* wafted onto the sidewalks, which had also been taken over with colourful wares.

Freddy drove us around to see a few sights and also took us to Windsor Castle. The castle was founded by William the Conqueror around 1080, which made it one of the oldest Royal Residences that had remained in continuous use by the monarchs of Great Britain. Like Edinburgh Castle, Windsor Castle was also rich in history, adorned with amazing artefacts and paintings, and I really enjoyed the profuse panorama it presented. But once again, all that walking about exhausted us and our interest began to flag. As we left the castle with tired feet, the guard detail had just changed and a group of them emerged, stomping their boots smartly and marched quickly past me. I started running after them like a prize idiot calling to Joe to click a photograph with me close to them, but they were just too fast.

One night Freddy treated us to a round of drinks on a boat that was moored close to Westminster Abbey and later took us to a Punjabi Pub in Southall which played loud blaring *bhangra* music. As was his wont, Freddy celebrated every Friday evening with some of his old-time pals and new-found friends, and we too enjoyed a Friday-party, where he served up his famous curry of chicken legs, and of course, spirits to keep us all in high spirits.

139

Chapter Ten

1997
BANGKOK'S GOLDEN BUDDHAS AND
PATTAYA'S BUSTLING BEACHES
"Just an ordinary day becomes adventure,
such sweet adventure"

We were going to celebrate our Silver Wedding in May that year so we should rightfully have been saving up for the celebration. However, when a chance to visit Thailand in January came our way, we decided to go, especially as we had not yet travelled to any eastern country. The package included return airfare on Cathay Pacific, six-day stay in 4-star hotels in Bangkok and Pattaya and all transportation. The cost would be just under Rs.31,000 per person so Joe, Vanessa and I all signed up for the trip. This was being arranged predominantly to see Chiara Lubich, Founder of the worldwide Focolare Movement, who had been invited to Bangkok. Having heard so much about Chiara, there was a natural wish to meet her in person. In what promised to be a historic occasion, an Honorary Doctorate in Social Communication was to be conferred on Chiara and a grand felicitation was being planned. Only those from India and Pakistan who were associated with the Focolare Movement were invited to form the entourage.

In 1997, Bangkok's Suvarnabhumi (Golden Land) airport was nothing to write home about. Ten years later I believe it was quite transformed and really worth seeing, but I don't know if I would want to go back for another visit. Of all the large group travelling from India, I was the only one whose luggage went missing – it had inconsiderately gone on to Hong Kong. This was the first time something like this had happened to me in all our travels (not to mention the time when the contents of our suitcases were being pilfered at Heathrow!) We registered a complaint but the authorities were not very helpful. With no night clothes and worse still, nothing for the function the next day, I finally went to bed with one half of Joe's pyjama suit. At 2 am we were woken up and the much-travelled suitcase was handed over to me.

The main function for Chiara was held on 5 January and, as expected, it was impressive. There was a big felicitation for her and the hall was packed to capacity, the locals far outnumbering our large contingent. Chiara was awarded a Doctorate in recognition of 'the power of communication of her message of peace and unity'. I tried several times to be in the front row so that I could greet her as she passed but there were just too many people around her. The next day we all attended another function. As we were waiting for Chiara to arrive I positioned myself where I thought I might have a chance to see her face-to-face, but she passed by not even looking in my direction. I noted the path she was taking and quickly re-positioned myself along that route. She was shaking the hand of the boy in front of me when I also put my hand out – and she took it. Joe was standing elsewhere wearing a Gandhi cap but she noticed him and gave him a second look.

Much of that morning's programme escapes my memory. However it was followed by a very grand lunch. We were eight to a table and each course was served in a large platter which was placed in the centre, from which we had to help ourselves. There were several courses and Joe managed very well with the chopsticks, but I stuck to traditional cutlery. We were the only two Indians at this table and we both noticed the expressions of the other diners when a large fish was placed in the centre of the table. As Joe and I are both not too fond of fish we took just a little to be polite. I couldn't help gaping at the others as I saw them dig in and demolish the fish, head, eyes and all! That's when we gave up and excused ourselves.

We were told that an unusual treat was in store for us when we were taken to see a 'special' concert. Certainly the various acts, the music and dancing too were very enjoyable, but we didn't see what was so 'special'. We did notice that the costumes were gorgeous and carried to perfection by the beautiful cast, with revealing décolletage and alluring rounded bottoms. The surprise finale was the revelation that what we had been watching was a gay performance by an all-male cast! After the concert we met some of them up close and they were not anywhere near beautiful, especially without their make up. All-in-all it was an entertaining and 'gay' evening. This show seems to have become a must for all tourists to Bangkok.

On one sightseeing outing we were amazed to hear the story of one of the many Buddha statues we saw in Bangkok. When reconstruction work was undertaken near Chinatown on the banks of the Chao Phraya River in the 1930s, an old abandoned temple there was slated for demolition. This temple contained a large gold-painted stucco statue of the Buddha, and though it was not remarkable in any way, nobody even once thought it should be destroyed. Instead, it was shifted to a temple of little importance known as Wat Traimit. The statue was too big to house inside the temple, so it was kept under a plain tin roof, where it remained for 20 years. The Wat Traimit temple was rebuilt and enlarged in 1955 and the monks decided to move the statue inside the new structure. Unfortunately, in the process, a cable on the crane snapped, and the statue fell into the mud. This was considered a bad omen and the workers fled the place leaving the statue where it was. As if to confirm the omen, there was a terrible storm and it rained the whole night, flooding the entire city. Next morning, when the head monk went to assess the damage, he noticed an open crack in the wet plaster of the statue and something shining beneath it. Further excavation and examination led to the discovery that the statue was made of gold!

The Golden Buddha weighs an incredible 550 kg and is 3 mts high. It is believed to have been fashioned in the 13th century during the

Sukhothai Dynasty period. When the Burmese were besieging Ayutthaya where the statue was first installed, it was quickly covered with plaster and painted over and then moved to Bangkok. For 200 years the true 'nature' of this Buddha was forgotten till an accident revealed it once more. (This was one of Joe's regular seminar stories so he was immensely glad to see the Buddha.)

Among the memorable outings we had in Bangkok, was one to a crocodile farm. We saw some people who were bold enough to enter the enclosure to pet the crocodiles, which were apparently trained not to attack, or just too well-fed to exert. I certainly would not venture to try that out. Joe used to catch snakes during his teaching days in Lonavala (a hill-station in Maharashtra) so he posed for a photo with a python curled around his neck and body. Again, something you could never get me to do. Instead, Vanessa and I posed with a real live tiger. We sat behind that magnificent creature and actually petted his head and body which was awesome to touch. The photo has captured nice bright smiles on both our faces. Thank goodness we could not see the look on the tiger's face or we'd have run a mile off. Today, I can't imagine how we posed for that photo without a second thought.

The maximum visitor cluster was around a huge orang-utan who seemed a born entertainer. Vanessa and I both posed with him. He twined his arms around us in turn and hugged us close. When he had to pose with a fair-skinned girl, he kept hugging and kissing her and would not hold still for the cameraman till his handler shouted at him. The next moment he was back to his antics. This happened repeatedly and finally, even though he faced forward, he twisted his lips towards the lady, pursed his mouth to form a kiss and made a loud kissing sound. How we all laughed! Now that I think of it, it is quite possible that his trainer was giving him some signal to behave in that fashion with some people in order to draw the crowds.

I don't recall having any tour guide with us (unless our coach driver acted as one) so I don't know how we all landed up at a gems factory.

143

When we were told that they would also be serving beer and soft drinks on the house, it made the visit a bit more interesting to many of us. No doubt the jewellery on display was enticing and the designs were beautiful but the beer was lousy. What made it irritating was having a salesperson on your tail from the time you entered till you felt compelled to buy. This was our first such experience. Later we realized that tour guides the world over have their hidden agenda and they take their groups, willing or not, to particular sales outlets. The sales people in these outlets have a universal annoying habit. They work on commission, so once they target a customer they stick to him or her till the bitter end. You can walk to any part of the showroom or round in circles countless times, walk backwards or forwards but you can be sure that your shadow will cling to you every step of the way. We had a particularly irritating female dogging us. However, it was not because of her but in spite of her that we bought two rings that we liked. It was such a relief to get away from there. Having been warned here in Bangkok, I made sure in the future that whenever a tour guide took us to such places, I remained firmly seated in one place without being annoyed by anyone and also got a chance to rest my feet in peace.

Shopping in Bangkok was not a pleasant experience as we found that many of the shopkeepers in market areas could not be trusted. I remember asking the price of a two-piece outfit I wanted to buy; when I paid for it, I was given just one half of it and the woman also refused to return my money. One lady in our group was keen on buying artificial flowers; she selected a bunch, handed over a currency note and continued looking at other flowers. When she asked for her change, she was flatly told that she had not made any payment and more money was demanded from her. It is not a small sum I am talking about; it was US $100! The other shopkeepers stood by their dishonest colleague and nobody would help. One gentleman, who was also shopping, quietly told us that we should make a complaint because this was done regularly, but we were all too disgusted. Nor did we have the time. When we were back to in Mumbai I wrote to the Ministry of Tourism in Bangkok as also to the King of Thailand, but never received any response. However, The Times of India printed two of my letters complaining about this.

I had been looking for material that would be suitable for my silver wedding gown but I didn't see anything that caught my fancy. It was only on our last day in Bangkok that I found a market selling mainly fabrics. Even here I almost gave up till I finally saw something I liked. Unfortunately, the man had only a small piece left and nothing else in stock but I decided to take it anyway; I also bought a matching silver fabric just in case I needed it to make up the shortfall. I knew I could improvise with those two pieces – and the gown turned out perfect. Come to think of it, when buying material for my wedding gown too, the guipure lace I selected was insufficient but Joe's mum, the famous Lydia Dressmaker, managed to turn out a simple and elegant gown using the material very cleverly.

We were put up at the Hotel Ambassador in Bangkok and every morning they served an elaborate breakfast spread the length of the long hall, with a variety of cuisines. I stuck to my usual eggs, bacon and rolls and a glass of orange juice. It was only on the last day when we had to travel and had no time to get sandwiches for the journey that we thought of smuggling a few rolls out of the hall. What we discovered was that others had been doing it every day and were surprised to hear that we had not joined the brigade earlier!

After three nights in Bangkok we left for Pattaya and checked in at Hotel Golden Beach. This is where I lost the beautiful sunglasses I had bought in Italy four years ago for L45,000. I left them on the sofa in the hotel lounge while sitting there and forgot about them, and that was the last I ever saw of them. I guess it was time to buy a new pair and I found a very techni-coloured pair which turned out to be quite the rage. Strangely enough, these too were stolen from my handbag while I was doing some election duty in Mumbai.

The days we spent in Pattaya were relaxing. Joe and Vanessa were daring enough to go para sailing, which they found exhilarating. It was much too scary for me. I confess I am afraid of water and so I did not even go for a ride on the Banana Boat which topples the riders into the sea at one point. However I did attempt going for a little dip only because you could see through the crystal clear blue waters right down to the sand beneath your feet. When we went to Coral Island we had to transfer to a smaller boat in mid-ocean, and I can tell you that was some scary ordeal, especially for the older folk who had to be practically lifted and physically carried across. Once settled in the glass-bottomed boat, all our fears dissolved as we gazed through to the depths of the clear sparkling waters and marvelled at the coral reefs way below with colourful fish darting about.

On the last morning, we all checked out of the hotel immediately after breakfast. We had been warned to leave several hours earlier than needed because traffic in Bangkok was unpredictable and we could miss our flight if we were caught in traffic that often moved at a snail's pace. We took our places in the coach for the long drive to the airport and discovered that two persons were missing. Almost half an hour passed during which many became jittery about reaching in time and some suggested that we leave without them. As the discussion hotted up, the duo appeared – they had gone to pick up something they had seen the previous day, and had to wait till the shop opened! Thankfully we made it to the airport in time.

146

Chapter Eleven

1999
MARRIAGES ARE MADE CLOSE TO HEAVEN
– ATOP THE EMPIRE STATE BUILDING
"Time can't erase the memory of these magic moments filled with love"

 W ho could have guessed that what transpired at the top of the Empire State Building in New York would lead up to our second visit to Scotland? The tale needs telling, even if it means an inordinately long 'introduction'.

It was wonderful enough to have been able to go to Scotland even once, in July 1996. At that time we had met Fr. Gerry Prior's parents and also his sister, Lynn, and her boyfriend, Jim Fraser. We had extended an invitation to all of them to come and visit us in India so when Jim phoned us a few months later to tell us that he had accepted an assignment in Hong Kong and asked if he and Lynn could come and stay with us on their way back, we were very happy.

They arrived in June of 1997. Joe was out of town for a training programme, so it was left to me to go to the airport to receive them. We had applied for permission to convert a parking stilt in the building to an enclosed garage and were told that we would have to produce registration papers to prove we owned a car (for which the garage was needed!). We did not own a vehicle. A decade earlier we had disposed of our last car as we had come to the conclusion that in Mumbai it was saner, healthier and more economical to hire a car when required rather than own and drive one. Our next door neighbour, Bronwyn, provided the solution by getting us an ancient Fiat for just Rs.20,000. As you could imagine, it came with several operational limitations, but it came also with the all-important registration papers.

Our office assistant, Ashok, whose great ambition in life was to be a chauffeur, was enthusiastic to the point of convincing me to allow him to ferry me to the international airport in that contraption. After welcoming Lynn and Jim, while wheeling their luggage out to the car park, I got cold feet and began apologizing for the transport arrangements. Jim's immediate reaction on seeing the car was, 'Wow, do you mean we actually get to ride in this? It's more with-it than a stretch limo!' His words allayed my fears, but when one door refused to open and Jim had to get into the driver's seat and slide across to the passenger side, I felt mortified beyond words. However Jim seemed genuinely seduced and assured me that if he could just take that quaint old Fiat back with them to Scotland and offer people rides up and down the King's Mile, he could make a fortune!

When walking out on the streets they were often besieged by urchins and beggars. Both were troubled to see such poverty, Lynn to the extent that she would invariably start to weep. No amount of our telling her that many were professional beggars, who earned an easy living in this way rather than work, stopped her tears. No number of warnings that if she gave to one, she would be mobbed by many more who would not leave her alone, ever stopped her giving. This prompted us to take them to meet street children at Don Bosco Shelter in Wadala. The visit seemed to have moved them deeply.

Whenever Lynn and Jim were happy about something, which was pretty often, both of them would stop, wherever they were, and dance with each other. They did this at restaurants, waltzing out after a meal, in stores after purchasing something they fancied, even on the open road when they saw something interesting. They were not one bit embarrassed or self conscious and would laugh happily. Onlookers too could not help but also smile. This was a couple who enchanted everyone they met.

Lynn, Jim, Joe's mum and I all made a short trip to Matheran, the smallest hill station in India, which is about a 100 kms from Mumbai and located on the Western Ghats. The name Matheran means 'forest on the head' (of the mountain). I've always liked this place which is located at 800 mts above sea level and enjoys a cooler and less humid climate. According to me, the best hotel there was Lord's Central; the rooms were clean and cosy, the food there always wholesome and delicious. However, as we could not be accommodated there, we took the package deal at Brightlands Hotel, which had its own charm, though this was marred by the noisy transistor radios of some guests, which disrupted the peaceful atmosphere of those sylvan hills. As part of the package, the hotel had arranged for a car to pick us and take us up till the railway tracks in Matheran. Lynn termed the journey up the Ghats as 'our death-defying drive, speeding around corners with hundred metre drops'. (I wonder what she'd say after she reads our chapters on our visits to the Northeast!) Being an eco-sensitive region, Matheran is one of the few places in the world where motor vehicles are not allowed.

Often what we think others may not like, turns out to be just the opposite. Lynn and Jim found the Hindi karaoke nights at the hotel spectacular and enjoyed the food. And when we were caught in the rain on one of our long walks, even the thought of a black panther roaming the hills did not scare them. Joe had been unable to come with us because of work, but he surprised us all by arriving on the evening of my birthday while Lynn and Jim surprised me by ordering a bottle of champagne from the hotel. Unfortunately, the champagne turned out to be flat so we had to return it and of course there was no charge.

Now why did I make such a long introduction to the main topic? Because it has a direct bearing on our second and unexpected visit to Scotland in 1999. You see, in the course of our many conversations, Jim confided that he had proposed to Lynn countless times but she had not yet said 'Yes'. Jim told us that even his latest Mumbai-proposal to Lynn had not yet been accepted. That's when I told Lynn that if she finally said 'Yes' to Jim, we would somehow make it for the wedding.

The year after their Mumbai visit, Jim took Lynn to New York. Lynn later told us that she had planned the whole trip and what she was going to do. 'An Affair to Remember' was a favourite of many women and Lynn was a big fan of the movie and of the actors, Cary Grant and Deborah Kerr. She had carefully timed their own visit to the Empire State Building and they were the last to go up in the lift before closing time. However, this time it was Lynn who proposed to Jim and how I would have loved to see the look on Jim's face then! She did not see 'Sleepless in Seattle' with Tom Hanks and Meg Ryan till much later, but I couldn't help wondering just what it was about the Empire State Building that made it such a romantic rendezvous.

Lynn immediately relayed the news to us, leaving me no option but to keep my promise and just be there. I was delighted, but the tricky part was we were in no position to go because we were low on finances then. I was unsure of what to do because if we didn't book early we might not get seats at the last moment. So I went ahead, made all the enquiries and without telling Joe, even made tentative bookings on Gulf Air. It was literally one week before the wedding that Joe said the cash flow had improved and gave me the go ahead. I told him that everything was organized and he had only to pay for the tickets: Rs.52,014 for both of us. I quickly informed Lynn that we were going to make it after all. Joe then left town for two seminars (which paid for the tickets and other expenses!) while I rushed around organizing overseas insurance, foreign exchange and the packing. The day after Joe got back to town, we took off for London via Abu Dhabi.

Lynn and Jim's wedding was fixed for 26 March but we made it to Scotland on the 24th as there was to be a party that evening. Lynn's dad, Owen, was most excited about our coming and had written to say that he was looking forward to seeing us in our traditional Indian dress. As many of Lynn and Jim's friends from America, Italy, Hong Kong and even Iceland were going to be there, it promised to be an international event.

In 1999 we had no trouble carrying a large bunch of 100 red roses all the way from Mumbai, which amazingly remained fresh till we presented them to Lynn. She was so thrilled to get them and even to this day she has kept some of them which she carefully dried and preserved. If it were this day and age those roses would have ended in the garbage at Mumbai airport. Lynn and Jim had kept a canvas with a midnight blue background and all the guests at the party painted stars on it. This was later used at the wedding reception as a decoration and to mark our presence for the couple's day. Then as Joe had taken along some Indian music, we all ended up dancing in a frenzy to Daler Mehndi's '*Bolo-ta-ra-ra*'. We had so much fun that Lynn and some of the guests asked us to give them a copy of the music.

The wedding ceremony was conducted at St. John Vianney Church, in Gilmerton, with the bride's brother, Fr. Gerry, as celebrant. As expected, his homily was humorous and had us all laughing in church. However, the pronunciation of the marriage vows and the exchange of rings were solemn and moving. But when Joe went up into the sanctuary, red turban and all, to do a reading, eyebrows were raised; later some did ask how he could speak such good English! (When narrating this to a friend, she said her standard reply to such queries is a nonchalant, 'I picked it up during the flight coming in.') Anyone who has heard the genuine native Scots accent will know what a feat it is to understand their English!

As the bridal couple emerged from church after the ceremony, Jim threw a handful of coins to the young lads hanging about outside, and they all scrambled to collect them. This Scottish custom is known as 'poor-oot' (to pour out one's money) and symbolises the couple's new fortune in marriage. Another explanation is that the money thrown away will keep returning to the couple throughout their married life.

Instead of entering with gift items for the couple, guests had been requested, in a note sent with the informal wedding invitation, to give cash or cheques (in an envelope which had been thoughtfully enclosed). Every penny would be donated to a charity of Lynn and Jim's choosing. As the guests walked into the reception hall, they were asked to tie their envelopes with a golden thread to the branches of a leafless tree standing there. As some confided, this philanthropic touch inspired them to give more than they would have spent on a wedding present. This appears to have been true in most cases – we can personally vouch that the sum collected was indeed a large amount. I have already mentioned how affected Lynn and Jim were by the beggars on the streets of Mumbai, so it was no surprise when they announced to all present that they had decided to donate everything in the tree-envelopes to the street children of Mumbai. We had the pleasure of presenting this personally to Shelter Don Bosco in Mumbai.

I had also applied mehndi (henna) with fairly intricate designs on my hands, almost up to my elbows especially for the wedding. Some mistook these for gloves. (In fact, even on the flight coming in and then during our few days in England, I had strangers stopping to ask and to admire.) Many of the wedding guests were dressed in their traditional kilts and I made sure I had some photos with them. The wedding cake was in the shape of the Empire State Building (no surprise!) In addition, there were several other small cakes which a select few were invited to cut with the couple. We were one of the chosen pairs. To enliven the course of the long evening, there were two live bands. One had Alan, younger brother of Lynn, playing the piano with a group of the family's good friends who had practised all the favourite songs of Lynn and Jim for the occasion. The other was a 12-piece band made up of three generations of good Glasgow

Catholics, right from grandfather to granddaughter! So of course almost everyone was on the floor throughout the evening. The Scottish Highland dances were exhilarating even to watch and I wished I could have joined them. Well, we had experienced our first Scottish wedding and it was indeed 'verra' grand and a lot of fun.

The day after the wedding, we were invited to go with a few select wedding guests, to the Malt Whisky Society in Leith. This very exclusive club with exclusive membership, catered to true connoisseurs of very old matured Scotch. The place had a lovely ambience of old wood and leather. Each precious peg cost a pretty penny – maybe that accounted for the reverential silence in which some sipped their single malts. From there we went on to a restaurant for dinner spiced with much witty banter.

After the wedding festivities, Gerry asked us where we would like to go and without a second thought we said, 'The Lake District'. Agnes gently suggested we visit Pitlochry instead, but we were set on the Lake District because we had heard so much about it, and presumed, wrongly as it turned out, that the Lake District was a region in Scotland. Gerry was as gracious and as obliging as ever. We started out early the next morning. Along the way we stopped at Gretna Green, romanticized in many novels as the place to which young couples ran off to get married against the wishes of their parents.

We covered mile after mile with Gerry driving at breakneck speed but I felt we were getting no closer to our destination. I started to feel rather uneasy and told Gerry that perhaps we should turn back but he said it was quite okay as he loved driving. As Joe studied the motorist map, we came upon an awful discovery: after travelling from England to Scotland, we had asked Gerry to drive us back to England, which is where the Lake District was! We were both so terribly embarrassed that we had not done our homework before making that suggestion. Of course, Gerry never uttered a word of complaint for having to drive those endless miles and back. Instead he told us he now had an amusing anecdote to tell all his friends!

The Lake District, covering 2292 sq.kms is a mountainous region in North West England and is also known as 'The Lakes' or 'Lakeland.' Due to the heavy rainfall here, much of the land is often boggy and its geography makes it the dampest zone of England. We were glad that we were visiting during the dry months which were from March to June. The most visited part is called the Lake District National Park, which contains some of the deepest and longest lakes in England and also the highest mountain known as Scafell Pike. After driving around a while, we stopped by one of the lakes to have a picnic lunch, just opposite a chocolate shop selling delicious confections. The entire area was extravagantly beautiful; little wonder then that with Wordsworth, '*Beside the lake, beneath the trees ... I gazed – and gazed – but little thought what wealth the show to me had brought.*' Even so, I still have pangs of guilt when I think of how we made Gerry drive us all that distance and back for a one-day outing.

On the following day we were happy to meet Jean McDonnell again. She lived in Linlithgow, a name that recalled a lot of history I had read. Jean was a good friend of Fr. Gerry's and would very kindly make time for us when Gerry was busy. She took us to the Linlithgow Palace which was not too far from her home. This palace built in 1425 was the birthplace of Mary Queen of Scots and the residence of all the Stewart kings. It was past visiting hours when we reached, so we only strolled around in the gardens.

Soon it was time for us to leave Scotland and once again Gerry crowned our visit by taking us out for a fancy meal at a swanky Chinese restaurant in Linlithgow. On our last morning, Jim took us for a walk alongside a little stream and showed us the tree beside which he and Lynn often met. They used to sit on a branch that stretched out over the stream. I forgot to ask whether if, besides falling in love, they ever fell in. This was the place that Jim first proposed to Lynn and it was Jim's 'Yes' (a powerful word that gets you to places!) that had brought us back to Scotland a second time.

SOUTHAMPTON SOJOURN
"Give me five minutes more, only five minutes more"

Back in England we kept dipping into the delicious memories of Scotland, as we unpacked and re-packed to take off for Southampton. We have always remained grateful to Freddy for letting us use his house as a base where we could leave the bulk of our luggage, taking smaller bags for our trips to other places.

Unfortunately, the only weekend free for us to spend with Bash and Asha whom I have written about earlier, happened to be the long Easter weekend. That being so, we could not and would not miss attending the church services on all three important Holy Week days, Maundy Thursday, Good Friday and then the Easter vigil on Saturday. Our hosts had moved to a new house in Chandler's Ford, Eastleigh, and the Church was some distance away. Why I used the word 'unfortunately' becomes clear when I say that it was Bash who most graciously undertook to drive us to church and then come back to pick us up – on all three days. Poor Bash was kindness itself, but it embarrassed us no end. How we missed our Mumbai taxis and auto rickshaws available just round the corner!

On one of the days, Bash, Asha and their two boys, Nandu and Karthik, drove us to Farley Mount Country Park, which lies about four miles west of the city of Winchester. It was a large expanse of open country and woods and we had a leisurely long walk along the footpath that ran through the site up to the highest point known as Farley Mount, which gave the Park its name. The pyramid shaped monument at the top, also referred to as a 'Folly', was in honour of a horse named 'Beware Chalk Pit'. The inscription on the plaque at the monument told the story:

> *Underneath lies buried a horse, the property*
> *of Paulet St. John Esq., that in the month of*
> *September 1733 leaped into a chalk pit*
> *twenty-five feet deep afoxhunting with his*
> *master on his back and in October 1734*
> *he won the Hunters Plate on Worthy Downs*
> *and was rode by his owner and was entered*
> *in the name of 'Beware Chalk Pit'.*

A rare honour for a rare equine! The area was popular on windy days for kite flying, and we can vouch for that as we ourselves had to cling to our jackets, and Asha and I struggled to keep our wind-tossed hair from blowing all over our faces.

Despite all the to-and-froing of the weekend, we managed to take in a lot, and, as always, the Baskers went all out to ensure that we had a marvellous time. We left on Easter Monday to return to Freddy's, found time to meet with an old school friend, Joyce Stephens, wandered around Southall and Ealing for a bit, and enjoyed the party that Freddy always arranged before we departed. We were on our way home before we knew it. Our stay in England was very brief, but we used every minute well.

WALKING IN THE LORD'S FOOTSTEPS
"Put your hand in the hand of the Man from Galilee"

How happy I was when we were offered the opportunity of visiting the Holy Land in October 1999. It was my wish and desire to go to this Holy of Holy Lands, and even though we had already made one trip abroad to Scotland the same year, we just could not resist going on the second foreign expedition. The return fare Mumbai-Cairo-Tel Aviv-Cairo-Mumbai was just Rs.24,500 a head and the overall package was also attractive. That's one good thing about group travel, and having experienced one such trip to Bangkok we knew we could take the risk. We were about 35 altogether, and most were known to each other.

At the airport Joe discovered that he was the only male among all the women and he seriously wanted to turn tail and run home. He confessed later that it was a bit unnerving for him. To make matters worse, we had a long wait at the airport as the Egypt Air flight was late by more than four hours. We reached Cairo at 6.45 am (Egypt time) and shuffled through another long wait until visa formalities for the entire group were completed. That done, we moved on to the Caesar's Palace Hotel, where we were put up. The 'palace' bit was truly pretentious but the very comfortable beds made up for that – truly the best I ever slept in.

That evening we went for a cruise on the River Nile. The US $30 a head we paid covered a five-star buffet dinner and three floorshows, of which the whirling dervish was outstanding, but we missed seeing the sights along the Nile, which I would have much preferred. We returned to the hotel at 1 am, had a cold shower (the palace did not provide hot water, or maybe they had fixed times for it) and managed to sleep for five hours before rising to catch our flight to Tel Aviv.

After a pathetic breakfast supervised by a man with hawk eyes lest anyone took an extra egg, we rushed down to the lobby, only to be told that the flight was delayed. Some of us, Joe and I included, went back

157

to our rooms to catch up on our sleep as we were very tired, but nobody remembered to wake us in time, so five of us missed the pick-up bus and had to take a taxi to re-join the group.

That first day we visited Caesarea, the city built by Herod on the shores of the Mediterranean and named after Caesar Augustus. This was one of the great cities of the ancient world. Many scholars had questioned the actual existence of a Roman Governor with the name 'Pontius Pilate', the procurator who had ordered Jesus' crucifixion. But in June 1961, when Italian archaeologists were excavating an ancient Roman amphitheatre near Caesarea, they uncovered an interesting limestone block inscribed with a dedication to Tiberius Caesar from 'Pontius Pilate, Prefect of Judea'. Pontius Pilate is said to have lived in Caesarea from AD 29 to 36. As the city did not have any natural sources of water, the Romans constructed an aqueduct to bring water from the foothills of Mt. Carmel 13 kms away – we saw the remains of the aqueduct still standing on the beach.

From Caesarea, we drove to Tiberias, the largest town on the Sea of Galilee. Herod Antipas, son of Herod the Great, founded this city around AD 20. Many of the incidents recorded in the gospels took place around this area. We stayed at Hotel Haartman, which overlooked the Sea of Galilee. The rooms were cosy and pleasant but there was a very strict man overseeing the dinner served to us in the dining room; he would not let me move my plates or cutlery from their original place. The moment I moved a plate or spoon even a little bit, he would come and put it back where it had to be, according to him. After that, I was wondering if he would tell me what I should eat first and how to eat it. I dubbed him 'Hitler' but even with his unnerving attention, the meal was very good and he provided some entertainment for us.

After breakfast next morning, we drove to the Mount of Beatitudes from where you have a panoramic view of the Sea of Galilee. The

Church of the Beatitudes is situated on the crest of the Mount. An octagonal-shaped chapel in the church marks the spot where Jesus is said to have delivered the Sermon on the Mount. From here we drove to the Church of Multiplication of Loaves and Fishes. Known as Tabgha, which means lonely place, it commemorates one of the most well known miracles that Jesus performed – the feeding of the 5000. Jesus frequently withdrew to this place to pray or be with his disciples alone. The church has been built around a large rock that marks the place where the miracle is said to have taken place. This holy site remained hidden for more than 1300 years until archaeologists excavated parts of its walls and mosaics. The foundations of the original church which was built in the fourth century can be seen under clear glass panels near the altar. The floor mosaics at Tabgha are reputed to be among the most beautiful in the Holy Land.

Capernaum (Kfar Nahum), our next stop, was a prosperous fishing and trading village. Here we saw the ruins of the 4th century limestone synagogue, which probably stands on the site of the original synagogue where Jesus preached. Jewish symbols are still visible on the decorated carved lintels. Nearby are the ruins of the house of Peter's mother-in-law where he also lived. A modern circular church has been built over the ruins, and a side view of this gives the appearance of a fishing boat.

The Sea of Galilee is a deep blue freshwater lake, about 55 km in circumference, situated in the Jordan valley. At 208 mts below sea level, it is the lowest freshwater lake in the world. It looks so calm and tranquil at most times that it is difficult to believe it could ever be the scene of violent storms. This goes as far back as the times of Jesus when His disciples feared they were going to drown one night in the waves whipped up by a tempest. We had an interesting and long boat ride from Tabgha to Tiberias across the Sea of Galilee in a boat modelled on the ones used in Jesus' time.

At Yardenit – the place where Jesus was baptized by John the Baptist – we saw many pilgrims who had come from all over the world to immerse themselves in the holy waters. We witnessed people clad in white robes being fully immersed while being assisted by others. This is done in the belief that they are following in the tradition of the scriptures. The river Jordan was quite shallow in some places and easily fordable. It was a long drive from Yardenit back to our hotel for another evening with 'Hitler'. Not wanting to trouble him any more than he already appeared to be, I behaved myself.

At Nazareth, our first stop was the Church of The Miracle at Cana. It was here that Jesus performed his first miracle of converting water into wine. Then on to the Basilica of the Annunciation, which dominates the whole of Nazareth – it is the largest basilica in the Middle East. In the crypt of this basilica which was completed only in 1969, can be seen the remains of the four previous churches. These were all built on the spot where the Angel Gabriel is said to have appeared to the Virgin Mary. A marble altar now marks the spot and bears a Latin inscription, which translates: 'The Word was here made Flesh'. Beside this altar is an ancient column said to mark the spot where the Angel Gabriel stood. However, according to Greek Orthodox tradition, the Angel Gabriel met the Virgin Mary near the spring which issues from the interior of the Church of St. Gabriel, now known as Mary's Well, while she was drawing water for her household needs. Well, wherever the actual location of the annunciation, we just have to be very grateful that Mary said 'Yes' and agreed to be the Mother of God and thus gave the human race hope for salvation.

The one with the least mention in the entire Bible is St. Joseph, foster father of Jesus. We know that he was born in Bethlehem (because he took his family there for the census), that he fled to Egypt with Jesus and Mary to avoid Herod's wrath when he killed all the children below two years of age, and that he then returned to Nazareth, a quiet and nondescript village, where he worked as a carpenter. Little else is known about him, or how and when he died. However, there is the Church of St. Joseph in Nazareth, where his remains are said to be buried and we visited this church too. St. Joseph is Joe's patron saint (his full name is 'Joseph') so we had a special devotion here.

We travelled from Nazareth to the Jordan Valley and along the Jordan River to Jericho, the world's oldest city. It was here that Jesus met Zaccheus, a tax collector. Being short, he had climbed a sycamore tree to see Jesus better, and we are told that this man, who had cheated the public for so long, received salvation that day and resolved to make restitution to all whom he had wronged.

After lunch, we went to the Dead Sea, which is the lowest naturally accessible point on earth, about 450 mts below sea level! Nobody can ever meet death by drowning in the Dead Sea as the water is extremely salt. Of course we all went in for a 'floaty' dip and plastered our faces and body with the clayey mud underfoot, which is supposed to be very good for the skin so it was no wonder that many expensive cosmetics were being marketed as Dead Sea products.

O LITTLE TOWN OF BETHLEHEM
"Go, tell it on the mountain,
Over the hills and everywhere"

We continued on to Jerusalem and spent the night at the Bethlehem Inn Hotel. Originally called Ephrath, Bethlehem is revered as the birthplace of King David and of Jesus. After breakfast, we went to the Basilica of the Nativity which has been built above the cave where Jesus was said to have been born because His parents could not find room at any inn when they came to Bethlehem for the census ordered by the Roman authorities. The church looks almost like a fortress from the outside, which it probably was, to protect it from invaders. One has to bend almost double (not me, with my height!) to enter the Door of Humility, which is the entrance to the church. The original entrance can be recognized as it was partly sealed over in the 17th century to prevent the Muslim invaders from entering the Church riding on their horses. Most churches were destroyed in the 7th century during the Persian invasion, but this church was spared from desecration because of the mosaic on the façade, which depicted the three wise men wearing Persian clothing. Except for an elaborate altar up front, the interior of the Justinian Basilica in the Church of the Nativity was almost bare, with double rows of thick columns on either side. We had to stand in a slow-moving queue to go down narrow steps to the grotto of the nativity. This occupies a very small space and only a few visitors at a time could enter, accounting for the slow-moving line. A large silver star marks the actual site where Jesus is thought to have been born. This spot is under an altar from which several hanging lamps are arranged in a semi-circle.

Known as Jebus in the time of King David, Jerusalem is an important and pivotal city in the history of Israel. We entered the Holy City through the Dung Gate, which is located in the southern wall. The city had flourished under King Solomon and its prosperity, growth and religious importance tempted many to covet it, and those who did rule over it were the Byzantines, the Arabs and the Crusaders from the kingdoms of medieval Europe, the Mamelukes of Egypt, the Ottoman Turks, the Romans and lastly, the British. It is truly amazing to note how many coveted, conquered, ruled and lost the city. Each of these conquerors left their mark – some burnt and destroyed while some embellished and adorned. We stopped at the Western Wall, which has a very long and colourful history. Built by King Herod as a retaining wall for the Temple Mount, it was not considered holy at that time. Today it has acquired great religious significance for the Jews especially, who see it as a blend of past, present and future. The site is considered holy also by the Muslims because, according to tradition, Muhammed tethered his horse, Al Buraq, at this wall before he ascended to heaven. Instead of the narrow alleys that existed earlier, there was now a renovated large plaza. This wall is also known as the Weeping Wall and we actually saw many Jews praying and weeping – as they still mourn the destruction of the Temple.

The Temple Mount also has a very interesting history. King David first bought the land, which was called Mount Moriah, from a Jebusite. His son, King Solomon decided to build a House worthy of God on the site. Since the Mount was originally a narrow peak, Solomon built a stone wall framework to create enough space to build the first temple. Thus instead of a narrow peak, the Mount was transformed into a broad square and tradition holds that the Ark of the Covenant was placed in the Temple here. Mount Moriah, as most Christians, Jews and Moslems know, is the site of the proposed sacrifice of Abraham's son, Isaac. The Babylonians destroyed this temple, but 70 years later, the prophets Ezra and Nehemiah rebuilt it. Centuries later when the Kingdom of Judah fell, the Temple Mount was once more laid waste. The people who were exiled to Babylon longed to return to Jerusalem and it was their descendants who, returning from exile, immediately began construction of a temple. However, it was Herod the Great (not to be confused with Herod Agrippa) who built the second big temple, which was a most impressive structure. He did such a good job that the western and southern walls survive to this day.

In the year AD 70 the temple was gutted with fire by the Roman legions and Emperor Hadrian built a pagan temple on its remains. The Byzantines destroyed that and built a church, but after the Moslems conquered Jerusalem in the 7th century, the Temple Mount became a Moslem religious centre, and the two main mosques, the Dome of the Rock and the Al-Aqsa mosque, were constructed. When constructing the Dome of the Rock, the Moslems left the tip of Mount

Moriah untouched. This can be seen through a glass cover and hence its name. During the Crusades, the mosques were converted into churches, and when the Crusaders were expelled less than a century later, the Moslems took over again, and the management of the Temple Mount continues in their hands to this day. The Temple Mount is important for the Moslems who believe that the prophet Mohammed ascended to heaven from here. From the explanations given above, one can see why it is also a holy site for both Christians and Jews.

The Via Dolorosa or Road of Sadness, which is about a kilometre long, is marked by the 14 Stations of the Cross. It starts from close to the Temple Mount and winds its way through the Muslim and Christian Quarters. The road climbs uphill gently and may not present a problem for people walking uphill today, but Jesus was carrying a heavy cross on this journey and the paths up the hill would have been rocky and uneven. The last five stations, leading ultimately to the place of crucifixion, are close to one another and are now located inside the Church of the Holy Sepulchre, considered by hundreds of millions of Christians worldwide as the most sacred site in Jerusalem. It marks the place where Jesus was crucified and buried, and is the birthplace of Christianity, which changed the face of the entire world. Unbelievably, the Church of the Holy Sepulchre is now sub-divided into six! The three largest belong to the Greek Orthodox, Roman Catholic and Armenian denominations; the other three are Coptic, Ethiopian and Syrian. So each 'chapel' is under different control. As can be imagined, there have been continuous quarrels and fights through the centuries, and because of this, overall neglect is all too apparent.

I thought it rather strange that of these six, not one has control over the main entrance of the church even today. This is in the hands of two neutral Muslim families: the Joudehs and the Nuseibehs. This arrangement dating back to the time of the Third Crusade was one of the outcomes of the truce concluded in September 1192, by Richard the Lionhearted and Saladin, Sultan of Egypt and Syria. Saladin entrusted the Joudeh family with the key to the door of the church, and their neighbours, the Nuseibeh family, were entrusted with the task of locking and unlocking the door. To this day a Joudeh brings the key to the entrance and hands it over to a Nuseibeh to unlock the door.

As you enter the church, you come to the Tenth Station where Jesus was stripped of His garments and then the Eleventh Station where he was nailed to the Cross. The Twelfth Station is on the hallowed spot of the Crucifixion, the culmination of that painful journey where Jesus died on the Cross. We had to crawl under the altar to kiss the base of the Cross and, like the Women of Jerusalem, I could not hold back my tears. We could not stay long in this place because there were impatient queues and hordes of tourists and the place was almost like a fish market where there should have been a deep, deep, reverential silence. The Thirteenth Station was where Jesus was taken down from the Cross and placed on the Stone of Anointing. Here His body was laid out and prepared for burial.

A short distance away was the Fourteenth and last Station – the tomb where Jesus was laid to rest. We had to wait in a long line to visit the tomb. This is also called the Chapel of the Angel where the angel proclaimed the good news of Jesus' Resurrection on that first Easter morn. To enter the Tomb one had to bend almost double and only two or three people could enter at a time. The sacred rock where the body of Jesus lay from Good Friday until Easter Sunday is covered with marble. Though the space was very confining, it was an overwhelming feeling just being there! Even in that short time, I sensed a tremendous calm and peace. There was no hope of getting a picture of the full tomb on my ordinary camera that had no wide angle lens. One would have had to stand much farther back to get the full tomb in the picture and there was no space to move backwards so I can only think that when I clicked, it was a miracle that I managed to get a good photograph capturing almost the entire length of the tomb. Of all the opulent churches, museums, etc. that we have visited in several parts of the world, the Church of the Holy Sepulchre had the least in the way of material treasures, yet it can be considered the richest because of its sanctity.

The next morning, we drove to the Mount of Olives and first stopped in the Garden of Gethsemane. A large ancient and gnarled olive tree caught our attention and we wondered how much sacred history it had witnessed. This is where Jesus and his disciples spent the last hours before his arrest. Right across from the Mount of Olives, one could clearly see the Temple Mount and the city of Jerusalem. It was on the slopes of this Mount that Jesus was said to have wept over the city of Jerusalem, which would soon be destroyed. Between the Mount of Olives and the Temple Mount lies the Kidron Valley, which Jesus often traversed. We entered the Church of All Nations, also called the Basilica of the Agony, which was built on the ruins of the Byzantine and Crusader churches with contributions from 12 nations, hence its name.

One of the most fascinating places to visit was the Church of the Coenaculum on Mount Zion, which holds the Room of the Last Supper where Jesus ate the Passover meal with His disciples. This is also where He washed the feet of his Disciples. (I realise I am editing this very chapter on a Maundy Thursday when this scene was first enacted.) Joe and I wanted to get the feel of the Last Supper room when there were less noisy people around so during the break for lunch, we went back for a second visit to sit quietly and meditate.

After a short tour of New Jerusalem, our guide took us to Yad Vashem, the Jewish memorial to the Holocaust. This is located on Har Hazikaron, the Mount of Remembrance in Jerusalem. This vast, sprawling complex of museums, exhibits, archives, monuments, sculptures and memorials was established in 1953 as a memorial to the murdered six million Jews. Some of the exhibits we saw when we entered the first exhibition hall were of the death camps. They were just too heartbreaking and stomach-churning and we made a quick exit from there.

The notable exhibits at Yad Vashem for us, were The Hall of Remembrance, a tent-like structure on the floor of which were the names of the six death camps and some of the concentration camps and killing sites; the Children's Memorial, hollowed out from an underground cavern, was a tribute to the almost one and a half million Jewish children who perished during the Holocaust. The place was dark except for many lit candles that reflected infinitely in mirrors, and one could hear the names of the children being recited as you walked past. It gave me goose bumps being there. Very significantly, our Jewish guide made us spend the longest time at Yad Vashem, but it was well worth the visit.

Though our trip was hectic and a little chaotic, the Holy Land definitely brought me a little closer to understanding my faith. As for Joe, he was glad that he didn't change his mind – also because he ended up being the hero among all the ladies!

Chapter Twelve

2000
AHOY AMERICA
"I knew somewhere, sometime, somehow ..."

The year 2000, the year of the Golden Dragon, the year we were moving towards a new millennium, was the year I had the longest and most varied of holiday experiences. Vanessa, our younger daughter, and I both left home on 13 August, she to attend a Youth Fest in Rome with a group from Mumbai, and I to visit our elder daughter, Melissa, and her family in the States for the very first time. Expenses for my air ticket alone set me back a little over Rs.56,626 with a stopover in Rome on my return journey. Vanessa and I both travelled on the same Alitalia flight, but not side-by-side. Simonette Ferreira, who was also going to Rome to participate in the Fest, had a Business Class ticket (given by the company she worked for) but as she wanted to be with the youth, she asked if I 'minded' exchanging places with her. What a great sacrifice that was on my part to move from Economy to Business Class and do a friend a favour in the bargain! In Milan, we parted company, Vanessa to get the flight to Rome, and I, a flight to New York.

Mel and family were living in New Jersey at that time; Mel had moved from a Hill Road address in Mumbai to a Hill Street address in NJ and I thought that a strange coincidence.

When planning that trip to the States, I could not help thinking about visiting friends and family in nearby Canada. So after about 10 days with Melissa and Kerissa in New Jersey, I left for Toronto on the Amtrak train on 24 August. Kerman, our son-in-law, had left for India.

CANADA, HERE I COME – AGAIN!
"I feel so welcome each time that I return that my happy heart keeps laughin' like a clown"

Seven years had passed since my niece Debra and her family had put me up in Dubai. Now I would be staying with them again, but in Mississauga, Toronto, as they had migrated to Canada. Debra's sister, Allyson, and family had followed suit and I spent a weekend with them as well. One of the highlights of this visit was my first camping trip which they and their friends had organized. I don't recall the name of the place where we camped but I do know that everyone had great fun in spite of the workload for those in charge of preparing the meals in the great outdoors. The laughter, singing and flowing spirits helped to keep up the jollity. I was sorry that Joe had missed this camping experience which he would have loved, having been a boy scout in his school days.

From Canada we made a foray to the American side to visit a Marian Shrine and also the Niagara Falls but doubled back to the Canadian side where the view is more spectacular. The first time I went to Niagara in 1986, I was too scared to board a 'Maid of the Mist' boat that goes almost up to the thundering Falls. This time around, I decided to be more daring and I confess it was exhilarating. Despite the raincoats handed out to everyone on board, we got quite drenched with the heavy spray from the Falls, and we had to protect our cameras for the same reason. Even so, I managed to take pictures till we were quite close. Then it became impossible to keep my eyes open because of the heavy spray.

Almost every night in Toronto was party night, and often turned out to be an occasion to meet up with old friends. I was really happy to stay overnight at Yolande and Emilio Fernandes' house in Scarborough, and spend a happy night with Mario and Lorraine Gonsalves exchanging amusing anecdotes and reminiscing about their days in Mumbai and their well known band, Friendship Clan. I spent the last two days in Toronto with Olga and Ivan Caspersz. They had given up their beautiful home in Agincourt and were now living in a deluxe condo in Mississauga. In fact, I found that very many Indians had made their homes in Mississauga so it was no wonder that with so many desis around, most of them had settled in well and were not homesick.

Joe's cousins, Yucca and Len Bocarro, drove from Montreal to Toronto just to pick me up, and to take me to their home in Montreal. Yucca insisted on fattening me even more (like I needed it!) with her exotic breakfasts and tasty cooking. I just loved their two lovebirds, Bitlet and Niblet, and enjoyed playing with them. While Len chose to stay home most often, Yucca took me to visit many places. One was to the Saint Joseph's Oratory on the northern slope of Mount Royal (from which 'Montreal' derives its name). Here, Blessed Bro. Andre Bessette built a small chapel in 1904, and this kept expanding to the present huge basilica. Yucca was also keen to show me the Notre-Dame Basilica in the historic district of Old Montreal but when we reached there it was closed. I had heard that the interior was very colourful and grand and that the stained glass windows did not depict biblical scenes but the history of Montreal.

On the one Sunday I was in Montreal, instead of going to their regular church, Yucca and Len took me to a different parish for mass. As I walked in, my gaze turned towards the organist, and I immediately saw her face light up with a smile. Though I was meeting Marion Rodrigues after many years it was so nice to see that she still recognized me. Marion is a very talented pianist and she used to accompany me on the piano when I sang at our Parish Zonal Talent Contests in Bandra. She insisted that we meet up again as she wanted to treat us to a good meal and we arranged to do so after our return from Quebec.

Yucca had booked us tickets for a day trip to Quebec but since we reached the coach station early, we wandered around. By the time we got back to the coach, we found that all the good seats had gone and we had to sit separately. I have almost always met excellent people while on our travels abroad or in India, but there has been the odd exception; the one I sat next to on the coach to Quebec belonged to that second category as I was to discover much too late. She was pleasant enough to start with. Some of our conversations during the day were about the exotic East, and then her continued correspondence with me for a year after that gave me no indication that she was a psychiatric patient who should never have ventured to subsequently make a journey to India on her own or without informing me of her condition. I do not intend going into details about her or her stay with us, except to say that it was a nightmare. Thereafter, we were more careful about whom we befriended.

Quebec is the only Canadian province with a predominantly French-speaking population and the only one where the sole official language is French. Though very much a part of Canada, Quebec, it would appear, still likes to consider itself part of France. Our guide, confirming the 'French' affiliation, stressed that Quebec was pronounced 'Kebec'. We visited the older part of the city which was divided into the Upper Town with its old European atmosphere, and the Lower Town located on the waterfront. Our first stop was the National Battlefields Park. This 44-hectare park also encompasses the Plains of Abraham, a historic area and the site of a great battle in 1759.

The Hotel Chateau Frontenac stood out majestically against the skyline atop a tall cape overlooking the Saint Lawrence River. Alfred Hitchcock's thriller movie 'I Confess,' starring Montgomery Cliff and Anne Baxter was filmed in this hotel in 1953 and its very location added a further air of mystery to the movie. After strolling along the Dufferin Terrace promenade which adjoins Chateau Frontenac, we stopped there to have our sandwich lunch before strolling down the charming old world streets to look at the sights and the shops. One was selling beautifully carved wooden statues and they had a cluster of life size Red Indians just outside their shop. As I was wearing a white flannel jumper, I posed amid that group as they too were all clad in white. I blended in well with them, even down to the brown skin, so you could barely tell us apart! (Years later, in a 'Just for Laughs Gags' show, we saw someone posing among the very same statues and scaring the hell out of onlookers by suddenly 'coming alive'.)

I was thoroughly charmed with my visit to this city. When we strolled down the Artists' Laneway, a small side street filled with artists selling their paintings by the roadside, Yucca couldn't resist buying a small painting which she liked very much. It was while she was signing for her purchase and she asked what date it was that I piped up and said it was 11 September. The artist shook his head firmly and said it was the 12th and I told him he was making a mistake because I had booked my return ticket to New York for 12 September. My heart almost stopped beating when it was confirmed that it was I who was wrong! Yes, Yucca had been kind enough to ask me from the start, to postpone my departure, but I just cannot imagine how I had lost track of dates. Besides, we had agreed to meet Marion that evening for dinner. When we got back from Quebec, Yucca immediately called up and spoke to someone at the railway office. She explained that I was ill and hence could not make the journey that morning, and she managed to get my ticket endorsed for 14 September. Well, you could say that I had made myself ill with worry! That sorted out, we went off to meet Marion and two of her other friends at Homards, where she treated us to a delicious seafood dinner. And on my last night in Montreal, Yucca drove us to a restaurant in town where we all had a great meal.

The next morning Yucca and Len both came to drop me off at the train station and made sure I got the right train to New York on the right date! The four days I had set aside for Montreal had stretched to six days by a happy mistake. But when you come to think of it, should one really think of looking at a calendar when on holiday?

MANHATTAN AND MEMORIES
"All my best memories come back clearly to me
some can even make me cry"

I was back in the States, this time not in New Jersey but in New York. Yes, while I was in Canada, Mel and Kerman had moved to a new apartment in Walden Terrace in Rego Park, New York. With the extra baggage I had collected in Canada, I was glad that the new apartment was not too far from the metro. I was also happy to find that the house was within walking distance of the Church, which made it most convenient to attend the midday mass at Our Lady of the Angelus Church.

Joe arrived in New York on 29 September, and apart from many excursions to Manhattan and many shopping expeditions to various malls, we also visited the Empire State Building for the first time. Best of all we had the opportunity to spend lots of time with our beautiful and very cute 4-year old granddaughter, Kerissa. I was happy to see that the many new dresses I had sewn fit her well and looked so good on her.

On 6 October we were all invited to Hira and Toos Daruvala's house in Scarsdale for dinner. We accepted even though it was far from where we lived, because we also had the opportunity to meet Hira's parents, Kaiki Alpaiwalla (my ex-boss in A.F. Ferguson & Co.) and his wife, Zarine Alpaiwalla, who were spending time with their daughter and grandchildren. We really enjoyed that evening with them, never imagining that it would be the last time I saw Mr. Alpaiwalla alive. He passed away exactly a month later, a day after his birthday. I really believe that it is the Lord who arranges these meetings for us and I am so glad we agreed to the visit.

On our last night in New York, Mel and Kerman took us to the famous 'Serendipity' restaurant (also made famous by the film of the same name). This place is a hangout for many celebrities and is well known for their out-of-the-world desserts. We ordered one which three of us shared as it turned out to be almost the size of Kerissa's head, and far too much for one person.

Joe and I left New York on different airlines on different days. He went via London and I via Milan, but we both met up in Rome on the same day, 13 October.

FRIENDS UNLIMITED
"There's grinin' and mandolinin' in sunny Italy"

The excitement of being back in the fabulous and eternal city of Rome was doubled with the delight of finding Nadja and Gianni Fontana waiting for us. They had motored down from Switzerland to meet us. We got acquainted with this couple in Goa while we were conducting a seminar at the Renaissance Hotel at Varca. They also happened to be on the same flight we took to Mumbai, and as there was a taxi strike on that day, we were able to be of assistance to them at the airport. We were touched that they took the trouble not only to meet us at the Leonardo da Vinci airport, but also to then drive us to Ostia Antica where they offered us an apartment to stay for as long as we liked. Having arrived from the States we had too much luggage to haul around, so we were immensely thankful that we could leave our cumbersome suitcases there. After lunch, we packed a small bag and they drove us to Centro Mariapolis in Castelgandolfo before they returned to Switzerland that same evening. It is not often you come across such overwhelming kindness. How many would do that for their friends? And we were practically strangers!

On our arrival at Castelgandolfo we met up with the delegates who had arrived from India and from various other countries for the Jubilee of the Families.   On the first day of the Jubilee there was to be a grand meeting with the Holy Father and families from all over the world. St. Peter's Square was packed with humanity in every direction one looked. A rich velvet curtain covered the main entrance to St. Peter's Basilica, which was referred to as the Millennium Jubilee Door. We had a long wait before the Holy Father, John Paul II, arrived in his famous Popemobile, driving through the crowds. The Indian group again had pride of place right on the patio outside the church. The celebrations started and people from different countries began to give their testimonies, including a family from our own group. This Pope was indeed a favourite of the masses and I loved him too.

The next day there was a special mass for the families, again in the square outside the church, but as we made our way there after alighting from the bus, the heavens opened and it poured, and continued pouring. Much as we wanted to be present for that mass, we couldn't risk getting more wet than we already were, and then remaining in those clothes for hours. Instead we found shelter in the parking complex and followed the mass on indoor TV screens. We heard later that the people in the square were soaked through and consequently many fell ill.

The three days at Castelgandolfo passed quickly. We met lots of new people and some old friends with whom we had rubbed shoulders in 1993. We left on the 17th and took the train from Castelgandolfo to Roma Termini, where we changed trains to go to Ostia Antica. On the train to Ostia, we encountered someone trying to pickpocket Joe but he got off the train when he realised we were on to him. After spending the night in the flat at Ostia Antica, we packed a bag and left to take the Euro Star from Rome to Ora. The train fare cost us L86,000 each.

Mario and his uncle, Fr. Luigi Jellici (who also happened to be in Tesero at the time), met us at the station and drove us up to Tesero. This time we stayed on the upper floor of the Jellici home as Fr. Luigi was staying in the one we had previously occupied. Whenever the

Jellicis were busy with work, Fr. Luigi happily took us round the village where he had grown up and where he seemed to know everyone. At almost every home we passed someone would pop out of a window to call to him and ask him to come in. Of course they all welcomed us too. One of them was a lovely lady named Maria Rosa Doliana. In this way we sampled lots of wines, cheeses, ham, and even polenta, the thick cornmeal porridge Italians love. Fr. Luigi showed us the tiny chapel where he had received his vocation to the priesthood, and the site of the Stava tragedy which I described earlier; we also made a trip to his friend Tino's farm in the hills and were invited to many lunches and dinners.

One afternoon Mario and Rita organized a fabulous lunch at a special German restaurant in the mountains. Here we met up with Gino, Martino and Elia, who had accompanied Mario and Claudio to India in 1994 when, fortunately, we had our large duplex apartment to house them all. Now we were meeting Claudio's fiancée, Lorenza, and Gino's wife, Clelia for the first time. It was wonderful catching up with the old friends and bonding with the new; the food was delicious and the wines were excellent. The entire afternoon which stretched into evening, called for what Joe refers to as the '*Gino Mudra*'. During his stay with us in India, Gino Mich would use this typical word-gesture move which we loved to imitate: Join the tips of forefinger and thumb of each hand, to form a circle, raise both hands, about three inches apart, up to chest level, the other three fingers extended, palms facing outwards, smile, and say a drawn-out '*Perfetto*' while moving both hands apart as if stretching a ribbon. (No royalty claims for this mudra!)

Though we had not asked, Mario on his own took us again to the Shrine of the Madonna di Pietralba. When we prayed at this shrine in 1993, we had hoped we would be able to return with our thanksgiving if our prayers were heard – and they were. Prayers offered, we strolled around picturesque South-Tirol before driving back by a different route.

On another evening, the handsome Gino Mich invited us all for dinner to his Albergo Alpino in the town of Varenna. All those who were at the special lunch at the German restaurant showed up again, as well as Tino's family. Gino and Clelia spared no effort in serving up a lavish meal served in great style, while we downed uncounted bottles of red and white wine. Hence one can imagine the jollity and laughter around the table well after the meal was over.

The next day saw us off to the neighbouring town of Cavalese, and while Mario ran some errands there, Rita, Joe and I strolled about in the parks which were carpeted with bright yellow autumn leaves which made it look as if the sun had burst and splattered the ground. On our last night in Tesero, the Jellicis treated us to pizzas at a restaurant. The pizzas were thin and crisp, totally unlike the thick bread base we land up with in India. And back home, we were presented with gifts – a bottle of Amaretto which we love, a book on the famous Dolomites, and another book of the many Christmas cribs that are on display in Tesero each year. We learnt that India was not represented there so when we returned to Mumbai, we made it a point to locate a Christmas crib of typically Indian figures fashioned of cloth. We mailed the parcel to Tesero, and Mario sent us photographs of the Indian crib on display with the others that year.

We left Tesero on 25 October and took the train from Ora to Milan; our tickets cost us L38,200 per head. In our one week in Tesero we had partied to the full and done so much that it felt as if we had stayed for a much longer time. At Milan we met Nadja Fontana, who was waiting to take us by another train to their home in Lugano, Switzerland – our holiday was far from over!

SWISS SURPRISE
"I know that I'll be contented with yesterday's memories"

The clichéd 'dream come true' would appear to be the ideal opening words for this chapter – but what does one say if there never was a dream in the first place? Switzerland was a country we had only read about and could identify on a map, but to be actually on our way there!!! When I started out on my trip in August 2000, I knew I would be visiting the United States, Canada and Italy. I had not even given Switzerland a thought when planning our itinerary.

Here's how it came about: When bidding farewell to Gianni and Nadja in India, we were surprised to see Gianni become moist-eyed as he confessed that he had come to India only to please Nadja who had been keen to visit Sai Baba in Puttarpathi. He had always thought of India as 'a dirty place, a land of beggars'. What he saw and experienced, particularly in the unasked help we extended to them, had touched them both deeply. As we held hands before parting, he told us, not only did we have a standing invitation to visit them, but also if Vanessa wanted to study in Switzerland, she was welcome to stay with them. Lastly he made us promise, if ever we planned to come to Italy, to inform him.

One sunny day we called from New York to say 'hello' to our friends in Switzerland. We told them we planned to spend some days in Rome and many more in Tesoro. Gianni immediately asked us to come to Switzerland. We told him that was out of the question for the simple reason that we did not have visas for Switzerland and it was a known fact that visas were only issued in one's home country. However, there was no changing Gianni's mind. For the soft spoken giant we knew him to be, we found the vehemence of his insistence most unusual. He waved aside all our protests and told us to just go to the Swiss Consulate in New York and he would do the rest. Out of politeness, we agreed, knowing for certain that our request would meet with a polite but firm refusal. That is exactly what happened. The official at the consulate told us that we should have applied for visas in India, and they could not issue us visas in the USA. But while we were still at the consulate, Gianni phoned and told them that he took full responsibility for us and that they should issue us visas come what may. What else he said and did, I really do not know.

The outcome was we were informed that an exception was being made for us so we hurried out and hurried back with our photographs. Defying all the odds, our visas were granted, and on that very day, sparing us the trouble of making a second trip to the consulate. All thanks to Gianni! Of course we had to make adjustments in our travel schedule after this. As mentioned in the earlier chapter, not content with organizing our visas and the invitation to Switzerland, they had also driven down to meet us in Rome and had given us an apartment in Ostia to stay.

Nadja, who came to Milan to pick us up, was glad there was time to show us the Duomo di Milano. This beautiful and impressive Gothic Cathedral is located in the main square of Milan and is one of the most famous buildings in Europe. After a quick round of the cathedral, we walked through the also famous Galleria Vittorio Emmanuele shopping mall with its arching glass and cast iron roof covering the promenade. This is one of the most expensive places to shop so we contented ourselves with just enjoying the fashionable sights with absolutely no desire to buy anything. This was our one and only brief visit to Milan city as we left soon after to catch our train to Lugano.

We paid L22,900 per head for our train tickets from Milan to Lugano and the train journey took about an hour. Our reunion with Gianni was emotional and I recalled that he had tears in his eyes when we parted in Mumbai as well. The building in which the Fontanas had their classy duplex apartment had a lift for the car so that you could park it on your own floor. That quite fascinated me.

Lugano is located in the alpine region of southeast Switzerland, with the city centre just 8 kms from the Italian border on the banks of the beautiful Lake Lugano. It was not difficult to guess why it is called the 'Monte Carlo of Switzerland', and attracts so many celebrities and tourists. We were surprised to learn that Lugano was the third biggest financial centre in Switzerland, where all the major banks were located. And there we were with no money to withdraw or deposit in any of them!

One morning Nadja dropped us off for a ramble in the city, telling us to wait for her at a particular bus stop at a fixed time. We were not to be late on any account as she could not stop to park anywhere. We strolled through the market and shopping centre, then ambled around Lake Lugano, and took a long walk on a pleasant promenade, this time on an orange carpet of autumn leaves (it was the end of October by then). To be on the safe side, we were back at the bus stop rendezvous nice and early. We knew the Swiss were sticklers for precision and timing but had no idea to what extent they took this till we experienced it for ourselves. An electronic sign board at the stop displayed which bus was due next and the time it would take to arrive at the stop. We were astounded to note that every single bus arrived precisely at the time shown, give or take a couple of seconds. You could regulate your watch by the bus!

On another fine morning, Gianni said he was going to drive us all the way to Lucerne and then on to Engelberg to visit the famous Mount Titlis. It took us around four hours to cover the 172 kms. On the way we passed through many tunnels, including the St. Gotthard Tunnel, which, at 16.3 kms was the longest tunnel in the world at that time. It had taken 11 years to construct and was completed in 1980. Then the honour was claimed by the Seikan Tunnel in Japan which is 53.85 kms long with 23.3 kms running below the seabed. However, the Gotthard Base Tunnel in Switzerland will once again hold the record for the longest tunnel in the world when it opens to traffic in 2016. Gianni also mentioned that when the heavy European trucks started coming into Switzerland, the Swiss government built completely new roads to take the weight of these trucks as they were worried their regular roads would get damaged.

We reached the foot of the 3238-metre high Mount Titlis, and Gianni left us for a while, returning with some high official. We were introduced and after some pleasantries, we were told that he had arranged for us to be taken up Titlis. Bypassing the queue of tourists at the ticket-window we were led to an ornate cable car which, we were informed, had been custom built for the visit of the King and Queen of Sweden. A plaque inside recorded the event and the date which, unfortunately, I did not note down. The car was stocked with beers and soft drinks and we were allowed to indulge ourselves. We felt quite privileged. To reach the top we had to transfer to a second car and then to the last, the special Rotair cable car, which was the first in the world. As its name suggested, its floor rotated, and as it ascended it provided a truly panoramic 360 degree view of the Mount Titlis glacier and the surroundings. From the summit, the spread of vista upon vista of breathtaking beauty was a feast for the eyes.

To reach The Glacier Grotto, we shivered our way through a 150-metre long tunnel. There was yet another, 20 metres long, leading under the surface of the glacier. There were caves within the tunnels, all well illuminated, but too cold for comfort. At the summit of Mount Titlis there were five restaurants and Gianni treated us to a tasty lunch at one of them before we left the ice'n snow paradise. Waiting for the ski lifts we encountered hordes of Indian tourists who had come from London, all talking at high decibel levels (reminiscent of stock market scenes) like there was no one around besides them.

Another four hours of fast driving brought us home to the end of an enchanting day, or so we thought. While we were enjoying our day's outing, Nadja, a Brazilian by birth (she had been the secretary of Pele, the football legend) had been busy organizing a Brazilian Night at the Toppo Rosso (Red Rat) restaurant. It was sheer delight to watch the many samba dancers. Even the very plump ones displayed graceful rhythm when they danced. The intricate legwork looks easy when watching others on the floor, but we were told that it takes years of practice at the samba schools to master this dance and even then, not all become proficient in it. Nadja sprang a surprise item with a cabaret by two professional Brazilian samba dancers who had huge elaborate headwear but were very scantily clad. One of the dancers was very fascinated with Joe and kept raising her eyebrows and winking and smiling at him, completely ignoring my presence! Realizing that we were visitors, these two dancers pulled Joe out to dance with them at the end of their performance. But they did get a surprise when Joe did his famous limbo back bend for them.

On the day before we left Lugano, we were taken to a chocolate factory where one was allowed to eat as much as one could on the premises. That, coupled with the attractive 'factory price' was a strong inducement to buy. Busloads came regularly from Italy just to get their stock of chocolates from there. We were definitely tempted to buy a load when we saw the different varieties but we had to keep our luggage restrictions in mind. Even though Gianni kept urging us to take more we stuck to a sensible amount. At the end Gianni insisted on paying for all we had selected and we just could not argue with him. Wasn't that 'sweet' of him?

On 29 October, our last evening in Lugano, Nadja and Gianni treated us to dinner at a cosy hilltop restaurant; after that we left to board the night train to Rome. We had spent five glorious days with Gianni and Nadja Fontana who had gone out of their way to take us to Switzerland and then spared no effort to make sure we had a memorable visit. It is always wonderful to have your dreams come true, and in Lugano we certainly got more than we had dreamed of!

A STRANGER IS A FRIEND YOU NEVER KNEW
"So hold me in your dreams till I come back to you"

The morning train brought us from Switzerland to Rome and we transferred to the local train to return to Ostia. We spent another day relaxing there and also went to the market to do some shopping.

We had been instructed to leave the key to the flat we were occupying with the neighbours, Alfredo and Sueli Barone. As we had to leave early the next morning, we went to meet the couple, who turned out to be welcoming and very helpful people. We also enquired about getting a taxi to take us to the airport. They made several calls for us but the gentleman finally told us that he himself would drop us to the airport rather than let us spend the small fortune that was being asked by the taxi operators. We were very grateful and showed our appreciation by presenting them with a bottle of wine and a box of panetonne, which is a typical Italian cake-bread. The Barones had a small car but somehow we managed to fit in all our huge suitcases (don't forget we were returning from the State!) while I squeezed into one corner of the back seat, and we trundled off. Joe had to go to London to get his return Air India flight home and I had to change aircraft at Milan for my flight to Mumbai. Only when I was on the aircraft did I remember that I had left my gold charm bracelet behind, on the dining table in the flat! However, this was kept safely for me till I got it back the following year when we met Nadja and Gianni again for a day in Milan.

While I was waiting at Milan airport for my flight to be called, I thought I would use my time fruitfully by saying my morning prayers so I didn't pay attention to the lady who walked towards me and chose to sit right next to me. When I glanced up, I did notice that she was dressed smartly and her hair was also well groomed. I returned her smile politely but did not attempt any conversation till I had completed my prayers and closed my book. Then we got talking about travel, flights and general stuff. I learnt that she was on her way back to New York from Germany and I told her that I had also been to see my daughter in New York and was now on my way home after visits to other places. I could sense she was a little emotional and she mentioned that she had had a lovely holiday in Germany with her friends and had felt sad to leave them (much later she told me that the lady, the wife of a doctor, had been diagnosed with cancer).

Both our flights had been delayed so we had an even longer time to chat; we found we had many common areas of interest. By then we had spent close to an hour together and when she took out the sandwich she was carrying with her and insisted I share it, it seemed the most natural thing to do. In retrospect, I knew it was rather foolish to accept food from a total stranger, and at an airport of all places, but then, fortunately for me, Joan O'Donnell turned out to be no stranger but a good friend with whom I've kept in touch from then on, and we meet regularly every time I am in New York. We still reminisce and talk about that meeting of minds at Milan airport.

When I sent Joan this extract, she wrote back saying she was delighted that she had found mention in my book and told me not to forget to add that I had spontaneously given her a little silver dolphin bracelet which I had with me. She sweetly added: 'Yes, you are right, I was feeling very sad leaving Germany and you indeed not only brightened my spirits but my whole plane trip back to New York.'

Chapter Thirteen

2001
THAT'S AMORE – AN ITALIAN WEDDING
"This is the moment, I've waited for"

Another item on our 'wish list' was about to come true! We had heard that an Italian wedding was an experience to die for, and we had always hoped we would be able to attend one. We were granted our wish in 2001 when Mario and Rita Jellici invited us to their son Claudio's wedding on 9 June. We were so looking forward to the event – this would be our third visit to Italy.

Joe was scheduled to team up with Dr. Walter Picardo to conduct their 'You Have a Dream' programme in Arizona, and so he left home a few days before I did. We were to meet at Milan airport. However, on his return journey, he travelled from Arizona to New York but could not get a seat on the Air India flight from New York to Milan, via London (as he was a sub-load passenger). There was no way of contacting me since I was already winging my way to Milan (those were pre-mobile days anyway). Rushing from airline counter to airline counter, with luggage in tow, he found all flights going full. His relief at being told that seats were available on American Airlines was short-lived as they would not accept his Visa credit card. A frantic phone call brought our daughter Melissa with husband Kerman to JFK airport. His 'acceptable' American Express card was swiped for US $600 to put Joe on the plane. That ordeal and the whopping amount spent in precious dollars made him conclude that the benefit of a 'free' ticket was not worth the stress and tension it could entail.

I had booked a Mumbai-Milan return ticket on Alitalia for Rs.39,325. I boarded the flight on 7 June and touched down in Milan quite early in the morning. Not having slept the previous night and despite my best efforts to stay awake, I promptly fell asleep on one of the airport seats that faced the arrival gates, while waiting for Joe's flight to arrive from the States. I was startled awake by someone whispering in my ear in Italian. In my confusion, I took some time to realize that it was none other than Joe, and not some romantic Italian who had found a 'sleeping beauty' irresistible! After making enquiries at various counters, we paid L51,100 for two tickets and boarded the train that took us up to Ora, where Mario had arranged to have us met and driven up to Tesero.

The marriage ceremony took place on 9 June in the Basilica of Santi Filippo e Giacomo, located in the picturesque town of Predazzo, which is surrounded by verdant mountains on all sides. The groom's granduncle, Fr. Luigi Jellici, celebrated the mass in Italian, and I was thrilled when, during the sermon, he quoted from one of my articles, 'Tax Free Benefits.' It was about learning to appreciate and acknowledge people while they are still alive rather than covering their graves with flowers after they were dead.

The reception that followed was held at a neighbouring hotel where champagne flowed and gourmet snacks were served. As we were taking in what, for us, was an unusual sight of several wedding cakes spread out in an artistic display on many different levels, we were told that a '*scherzo*' (prank or fun event) was about to begin. Claudio was being directed to climb up a rope which had been rigged from the rafters of the hotel, to 'rescue' Lorenza, who was waiting for him, in all her bridal finery, on the second storey above. But first, he was made to strip down to his underwear and don his mountaineering gear. As part of the play-acting, a doctor, suitably dressed to leave no one in any doubt about his profession, was on standby. Encouraged by the cheers of the guests and the enticing smile of his bride, Claudio swarmed up the rope expertly. Lorenza, of course, did not risk being carried down the rope by her husband and walked down the stairs before he could reach her. All agreed that Claudio had done an excellent job and he was applauded for being such a good sport.

Incidentally Lorenza herself was known as 'thousand-sport Lorenza' for her prowess in very many games. Such fun events seem to be a regular feature of wedding celebrations in Italy. They are organized by friends of the couple who are given free rein to let loose their creative minds in thinking up pranks to play on them.

Claudio and Lorenza's wedding reception was followed by a sit down dinner for family and select friends and we were given places of honour with the immediate family at the head table. Large platters with lacy paper doilies had been laid out. A swarm of waiters and waitresses, each bearing four plates, appeared and, starting with the bridal table, deposited the first course on our platters. The same drill was repeated as course followed sumptuous course, with the wines flowing freely, till, after the fourth or fifth, we lost track; we do remember though, being served a sorbet to cleanse our palates before switching wines.

We soon learnt that the secret to relish such an epic feast, was to get up from one's seat and saunter around, chatting with the other guests. Besides, several skits and party activities had been lined up for the evening to provide breathers between courses. It was fun watching the two mothers-in-law feeding their new in-laws either some porridge or gelato from behind, so they had to be careful that the spoon reached the mouths and not elsewhere! Mario's mischievous uncle, Fr. Luigi, provided us with even more entertainment on the side. Noticing that his brother-in-law was dozing peacefully between courses, he slipped some cutlery into his pocket, and then impishly urged the hotel staff to check him before he left the hotel! The end of the meal was not the end of the celebrations because the younger folk trooped into the disco in the same hotel and continued dancing until the wee hours of the morning. After joining them for some time, we left to get our beauty sleep.

On 10 June morning, we were invited by Fr. Luigi's friends to their mountain retreat for a picnic. They had also invited quite a few of their friends and each had brought along a dish so that there was a wide variety of foods and wine. It was a great outing and very enjoyable. In the evening we were scheduled to go to Trent as we had heard that Chiara Lubich, the Founder of the Focolare Movement, (I wrote a lot about this in my earlier chapters on Rome), was going to be there for a function organized by the Movement. Fr. Luigi's friend, Gian Pietro, offered to drive us there. Before leaving for Trent, we had agreed to stop in Varenna for tea with Gino and his family. Their hotel was under renovation so they had all moved to another smaller residence higher up the hill. Gino had prepared a lavish spread, but we were still too stuffed from the afternoon's picnic lunch to do justice to his hospitality. It was a joyous interlude because, as usual, Gino clowned around and made us all laugh.

By the time we reached Trent, the function was ending. As Chiara was leaving the venue, Fr. Luigi, with one hand clasping Joe's wrist and the other mine, tried to push his way through the crowd to reach her. We felt it embarrassing and held him back. He scolded me later for stopping him because he said he would have definitely succeeded in getting us to meet Chiara face-to-face.

We took another route back to Tesero and stopped at the Foradori Vineyards at Mezzocorona. Carlo, the person in charge, took us on a leisurely detailed tour of the vineyards and then the cellars, describing the process of wine making. Next, he gave us different wines to taste. As if that wasn't enough, he insisted on taking us to his house to sample even more wines and taste his special homemade salami. What a long, eventful and memorable day that turned out to be.

On 11 June, to celebrate their 30th wedding anniversary which was on the previous day, Mario and Rita hosted a dinner for a few of their relatives and friends, up in a rustic mountain restaurant called Agritur

Maso Zanon. Some guests had brought flower bouquets for the recently married couple, for Mario and Rita and also for me, as it was my birthday. Of all the parties we had had thus far, this one turned out to be the most fun-filled. We sang, we danced, we joked and we clowned around long after a sumptuous meal and gallons of wine. Joe had brought along one of our party cassettes so we showed them how to do the Hokey Pokey, the Fiesta, the Birdy dance, and even the *bhangra* (a Punjabi folk dance). The restaurant owners did not throw us out at closing time as they were enjoying the fun as much as we were and had even moved several tables to clear a space so all could dance. This was indeed a fantastic, unforgettable birthday for me. But that was the last time we saw our dear Gino. Mario gave us the news some years later that he had died of cancer. Well, we guess he is now entertaining a higher audience. We miss him.

The next day Fr. Luigi took us to the Jellici ancestral home in the village. It was a huge, centuries-old mansion which had been taken over as a heritage property, but he arranged for us to go inside. He showed us the room where he and his sisters and brothers were born. The room had a huge green porcelain type heater. Every room held its own memories for Fr. Luigi who became very nostalgic as he recounted details to us while moving from room to room, even climbing up into the loft where the children used to play. At the age of 93 in 2008, he was still making trips to Italy. God bless him!

On 13 June, Mario, Rita, Fr. Luigi, Joe and I drove to Penegal through the Mendola Pass. At Penegal we climbed a high tower that gave us a panoramic view of Bolzano below. We stopped for an outdoor lunch at Hotel Paradiso near the town of Fondo on the way to Sanctuario San Romedio in the Trent province. This ancient Church built in the 18th century was embedded between towering rocks. We had to climb 120 steps to reach the top where a priest celebrated Mass for us. It was a very peaceful place that induced contemplation and, best of all, it was insulated from noisy tourists.

It was a big day for the parish of St. Elias in Tesero on 14 June when they celebrated the Feast Day. For every Italian village, this is a big event and all shops remain shut the entire day. The Church was well decorated inside and out. After mass there was a little feast oganized outside the Church. Parishioners served up delicious home-made goodies (including *Grostoli*, a kind of 'papad', dusted with ground sugar, which was my favourite) wine and soft drinks. Later we moved to the school compound where picnic tables were laid out and gaily-clad people were gathered around them eating and drinking, laughing and joking. There was the village band dressed in very Austrian-looking uniforms, playing and entertaining the crowd, while the children enjoyed themselves playing on the swings and roundabouts. A wondrous magical spirit seemed to have entranced the entire village, including us, and we were happy to be part of it.

After our meeting with Maria Rosa Doliana the previous year, it was lovely to meet her again. She was so full of warmth and joy at meeting us and insisted we have dinner at her house one evening. We left some of our Indian outfits with her to be used/sold/given to the Focolare of which she was an enthused member. That lady stands out in our minds as a beautiful example of what it is to love others. With so much happening, our week in Tesero went by very quickly. We had come mainly for the big event of Claudio and Lorenza's wedding and all the other parties and happy events were added bonuses. This, our first and probably only Italian wedding, had exceeded all our expectations and I can truly say that it was indeed magnificent and one of its kind.

FRIENDS IN NEED AND DEED
"Everybody finds somebody someplace"

We left Tesero on 15 June and took the train from Ora to Milan, where we had arranged to meet Nadja and Gianni Fontana (mentioned in our earlier chapter). Our flight to England was later that night so we had the whole day to spend with them. They drove us to a very picturesque lakeside resort some distance from Milan city. I'm not very sure of the name, but it could have been Lake Como. It was a very beautiful setting with quaint side streets. We had a cosy lunch at one of the many cafes and later enjoyed Italian gelato as we strolled along the narrow side lanes dotted with small shops that attracted tourists. More than anything, it was good meeting up with these friends once again, less than a year after our visit with them in Switzerland, and we quickly caught up on our news.

We were so engrossed in our conversation that we lost track of time and as Gianni drove us back at high speed, we had some anxious moments wondering whether we would make it to Malpensa airport in time for our flight to London. We barely did, and our last farewells were hurried. We had managed to spend a wonderful day together, and it had ended all too quickly. After this, we lost touch with them because they had moved to Brazil – but renewed contact by a miraculous chance in 2012, just before the publication of this book.

One reason for the Fontanas meeting us in Milan was to give me back the gold bracelet, which I had left behind in the flat in Ostia the previous year. I had promptly put it back on my wrist but it fell off again at the airport when re-packing some of our stuff. I wondered if this bracelet was jinxed on my hand; I put it away carefully and did not use it again till my next trip to Italy the following year.

FOREVER UNFORGETTABLE IN EVERY WAY
"Gonna make a Sentimental Journey,
to renew old memories"

We had no intention of visiting London or Scotland in 2001 but as we made plans to travel to Italy for the wedding, London seemed just a hop, skip and a jump away – and another hop, skip and jump from London would take us to Scotland! My return ticket on Alitalia included the London stopover, and Joe's complimentary Air India ticket also included a London stopover. This time we stayed with my sister, Mabel, and her husband, Aubrey Jiggins. They had moved from their place in Northcote Road, West Croydon, which had also briefly been home to me in 1970, and were now living in Wallington, another suburb of Croydon. They took us around to see some of the sights, but as we had already been to the major tourist spots in London, I am commenting on just two of the places we visited.

The London Eye or Millennium Wheel, as it is commonly known, was a more recent attraction and has now become one of the unmistakeable landmarks of London, and a draw for most tourists to the city. At first glance it resembles a huge multi-spoked bicycle wheel, visible from several parts of London. As we made our way across the Westminster Bridge, it loomed even larger. Located on the banks of the River Thames, this giant Ferris wheel is 135-metres tall and carries 32 sealed air-conditioned passenger capsules, each representing a London Borough. Mabel and Aubrey bought us tickets for a ride. At that time, British Airways was running the show and I couldn't help feeling that we were boarding a plane as we were even given boarding passes to step on. Each ovoid capsule had a carrying capacity of 25 persons and weighed 10,000 kg. Although seating was provided, few chose to sit – after all, we were there mainly for the view rather than for the ride. The clear glass walls allow for some spectacular sights. It took about half an hour for the wheel to complete a rotation and it remained in non-stop motion, because the rotation rate of 26 cms per second was slow enough to allow passengers to walk on and off the capsules at ground level.

Located in the heart of London's West End, Covent Garden has become one of the noted entertainment and leisure destinations. This Italian-style piazza is filled with many restaurants, bars, fancy boutiques, shops and street performers even from around the world. This is one of the famous places that most tourists have visited and, like me, many might have wondered if the name had derived from the word 'Convent'. It appears I was right because many years ago it was a Convent Garden. With vocations to the religious life dwindling or becoming 'old fashioned' there were fewer entrants to the convents and seminaries. As a result, these institutions closed and the premises were used for other purposes. We even saw one church in England which had been converted to residences and, sadly, I believe there are many more going the same way!

When I first came across the name 'Edinburgh' in a school lesson, I clearly remember thinking how far away it must be, in a very distant land, almost as if on another planet. I remember that I still retained a bit of that awe when we talked about going to Scotland – and Edinburgh in particular – for the first time in 1996. That first trip was simply wonderful. The second in 1999 for Lynn and Jim's wedding was an unexpected bonus, and now here I was making my third trip to rekindle those happy memories. For more than one reason I felt sorry that Joe had to leave to return to India after London and so he missed out on this marvellous visit. Instead, Mabel and Aubrey accompanied me and we stayed with Fr. Gerry Prior at St. Peter's Parish in West Lothian.

We took the coach from Birmingham all the way up to Edinburgh, and the return tickets cost us £36 each. Though it was a long journey, we did not feel tired in the least. I guess that was because the coach was really comfortable, though the driver looked like he was on a diet of vinegar and might have made the journey rather sour if we let him.

First, he scolded me for entering the bus without waiting for his permission. Later he scolded passengers for walking about while the bus was in motion and asked people not to smoke inside the bus. He finally stopped the bus at a siding and announced that if the passengers did not stop smoking he would have to offload them (right up front, he could catch the whiff of smoke of someone puffing at the rear end of the bus). Fortunately, we got another driver halfway through the journey.

We reached Scotland a little too late to enjoy the Italian dinner night that was organized in the Parish of St. Peter's, but the next day we gladly went on the picnic organized for the senior citizens of the parish. I don't remember all the lovely places we visited but we sure had a lot of fun. We ended up at the British Region Pub in Portobello where we spent the evening with lots of singing – and drinking, of course! Most were surprised that I knew the words of almost all the songs they were belting out. As there were still lots of spirits left over from the cache for the day's outing, those who felt like it continued to raise their spirits in the bus!

We spent a good part of the next day with Jean McDonnell who took us to Linlithgow Palace. This time we went during the morning hours and so we could go in for a tour, which I enjoyed. This palace was used a lot by Mary, Queen of Scots. Mary was only six days old when her father died and left her to become Queen of the Scots. Her colourful history unfortunately ended in her being tried for treason and executed by her cousin, Elizabeth I, a Protestant, who feared being deposed by Mary who was considered the rightful queen of England by English Catholics. But in the end, it was Mary's son, James VI of Scotland, who succeeded Elizabeth I and became James I of England.

When Fr. Gerry was free of his Sunday duties, he drove us to Haddington Cathedral. This is one of the largest and most impressive churches in Scotland, being 64 mts in length. From here, we went on to Nunra Abbey, which was run by the Cistercian Monks. Visitors are not encouraged but we managed to see the chapel where a solitary monk was praying; he discreetly left as soon as we entered.

Kinnoul Hill in Perth, where Fr. Gerry drove us next, was his favourite hideout. These thickly wooded hills, called Hermitage, are outside Dunkeld. He told us that whenever he needed to think or be by himself he went there. The area was lush with greenery, huge tall old trees and a gushing waterfall. What was believed until recently to be the tallest tree in the UK stands in these woods; it lost its title to a tree in Moniack near Inverness. I could see why Fr. Gerry was in love with this place – it exuded peace and tranquillity.

One evening, Fr. Gerry's friend, Eddie Neil, a police officer, came over in his Mercedes police car together with his police partner, Caroline McKay. They showed us the workings of the hi-tech car and I even got to pose inside the car wearing Caroline's police cap. When they clapped the handcuffs on me, I laughed because I could easily slip them off my tiny wrists without having to unlock them!

Pitlochry was a relatively new town dating from the mid-19th century. After Queen Victoria's visit there in 1844, it grew into the tourist town of today. Our first stop was the famous Salmon Ladder. Each year between April and October (when the river levels rise after heavy rains), an average of 5,400 adult salmon fight their way upstream from their Atlantic feeding grounds to spawn in the upper reaches of the River Tummel. Once they enter fresh water, they don't eat anything – this can sometimes be for months – and with the falling temperature their endurance goes down. The salmon (their name is derived from the Latin for 'leap') work their way upriver, leaping repeatedly over all obstructions, even waterfalls, but they have to rest for a period in between each jump. To by-pass the Hydroelectric dam at Pitlochry they swim up the 'fish ladder', a series of interconnected pools, rising in steps from pool to pool until they have climbed the height of the dam, but despite their persistence, only a few get through. Three patches of slack water provide for breaks in the struggle against the current. Through large plate glass windows in the viewing area, we were able to watch the brave salmon fighting their way upwards and against the strong current. It was inspiring to see their determination, but I thought the life cycle of the salmon a bit sad. Consider this: they are born in one spot, then leave for the ocean and after about four or five years, they return, fighting to reach the same spot where they were born, this time to die after spawning.

There was a lot more to see and do in Pitlochry but we went on to Edradour, the smallest distillery in Scotland. After waiting for sufficient numbers to form a group, we were taken on a tour of the distillery and I saw for the first time how Scotch whisky was made in those huge vats where you could easily drown if you fell in. I guess some might consider that a nice way to go! The whiff of scotch was so strong that I kept wondering if we might get high on that alone. At the end of the tour, all of us were given a wee (and I mean 'wee') peg of the single malt whisky to sample; though it barely tickled our tongues, it induced several in the group to buy a bottle or two, high-priced though they were.

On our last night in Scotland, Fr. Gerry took Jean and us for a terrific dinner to The Bridge Restaurant, which was on the other bank of the river, flowing alongside Haddington Cathedral. It was quite an exclusive – and expensive – place. We were concerned about the rates, but once again generous Fr. Gerry assured us that this came out of his 'onions and potatoes' money for just such outings with friends.
Our five days in Scotland ended all too soon and it was time to return to London. Fr. Gerry had been an excellent host and had endeared himself also to Mabel and Aubrey. On 26 June, having said our goodbyes to his delightful dog, Tess, we left with Fr. Gerry who accompanied us by train from Livingstone to Waverly Station and from there to the coach station at St. Andrew's Square, Southside,

where we said our final goodbye to him.   Another four days in England and I was back in Mumbai on 30 June.

****

In June 2002, less than a year after we parted from him we were utterly stunned and saddened to get the news of Fr. Gerry's death. How sorry Joe was that he could not accompany us to Scotland on this last trip. Gerry's sudden passing left his parents, family, friends and parishioners devastated.   His death remains one of God's great mysteries for us.   May He who oversees our destinies bless and rest this wonderful, loving, generous, kind and good soul.

Chapter Fourteen

2002-2003
THE UNIVERSITY OF DIVERSITY
"Take a look at yourself and you can look at others differently"

After many travels in India this year, Joe and I were on our way to Rome on 14 June for the Hindu-Christian symposium organized by the Focolare Movement. This time we paid Rs.26,135 for each of our Mumbai-Rome-Mumbai tickets, and did not make any other side trips as we usually do.

The symposium was held at Castelgandolfo, and there was a group of Hindus from India attending together with Focolare members from different parts of India and the world. Cardinal Ivan Dias was already in Rome so he could join us for one of the sessions. The highlights of that incredible week were our meetings with Chiara Lubich and then with the Holy Father, John Paul II. I was thrilled to be given the opportunity of being so close to the Pontiff when, after a public audience at the Vatican, our group from India was called up to take a special photo with him. I had always wished to meet John Paul II, so one of my life's longings was fulfilled! The next day a photograph of the group appeared in the Vatican newspaper L'Osservatore, but my focus was only on holding and kissing the hand of the Holy Father.

On the following day we had a meeting at the Vatican office of the Pontifical Council for Interreligious Dialogue. We were presented to Francis Cardinal Arinze, who was then in charge of interreligious dialogue. As Joe was dressed in an Indian outfit and we were among many Hindus, he introduced himself to the cardinal by saying, 'Your Eminence, I am a Catholic'. The cardinal, who has a great sense of humour, reacted with a hearty, 'Ho-ho, ho, so am I!' After the meeting we had a group photo taken. This was directly under a large painting of Pope Paul VI greeting world leaders and heads of various religions, and closest to the Pontiff, was Mahatma Gandhi.

I am not dwelling on the proceedings of the actual symposium which involved several sessions with presentations of papers both by Hindus and Christians, followed by discussions, which would not be of interest to most. After the days of serious business of 'Dialogue', we were treated to additional glimpses of Italy. Fittingly, our first stop was Assisi. This was the venue selected by Pope John Paul II to bring together more than 120 representatives of different religions and christian denominations for a World Day of Prayer and Peace in October 1986 (the United Nations International Year of Peace) and again in January 2002. The Holy Father considered a spirit of mutual understanding and tolerance as prerequisites to a peaceful world. One might ask, 'Why Assisi?' For those who have never heard of St. Francis of Assisi (AD 1182-1226) he was known as the gentle saint who promoted the values of love, the simple life and respect for Nature and all of God's creation. Although born of wealthy parents, Francis gave up everything at the young age of 19 to devote his life to the poor. It was St. Francis who was the first known person to have received the stigmata (the five wounds of Christ). I am particularly fond of the beautiful prayer for peace that he composed:

Lord, make me an instrument of Your Peace
Where there is hatred, let me sow love;
Where there is injury, pardon;
Where there is doubt, faith;
Where there is despair, hope;
Where there is darkness, light;
Where there is sadness, joy.
O Divine Master, grant that I may seek not so much to be
consoled as to console; to be understood as to understand;
to be loved as to love; for it is in giving that we receive;
it is in pardoning that we are pardoned,
and it is in dying that we are born to Eternal Life.
Amen
199

I made it a point to find out some facts about Basilica of St. Francis, and learnt that the land donated for the church to be built was known as the 'Hill of Hell' because it was here that criminals were put to death, probably very much like 'Golgotha' in the time of Jesus. Today the hill is called 'Hill of Paradise'. We also learnt that St. Francis' remains had been concealed under the altar of the Lower Basilica for fear that they might be stolen and dispersed as relics during the fighting between the noble families of Assisi and Perugia in the 15th century. For centuries the body lay hidden until the tomb was finally discovered on 8 December 1818 after Pope Pius VII gave his permission to excavate the area beneath the altar. The sarcophagus contained a stone used as a pillow for the body of the saint and eleven silver coins of that era. The coins authenticated the times of the birth, death and burial of St. Francis. Fittingly, St. Francis of Assisi was declared the patron saint of Italy by Pope Pius XII in 1939.

From Assisi we drove to Loppiano, located on the Tuscan hills of Incisa Valdarno, near Florence. This permanent 'Mariapolis' (City of Mary) is like a little town by itself. It is a beehive of schools for the formation of those associated in varying degrees of dedication to living the ideals of the Focolare Movement. People from 70 nations (christians and other religions) come together at Loppiano, to form a new society based on the evangelical law of love. This was our second visit to Loppiano, but we still enjoyed making the rounds again with the others and seeing the different work centres. I remember that many of the Italians who were present at an evening's entertainment arranged for us, wanted to know if Joe's beard had been glued on, because they said it was too neat and well trimmed to be a natural growth!

Our week in Italy ended, almost before it began – or so it seemed to us – and we departed from Loppiano early on the morning of 21 June to catch the first flight out from Florence at 0645 hours. A friend agreed to drop us off at the airport at an unearthly hour, and till today I have no idea at which point in the journey that gold charm bracelet, lost and found several times over, but destined not to be mine, was finally lost forever.

ROLL OUT THOSE LAZY, HAZY, CRAZY DAYS IN NEW YORK
"I'm crossing you in style some day"

While planning our trip to Rome in 2002, Joe and I had thought of going onward to New York to see our older daughter, Melissa and her family, especially since our grandchild, Kerissa, would be having her school vacations. However, we found the combined airfares way too high so we dropped the idea. Besides, with all the travelling we had undertaken from January to June that year (once to Bangalore, four trips to Pune, and two to Goa) I was a bit tired and was looking forward to staying put for some time. But that was not to be.

Melissa kept phoning to tell us how disappointed Kerissa was that after travelling halfway to New York we had gone back. So we had a re-think, with Joe feeling that at least one of us should go – and guess who got the pleasure trip? Fortunately, I had a 10-year US visa and I was also very kindly given a buddy ticket on Delta Airlines by one of Melissa's friends, Sunanda Braganza. Though the taxes on this ticket worked out to Rs.22,150 I had the great joy and luxury of travelling first class both ways. I just had to organise a French visa (as the flight went via Paris and I was a sub-load passenger), insurance, and a little spending money. Barely a fortnight after returning from Rome, with just four or five days to prepare for this trip, I left for New York on the morning of 4 July.

Mel and family had moved to a new house on 63rd Road, in Forest Hills, not far from their previous place in Rego Park. I was delighted to find that our grandchild, Kerissa, seemed to have inherited a tremendous sense of humour and kept me amused with her non-stop chatter, especially at bedtime when I was smothered with her hugs and kisses and her uninhibited love and affection. We missed Joe who was unable to snatch even a few weeks with us but he managed to stay sane by running up high telephone bills and keeping busy with several programmes which took him out of town.

I had landed in America 10 months after the 9/11 World Trade Centre (WTC) terror attacks, which were still fresh in the minds of people. Our son-in-law, Kerman, told us how he and some colleagues from his office (which was round the corner from WTC) had heard there was a massive fire at WTC and went out to check what was happening. The scene was pretty chaotic but they and the other bystanders had absolutely no realization that it was an orchestrated terror attack. It was as they were watching the conflagration grow and speculating what had caused it that they saw the first tower start to collapse. The police were shouting to people to move away, but by the time they found their legs and started to run, a thick cloud of dust, smoke and ash as tall as the skyscrapers themselves had turned the day into a dark night. Worse still, like a monster from a horror movie, it was chasing the crowd now fleeing in panic. Nobody could see even a foot ahead once overtaken by the cloud. Fortunately there were no fatalities in that blind stampede. Kerman said that he instinctively ran in the direction of the sea, planning to jump in, but on reaching the pier safely he found it was not necessary.

I too remembered the day well. Back in India, we had just completed a seminar for personnel of the Bank of America at 'The Retreat' in Marve, Malad, a suburb of Mumbai. On our way back, I dropped Joe off at the airport to catch a flight to Bangalore for another seminar, this time for Transamerica Apple Distribution Finance. As events unfolded I thought it rather uncanny that both companies had an 'America' connection! I was unaware of what had happened in America till someone phoned me to ask if all was well with Melissa and family and that's when I switched on the TV and saw those unreal pictures. People were glued to their screens, and Joe looking at a TV monitor at the airport in Mumbai was also caught on camera in a news update, and that triggered more phone calls ...

In New York, I paid a visit to the actual site where the two missing WTC towers had left a gaping hole in the skyline. We could not go right up to Ground Zero which had been cordoned off, but we stopped to inspect the railings of the buildings closest to the site. These were festooned with American flags, flowers, photos of those who had perished in the disaster, souvenirs, cuddly toys and even articles of clothing left by family and friends or even by those who had not lost any of their loved ones. Every inch was covered and the tributes had overflowed on to the pavements. This was a manifestation of an outpouring of helpless grief, and we could feel it too.

I was happy to meet up with Joan O'Donnell who featured in an earlier chapter. She came over to Mel's house for lunch one day, and on another I met her in town and she took me to lunch, after which we walked a great deal around the city and landed up at Rockefeller Plaza where she went to skate occasionally. On another day Mel and family took me for a ride on the Staten Island Ferry. There is no charge for this ferry service which runs from the Whitehall Terminal at the southernmost tip of Manhattan near Battery Park to Staten Island and back. It covers the 8 kms in 25 minutes each way, passing the Statue of Liberty as she stands alone and aloof. Another day Mel and I saw Kathleen Turner do the full Monty in the Broadway adaptation of 'The Graduate', and then I took in 'Aida' with 6-year old Kerissa, who regaled me with the story (in case I did not understand any of it!). Even at that age she had grasped and understood this classic musical.

To celebrate the Parsi New Year in August, Kerman's cousins, Maharukh and Gev Billimoria, invited us over to Connecticut, where we spent practically the whole day feasting. Maharukh still couldn't get over how we had accidentally met in a jeweller's shop in Bandra, Mumbai, when they were on holiday in India. Gev, a Chartered Accountant, had also worked with me in A.F. Ferguson & Co., and though I did not recognize him, I had not forgotten his distinctive deep voice. Maharukh had been even more thrilled when she discovered that our daughter, Melissa, was married to her nephew, and from then on, as far as she was concerned, we were family too!

Soon I was getting ready to return to Mumbai and it was only when going through my papers to check that everything was in order that I discovered that the Delta staff in Mumbai had torn the wrong leaf out of my ticket booklet so now I was left with the Mumbai-New York leaf instead of the New York-Mumbai one. Mel felt this would cause no problems but I felt very uneasy and insisted on getting the matter sorted out at the Delta office, where they issued a fresh ticket after several phone calls to India and more than an hour's wait. I returned to Mumbai on 28 August and was laid up in bed for most of September with agonizing slipped disc pains, which I think I can blame squarely on having had to heft my heavy luggage several times on and off the counters at New York airport because of stringent security measures that called for repeated checking. Simultaneously, I had a severe toothache, but decided to postpone the extraction till my slipped disc problem got handled first. And though I wept with the pain, I fortunately recovered fairly quickly from both ailments. I guess I was making up for all those lazy, crazy days I had spent in New York!

A WHITE, WHITE CHRISTMAS!
"Let It Snow! Let It Snow! Let It Snow!"

With no intention of travelling anywhere for the remainder of the year, my plans were soon changed once again, when I received an SOS from Melissa, to help with her small venture of sending out mail order gift baskets. Not one to refuse what I considered a challenge, I left for New York again on 3 December 2002 with Joe's blessings – and funding! I travelled on Kuwait Airways as I managed to get a return ticket for just Rs.33,500. I had a little balance left over from the previous trip so I did not bother to take more foreign exchange as I did not intend to do any shopping. Kerman met me at JFK Airport, and though he had thoughtfully brought along a warm coat for me, I was almost knocked off my feet with the chill blast of winter air when we stepped out of the airport.

With barely time to settle in, we started working on the 'Magical Gift Baskets' – that was the name of Melissa's project. It was one mad rush of continuous work with not a moment to think of making any Christmas sweets or even partying before Christmas. It didn't take me long to realize that Mel had taken on far too big a project to handle on her own. Neither of us had realised the extent of the logistics involved, right from ordering stuff over the net, stocking and labelling, filling, sealing and decorating the gift baskets, to preparing them for delivery (another major process in itself). And all this just by ourselves when what was needed was a small army. It was no wonder that Mel had to re-consider continuing with the venture. Anyway, I had no regrets as I had the opportunity to spend more time with them and also to experience my first winter and also my first Christmas in the States.

And what a winter that was the worst in 26 years, with several blizzards and snow storms, one on Christmas Day itself. How well I remember it! We had all been invited over for Christmas lunch by one of their friends, Sophie Fernandes. When we left home, it was a clear day, but once it started snowing it did not stop, and by the time we were leaving to go back home, everything was covered under a thick blanket of snow and we had to search for the car. Kerman finally located his car but that was the least of it, Kerman finally located his car but that was the least of it, because driving through that snowstorm demanded extraordinary skills. There was hardly anybody out on the streets and we had to literally inch our way home as visibility was down to practically zero. Though it was Kerman who had the tension of driving, it was scarcely less tense for the rest of us. Yet I was just too flabbergasted to see a Chinese lad struggling through that snowstorm on his bicycle to make a delivery! I guess there's no such word as 'impossible' for the Chinese!

Joe decided to join us in mid-February to celebrate Kerissa's seventh birthday. We usually travel together and it is always I who fill in the details in the embarkation cards before we land, including the address of where we would be staying. Unfortunately, Joe did not have this information handy with him and so he was detained by Immigration officials who said that unless he filled in the address they would not let him through. Joe gave them phone number of the house but of course there was nobody at home as we were all at the airport waiting for him. To make matters worse, Joe could not remember Mel's cell phone number nor was he allowed to make a call from where he was.

Waiting outside, we began to get really worried seeing that practically all the passengers had exited and there was still no sign of Joe. In the meantime Joe had met an Indian staff member of Air India and told her what had happened. She explained that passengers were not allowed to phone from the immigration clearance area, but then proved exceptionally helpful; she led him to a far corner, gave him her cell phone to use, and shielded him from view as he called. But Joe still could not remember Mel's cell phone number. After several wrong calls, he finally managed to get it right and was relieved to get the address from Mel. It was only then that he was let through. Kerman, who worked for a law firm which specialized in immigration matters, later told us that such a lapse was considered quite serious and could have resulted in Joe being put on the next flight back to Mumbai.

On Kerissa's birthday we had another blizzard and the snow was piled up high outside the door. Joe and I had novel experiences of shovelling snow to clear a pathway. What looked like fun in movies was really backbreaking work and not that much fun! Later, we had a proper birthday party for Kerissa at Hampton Bays where Kerman's sister, Delna Mehta, and her family lived. Many other friends also joined us for the party so we ended up having lots of fun despite the snow outside. In fact, we made many overnight trips to the Hamptons while we were there, so snow or no snow, there was no moratorium on parties and fun.

When in New York, we like to see at least one Broadway show even though we find them very highly priced. On this visit, it was Mel and Kerman who insisted on treating us to front row seats for 'The Phantom of the Opera', which was stupendous, especially for the sets and some dramatic scenes that could scare the hell out of the audience in the front rows.

Snow, blizzards and the cold notwithstanding, this had been our first great winter experience in America – but we were happy to return to our own warmer climes. As always!

Chapter Fifteen

2004
TRAVELS IN THE U.S. OF A
"To be where little cable cars, climb halfway to the stars"

So many wonderful things happened for us in 2004! After selling our duplex apartment, which was much too big for us, paying for the smaller apartment we moved to, and clearing all our outstanding loans and debts (of which there were quite a few), we had money enough to think of some exotic travel – and fortunately, enough to afford the further surprise that was in store for us that year.

We were scheduling a visit to the States in May when our daughter, Vanessa, sweetly told us that she was thinking of getting married in June! We were ready to cancel our trip but Vanessa agreed to change her date instead (also because the monsoons in Mumbai make June a 'no-no' month for wedding celebrations). Her next choice was early October, which is also one of the hottest months of the year, and though we pleaded for November, Vanessa was determined that there would be no pushback from that date, because her fiance, Sanjay, was scheduled to leave for London on work in October. As we would be spending a fairly long time abroad, we would have just two months after we returned to prepare for the wedding so I worked on both fronts simultaneously – arranged for visas, insurance, tickets, kept in e-mail touch with contacts abroad, bought gifts, packed, and made bookings for the church, reception, band and caterers, while also organizing the wedding cards, and other miscellaneous details.

We left for New York on 17 May by Air India. The fare came to Rs.36,000 + Rs.210 Tax +Rs.5,500 high season tax because, we were told, our return date fell in the 'high season'. This gave us a jolt as we were supposed to get hugely discounted tickets from this travel agent who was recommended by a friend. I wonder if he made up for the promised discount by piling on more by way of taxes till we ended up paying Rs.44,710 for each of our tickets.

In June, Melissa and Kerman organized a wonderful surprise party for my birthday. As Mel has earned quite a reputation for organizing 'surprise' parties, I had my suspicions, which were confirmed when they bundled Joe and me off to church for evening mass. Besides getting many gifts from the guests, I received lavish presents from Mel, Kerman and Kerissa, including a heart-shaped diamond pendant and gold chain and also front row seats for Joe and me for 'Fiddler on the Roof'. That Broadway Show was just too fantastic for words – wonderful acting by all, particularly Alfred Molina in the lead role of Tevye, for which he received a Tony Award for Best Actor in a Musical. The orchestra played with such gusto and heart thumping beat that it made us want to jump up and join in the dancing! Another superb musical we saw was 'Chicago'.

After a month of lazing around in New York, Joe and I left for Pittsburgh by the Greyhound bus. We had been invited to visit Kerman's relatives, Farhad and Shahnaaz Cama. They had a lovely home in a serene, peaceful neighbourhood. Our hosts were most hospitable and smothered us with their kindness and almost embarrassing generosity. On our first night there, they took us to Mount Washington, which was once the site of many prosperous coal mines. It offered a spectacular view of downtown Pittsburgh as well as its three rivers. The Camas insisted we take a ride in the incline car, or funicular. For the thrill of it, we travelled in the original 1877 ornate wooden cable car on the Duquesne Incline and returned by the same route to the top.

While Farhad was away at work, Shahnaaz made time to take us to the Carnegie Museum of Natural History, which has the world's largest collection of Jurassic dinosaurs, mounted in most realistic displays. Another section showcased the best geological specimens we've ever seen. From there we went to the Phipps Conservatory and Botanical

Gardens; the Victorian greenhouse contained some exotic plants, succulents, bonsai and a profusion of fascinating orchids over which Joe went crazy. The walk-through Butterfly Forest provided another colourful treat.

The Cama's daughter, Shireen, accompanied us to see the famous Falling Waters, one of Frank Lloyd Wright's architectural masterpieces. Edgar Kaufmann Jr., of the wealthy Kaufmann's Department Stores family, had briefly studied architecture under Wright. When the cabins on the estate they owned outside Pittsburgh deteriorated, he prevailed upon his father to have a new residence built, to Wright's design specifications. Falling Waters, the main house, was eventually constructed in October 1937. This multi-level structure, which has strong horizontal and vertical lines, was fashioned using stone, concrete and glass, and cantilevered over an actual waterfall. This remained the family's weekend home till 1963 after which it was donated to Western Pennsylvania Conservancy, which then opened it to the public as a museum. I read later that the mother of Frank Lloyd Wright was very sure her baby would be a boy, and that he would become an architect. Even before Frank was born, his mother placed about a dozen wood engravings of old English cathedrals on the walls of the room that was to be the nursery, and the rest, as they say, is history. It's our personal belief (Joe's and mine) and also our experience, that one's destiny can be created, and visual imprinting is a key factor in this process.

Though the time we spent in Pittsburgh was short, we had managed to see and do quite a lot. The Camas truly showed us wonderful hospitality and we left with a warm glow in our hearts.

CANDID CANADA
"Tis grace hath brought me safe thus far,
and grace will lead me home"

We made our way from Pittsburgh to Toronto, Canada, on 20 June, again by Greyhound coach.   My niece, Debra, and her husband, David, met us at the bus station. I had stayed with them in 1993 when they lived in Dubai, and then again in 2000 when I went to Canada alone. This was Joe's first visit and my third. We stayed with them for a week, and while they were at work/school, we found our way to Niagara Falls where we spent the entire day. We bought a ticket that allowed us a combination of several things – a trip on the Maid of the Mist to the Falls, a journey behind the Falls and visits to the Botanical Gardens and Butterfly Enclosure.

Although I had been on the Maid of the Mist in 2000, I went a second time with Joe and enjoyed this experience just as much – and again ended up thoroughly drenched! These special boats have very high powered double engines, which is why they can go against the powerful current almost up to the Falls. As for the journey behind the Falls, the thought of actually going behind that relentless flow of water gave me a fascinating, fearful feeling. I hesitated every step of the way. Water scares me; so do heights, but I finally found the courage to face the double dare. We entered the elevator and were taken down to the area behind the Horseshoe Falls. Here too we were given rain ponchos to wear before descending further. Emerging from the elevator we walked through the tunnel, stopping at two observation points known as The Great Falls and The Cataract Portals. Standing behind a guardrail at a safe distance from the precipice we watched the cascading water gushing past with tremendous force. The stupendous flow was accompanied by persistent gusts of wind, which in turn generated quite a spray. I kept wondering if the rock ceiling dripping water above me could collapse or if I might get sucked out through the openings behind the curtain of falling water. It was an awesome sensation that defies words. At the end of the tunnel we came to another observation deck right next to the Horseshoe Falls and from this point we felt as if we could reach out and touch the falling water even as we were bathed with continuous heavy spray. The more adventurous in our group went on to the observation deck which was higher up. I was happy with the safer option of staying back.

It is sensible to keep in mind that scheduling too many things all for one day is not a good idea. If you have to walk around a lot, it can be very tiring, as we soon discovered after our first two forays; hence the Botanical Gardens and Butterfly Enclosure were covered very fleetingly.

During the remainder of our stay in Toronto we met many old friends. Olga and Ivan Caspersz treated us to an elaborate Chinese buffet lunch, with a range of regular fare and fancy dishes, not to mention the variety of tempting desserts, and Gary (their son) and Noella had us over for dinner one evening. Marise and Brian Mascarenhas drove us back to Niagara Falls to dine at a revolving restaurant that offered a spectacular view of the Falls at night; this was follwed by another fun night at Mario and Lorraine Gonsalves' house; Mario was happy to see Joe this time as they had worked at the same pharmaceutical company in Mumbai.

Many of our family and friends had settled in Canada and we were glad to see the commendable levels of prosperity they had achieved (some, starting practically from scratch). Even more, they had done a great job of integrating and making themselves completely at home there. Conversations with them sometimes veered round to the question of whether the two of us had missed the boat by not emigrating. At times we were even bombarded with proofs of what a marvellous life we could have had there. This happened in England and America too. We did not contest their points or doubt their good intentions, but said that despite all the negative aspects of life back home, we have never succeeded in cutting that strong umbilical cord that binds and holds us to India. And if our words failed to carry conviction with them, we would fall back on silence, which was often more eloquent than speech.

⚜

THE GOLDEN CITY BY THE BAY
"Won't you come along with me to ..."

We returned to New York in time for Kerissa's tonsils and adenoids operation. It was the first time we ever saw the child cry so much because of the pain, and it broke our hearts. Fortunately, she healed quickly but was not up to coming with us to San Francisco and Alaska, as was earlier planned.

Joe and I left on 4 July by Continental Airlines and we stayed with Vivian and Ariosto Coelho in their home in San Bruno. (Ariosto was one of Joe's students when he was teaching in Don Bosco's, Lonavala, in the early 1960s.) Vivian had very kindly sent us hugely discounted air tickets from New Jersey to San Francisco, which was a great blessing. They had extended an invitation for us to visit them many years ago, and finally we were there. Ariosto is an avid gardener and it was such a delight to see their garden with trees laden with juicy peaches, apricots, pears and other fruits, and even a strawberry patch. We could not resist sampling them all.

In between sightseeing trips in San Francisco, we made a quick dash to visit Sherry (Joe's godchild) and Sudhir Bhatia, in their home at Walnut Creek. Some days Vivian drove us around to see the sights, other days Ariosto accompanied us and on some days, we wandered off on our own. We were thrilled to actually walk on the Golden Gate Bridge, ramble around Fisherman's Wharf and Pier 39, visit China

213

Town, Stanford University, and spend a whole day at beautiful Carmel, after which we drove back to San Bruno by a very scenic route and stopped many times along the way to take photographs. On one evening, Vivian's brother, Michael Marrone, invited us out for dinner in a swanky restaurant close to the airport from where we could watch planes land every few minutes, right at the edge of the Bay. But all the wining and dining and visiting we did were simply preludes to the main star attraction of our visit to the West Coast, so read on.

NORTH TO ALASKA
"A dream is a wish your heart makes"

So far I've spoken about many of my dreams-come-true over the years: Nagaland, Shillong, Rome, Venice, Lourdes, Scotland, The Holy Land, Switzerland ... Now we were about to savour yet another – an Alaskan Cruise! In fact, this was to prove the highlight of our trip to America this year. We were over the moon when Vivian Coelho told us she had arranged for us to accompany them on this much-raved-about cruise. She even organized first class air travel for us from San Francisco to Vancouver on Alaska Airlines. Our group comprised Ariosto and Vivian Coelho, Bob and Gail Jarmusz (friends of theirs) and Joe and me. After landing in Vancouver on 12 July, rather than take two taxis, we hired a limousine to take us all to the port. This was my first time in a limo and it felt great to be sitting in one, revelling in the luxurious setting.

Joe and I had obtained single entry visas for Canada. We reckoned, and we were told that though the cruise took off from Vancouver in Canada and sailed to Alaska in America, for all practical purposes we would be in transit all the while and so multiple entry visas would not be necessary; besides, they cost much more. However, when we presented our passports to the Canadian official before we could board the ship, he pointed out that our visas permitted only a single entry into Canada and this had been expended when we went to Toronto. We explained the reasoning behind our taking single entry visas and he studied us for some time, evidently debating what to do. He then scored a line across our Canadian visa pages (so that we could not use them again) and finally allowed us to go through! In retrospect, it was foolish of us not to get multiple visas because our entire trip would have been wasted had we been refused entry and sent back! In fact we could have been denied entry when we landed in Vancouver, but being in a group with American passport holders, who do not require visas for Canada, possibly we too were taken for Americans and allowed to walk through.

We were both just too thrilled to be embarking on this exotic cruise, especially as we also got it at a very affordable price. Boarding the ship was very much like going through airport formalities at departure time, and very efficiently managed. I was awed by the size of the Sun Princess – it was huge, at least three football fields in length and towered 14 decks high (we were on the 12th). Besides the main eating deck on the 14th floor there was a choice of many eating places, with finc-dining restaurants, pizza parlours, a variety of watering holes, and best of all, there was round the clock eating (gorging!). What took our fancy was the spectrum of entertainment, including fantastic stage shows on a par with Broadway, karaoke evenings, enlightening art auctions, a fully equipped gym and fabulous swimming pools ... Then there was a casino, and beauty salons, boutiques, interesting demonstrations like one on culinary arts and more. All for free. The only item one had to pay for was the liquor, and of course purchases made at stores. We became regulars at the Trivia quiz contests conducted during the afternoons, and we did extremely well at them, collecting many interesting prizes each time!

As part of the entertainment organised, there was one Talent Night when the crew put on a super show for us, followed by another when passengers were invited to perform. Joe put up a modern skit of St. George and the Dragon, picking volunteers from the audience, and everyone enjoyed it a lot and told him so. I'm sure they were surprised at his command of English because most people who have never left their own country cannot believe that people from India can speak the Queen's English. Unfortunately, I could not show off my talent as I had lost my 'singing' voice before I left home. I had foolishly done some varnishing in a room without good ventilation and the fumes had apparently affected my vocal chords. It took several years before I could sing normally again.

Our ship first docked at Ketchikan where time seemed to have stood still. Ketchikan comes from the Tlingit name for the creek, Kitschkhin, which flows through the town. The town seems wedged between the water and the forested mountains, and carved and painted totem poles seemed to have sprouted all over. As we treaded those boardwalks past houses that were partly propped on wooden pilings we felt almost like extras in an old western movie. Located along the boardwalk and painted a bright green was the well advertised 'Dolly's House'. Madam Dolly Arthur owned and occupied that place for 50 years and hers was the most popular brothel in town. Dolly's House had become a museum and gift shop and proved a great favourite with tourists curious to see such a well-preserved house, maintained much the way it was when it opened for business in 1919.

Our second port of call was Juneau, the capital of Alaska. This was located on a small strip of land between the sea and high mountains, and there was no way to reach the outside world except by airplane, and of course, by sea. Juneau was only 45 miles from end to end and it might have remained undisturbed and undiscovered but for the gold prospector Joe Juneau who, together with Richard Harris, was told by a Tlingit chief called Kowee, where to look for gold in the late 1800s. Although plenty of gold was found, Juneau and Harris did not follow the gold to its source, and it was only at Kowee's urging that the mother lode was eventually found. Within a few years, more gold was mined from here than the price the United States paid to purchase Alaska from Russia! So, had I been consulted about the naming of this town, I would have called it 'Kowee'!

Juneau grew into a boomtown while the gold in the stream beds lasted, but their economy then came to be based on fishing, large scale hard-rock mining and, of course, tourism. When many cruise ships dock at the same time, the number of visitors can be overwhelming to the residents. The locals lived in quiet neighbourhoods closer to the woods and mountains, heavily populated by brown bear, eagles and 114 species of birds. We would have loved to inspect the 5145 sq.km of glacial ice fields which form the backyard of Juneau, bordering Canada, but we could not afford the helicopter ride.

As could be expected, the streets near the docks had been almost completely taken over by souvenir shops and other tourist-related activities. Most of these were owned by seasonal inhabitants who were not from Alaska but arrived every summer and left after the tourist rush ended. Would you believe that the native Alaskan souvenirs sold in the shops were not made in Alaska? We discovered the ubiquitous 'Made in China' label on almost every item we looked at, including the Alaskan crib set we bought. It has been my practice to pick up one good ethnic souvenir from each of the different places we've been to, and in Alaska I bought an expensive and heavy piece of pyrite and quartz sculpture that caught my eye. Somehow I think that could not have been made in China, though one never could say – the clever Chinese can reproduce practically anything.

Skagway, our third port of call, is a corruption of the Tlingit 'Skagua' which means 'windy place'. It was known as the Gateway to the

Klondike because during the gold rush era, prospectors had to travel through Skagway to get to the Yukon Territory. The warden who accompanied us around the town told us that Skagway was experiencing a second gold rush which was even better than the first – he was referring to the influx of tourists who were pouring in more money than the gold rush ever brought!

In Skagway's historical district we viewed some of the 100 or so buildings that still existed from the days of the gold rush. One of them, the Red Onion Saloon, had been built in 1897. It was located on the corner of 2nd and Broadway Streets where it had been moved from its earlier location. This was accomplished by mounting the entire building on rolling logs and having it drawn down the street by a horse. As it had been dragged backwards, rather than try to turn the building around, the front and the rear facades of the building were sawed off and switched. In the heyday of the Klondike Gold Rush, there used to be a saloon on the ground floor which miners frequented in order to quench more than their thirst, as the upper floor acquired a reputation for being one of the finest bordellos in Skagway.

Unsavoury and unscrupulous characters of every shade and hue poured into Skagway, and during the closing years of the 19th century it became a den of corruption and utter lawlessness. Disorderly fighting, harlotry and drunken revelry were commonplace and it was little better than a hell on earth. This left the door wide open for the rise of Jefferson Randolph 'Soapy' Smith, the most colourful character of that period. Not unlike many of our politicians today, Soapy Smith was nothing but a sophisticated swindler. He managed to fool many into believing he was a kind and generous benefactor to the widows and needy, even while he operated a ring of thieves who swindled prospectors. The telegraph service to and from Skagway commenced only after 1901, but Soapy's 'telegraph office' operated well before that time and he charged $5 to send a message anywhere in the world. Unsuspecting prospectors used his telegraph office to send news to their families. Soapy ran many other scams till he was finally shot and killed in 1898 and was buried in the Gold Rush Cemetery.

All the three towns where our ship docked had very small resident populations, and tourists often far outnumbered the locals. Though we had gone prepared for bitterly cold weather, it was actually sunny and HOT! Even the natives were surprised to have such pleasant weather because it was usually cold and gloomy for most of the year. The only time we felt the chill was when our ship entered Glacier Bay and College Fjord. It was an unforgettable experience – almost like being in a church – as we glided smoothly and soundlessly between huge awe-inspiring glaciers. Everyone on board seemed to be dumbstruck, just watching and clicking. What an awesome, awesome feeling that was! As we neared the glaciers, the ship's engines were switched off, as even those vibrations could cause huge portions of the glaciers to break off. In fact, special officials came on board the ship at a certain point to ensure that these rules were strictly followed. We saw some small portions of the glaciers break off with sounds like loud gunshots or bursting crackers .

Our cruise ended at Whittier, from where we took a coach to Anchorage, paying $55 a head. From Anchorage, we returned to San Francisco by air, again travelling first class. Unfortunately, this was the last cruise for Gail. Three months later she had a massive heart attack and dropped dead in her living room, leaving Bob inconsolable. We too were shocked by the news.

I know that many will agree with me when I say that we were extremely lucky and blessed to have been able to go to Alaska without having to spend the really big bucks that one should be prepared to spend for trips like these. For me, to think it, is to 'create' it and allow it to manifest itself, as the mother of Frank Lloyd Wright also did. That's one of the secrets of how we have managed to achieve so much in our lives, and I'm not referring only to travelling. The most common reaction when we present this concept is scepticism, but it strikes a chord with those who have also achieved. In all probability they have used the same principle to a lesser or even greater extent. Of course, the steps from 'thinking' to 'creating by manifesting' also involve 'doing what is necessary' to allow it to happen.

As our plane taxied to take off from San Francisco to New York, the words I had sung so often came unbidden to my lips: 'I left my heart in San Francisco ...'. Well, not all of my heart, but certainly a wee part of it.

During our last 10 days in New York, there were several good-bye parties and then frenzied packing, and soon, on 1 August, we were on our way back to Mumbai, carrying so many experiences to sort out and savour.

Me, outside the Fernandes'
bungalow at Cobravaddo

Children caring for their
siblings in Kohima village

Fr. K.V. Devasia sdb in Naga costume

With the boarding school children at Mon

*Joe and me with Bro. Bimal Lakra at his
Diaconate Ordination in Shillong*

*The first primitive building of SAN-KER, in Shillong
with Dr. Sandi, extreme right and Nola in the centre*

On our way to Cherrapunjee

*Outside the Kohima Museum
in front of a Naga village gate*

*Joe wearing
Naga headdress*

The ceremonial war drum in Kohima Museum

Melissa and Vanessa with a mithun statue at Kohima Museum

In front of the thatched roof palace. L to R: me, Joe,
the King of Chui, Ah Ching his son, Melissa and Vanessa

Posing in the bizarre house of skulls, Chui Village

The King of Chui in full regalia, with son, Ah Ching

With Sheriff Tom Higgins at the Lorelei Dance, USA

The late Hedy and the late Harold Hausch, USA

With the Provincial and a group of young priests at Pastoral Centre, Shillong. Fr. Joseph Thelekkatt is in the front row on the extreme right

Rani examining my head for tit-bits, Shillong

Me, in three different tribal costumes, Shillong

*With Fr. Mathew Pulingathil and seminarians
at Salesian College, Sonada*

Joe and me with the driver's children, Sonada

Ghoom railway station

The Darjeeling Toy Train

*With delegates
from Africa and
Ukraine, in Rome*

*With delegates from
Mexico, in Rome*

*In St. Peter's Square,
Vatican City*

*Joe and me with
Queen Christina,
Mafua of Fontem,
in Castelgandolfo*

The Cemetery at Tesero filled with the love of the living

Felix deFlorian, and the Stava Tragedy monument he designed

Rita, Joe and me on a carpet of flowers, Tesero

Fabio, Rita, Joe and me outside the beautiful Jellici home in Tesero

Joe and me in the balcony of Casa Jellici, Tesero

*Me, Rita, Mario and
Fabio outside
St. Mark's Basilica,
Venice*

*On the Marmolada Peak:
Rita, me, Joe, Tarcisio, Lucia and Marcello*

Gondolier in Venice

*Joe on the steps of
Sacre-Coeur, Montmarte*

Joe under the Eiffel Tower

*Lighting a candle for
family and friends
at the Lourdes Grotto*

*Dominique, Louise
and Anne-Marie
Hascher, Paris*

At Stonehenge

Gerry cutting his birthday cake,
West Lothian, Scotland

Joe and me with guardsmen
outside Edinburgh Castle

Chasing the guards at Windsor Castle

Vanessa and me posing with a live tiger in Bangkok

Joe with a python, Bangkok

An amorous Orangutan, Bangkok

Dancing to 'Bolo-ta-ra-ra' at the pre-wedding party in Scotland

*Joe and me with
Jim Fraser outside
St. John Vianney
Church, Edinburgh*

The 'cool' bridal couple, Lynn and Jim Fraser, Edinburgh

With some of the wedding guests in their Scottish kilts, Edinburgh

The group travelling from Tabgha to Tiberius on the Sea of Galilee

The Star of Bethlehem marking the spot of Jesus' birth

Entrance to the tomb, Jerusalem

The Sepulchre of Jesus Christ

One brown Indian among four Red Indians in Quebec

At Hira and Toos Daruvala's house in Scarsdale – our last meeting with Mr. K.R. Alpwaiwallla (third from right)

Kerissa, me and Mel enjoying dessert in 'Serendipity', New York

Rita, Joe and me with the Dolomites in the background

Our Italian friends after a grand lunch

Dinner with Nadja and Gianni Fontana, Lugano, Switzerland

Just married – sporting Lorenza and Claudio Jellici, Predazzo

The mothers-in-law feeding their new relatives, Predazzo

Fr. Gerry Prior near
Haddington Cathedral, Scotland

Me in the driver's seat with
Police Officer Caroline McKay
standing by, Scotland

At Fr. Gerry's ordination. L to R: Sharon and Mike, Agnes,
Fr. Gerry, Owen, Lynn and Alan Prior in Scotland

A hundred roses from India for Chiara Lubich, Castelgandolfo

With Francis Cardinal Arinze at a lunch meeting, Rome

The delegates of the Hindu-Christian Meet at Centro Mariapolis, Castelgandolfo

The group from India with The Holy Father, John Paul II

*At the Vatican office of the Pontifical Council
for Interreligious Dialogue*

A make-shift memorial for the victims of the WTC disaster, New York

On the Staten Island Ferry with Melissa, Kerman and Kerissa

Joan O'Donnell at my "surprise" birthday party, NY

In the dining room of the Sun Princess, en route to Alaska L to R: Bob and Gail Jarmusz, Ariosto, Joe, me and Vivian Coelho

In Ketchikan, Alaska – Madam Dolly Arthur's house on the right

One of the many carved totem poles in Ketchikan, Alaska

The notorious Red Onion Saloon in Skagway, Alaska

Watching the glaciers in awe in Glacier Bay, Alaska

A panoramic view of Aizwal, Mizoram

In Clock Tower Square, Thimphu

Sikkimese kids making sure Santa's beard is real

The Don Bosco Church in Mirik

The welcome dance at the start of the service in Mirik

Our last meeting with the irrepressible Don Luigi Jellici in Mirik

In Tiananmen Square, Beijing

Struggling to climb the Great Wall, Beijing

Posing with the Kung-fu artistes, Beijing

Joe, Ingrid Creado and me with the Terracotta Warriors, Xian

Joe chanting on the Circular Mound Altar, Beijing

The Temple of Heaven, Beijing

Fine dining with Vanessa and Sanjay (not in picture) in Gibraltar

The tip of The Rock of Gibraltar

Chatting with a Barbary Ape, in Gibraltar

The Corrie ten Boom Museum – entrance to the hiding place through a laundry cupboard, Haarlem

The Anne Frank Museum, Amsterdam

Joe, Vanessa and Sanjay in a canal boat, Amsterdam

The Hague Parliament Buildi
Madurodam

Tableau of the Little Dutch
Boy plugging the dyke,
Madurodam

Miniature city
at Madurodam

*The Long Road
to Mombasa*

*Joe with a
Masai couple,
Mombasa*

Mother and child, Mombasa

Taking his brother for a ride

The mammoth elephant that took us by surprise, Manyara Park, Tanzania

Cheetah cubs, Manyara Park, Tanzania

The leopard guarding her prey hidden above

The Seronera Lodge built within and around the kopjes

Ajabe tribals making fire, Lake Eyasi

A baobab tree

Interrupted lunch, Arusha Park

Petting a cheetah – 'Mr. Nice' in Nairobi Safari Park

Road for vehicular traffic intersecting the runway at Gibraltar airport

Looking at Africa in the distance from Europa Point, Gibraltar

View from Vanessa and Sanjay's apartment in Gibraltar

Tableau inside the Rock, Gibraltar

*The Prince Henry
Monument to
New World Discoveries,
designed in the shape
of a caravel, Lisbon*

*At the Fatima Shrine
in Portugal
L to R: Sanjay, Vanessa,
Livia Lobo and Joe*

*The fascination
of a 'Fado', Lisbon*

*Joe in the Plaza
de Espana, Seville*

Outside the Plaza de Toros de la RealMaestranza, the oldest bull ring in Spain, Seville

The Giralda, now part of the Cathedral of Seville

The 19-metre high altar overlaid with 2400 kgs of gold, Seville

Flamenco dancer at El Arenal

Joe in a cycle trishaw in Malacca

The Convention Centre in Kuala Lumpur

Joe and me outside the King's Palace in Kuala Lumpur

Cheong Fatt Tze Mansion, Penang

Kek Lok Si Temple, Penang

Pagoda of the 10,000 Buddhas, Penang

Boat ride in Langkawi – Joe and me with Rod and Jen Serrell

At Trump Palace, Atlantic City.
L to R: Melissa, Kerissa, me and Joe

The Sans Souci Palace, Potsdam, Germany

The simple grave of Frederick the Great, the 'Potato King', Potsdam

Sanjay, Vanessa and me near the Brandenberg Gate, Berlin

Section of the Berlin Wall on display

Checkpoint Charlie, Berlin

Vanessa and Sanjay with Gaia, the latest addition to the family, St. Mary's Hospital, Paddington, UK

Three generations: Kerissa, baby Gaia, Vanessa, me and Melissa, Richmond, UK

The novitiate at Sechu-Zubza, Nagaland

Fr. MP Thomas (centre) with Salesian novices, Sechu-Zubza, Nagaland

Using mind over matter to smash a wooden plank, Sechu-Zubza, Nagaland

*Welcome gate
to Khonoma*

*On safari
at Kaziranga*

*The Picture of
Fr. Luigi Jellici outside
Don Bosco School,
Mirik*

Radiant Dawn and Adrian Mendez , UK

Travel seems to be in Gaia's genes, Richmond, UK

Johnny Arago and Joe at Park Guell, Barcelona

Entrance to Park Guell, Barcelona

Audry and Bel's house in the Girona mountains

The 12th century Roman Bridge built over the Fluvia River in Besalu

The double rainbows in the Girona sky

Village built on a volcanic hill near Girona

Spires of the Sagrada Familia Basilica, Barcelona

A section of the Sagrada Familia façade, Barcelona

The Tibidabo Shrine in Barcelona

The Majestic entrance to Tibidabo, Barcelona

At King's Park, Perth, Australia

In the Pinnacles Desert, Nambung National Park, Australia

With a koala bear in Yanchep Park, Perth, Australia

Story-time for Gaia and grandma in bed, Dublin

Outside Parliament House, Dublin

*Entrance to the prehistoric Newgrange monument,
County Meath, North of Dublin*

Opening gifts on Christmas morn, Forest Hills, New York

*Hira Daruvala and me
at The Cloisters, New York*

*At the Cloisters Museum
in New York*

Chorao Island seen from Pomburpa, Goa

The highest point on the Island

Jose Balduinho Coutinho

*Subhash Coutinho,
the brain behind
Chorao Island
Resort, Goa*

Mel and Kerissa in the swimming pool, Chorao Island Resort, Goa

Hornbills searching for a nesting place in the Chorao Island Resort, Goa

Goa "Sussegad"

The entrance porch of 'Osprey', Chorao Island Resort, Goa

Side entrance to 'Osprey'

View from the verandah of 'Osprey'

*Living Room,
'Osprey'*

*Dining area,
'Osprey'*

*Master
Bedroom,
'Osprey'*

Chapter Sixteen

2005-2006
WELCOME TO OUR WORLD
"Just like before it's yesterday once more"

The magnetic pull of the Northeast took us back there in 2005, after a gap of three years. We had decided that this was to be our last and final journey to those regions (famous last words), but there was another special reason for making this trip. We wished to make it a 'grand' tour, so I drew up an ambitious itinerary during which we would take in Dimapur (Nagaland), Guwahati and Silchar (Assam), Shillong (Meghalaya), Seling and Champhai (Mizoram), Mirik (West Bengal), Sikkim, and the exotic kingdom of Bhutan. Fr. Joseph Thelekkatt had informed us that they now had a guest room, and thanks to his accommodating kindness, we knew we could use Guwahati as a convenient base to store the bulk of our luggage while we travelled light to our various other destinations.

We left Mumbai on 19 March, and took the Indian Airlines flight to Kolkata (Calcutta had been transformed, at least in spelling). The connecting flight to Dimapur was delayed by two hours, which was nothing new to us. Our friend, Fr. M.P Thomas, was now the Provincial of the Dimapur Province, but he still made time to meet us in person at the airport.

After conducting a three-day seminar at the Salesian College we did some shopping in the local market. We found it flooded with foreign goods – a common feature in border territories. As Fr. MP had to tour his province regularly, we accompanied him to Jorhat where we had the opportunity to meet up with Fr. Scaria Nedumala at the Don Bosco Rua Home. I have to mention that the bakery they have set up on the premises makes the most awesome bread, and as we were there for the Maundy Thursday services, hot cross buns were distributed freely.

We were back in Dimapur for the Good Friday services and the Easter Vigil. I have deliberately not expanded on our stay in Nagaland and in Shillong as I have already written much about these places in earlier chapters.

After a week in Nagaland, we left for Guwahati, this time by road. We had to cover 280 kms, which was almost as much as the distance from Dimapur to Mon. We spent the many hours of travel in deep and interesting conversation with Fr. MP. On the outskirts of Guwahati, we halted at a rustic restaurant to rendezvous with Fr. Joseph Thelekkatt and a few others for dinner. After a pleasant evening together we drove to Guwahati and were delighted to find that the new guest room was en suite, spacious and well furnished. Fr. MP left us the next morning, journeying onwards to other parts of his province, while we stayed on.

We conducted three one-day seminars for three sets of teachers during our four days in Guwahati, and left for Shillong on 1 April, where we once again enjoyed the hospitality of Nola and Dr. Sandi Syiem. We were in Shillong for just two days but managed to meet many friends. We were invited to high tea at St. Margaret's Convent, Peachlands, with Mother Rose and Sr. Elizabeth Packumala, who was now the Provincial. Later we caught up with Fr. Paul Kootala and Archbishop Dominic Jala whom we had known as an enthusiastic young priest in 1991. His elevation to Bishop and then Archbishop had found favour with his local people.

When we left Shillong for Silchar on 3 April, it was with a few apprehensions, especially because we still remembered our attempt of 2002. But read on.

222

SENTIMENTS ON SILCHAR
"Lookin' back on how it was in years gone by, makes today seem rather sad, so much has changed"

The trip we had planned to Silchar when we made a brief visit to Guwahati and Shillong in 2002 had to be aborted just short of our destination. On that occasion we had driven up from Guwahati to Shillong where we stayed overnight at the Don Bosco School. Unfortunately, I caught a nasty cold that night; it could have been because of the sudden change in temperatures or the fact that I stepped out into the chill air immediately after a hot bath. However I did not let that deter us. We had set out early the following morning through wet and soggy weather. What had upset me even more was the scarred and pitted landscape, the result of a recent free-for-all rush to dig for coal in a most disorganized manner. In fact, along some stretches, it seemed we were going through a mining village.

Barely one and a half hour short of our destination, we had to pull up behind a huge line of vehicles – a landslide had brought all traffic to a standstill. This was a common hazard whilst travelling in the mountainous regions of the Northeast, especially when it rained heavily and the roads collapsed. I have written about some of these incidents in other chapters. We cooled our heels for quite a long time in the hope that the debris would be cleared soon and the road re-opened. However, we learnt, through messages relayed down the line that the landslide was massive and there was no saying how long it might take to restore traffic – hours or even days. So we took the decision to turn back. The deciding factor was the cold plaguing me and the fact that there were no toilets (forget decent) anywhere for miles around; for all we knew I might have been the only female in that vicinity. Besides, all our snacks had been consumed and the continuous torrential rain made visibility difficult. It was a dreary outlook on every front! We drove back to Shillong, making a much needed halt at a Don Bosco Institution on the way, and went straight on to Guwahati that same night after being on the road for the entire day.

Fr. Joseph Thelekkatt was quick to respond to our SOS and organized a room for us at a hotel near Don Bosco's (in 2002 they did not have any guest rooms). All we wanted was to have a good bath and a restful sleep. The hot water for our baths took its own time in being carried up (as the main heater had been turned off). Then a rat insisted on sharing our room – and bed – that night. The rat won, and we moved to another room. The unkindest cut of all was that in the morning we were presented with a big bill (minus apologies) for our 'luxury' stay. Poor Fr. Thelekkatt felt upset and embarrassed though he was in no way to blame.

Fr. Anthony Valluran, our friend in Silchar, was also upset that we had cancelled our visit, especially as he had prepared a big feast and a special programme for us. We promised to go back another time and that is what we were now doing – three years later!

When planning our visit in 2005, we decided to take a flight rather than face the ordeal of that long journey by road again, especially with thoughts of the landslide still lingering in my mind. I guess we should have anticipated that the flight on which we were booked would be cancelled – routinely! So once again we had no option but to brace ourselves for the long drive to Silchar from Shillong. The taxi charges were Rs.3,000 (return fare for a one-way drop). We made it without encountering any landslides along the way, though the vehicle made some strange noises throughout the journey, making us wonder if this time, we would be stalled by a car breakdown.

When we arrived, Fr. V. Anthony (as he is also referred to) gave us a warm welcome. He was in charge of building the new Don Bosco School in Ramnagar and this large institute was still under construction at the time.

Silchar is the second largest city in the state of Assam. The original inhabitants were the Meitei, Bishnupuriyas, Pangals, Rongmei Nagas and the Cacharis, who have now been reduced to a minority. The majority of the population comprises Bangladeshi immigrants. It is not difficult to understand why, as Silchar shares a border with Sylhet, which is part of Bangladesh. Also, Silchar is a commercially important city, being well connected by road, rail and air to the rest of the country, so traders from distant parts of India also settled there. As happens in most heavily populated areas (Mumbai included), the city had grown haphazardly with no evidence of civic sense. Almost everywhere one looked, there was dirt and garbage piled up or strewn around, and puddles of dirty water that had to be carefully skirted. The rainy season frequently brought added woes. With all those problems, Silchar still continued to see a steady influx of people from nearby adjoining areas because of the availability of better facilities in education and healthcare, and better commercial prospects. Little wonder that the real estate market was booming.

MAGIC BUT SCARY MOMENTS IN MIZORAM
"Something here inside, cannot be denied"

We had heard a lot about Mizoram but had never been there, despite the many times we had gone to the Northeast. When Fr. V. Anthony had been based there years ago, we kept turning down his invitations. I can only think it must have been because of the high cost of travel which we could not afford at that time. Now that we finally agreed to visit him, though based in Silchar, he promised he would take us to Mizoram.

On the very day after reaching Silchar, we started out for Mizoram. Though Fr. V. Anthony was adept at the wheel, he wisely took along a driver to relieve him on the long journey. Mizoram is one of the seven sister states in Northeast India and shares land borders with three other States, Tripura, Assam and Manipur, and two countries, Bangaldesh and Myanmar. The origins of the Mizos, like those of many other tribes in Northeast India, are shrouded in mystery. The generally accepted view is that they were part of a great wave of migration from China to Burma and then to India. Others believe that they originated in Mongolia, but nobody knows for sure. The Mizos have many tribes, the main being the Lushais, Pawis, Paithes, Raltes, Pang, Himars and Kukis. The community has been greatly influenced by Christianity, and together with their own language, English is widely spoken. Their literacy rate is one of the highest in India.

Mizoram means 'land of the highlanders'; there could be no more fitting name than this. This was my very first trip there and, after the first few days, I knew it would be my last. Make no mistake – it is a very picturesque region and, like most of the Northeast, very beautiful, with fascinating, panoramic vistas. What put the frights into me throughout the drives along the narrow winding roads, were the steep drops of hundreds of metres. How I prayed each time we passed the many memorial stones that marked the spots where some people, even full busloads had fallen to their deaths! Those grim markers served a double purpose – they were warnings not only to drive carefully, but also to live good lives because, at the very next bend could come the end! I know Vanessa's friends, Ruth and Rebecca Balchim, might not like to read my views on their beloved homeland, but what I have written is _my_ personal experience taken in the context of my great fear of heights.

Mizoram's terrain was the most varied in the eastern part of India. As many as 21 major hill ranges run through the length and breadth of the state. Their average height is 1000 mts; rivers have created deep gorges between the densely forested hill ranges. I don't know how they manage to cultivate the clearings on those cone-shaped hills, but adults and children both seemed to climb them with effortless ease. Even very small children rambled confidently about with no adult supervision.

Traditional Mizo houses are gravity-defying marvels of engineering. Made mostly of bamboo and wood, they are perched precariously at the edge of the road. From the entrance at road level, the houses extend outwards, overhanging a sheer drop. The rear portions are supported by stilts anchored in the hillside. Attached to practically every house were small pens with big fat pink pigs, which seemed to be asleep all day. After all, what did they have to look forward to, except ending up on the dinner table! Another common feature of the Mizo abodes was the profusion of orchids and geraniums in bloom.

We spent the night at Don Bosco's, Seling, and the next day after lunch with a Mizo family I gritted myself for the drive to Champhai about 194 kms away. Champhai has a common boundary with Myanmar and we found it hard to believe that we could cross over without visas or even passports! All it required was on-the-spot filling out of some simple forms, and without any difficulty, we obtained permission to enter. We drove across a bridge spanning a small stream, and we were in Myanmar! A rough ride of a few kilometres along torturous roads brought us to our destination, the almost heart-shaped Rih Dil Lake. Departed souls who have done good, we were told, cross over this lake to reach 'Pialral' or heaven. Mizoram too had interesting legends about their lakes. Palak Lake, the largest in Mizoram, was created as a result of an earthquake or a flood and locals believe that a village which was submerged when the lake was formed is still intact and vibrant in those deep waters (shades of Atlantis!). As for Tamdil Lake, legend has it that a huge mustard plant once stood there; when it was chopped down, jets of water sprayed from the plant and filled the area. The word 'Tamdil' means 'Lake of Mustard Plant'. It is said that all legends have some element of truth but how true these tales are, is anybody's guess. However, they make for good stories to attract tourists!

After a picnic tea at the lakeside, we drove back to Champhai where we spent the night in the Holy Cross parish house. The next morning we visited a few other places, checked out some shops selling loads of cheap Chinese goods, had a lavish lunch with another Mizo family, friends of Fr. Anthony, and returned to Seling for the night. On our return journey to Silchar we travelled via Aizawl, the capital of Mizoram. Aizawl, the largest city in Mizoram, is 140 kms from Silchar and located at an altitude of 1132 mts above sea level. Our first panoramic view of the city, like a collage of designer match boxes on the steep slopes of a sharp ridge, was breathtaking. Entire hillsides were studded with houses for as far as the eye could see. We contented ourselves with taking a photograph of this amazing sight as there wasn't enough time to foot it round the city.

Some other aspects of Mizo culture I picked up were truly edifying. Whenever there was a death in a family, the entire village rallied round; friends and relatives took charge of all arrangements, ensured that the family did not have to do a thing, brought food to feed visitors who came from afar, and they even kept the mourning family company for at least a week. The Mizos are natural musicians and have very melodious voices; at church services, I was told, the full community sings in one voice with nobody ever singing louder to take centre stage. How different from what happens in some churches where those deputed to lead the congregation in singing, use it as an opportunity to impress others by rendering the hymns in a manner that is far from conducive to a participative prayerful atmosphere.

Much as we liked the novel experience of visiting Mizoram (and even Myanmar) I can tell you it was a relief to be getting back to level ground again – in one piece; but even that, as we were soon to learn, was no guarantee for safety. We were nearing home, driving along the main road at a moderate speed, when a young boy dashed across the road in front of the vehicle. Fr. Anthony just about managed to swerve and brake in time. It took several moments for us to realize that we had miraculously escaped what would have been a fatal accident. Having just come through a series of heart-in-the-mouth episodes on the slopes of Mizoram, we did not expect to experience a more frightful shock in the plains of Silchar. (Fr. Anthony later told us that if the accident had occurred, there would have been no escape from the mob fury; the jeep would have been damaged and all those inside it beaten up.)

On that our last evening in Silchar we were all saddened by the news of the death of Pope John Paul II. He was one of my all time favourite Pontiffs and I had a great admiration for him. How glad I was that we had been able to meet him in Rome in 2002.

After another day of quiet relaxation at Don Bosco's, Fr. Anthony drove the 22 kms to Kumbhirgram where the airport was located. Fortunately, our flight was not cancelled, though it was delayed by several hours. When we reached Don Bosco's, Guwahati, they were busy following the prayer services for the Pope, which was being broadcast on TV. That was to be our last night in Guwahati which we had used as base camp. We went to bed early to be up well before dawn to catch the train to New Jalpaiguri, as our flight to Bagdogra had also been cancelled! It will be seen from my accounts that flight cancellations/delays in these regions are quite common, so one does need to factor this in when planning a trip. Fortunately for us, the railway station was just around the corner from Don Bosco's.

HAPPINESS IN THE HIMALAYAS
"When you're smiling, the whole world smiles with you"

As the train drew into the platform at New Jalpaiguri, we saw Fr. Mathew Pulingathil, already there waiting for us. After lunch, we drove to Nazareth Bhavan in Siliguri where we stayed the night.

229

Early the next morning we left to resume our unfinished journey of 1996. Yes, the exotic kingdom of Bhutan had kept beckoning to us across the unfulfilled years, and this time we had prepared months in advance. Our photographs and copies of our passports had been sent to Fr. Mathew who was now based in Mirik. However, there was no shortcut to having our entry permits processed. Someone had to go all the way to Phuntsholing to present the papers; I believe the entire process had taken some months.

We were back on the same route to Bhutan almost a decade after we first drove to Phuntsholing, the point of entry for travellers arriving from Kolkata and Siliguri. Phuntsholing is located close to the town of Jaigaon on the Indian border, and though it is the second largest town in Bhutan it is little more than a staging post for Indians and Bhutanese to do business, and had nothing to hold tourist interest. In fact any visitor, who made the mistake of considering Phuntsholing as representative of the rest of the country, would conclude that Bhutan was a nondescript land. Nothing could be further from the truth.

Formalities completed and entry permits stamped, we left Phuntsholing and set course for Thimphu. My expectation that a short drive would take us to the heart of Bhutan was ill-founded. We had to negotiate mile after endless mile through mountainous territory. There were vast stretches of desolate areas, but also some very scenic regions. We were stopped at several check posts along the way, and very occasionally we saw locals selling fruit and vegetables in makeshift stalls by the wayside.

Bhutan or Druk Yul, 'Land of the Thunder Dragon' to give it its awe-inspiring Bhutanese name, is located at the eastern end of the Himalayan range. It has contiguous borders with India on three sides, – south, east and west, and touches China to the north. The total area of the country is about 38,394 sq. kms. This is the area to which it has shrunk, from its original 47,000 square kms, after China created a new boundary demarcation in the north. Most of the population lives in the central highlands and is predominantly Buddhist, with Hinduism having the second-largest religious following. Bhutan has five distinct seasons: summer, monsoon, autumn, winter and spring. The north has year-round snow while the west has heavier monsoon rains.

As we passed some sheer walls of rock, Fr. Mathew told us about a special mineral found in Bhutan's mountains, but people were forbidden to collect it. One of its properties was to speed up the healing process when used on fractures. I was curious to know more and a little reading on the subject led me to discover that the mineral in question was known as Shilajit and it oozed from fissures in the rocks of the Himalayas during the summer months. It was found also in Afghanistan, China, Nepal, Pakistan, Tibet and Norway, and had to be 'harvested' from steep rock faces at altitudes from 1000 to 5000 metres. The Shilajit collected from different regions had different physiological properties. Ancient Ayurvedic texts lauded this mineral as one of Nature's wonder compounds, which was useful for a range of diseases including diabetes, tumours, epilepsy and even insanity.

After a six-hour journey we were finally in Thimphu, the Capital of Bhutan. We booked into Hotel Dragon Roots on Norzin Lam, just opposite the Clock Tower Square, which was located one level lower than the main thoroughfare. Shops, restaurants and retail arcades lined the streets on both levels. Elsewhere, there was a mix of apartment blocks, small family homes and family-owned stores. The currency is the ngultrum but Indian money was also accepted without question and I bought many of the colourful Bhutanese stamps (a coveted export item) from one of the shops.

Thimphu is one of the two national capitals in Asia that does not have traffic lights (the other being Pyongyang in North Korea.) A set of traffic lights was once installed by the local authorities but was removed before they became operational. Instead, the city now takes pride in its traffic police who direct traffic with dance-like movements of their hands.

We learnt that tourism in Bhutan is strictly regulated by the government; fortunately for us the regulations for Indians are more lenient than those for other nationalities. Indians with valid Indian passports are exempted from taking a visa and are granted entry permits. Apparently tourists had to go through a licensed Bhutanese tour company if they wished to go round the country or rent a car with a guide and driver. As there was little or no crime in Bhutan, even single women were safe touring on their own. Until the year 2005, foreigners were allowed to enter without a visa, after which a charge was levied. We were told that non-Indian foreigners had to pay visa fees of $200 a day which surprised us and we thought that exorbitant. Later we found out that the visa fee was only $20 but the tour charges could run as high as $240 per day per person. That's probably where the figures got mixed up. Most visitors enter Bhutan by air, landing at Paro. We had planned to drive there from Thimphu but after the already long journey from Phuntsholing we changed our minds. Also the hotel staff told us that Paro did not boast of anything significantly different from what we had already seen in Thimphu, so that settled it.

Before King Jigme Dorje Wangchuk developed Thimphu into a town and made Tashichoedzong the seat of Bhutan's government, it was just a small settlement. The city kept growing with the influx of people from rural areas and Thimphu now sprawls across the western slopes of the Wang Chuu River valley and contains many government offices. We were unable to visit Tashichoedzong, the imposing 17th century fortress-monastery as one had to make an application for this in advance.

The Memorial Chorten is an imposing Buddhist shrine dedicated to Bhutan's third king, Jigme Dorji Wangchuck, after his sudden death while travelling abroad. In these religious places, walking only in a clock-wise direction was permitted. It is also useful to know that pointing out to anything, especially a religious place or object, with a single finger was not allowed; the way to do it was with the open palm extended outwards.

The National Library housed an enormous collection of religious books and manuscripts, but the pride of place went to the largest published book in the world, 'Bhutan: A Visual Odyssey across the Last Himalayan Kingdom'. This masterpiece featured more than 100 pages of spectacular images of Bhutan, was as large as a ping-pong table measuring 1.5 x 2 mts and weighed more than 59 kgs. It was created by Michael Hawley of the MIT Media Lab and yes, it is featured in the Guinness Book of World Records.

We met a very forward-thinking young man at the National Folk Heritage Museum who appeared more keen than others to carry on talking with us. We discussed the GNH (I will come to that later) and even matters of religious freedom (we had heard whispers that one of the king's relatives had become a catholic priest and there was some talk of finally allowing Christian schools to be opened in Bhutan). However, though he tried to appear very forthright in his thinking and speech, he kept dodging direct answers, which left us wondering what he thought deep down inside.

Nearing the Voluntary Artists' Studio at Chang Lam, we noticed an artefact dangling over the main door. I thought it was just an overactive imagination on my part as I struggled not to recognize the object, but there was no escape from the truth. Many more, carved of wood in realistic detail and in various sizes and colours were displayed for sale on a table in the shop. To state it bluntly, it was the erect male organ. The phallus was supposed to ward off evil and every house and establishment sported one at the entrance and often even at the four corners. There is a long complicated story about a monk, and how this came to be regarded as such a potent force, but it still boggled my mind.

In Bhutan, 'Tradition' is highly revered and reflected in every aspect of life; they are indeed very strict about the dress code and their national dress. The women wear a *kira*, an ankle-length wrap around, somewhat like the Tibetan costume. This is combined with an inner blouse and an outer jacket. The men wear a *gho*, a long robe like an overlapping kimono with large lapels; it is held in place with a *kera*, a woven cloth belt wound around the waist, and hoisted up to knee length. The large pouch formed at the waist is used to store a bowl and betel nut or other food. The sleeves are long and loose with turned up white cuffs 5 cms wide. Knee-high stockings and closed shoes complete the ensemble. I quite liked the effect.

All houses and buildings in Bhutan were required by law to be designed in traditional style with Buddhist paintings and motifs and, as a result, they all had a festive appearance. Around the upper edges of the structure, just below the roof and above doors and windows, were elaborately painted timber cornices. Besides the floral, animal and religious motifs that were depicted, there were also large red phalluses suspended. What was most remarkable was the fact that no nails were used at all even though timber was used extensively in the construction. The family homes were generally three-storied – the ground floor for livestock, living quarters and storage on the floor above, and the topmost floor was reserved for a religious shrine and place of worship. Between the topmost floor and the roof there was space for open-air storage (like a refrigerator). The windows on the lower floor were smaller than those on the upper floors, and the staircase consisted of a single log of wood into which ledges were hewed on one side.

One evening we went for dinner to a restaurant recommended as much for its cuisine as for its setting. It was located at quite a height up a mountainside. After parking the jeep, we had to climb a steep flight of steps; I found my breathing had become very laboured. Even though I stopped along the way, pretending to enjoy the view (but in reality to catch my breath) my breathing would not return to normal and I was greatly distressed. Nobody else had experienced what I had, so I was even more determined not to mention it, presuming it was due simply to lack of exercise and a neglect of my health. Even after we reached the restaurant, it took over 15 minutes for my breathing to get back to a somewhat normal state. It was only much later when doing some further research on Bhutan that I felt I might have had acute mountain sickness (AMS) and realized also what a bad idea keeping silent had been, and what a dangerous turn it could have taken. I learnt that AMS is a 'constellation of symptoms that represents your body not being acclimatized to its current altitude'. Though this generally affects trekkers at altitudes of over 3000 mts, going above the 'ideal' altitude where one's body was in balance could also result in breathlessness and other symptoms with oxygen starvation. I do not doubt that the neglect of my health could also have contributed to the feeling. However, with my thyroid problem I was probably more vulnerable. I recall how, when I was working for Findus Food Products in Croydon, England (in 1971), I suffered from regular nose bleeds just going up in the lift to the 21st floor of the building which was also located on a hill.

The landlocked nation of Bhutan remained isolated from the rest of the world and emerged as a kingdom only in 1907. The one positive fallout of that isolation was that the environment was preserved from rampant destruction. On the flip side, it remained backward for just as long. It was as recently as 1999, that the ban on television and the internet was lifted, thus making Bhutan one of the last countries to be exposed to television. All along, the Bhutanese have been very determined to preserve their culture and religion from outside influences but the king realised that it was an important step in the modernization of his country; at the same time he also warned that its misuse could erode traditional Bhutanese values. As late as 2005, Bhutan did not have a single ATM, nor were credit cards accepted except at a few high end shops and hotels. Although Bhutan is now a changed nation with direct international flights, internet, mobile phone networks and cable TV, it has yet managed to integrate modernization with its ancient culture and traditions. And yes, some regal customs still persist. Anyone driving along the roads had to instantly pull over on noticing a vehicle belonging to the king, or his wives, or any of the royal family, to allow them to pass. (Their cars carried special number plates). No matter how slowly the privileged class were travelling, no commoner was permitted to overtake them or honk! We too pulled to the side of the road for one of the king's wives to pass; fortunately, her car was moving at a decent speed.

I am sure the miniscule Himalayan kingdom will continue to attract tourists – and satisfy their expectations. The inexpressible beauty of the place is physically exhilarating. Parts of Bhutan reminded us very much of Switzerland, with some peaks on the northern horizon rising 7,000 metres into the sky. To this day I carry the indelible impression of those snow-capped mountains, and the smiling faces of the people. This brings me to the explanation of GNH.

In 2006, Business Week magazine rated Bhutan as the happiest country in Asia and the eighth happiest in the world. This was based on a global survey conducted by the University of Leicester called, 'The World Map of Happiness.' Although it was said to have evolved over centuries in Bhutan, the nation had to thank King Jigme Singye Wangchuck for developing a unique economic policy known as Gross National Happiness (GNH), and formally launching it in 1972 as an alternative economic parameter. The king had been criticized for the stagnation of his country's economy, which previously relied solely on agriculture and forestry. Based on Buddhist principles, the philosophy of GNH advocates that economic goals alone should not be used to measure and define 'Development'. There are several other equally important dimensions like respect for all living things, ecology, community participation, and the need for balance in work, sleep and reflection or meditation. Policy makers began taking these factors into consideration in planning the country's development.

Bhutan today is the only country to measure happiness, and economists actually go there to study that philosophy in greater depth. While walking along the roads in Bhutan, people and even children regularly smiled at us, and generally exuded a look of happiness and contentment. GNH was working. They were all happy and so were we that we had an opportunity to visit a close and reclusive neighbour – and be blessed with a dose of Himalayan Happiness ourselves.

SANTA IN SIKKIM
"I may not have a lot to give but what I got I'll give to you"

With some of Bhutan's GNH rubbing off onto us, we left on 12 April to return to Siliguri. After refreshing showers, we re-packed our luggage which we entrusted to Fr. Mathew who was returning to Mirik because of work. Fr. Mathew had asked us to conduct two seminars for his teachers and, to combine training with an outing for them, he selected Sikkim as the venue. We were driven up to Malbasey in West Sikkim by another priest, a Fr. George, whom we had not met before.

The route to Sikkim was flanked by the River Teesta which flows along almost the entire length of the state. As we passed a particular spot, where, Fr. George said, the river was exceptionally difficult to ford, he pointed it out to us and then related this: Every attempt to construct a bridge there failed as the river floods washed away whatever had been erected. Finally, the army did succeed in building what they considered was a very strong and secure bridge, and they also put a huge banner across it, which read: 'What God could not do, man has achieved' or words to that effect. Less than a week later, the bridge with that pompous banner was carried away in the swirling waters. God will not be mocked!

Perhaps it was a good thing that we drove up to Malbasey when it was too dark to notice how steep the slopes were. I do not have much to write about Malbasey as we had little time to move around and explore after we conducted the seminar. Yes, it was a beautiful mountain location with scenic views, and one evening we were taken to see, of all things, a place known as Suicide Point but, thankfully, it didn't inspire us to do anything foolish.

Another evening we visited the boarding school where Joe spoke to the bigger students for an hour on easier methods of studying and memorizing. Later we thoroughly enjoyed interacting with the smaller children, many of whom were orphans or came from broken homes. They were rosy-cheeked and not only looked very cute but were truly delightful in their behaviour. When I told them that Joe was Santa Claus, they squealed with delight and swarmed all over him, till they all ended up on the floor. Joe was caught totally off-guard by that avalanche of little bodies. To make their visiting Santa a reality for them, we did ensure that the cheque we sent before Christmas to the superior in charge would be enough to cover gifts for them all.

When we left Malbasey after the seminars it was 2.45 pm and I can tell you that the drive down that steep mountain could be compared to a spin in the well of death. I did not know whether to keep my eyes shut – or open, so I would have enough time to save myself just in case we were going to take a tumble. The sight of the fast-flowing emerald-green Teesta River far below did not help to allay my fears. This river is like a trickle in some stretches where it moves lazily over rocks and huge boulders, but for the rest, it is deep, fast and furious. Part of the way, it is the border between Sikkim and West Bengal, and eventually merges with the Brahmaputra in Bangladesh.

From Malbasey, we drove directly to Mirik full of anticipation for the event that was to be the highlight of the trip at the tail-end of our visit to the Northeast.

THE LOVABLE DON LUIGI
"The years go by as quickly as a wink, enjoy yourself, enjoy yourself, it's later than you think"

It was 7 pm on 14 April by the time we reached Mirik, our last stop on that long journey we had begun in Mumbai on 19 March. This little town near Darjeeling was to play host to the celebrations of the Diamond Jubilee of Fr. Luigi Jellici's priesthood and also of his 90th birthday (which was actually in March). Many of our friends and relatives had met that 'young priest' who had made the journey to Mumbai for Vanessa's wedding in 2004. We had decided to be there for his big day and had slotted in all our visits to other places around this event.

The day began with an inspiring service in the little church on the hill. There was a host of priests and religious concelebrating, and I was glad to be the one chosen to do one of the readings during mass, while Joe was selected as one of the bearers in the Offertory procession. The mass was followed by a felicitation ceremony with many speeches, songs and dances by the school children and others. Then a long queue formed to garland and present gifts to Fr. Luigi. Finally, a feast-day buffet lunch was served in the school compound where we were happy to meet many old friends and several priests who had attended our seminars in Bandel, Sonada, Dimapur and elsewhere. Joe was immensely cheered when one of them told him how he still remembered the salient points of the seminar and had carefully retained all the notes he had made then, although he had discarded most of his other notes.

In Mirik, we had to walk up and down some fairly steep slopes to get from one point to another within the complex and my knees began to give me a lot of trouble as I struggled to walk, not so much uphill as downhill. I remember the pure agony it was, and when I got home the doctor told me that I had damaged the cartilage in both knees. Fortunately for me, homeopathic medication as also the MSM, Glucosamine and Chondroitin tablets I was recommended, soon put me right.

Our return flight from Bagdogra to Calcutta was delayed by over an hour and consequently the Calcutta-Mumbai flight also left late. Before the open skies policy, we travelled only on Indian Airlines and had no option but to get used to delayed and cancelled flights as a fact of life. Today, thankfully, one has a choice of airlines, which are fairly punctual.

We really felt privileged to be present at the celebrations in Mirik and to see how much Fr. Luigi was loved by one and all. Despite his advanced age, he was still very active and even made another visit to Italy after that. What a lovely end to our long, exciting, 'last and final' Northeast Visit 2005! And yet, before leaving Mirik we promised to make one more, really 'last and final' trip – and we did, in 2009, but it was two months too late.

RATS ON THE MENU
"(They) got no mansion, got no yacht, still (they're) happy with …"

In 2006, one of our daughter's friends, Raj Kalra, a pilot with Sahara Airlines at the time, very kindly gave me a free ticket which I could use to travel anywhere in India. Of course we chose to visit the Northeast again. Joe flew Indian Airlines on a paid ticket and we met up in Guwahati. We made a quick dash to Shillong and were back in Guwahati after two days. Fr. Joseph Thelekkatt then arranged an outing for us along with a few others, to Sashipur. This was in the north of Assam and on the way we stopped at a Don Bosco institution for lunch. From there we entered the kingdom of Bhutan, this time through Samdrup Jonghkar, another frontier town like Phuntsholing. This was located in the south-east of Bhutan, and served as a convenient entry point for visitors passing through Assam. The journey between Guwahati and Samdrup Jonghkar took about three hours. The guards stationed near the enormous, beautifully decorated gates, did not stop us because we were Indians and also because without a proper entry permit, there was no way one could go beyond a certain point. We rambled around for a while, bought some beers, wine and a few noodle snacks, and then left.

On our return we passed through a place adjacent to the border of Bhutan called Kumarikatta. Perhaps a young maiden (*kumari*) had been sacrificed (*katta*) there. We were told that here the people ate rats, and of course we did not believe this to be true. But as we passed through the market we saw some vendors actually selling rats which were kept in cages. Later, over high tea at another Don Bosco institution, we verified and confirmed that the locals did indeed eat rats. We then recalled that some years previously an article appeared in a national magazine about a village (probably the same one we were visiting) being so poor that its inhabitants were reduced to eating rats. There was quite an outcry over this dramatic news but it turned out that the reporter had not done her research properly. Yes, the people were eating rats, but they were doing so voluntarily as they were fond of that 'delicacy'. Later I read that the Romans too were fond of eating dormice. The upper classes raised these rodents domestically in specially designed cages and they were fed a mixture of nuts. Well, to each his own!

Chapter Seventeen

2005
CHINESE INTERLUDES
"I'd like to get you, on a slow boat to"

China was another country we had little hope of ever reaching, but still we added it to our wish list. So when talk of China came up at a party we became very interested especially when Fleur David, who lived part of the time in China, told us that she could organise a tour for us if we formed a group of 10. There and then we asked her to count us in and tried to enthuse others to also join. Many were interested and said they would let us know, but as the days stretched into weeks, one by one they said they would not be able to make it. Fleur then contacted us to ask if we would like join some others for whom she had finalized a tour programme. The charges would be US$1,600 per head for 14 days, and it seemed like a very good deal for what we were being promised. The itinerary covered Shanghai, Suzhou, Hangzhou, Guangzhou, Guilin, Yangsho, Xi'an and Beijing. We would have to make our own air travel arrangements to and from Shanghai, the first and last port of call. The tour included five internal flights, stays at 4- or 5-star hotels, three large meals daily, entry to all tourist spots, travel by coach, train and river boat, including airport pickup and drop. Tips were not included. We thought it was just too good a deal to miss!

Getting our Chinese visas was not difficult and took a little over a day. Our flight arrangements needed more of a run-around. We had first booked and even paid for our tickets on China Eastern Airlines, but they suddenly discontinued service from Mumbai. They would be operating flights only from Delhi, and the Mumbai-Delhi-Mumbai sectors would be at our own expense. Mercifully they did not make a fuss about refunding our money. We then booked ourselves on Air India, paying Rs.46,888 for both our return tickets. The routing was still via Delhi and Bangkok. We were happy when Joe's cousin, Neil

Creado, and his wife, Ingrid, decided to join the tour at the last minute. Our journey was uneventful except that it was quite a pleasant surprise for me to hear one of my songs being played on the Air India flight as we were about to land in Shanghai! Years ago I had sung this silly little song, 'Under the Lilac' amongst others, for a compilation of party songs which were recorded and sold commercially.

Besides Neil and Ingrid, Joe and myself being on this flight, there was also another in our group who joined in at Delhi. Having held very senior ranks in the Mumbai Municipal Corporation and later in Air India, he expected everyone to treat him as though he was still occupying those chairs. For one, he was most upset that it was Joe's name on the welcome board at the Shanghai airport and not his (a multi-syllable tongue-twisting name which must have made it off-putting for the person meeting us to write or pronounce) and from the airport to the hotel he kept grilling us about this, as if we had asked someone to put Joe's name on that board. This behaviour and attitude set the tone for the rest of the tour. Another ex-senior member of the Indian Ministry was also part of the group and was used to giving and not taking orders, so he and his wife would often make decisions for everyone else without any of us being consulted. Obnoxious is the only word I can think of and I'm not going to spoil this narrative by spending any time remarking on their generally inconsiderate behaviour.

China was truly an amazing experience. We had heard tales of the country's modernization, but nothing prepared us for the reality bite. What we saw in Shanghai was another Manhattan in the making, and far past the embryonic stage. No doubt the Chinese have made this city a showpiece for the world, and hats off to them. It was not just the skyscrapers but also the wide roads, the mazes of crisscrossing flyovers, a sprawling, modern airport, profuse greenery, beautiful islands of multi-coloured flowers arranged artistically, open plazas, riverside promenades – and all so invitingly clean, with workers continuously sweeping or cleaning those areas.

Preparations for the 2008 Olympics were on in full swing with major construction work in all the big cities, especially Shanghai and Beijing. Waiters (anyone who served you in any capacity was called a 'waiter') had all been told to learn English before the Olympics on pain of being fired from their jobs. Such phenomenal progress must have a downside. It was easy to guess that Big Brother had his eyes open and controlled things. Nobody talked about it openly but all that construction could not have been accomplished without displacing thousands from their homes and livelihood. Some of our friends also chided us for wanting to visit a Communist country and spending our money there. My interest was not so much to shop or spend my money there as to get a first-hand experience of the people and the place. China has some very beautiful places and the natural scenery can be quite spectacular. For years this was all hidden from the rest of the world and now that they had opened their doors people were pouring in to see while the seeing was good, in case the doors shut once again.

Buddhism is the main religion, but there are some followers of Islam and a sprinkling of Christians. Talking to our young guides, we could deduce that the youth were areligious if not atheistic. We also got the impression that what we saw of China was what we were allowed to see, tourism being under governmental control. Well, all said and done, they certainly seemed to be going about it the right way when it came to pulling in the big bucks, because tourists from around the world were pouring into China in a continuous stream. They all go back with glowing reports, the most powerful form of advertising. Some of the tourists we met and spoke to in China, sadly did not have very complimentary things to say about India vis-à-vis China in terms of tourist amenities. Much as we love our country, we had to concede to their views.

In Shanghai, we first rambled around the beautiful Yu Garden, visited the old city bazaar and bought a few souvenirs, took the lift up to the top of the Oriental Pearl TV Tower and then we all decided to take a trip on the Shanghai Maglev Train. Running, or should I say 'flying' at a speed of 430 kms per hour, it covered the 30-km distance from Longyang station in Shanghai to the Pudong international airport in an incredible eight minutes! This ride was not included in the tour package, but we all wanted the experience of travelling on such a fast train.

On our first night in Shanghai we were taken to an acrobatic show which was very much like a circus performance, but the feats performed on stage were more incredible than any we had ever seen. The next morning we set out on a whole-day city tour of Shanghai, and spent quite some time at the museum (which offered a fascinating peep into the culture and history of the country) People Square, the Jade Buddha Temple and finally shopping at Nanjing Road and the Xiangyang Market.

The next morning we left by coach for Suzhou, a famous historical and cultural centre, known as Wu in ancient times, and we stayed at the Suzhou Hotel. It was also known as the Venice of the East because of its network of rivers and canals with as many as 168 bridges, but we saw little of all this in our restricted time there. We only covered Tiger Hill, Wangshi Garden and the ancient Panmen Gate.

The 'heavyweights' in our group had decided that we should experience every form of travel so the following morning we went to the railway station to catch the train to Hangzhou. They had not factored in the ages of the group members or how they would manage with their huge suitcases. As Joe and I (both in our 60s!) were the youngest, we ended by helping the others with their heavy cases up and down stairs and subways, just about making it to our platform in time to board the train. Once settled in at the Hangzhou Sunny Hotel, we were taken by coach to the Linyin monastery and the Yue Fei Temple. Both these were very rushed visits and I suspect the guide must have been in a hurry to go elsewhere. The Yue Fei Temple, first built in 1221, contained the tomb of Yue Fei, who was an outstanding national hero. Above a huge statue of his was an inscription in Chinese that translated to read 'Recover our Lost Territories'. I wondered if this could have been the inspiration to take his exhortation to heart and go after Tibet and Arunachal Pradesh!

As it started to rain, we skipped the cruise that was planned on the West Lake and instead went to the Dragonwell Tea Plantations. There we were given a long spiel by a garrulous lady who convinced us to buy lots of expensive green tea that was said to have many uses, like curing obesity and also helping in rejuvenation. We were told that in the days of the emperor, who owned the gardens, only virgins were allowed to pick the tea leaves, with their lips, and at night these were placed on their breasts. I guess the emperor liked his morning cup of tea with a little spice.

That night Joe and I went across the road from our hotel to their extension and had fantastic foot massages at a discounted rate for hotel guests. When the others heard of our experience they wished they had thought of it too. After a restful night, we left for a day tour of the city. I must mention the Liu He (Six Harmony) Pagoda, a wood-brick structure first constructed in the year 970 and rebuilt in 1153. From the outside, this unusual octagonal pagoda, which was about 60 metres high, appeared to have 13 storeys, but inside there were just seven. After rambling around some more we left immediately after lunch to get our flight to Guangzhou.

The 5-star Guangzhou White Swan Hotel had very beautiful jade sculptures on display and for sale around the large lobby. Some were huge and the prices seemed very reasonable. Each item would have easily fetched five times its price in India. Compared to Suzhou and Hangzhou, Guangzhou was rather a bustling city and our hotel was filled with westerners, mainly American. This intrigued us a bit till we went to the dining area for our meals and saw practically every couple there with a Chinese infant they had come to adopt. Some couples with children of their own were adopting a second or third child from China. What was even more amazing was that all the children they were taking away to a new life were 'special' in one way or another – physically or mentally. We were touched to see the adoptive parents showing so much concern and taking such care in feeding them. We had heard some horrific stories of what took place when the country was trying to keep the population rate down. We wondered if some of these children being given up for adoption were products of those cruel days.

The morning's tour of the city took us to the beautiful Yuexiu Park; we rambled through the exquisite gardens and laboured uphill to the famous Five Rams Statue, a symbol of Guangzhou, which commemorates the rams on which five heavenly beings rode into Guangzhou to bless the city. We visited the 72 Martyrs Mausoleum and Dr. Sun Yat-Sen Memorial Hall, before being transferred to the airport for our flight to Guilin.

In Guilin we stayed overnight at the Plaza Hotel and in the morning we boarded a riverboat on the Li River. This slow-moving river is a tributary of the Zhujiang River which originates in the mountains north of Guilin, and meanders over 83 kms to Yangshuo, which was our destination. The Guilin landscape was unique with hills of a distinctive shape which we had never seen elsewhere before – it was as if giant inverted ice-cream cones with rounded tops had sprouted out of the earth, some in clusters, but many in isolated splendour. The often-quoted line of the poet Han Yu says it best: '... the river winds like a green silk ribbon, while the hills are like jade hairpins'. The geological story is that these 'Karst' hills were formed under the sea and then thrust to the surface of the earth millions of years ago. Many had interesting names like Fighting Cocks Hill, Father and Son Cave, Yearning-for-Husband's Return Rock (the crest of the hill facing the river looked like a woman carrying her baby and waiting for someone) Strange One-side Ferry, Yellow Cloth in the Water, and even a Page Boy Hill. As several tourist-filled boats floated down the river, many small skiffs each manned by a single oarsman, would manoeuvre along the outside edge of the boat, skilfully hook up and entice tourists to buy their handicraft. These were mostly coloured crystal pillars and wood carvings which were really good, and the price could be beaten down to a fraction of what was first quoted.

At the end of that most delightful cruise we booked into the Yangshuo Paradise Resort. Joe and I had decided to go slow on buying anything until the end of our tour, simply because we were told we could carry only limited luggage on the internal flights. And we wisely followed this advice. Others struggled all through with heavy baggage while envying us our single small strollers, and they also had to pay for excess luggage at most of the airports. Now in Yangshuo we finally went shopping and bought two suitcases and dumped our strollers and the few odd knick-knacks we had picked up along the way into them.

That night we went to a late night Water Acrobatic Show known as Impression Liu Sanjie. This stunningly fantastic show involved over 600 performers who used the Li River as a natural theatre. Despite gliding along on long skiffs in the river, sometimes in darkness and holding small flickering lamps in their hands, they maintained perfect balance, and their performances seemed so effortless and graceful. They combined Sanjie Liu's folk songs and their exotic fishing culture, which was said to reflect the harmony between human beings and Nature. The lighting effects and the music made it a magical evening. The ceramic seats on the river bank were not too comfortable and reminded me of toilets, but as the show lasted for a little over an hour, we were not unduly inconvenienced. Joe and I rated the performance as sensational so we were surprised to hear some in our group say that they were disappointed and had expected something better. This show was not included in the tour and we paid for it ourselves, but it was money truly well spent.

We returned to Guilin by coach the next morning and descended into the Reed Flute Caves where the clever lighting inside the caves brought out the natural beauty of surreal colours. We saw Fubo Hill, also called Subduing Wave Hill as it stands half on land and half in the river, Elephant Trunk Hill, which looks just like an elephant with its trunk in the River Li, and then left for the airport for our flight to Xi'an, where we stayed at Tang Cheng Hotel.

Xi'an, known as Chang'an in ancient China, was one of the seven ancient capitals of the country. This was the starting point of the ancient Silk Road and it was also the capital of 13 successive dynasties. The area therefore has a rich cultural heritage. Most fascinating was the army of Terracotta Warriors, with chariots and horses, arrayed in serried ranks within three deep pits in a museum, spread over 20,000 sq. mts. These were all buried with the first Emperor of China, Qin Shi Huang, who died in 210 or 209 BC. They were intended to protect him in the afterlife. It was only in 1974 that local farmers digging for a well uncovered some of these. This in turn, led Chinese archaeologists to investigate further and unearth this amazing find of the largest collection of pottery figures ever discovered in China. They estimated that the total number must have comprised 8,000 soldiers, 130 chariots with 520 horses and 150 cavalry horses, but most of these still lie buried.

From there we went to the famous Buddhist Big Wild Goose Pagoda which stood 64 mts high; it had been renovated several times during different dynastic rules. The Ancient City Wall which we visited next was the largest and best-preserved ancient city wall in China. It had been constructed on the base of the earlier walls erected during the Sui (581-618) and Tang (618-907) dynasties. The wall had a perimeter of 13.7 km. It was a solid rectangle, 12 mts high and 16 to18 mts wide at the base. While strolling on the top of the wall, which was like walking down a wide street, we took many photographs before deciding to enter an Art Exhibition out of idle curiosity. Our idle curiosity turned to deep interest when we saw four wooden lacquered panels with jade figurines and delicate mother-of-pearl inlay depicting the four seasons. In a moment of spontaneous madness, with less than 10 minutes left to reach our bus, we took the decision to buy the set, bargained the price down from 8,000 Yuan to 6,000 Yuan, paid with our credit card, gave our address and instructions for shipping them to India and dashed out. But even as we were leaving I realised that we could have got them for much less.

When the others in the bus heard what we had done, they too wanted to turn back and have a look and perhaps also buy the same items, but we were caught in traffic on a long one-way road, with not enough time to change the schedule. Joe and I had not stopped for a moment to ask ourselves if we were making a rash or foolish decision, and then everyone piled onto us, saying that in all probability we had seen the last of those panels, and we could kiss our money goodbye. Nor was there any way we could follow up with the sellers. That had us worried for exactly five minutes; then we decided not to let anyone rain on our parade and resolved to put our doubts aside and enjoy the rest of our trip.

That last night in Xi'an we enjoyed a stage show of Tang Dynasty Singing and Dancing. It was very entertaining and we even bought the CD of their music. We saw the Famen Temple and the Stone Tablets of Xi'an the next morning. The Museum of the Stone Stele Forest is built in the classical Chinese style and is famous for its inscribed stone steles. There was no time to stop at the Bell Tower so we just drove around it and then headed for the airport to catch our flight to Beijing, where we stayed at the Plaza Hotel.

One of the first things we did in Beijing was to visit the Forbidden City of the Emperors. As we walked along Tiananmen Square I asked our guide if this was the place of the massacre and he quickly shushed me saying we should not speak there. I persisted and he finally said he would tell me later in the bus (which he never did). Instead, it was the government official from our group who whispered and pointed out to me where exactly the massacre took place. His information also proved to be incorrect because when we met a Chinese doctor in London in 2009 she informed us that she had been a student in Beijing and present at the time of the incident. It was not within the Square; before the students could enter Tiananmen Square they were fired upon in an adjacent area.

Chairman Mao's large photo dominated the square and you could not escape his penetrating gaze. Under those watchful eyes we passed through the gate and entered the Forbidden City, which remained the home of the Emperor and his household for almost five centuries, from the Ming to the Qing (different from the Qin dynasty) Dynasties. Located in the heart of Beijing, the City covered an area of 720,000 square metres and had 980 buildings with 8,707 bays of rooms still surviving. It had the largest collection of preserved ancient wooden structures in the world, and more than a million workers were employed in its construction, which took 15 years. I looked closely at the emperor's quarters and those belonging to his special wives and concubines, and I wondered how tiny some of them must have been, judging from the size of their beds. The Forbidden City, which exemplifies traditional Chinese palatial architecture, is now the Palace Museum. I noticed that the roof tiles of the palace buildings were gold in colour unlike other buildings in the rest of China.

The Forbidden City was so called because nobody could enter or leave the palace without the Emperor's permission. It was the centre of the ancient walled city of Beijing and was enclosed within a larger walled area known as the Imperial City, which in turn was enclosed by the Inner City and then the Outer. It was quite special to be able to see this place that was closed even to the local Chinese people for centuries.

We passed on to The Temple of Heaven where the emperors of the Ming and Qing dynasties worshipped heaven and prayed for bumper crops. It was considered a masterpiece of the period and the only existing example of China's ancient Mingdang style of architecture. The place known as Tiantan Park covered an area of 273 hectares. We entered from the northern end where the surrounding wall was semi-circular whereas the southern part was square. The pattern was symbolic of the ancient belief that heaven was round and the earth square. The Park contained two main groups of buildings – the northern structure was the Hall of Prayer for Good Harvests and the southern structure was the Circular Mound Altar. The Hall of Prayer, a round structure 38.2 mts high and 24.2 mts in diameter, had a triple-eaved roof, each covered with blue glazed tiles, and looked very serene and yet imposing. Supporting the roof were huge pillars symbolizing the four seasons, the 12 months of the year, the 12 divisions of day and night, and all the constellations. The Circular Mound Altar served as a place for holding the ceremony of worshipping Heaven on the winter solstice each year. The steps of each flight leading to the Mound, the slabs of each tier and balustrades, arranged in multiples of the number nine, symbolized the nine layers of heaven. We all took turns standing on the circular slab and chanting, singing or praying aloud on it.

That night we were due to go for a Beijing Duck dinner but the 'heavyweights' wanted to have a dumplings dinner instead; this was an 'extra' we had to pay for as it was not included in the cost of our tour. It turned out to be a double disappointment because the dumpling dinner was not to my liking (and I think a general let down for the decision-takers too) and I really missed the Beijing Duck to which I was so looking forward.

Here I'd like to touch on the meal service. It was evident that China had prepared well to cater to vast hordes of tourists; they had constructed restaurants of three- and four-storeys, each floor being larger than even the largest restaurants we had seen in India. Wherever we went, we found these eating places invariably full. They had arrangements to seat vegetarians separately, and even reserved floors for Muslims to have their special meals and a prayer room too. The round dining tables were capacious and could seat 10 or more diners comfortably. At every meal at least eight different dishes were served and if you did not care for one particular dish there was ample choice to satisfy your appetite. We were also given a drink with each meal – the choice being a glass of beer, or mineral water or a soft drink; and the cups of green tea were refilled times without number. Four of us were extremely happy with the quality and the variety of food and the attentive service but we had to hear embarrassing complaints about dishes not being served piping hot, how the food was nothing compared to what they got in India, and the need to send the tea back to the kitchen to be made really hot. This, at nearly every meal!

Some travellers might have considered it an honour to be thrown together in the august company of high ranking bureaucrats, as we were on this tour; believe me, some such personalities seem unable to step out of the corridors of power and walk among common men, even during a tour in a foreign land. One was indignant that in spite of reeling out the eminent positions he had held, the airline official insisted that he pay for excess baggage on an internal flight. I could have gone on with numerous other instances of what happened along the way, but ... better to travel with simple people to simply enjoy!

A one-day excursion took us to the Great Wall and then the Ming Tombs. I felt proud to be one of the four in our group who negotiated the steep steps on a stretch of the Great Wall of China. My biggest thrill and achievement was to climb to a height of about 1828 mts, sometimes hauling myself up by the railings – and the next few days the muscles in my arms ached pleasantly. Even I was surprised that I managed to climb so high though I can tell you it was scarier trying to come back down; some people had to sit for a while to recover from their dizziness. Most of our group, after reaching the base of the Wall, declared they had seen it and then looked for a café (as there were no bars) to while away the time till we returned. What, I wondered, was the purpose of coming to China!

That night we paid to see 'The Legend of Kung Fu' at the Red Theatre. The story began with the initiation of a little monk when he arrived at the temple and was given the name of Chun Yi, the pure one. He studied Zen and Kung Fu and grew into a man; years of disciplined training and concentration had made his body as tough as iron. Then Chun Yi got diverted, chasing after a beautiful fairy he had created in his mind and thus distracted from his Buddhist disciplines till great remorse overcame him. To become a warrior monk, Chun Yi had then to accomplish the final task of passing through the temple gate, a glorious but difficult ritual. Chun Yi finally achieved this and his old master passed on the stave of succession to him. We witnessed fascinating displays of martial arts; the monks' graceful movements packed incredible strength, and though in our seminars we teach participants to smash panels of wood with bare hands, and even hit a pin with open palm and bend it, Joe was amazed to see the actors breaking metal rods on their bare heads. After the play, the actors posed with us for photos, but when least expected, they would suddenly leap and take a kung fu stance or execute a move that startled us and made us jump. It truly was a terrific show.

On our last day in Beijing we visited the summer palace briefly and the silk market before our flight to Shanghai. We had a nice large room and a huge bathroom at The Bund Hotel. In the morning we went to the Old City Bazaar area for our last shopping spree and then on to Nanjing Road where we bought a sleek Kodak digital camera for our daughter, Vanessa, who wanted that particular model. I picked up quite a few decorative artificial flowers in the flower market and some nice 'almost genuine' watches in the fake market! Sellers had no qualms about accosting one and asking how much one had paid for an item, and then offering the identical piece at a lower price. One of our group almost had an apoplectic fit when he was asked how much he had paid for the Rado watch he was sporting and told in the same breath that the seller had a much more realistic copy which he could have at a 'good price.' What our man was wearing was an honest-to-goodness genuine Rado!

The Chinese sense of aesthetics is evident everywhere – in buildings, gardens, palaces, even the plazas and streets. We found nothing garish or hurtful to the eye and even the most mundane, common items were given an artistic touch. Though not as blatant as Bangkok, I would recommend that tourists be wary of being cheated by wayside hawkers who are known to return fake money as change in exchange for a large denomination notes. Fortunately we were warned of this in time. This chapter gives the barest gist of all that we saw, did and felt in China. There was, though, one disconcerting discovery: relatively few Chinese had heard about India; many did not know of its existence even though we tried telling them we were neighbours. So much for the education system!

Given the chance to return for another visit, would we go? Most definitely!

****

A week after returning from China, we were asked to come to the locak post office to collect a parcel from abroad. We were truly puzzled. Quite frankly, we had forgotten for the moment about the panels we had ordered and paid for in China. Then it struck us and Joe was apprehensive about being asked to pay a big sum as customs duty. However, at the post office all he was told to do was sign for the package! Joe was just too amazed and tipped the man heavily. The panels were packed so well, that there was not a scratch on them. They adorn our walls in the sitting room and look positively gorgeous. However, soon they will be packed up once again, awaiting transportation to our new house in Goa.

Chapter Eighteen

2006
HOME AWAY FROM HOME
"Magic moments, mem'ries we've been sharin'"

Soon after our daughter Vanessa was married in 2004, her husband, Sanjay, moved to London where his job took him, and Vanessa followed within a couple of months. After they had settled in, they extended an invitation to us, but we had already made plans to visit China in 2005. Travel-wise, I had had my fill of London but even so, family is family and this time we were going not to see London but our children. Further attractions they put out were side trips to Gibraltar and Holland. We bought our two return tickets on British Airways for Rs.50,796 and left on 15 February.

We would normally not think of going to England when it was still winter there, but England was the half-way point where we could also meet our daughter, Melissa, and grandchild, Kerissa, who were arriving from the States to celebrate Kerissa's tenth birthday, which coincided with her school spring break. They arrived in England two days after we did. It was so good to be together, and the warmth and happiness we generated was enough to ward off the cold outside. Vanessa and Sanjay invited friends over and arranged a memorable birthday bash for Kerissa – drinks and snacks at home followed by an elaborate dinner at a nearby restaurant.

This was Melissa and Kerissa's first visit to London so Vanessa took them on the round of some of the interesting tourist spots. The weather was too cold for us to make many outdoor trips, but we did all go into London to Madame Tussaud's Museum. The entry prices had more than trebled since I went there in 1970, but of course Vanessa, our generous hostess, insisted on doing the honours. While Madame Tussaud's had upgraded and installed new exhibits, including our

Bollywood stars, Amitabh Bachhan and Aishwarya Rai, I frankly much preferred the quality of work that I saw in 1970. The figures then looked more authentic and you could barely tell apart the wax figures from real humans.

That short week together flew by much too quickly with late breakfasts, crazy shopping and lazy dinners. All too soon Mel and Kerissa had to return to New York. Once they left, we generally stayed indoors (the cold was one big reason) with just occasional jaunts to the shopping malls. Vanessa and Sanjay had a beautiful large apartment on the first floor of an old Victorian house in North Ealing and as big a collection of DVDs as a lending library so I spent most of my time 'vegging' out in front of the TV since I rarely get a chance to do that in Mumbai. I managed to view a great number of movies and sitcom collections; best of all were my favourite Poirot series which I enjoy watching again because often I cannot remember the endings – which is why I still enjoy them all over again! I loved all Agatha Christie's books. Joe, instead, would often brave the cold to go wandering around on his own to Ealing Abbey for Christian meditation with a group. The 20-minute walk to the Abbey for mass each week could be pure agony in the chilling cold and Vanessa often spoilt us by calling for a cab. All my plans to go for daily mass during Lent had to be abandoned because of this.

Sanjay was making regular weekend trips to Gibraltar on work and we were really happy when he told us he had arranged for us to also accompany him on one such trip. We had not applied for a visa for Gibraltar from Mumbai as we were misinformed that we had to apply for it in London. However, when we went to the consulate in London they told us that we should have applied in India, the country of our origin, and that if we had had a one-year UK visa that would have automatically entitled us to enter Gibraltar without another separate visa. We had taken only a six months' UK visa because one, there's a huge difference in visa rates for six months and one year; two, we definitely had no intention of visiting the UK more than once that year, and three, we did not know about this rule till we went to the UK Consulate in London. The first official we dealt with was very kind and helpful but when he went on leave, another official gave us a hard time. We had told him that we had already made our travel bookings to leave for Gibraltar on 23 March, and he said he didn't care. We may or may not get the visas. After marking buttons, we had no option but to cool our heels till 'His Majesty' made up his mind about whether he could trust us not to stay on in Gibraltar and make it our permanent home! It was only on the day before our departure that we finally got our passports back, with the visas stamped for the exact number of days we said we would be in Gibraltar and not a day more. We had to shell out £48 for them but all four of us left from Gatwick airport on 23 March.

ROCKING AROUND THE ROCK OF GIBRALTAR
"The beginnin' has just begun
when the sun goes down"

The British Airways flight from London to Gibraltar took approximately two hours and 45 minutes. At Gibraltar immigration, there was another consultation about the stamp on our passports and we were asked to wait (till they probably checked if we were truly booked at the Hotel we named!).

The airport is very small and has just one landing strip. This runs west to east along the narrow northern part of Gibraltar. The Spanish border is immediately to the north of the airport. The plane lands at the very edge of the bay making you wonder whether you are going to touch down in the sea. The runway is intersected by Winston

Churchill Avenue, a busy road that leads to Spain, so traffic must come to a standstill well before a plane lands or takes off. That's why Sanjay often missed his flights back to London. Being immersed in meetings he would rush to the airport at the last minute, only to find that the intersection to get to the airport was already closed. Just as well for Gibraltarians there are only two or three flights a day!

Once out of the airport, we took a taxi to Caleta Hotel which is located on the east side of the Rock. It overlooks the Catalan Bay and the Mediterranean Sea. Our rooms had overhanging balconies which made us feel we were in the middle of the sea. We never tired of watching the hundreds of birds gently floating on the water or sometimes swooping down and squabbling for fish, and each night the cool breeze and the soothing sound of the waves lapping gently against the rocks lulled us to sleep.

The Main Street which goes right through the City Centre from one end to the other is long and narrow, free of traffic for the most part, with benches placed along the way to rest in-between long shopping sprees. There are enticing shops on either side of the road that cater to the hordes of tourists that come in on the cruise liners. The street has most of the well-known British stores on a smaller scale. I was amazed to find that the Sindhi community owns almost 80% of the shops lining Main Street. What I found strange was to see so many gold and jewellery shops. I know that Indians are very fond of the yellow metal and I thought that most westerners are not, but I guess those shops proved me wrong.

Gibraltar is actually a land extension of Spain, located near the southernmost tip of the Iberian Peninsula, overlooking the Strait of Gibraltar. Known as the last point of Europe, there are just 14 miles separating it from Tangiers, the north-western tip of Africa. In the year 711, the Moors, who were led by General Tarik-ibn-Ziyad, conquered Gibraltar, and that is how the place was named 'Jebel

Tarik'. The Arab name 'Jebel Tarik' means 'Tarik's mountain' and this was corrupted into 'Gibraltar'. (The British did the same with most names in India and all the other territories they conquered.) An ancient Moorish castle dating back to 1333 is still standing on the north-western slope. Earlier, Gibraltar was known as Mons Calpe, one of the Pillars of Hercules, but it is now commonly known as Gib or The Rock.

Gibraltar is now a self-governing British overseas territory and has been a major bone of contention in Anglo-Spanish relations for centuries. A little more explanation is called for here in order to understand why this is so. Under the 1713 Treaty of Utrecht, Gibraltar was ceded by Spain to the Crown of Great Britain in perpetuity. Later Spain sought its return but the majority of Gibraltarians strongly opposed this, and the British government said that it respected their wishes! The Government of Spain in turn opposed the referendum and then completely closed the border with Gibraltar and severed all communication links. From time to time, Spain renews its claim to sovereignty over Gibraltar. When it was announced that Prince Charles and Lady Diana would start their honeymoon from Gibraltar, the Spanish Government said that King Juan Carlos and Queen Sofia had declined their invitation to the ceremony as an act of protest. I guess Gibraltar will continue to be a thorn in the side of Spain. It is not difficult to understand why the British have refused to give up Gibraltar despite many wars being fought over it for centuries. Its location makes it ideal to rebuff invaders from land and sea; during World War II the Rock was turned into a most effective fortress.

Gibraltar is famous the world over for the dolphin populations that come to the bay for food, shelter and to breed in their hundreds. Joe and I went on the Dolphin Adventure boat cruise to catch a glimpse of them. The wind was very strong and the boat was speeding along so we had to hold on tight, especially when another boat or ferry passed us because they left a wake that would rock our boat even more. We were disappointed when we did not see any dolphins for quite some time. However, we finally caught up with a school of them that frolicked alongside our boat. It was fun to watch these happy and social creatures.

After this we took a private guided tour of the Rock. Many have heard of the Rock of Gibraltar, but it is truly surprising to discover how very few people actually know that there's a place called Gibraltar, and there are many who have absolutely no idea where it is located. I too remember hearing about the Rock of Gibraltar in school and that it was somewhere near Spain, but that's about as far as my knowledge went – till Sanjay's work took him there almost every week and Vanessa often accompanied him. Vanessa used to grumble that Gibraltar was so small that even Bandra was bigger! Now that we were actually there, we disagreed and thought it was charming and very picturesque with lots to see and do. (Vanessa fell in love with Gibraltar much later, when she and Sanjay had moved there from London in 2007.)

The Rock occupies almost two-thirds of the place and dominates everything around it. Wherever you go, you are in the shadow of the Rock. The highest point of the Rock, which is of limestone, rises to a height of 426 mts A narrow coastal lowland surrounds the Rock and the entire territory covers about 6843 sq. kms and shares a 1.2 kms land border with Spain. Inside the Rock there are many tunnelled roads, which are operated by the military and closed to the public. The Great Siege Tunnels were excavated by the British army from 1782 and these unique Upper Galleries formed part of what was considered the most impressive defence system anywhere, and made Gibraltar literally impregnable. The upward climb can be a little hard for the not so fit, but one can halt along the way to admire the little tableaus, together with sound effects, that bring to life the scenes of old. At one point we stopped to look inside a closed door with bars on it. A dummy soldier dressed in the uniform of that era stood just inside the door holding up a lantern, and when one least expects it, he shouts, 'Who goes there?' It scares most people who are not prepared for it. We were unable to see the World War II tunnels from where Gen. Eisenhower planned the invasion of North Africa.

St. Michael's Cave inside the Rock is located more than 300 mts above sea level and is known to be one of the most spectacular natural phenomena in Europe. It has fantastic stalactites and stalagmites, many of which have joined to form large pillars. A cross section of one of these shows beautiful grains with intricate swirls and patterns. A sound and light system that has been installed enhances the caves' natural features. The large main chamber is now being used as an auditorium where concerts, fashion shows and other events are held, but during the war it was prepared as an emergency hospital. Fortunately, there was never need to use it. The upper hall is connected by a series of winding passages to many lower chambers.

Perhaps the best known of Gibraltar's attractions, are the famous tailless monkeys known as Barbary Apes, or macaques. These apes are actually native to North Africa and their presence in Gibraltar goes back hundreds of years. One legend says that they travelled from their native Morocco via a subterranean tunnel beneath the Strait, ending in St. Michael's Cave. There could be some truth in this because the Lower St. Michael's Cave which we could not see does end in a subterranean lake and extends for several kilometres. A more simple explanation would be that they came by ship with the Moors. A pack of them are resident at the Ape's Den but five other packs are said to live in the wild on the steep slopes of the Rock. These apes are a very bold lot. When we reached Ape's Den, many of them climbed onto the vehicles and perched on the windows or hung onto the drivers' arms. One also jumped onto our vehicle and held on to the driver. Our driver talked to it as though he was talking to an old friend till the monkey finally jumped off. We were warned not to get too friendly with them so while we enjoyed watching the mischievous antics of the hyperactive younger ones, we kept our distance. However, while bending over a wall to get a good snapshot near a steep cliff, I let out a piercing scream – a monkey had leaped onto my head, followed by another chasing him, probably in a game of tag. It was only an hour later that I discovered that the expensive cap I had bought just that morning had disappeared (it probably fell over the wall and now a different monkey must be wearing it). I felt so sad at losing my cap that Vanessa promptly bought me a new one. To 'cap' it all, Vanessa and Sanjay gifted us the entire Gibraltar trip, including those lavish lunches and extravagant dinners with copious amounts of select wines.

We did so want to hop across the border to Spain – it looked as simple as crossing a street, which it actually was. But though we had a Schengen visa that would allow us entry to Spain, our visa for Gibraltar had only a single entry so we could not take the chance of not being re-admitted.

A plaque in the inner courtyard garden of Caleta Hotel reads: 'Take nothing but photographs, Leave nothing but footprints, Kill nothing but time.' We followed the first two but not the last. We did not have to kill time as we used every moment of our three days preciously.

THE NOVELTIES OF THE NETHERLANDS
"When it's spring again
I'll bring again, Tulips from …"

I've always associated Holland with tulips, windmills and those thick clogs that the Dutch were noted for. But those were not our first sightings when we arrived at Schipol airport in Amsterdam on 3 April, exactly a week after returning from Gibraltar. It was our friend, Livia Lobo, another of my ex-colleagues from A.F. Ferguson & Co., who was waiting to meet and welcome us. Livia was working in Norfolkline in a high profile job and was posted at Den Haag (The Hague) in The Netherlands.

From our base in London, it was easier to make these side trips to Europe. We paid £152.60 for our two return tickets on British Midlands from London to Amsterdam. Our 75-minute flight was uneventful but it was a fairly long drive from the airport to Livia's prestigious flat in Den Haag. She was a gracious hostess and went out of her way to ensure we had a grand time, taking a day off to show us around The Hague where we saw some amazing constructs.

One of the first places we went to was the Panorama Mesdag, which was one such amazing construct. From the outside you cannot tell what a fascinating exhibit you are going to see inside – it was like stepping into the largest painting of the Netherlands with a 360 degree view. As its name implies, it is a 'panorama' that was created by Hendrik Willem Mesdag who was a notable marine painter. This particular panorama was a cylindrical painting known as a Cyclorama, but around this time, this type of paintings were going out of style so when the Belgian company that hired Mesdag to paint the panorama went bust, Mesdag purchased the painting despite the heavy losses it entailed. Then, with the help of his wife and some of his student painters, he completed it in 1881. It is 14 mts high, about 40 mts in diameter, with a 120-metre circumference. From an observation gallery in the centre of the room we had the illusion that we were on a high sand dune looking at the sea, beaches and the village of Scheveningen as it was at the end of the 19th century. Thanks to Mesdag the panorama has not only survived but is now the oldest in its original location. I would definitely recommend a visit to this museum when in The Hague.

Later we walked through the town and saw the Dutch parliament buildings which have been the centre of government of The Netherlands for centuries. The look was that of a medieval church. We also walked past Queen Beatrix's working Palace. It was not very large and there were no visible signs of high security. We then took a tram to Madurodam, one of Holland's most popular destinations. If you do not have time to go around Holland, you can 'see' the entire country here in one day! This miniature city highlights all the qualities of Dutch culture and contain the major landmarks of Holland, like the Peace Palace of the Hague, the Royal Palace on the Amsterdam Dam Square, the canal houses of Amsterdam, the Alkmaar cheese market, and parts of the Delta works. The ornamental bridges resemble the originals perfectly, as do the fully functional harbour, the trains that run on the world's largest miniature railway and Amsterdam's Schipol airport complete with airplanes and even a miniature Concorde. There are also manicured gardens with living flowers and plants, some bearing fruit of the same scaled-down size! We were told that some of the exhibits take four years or more to construct but everything is built and constructed with precision, detail and skill on a scale of 1:25 so they are not toys.

As Livia had to resume work the next day, she taught us how to get about on our own by bus, tram and train. Joe and I then made day trips to Rotterdam, Haarlem and Amsterdam on three different days, while in the evenings Livia would drive us around The Hague and point out the interesting buildings, including The Peace Palace which is the seat of the International Court of Justice that settles disputes between countries.

Rotterdam is an amazing shipping port with the world's heaviest traffic. We know that the best way to see the city is on foot so we picked up a map from the tourist office and checked out the important landmarks and things to see and do. We decided that we would first take a boat trip through the waterways of Rotterdam on the Spido Boat, which is named after the Dutch explorer who travelled the South Pacific Ocean and the Indian Ocean. As we walked towards the place, we passed the Erasmusbrug (Erasmus Bridge), which is one of the many striking bridges in Holland with an outstanding structure. The Spido office is very close to this bridge. After buying our tickets, we were about to board, when we were stopped by two pretty girls. They asked where we were from, where we were staying and our views of the city. They were reporters for 'NL10', a tourist magazine. Later they were sweet enough to post two copies of the magazine to our Mumbai address which had their article and a large photo of the two of us. Of course it was in Dutch and that was Greek to us!

Rotterdam is the largest container port in the world where several transport firms operate. As our boat cruised down the waterway, we saw proof of this. Huge containers were stocked endlessly one over the other for as far as eye could see. The Dutch seem to be the best in Water Management (living as they do in The Netherlands which is a water-logged country) and they have some pretty fantastic systems in place like the Delta Works, to protect the country against high storm tides. We saw many of Rotterdam's landmarks as we passed and when we got off the boat, we made for the 'Euromast', a 185-metre high tower. A turbo lift takes you up to a height of 100 mts. We chose to ride in the Space Cabin that revolves slowly till it reaches a height of almost 200 mts. The floor is partly glass and you can look down through it and also around to get a full view of the city. It was scary at times and I tried not to look down too often. After going to a few more touristy places, we returned to The Hague.

In Haarlem, the highlight for us was the Corrie ten Boom Museum. Corrie's father, Willem, had started a clock and watch shop and the family lived on the two floors above the shop. The ten Boom family had dedicated their lives to Christian service and to their fellow men, and their home was an 'open house' for anyone in need of help. During the Second World War, their home became a refuge and hiding place for those being sought by the enemy. The ten Boom family risked their lives by helping these refugees and becoming the centre of underground activities. In this way, they and their friends saved hundreds of lives. They managed all this in the small rooms they occupied.

In February 1944 the family was betrayed and the Gestapo, the Nazi secret police, raided the house. Six members of the ten Boom family were arrested as also 30 others who came there unaware of the betrayal. Although an in-depth search was made, the Gestapo did not find the four Jews and two members of the Resistance who were hiding in the house. We saw the hiding place which was cleverly concealed in Corrie's bedroom. It was inconceivable how six adults could have remained hidden in that confined space without food, water or proper ventilation, and without being able to even lie down. The entrance to the room was through a laundry cupboard which had a sliding door at the rear bottom through which one had to crawl. The Gestapo remained in the house for some days as they were convinced there were Jews hiding there. As the refugees could not be found the Gestapo hoped to starve them till they surrendered. Fortunately the Resistance managed to liberate them after two and a half days. In keeping with its long history, the clock shop still exists on the ground floor of the ten Boom House.

The next day we met up with Vanessa and Sanjay in Amsterdam. Sanjay was there on work so they stayed in a hotel on Dam Square, but we met as often as we could. Sanjay managed to make time in-between his meetings to come out with us so we first took a coach tour of the city before going for a boat cruise on the innumerable canals that criss-cross Amsterdam.

There are over 50 museums in Amsterdam but not all contain paintings by famous artists. Besides the most famous ones like the Rijksmuseum (which is the largest museum in The Netherlands) the

Van Gogh Museum and the Stedelijk Museum, there are museums for Houseboats, Coffee and Tea, Bags and Purses, Diamonds, Computers, etc. and some bizarre ones for Vodka, Sex, Torture, Erotica, Drugs, and even a Dutch Funeral Museum! Our interest was in the Van Gogh Museum and the Rijksmuseum. We did queue up outside each in turn, but eventually did not enter. The long lines were moving at snail's pace. A quick calculation showed that we would get hardly any time inside to view the exhibits as they both had early closing times. Besides, the entry tickets did cost a pretty penny so we decided it was not worth the wait or the money.

Whatever else we could or could not do, I was determined to see the Anne Frank house from the inside so we made our way there and found a very long queue that snaked and curled around the building. This place seemed to have the largest number of tourists but I was not going to leave Amsterdam without entering it. I had expected to see a ramshackle old house but the outside is now like a fortress of steel which preserves the inside in almost original condition.

Most people know the story of Anne Frank and her famous Diary but, strange as it may sound, there are still many who have absolutely no idea of the Second World War and the atrocities committed by Hitler. So for their benefit I recount the story of Anne Frank in brief. The Frank Family, who lived in Frankfurt, Germany, fled to the Netherlands when Hitler came to power in 1933. The family, like many other Jews, felt unsafe in Amsterdam when the Nazis occupied the country in 1940, and they decided to go into hiding to escape persecution. Their hiding place was in the office annex of Anne's father, and located to the rear of the building, which was in the centre of Amsterdam. Four others joined them in this hideout. A few trusted employees of Anne's father alone knew of this arrangement and brought the family food and other essentials. Anne made poignant entries in her diary about every day of their life in the annex, the isolation and the constant fear of being discovered. We saw the original diary on display. After more than two years of living this way, they were betrayed and deported to various concentration camps. Of the eight people, only Anne's father, Otto Frank, survived the Auschwitz extermination camp. He returned to Amsterdam in June 1945 and later decided to publish his daughter's diary which had been found by his helper, Miep Gies, who gave it to him after she was sure that his daughters were no longer alive. It was Otto Frank who was responsible for making the Secret Annex accessible to the public as a museum.

The Red Light District of Amsterdam, like most Red Light areas all over the world, gets its name from the red lights that glow in the windows to announce that prostitution is legal. In Amsterdam this area is close to Centraal Station, the city's main train terminal, so for the hordes of tourists who arrive by train this area is an inviting first stop. Many people, including senior citizens fresh off cruise ships, find this a very interesting place to visit and make a beeline there. Besides those interested in doing business, there are plenty of voyeurs and so there's lots of nervous giggling and pointing to all the fleshy sights to be seen through huge glass windows where scantily clad, and sometimes topless, female sex workers disport themselves to attract customers. You can stare all you want but you are most definitely not allowed to take any photos. My natural curiosity also made me gawk like a teenager but I could not help wondering what must be going through the minds of those women. I may sound like a damp squib but, frankly, as we walked through this area, searching for, of all things, a church, it was rather a depressing sight to see so many beautiful and also young girls displaying themselves like cattle at an auction.

The church we were looking for was known as the Museum of Our Lord in the Attic Church. Strange name for a church I know, and that's one reason we wanted to see it for ourselves. We were told that it was located near the Red Light District which was the site of the city's original settlement going back to the 13th century. After the Rijksmuseum, this Church was the city's oldest museum and was built during the Reformation when Catholics were forbidden to hold public services. Unfortunately, we could not locate the church in time (because it had also taken us a long time to find the Red Light District) and by then it was also too late, so we made our way to the station to get our train back to Den Haag.

Vanessa came to visit with Livia on the last day of our stay, and after a delicious lunch, Livia took us on one of those huge Norfolkline ships. We were privileged to meet the captain who personally demonstrated all the hi-tech navigation equipment. Then we strolled by the docks and sampled the famous Dutch pannekoeken (pancakes) which is as common to Holland as fish and chips is to England and burger and fries to America. Vanessa then left to re-join Sanjay in Amsterdam. We returned to London after a packed six days in Holland. I do not think I have ever walked as much anywhere as we walked in The Netherlands, and every night I had happy, sore feet!

ABUNDANCE IN THE SPRING
"We may be oceans away, you feel my love ..."

After returning from The Netherlands, we had another 10 days in London and by then the weather had begun to improve so we accepted invitations from our many friends. One day it was to Freddy Pitter's house in Southall for a late lunch. Another time our friends, Minnie (an ex-AFF office colleague) and Adi Bilimoria, invited us all for a delicious meal that we lingered over at their place on Muswell Hill, and another ex-colleague, Farida Gai who lived in Wimbledon had us over for a Parsi dhansak lunch. Instead of going over to visit Bash and Asha again, we called them over for a South Indian lunch that Vanessa took great pride in preparing. Both my sisters, Mabel and Lily, lived far from Ealing and the commute was not simple but we met them when we went over to Mabel's for lunch one day. And so the days passed feasting – and fasting. Fasting because we were in Lent and soon we were into the Holy Week services which we attended at Ealing Abbey, where we were happy to see a packed church all through.

Spring was slowly dispelling the winter cold and the variety of flowers bursting forth from the earth created a riot of colours. The daffodils came in many shades of yellow and, though the most common of flowers, they were beautiful to look at. Trees, which just a month earlier looked like barren dead logs, were now totally transformed, revelling in their multi-hued finery. I couldn't stop marvelling at how all this takes place without man having to move a finger.

Sanjay loves the greenery and the open outdoors so he made time to take us to Kew Gardens. I didn't realise what a large expanse the gardens covered and what a variety of plants and trees they housed. We also visited Richmond and went for a cruise down the Thames. It was beautiful to see the many graceful swans floating along or feeding on snippets thrown to them. When we reached Hampton Court we had lunch and took many photographs amidst a sea of daffodils that filled the gardens wherever you looked. We would have loved to enter Hampton Palace and look around but if we missed the last boat getting back, we would have a long way to travel back on our own.

We managed to see two terrific plays in the West End, 'Mary Poppins' and 'Les Miserables'. I expected the first to be childish but we were very impressed with the elaborate sets, acting and singing. The second play began on a dull, sad note and I was wishing we had picked another play, but then it turned out really super. Joe and I also went on a walking tour of London with an informative guide. Starting from the Tower of London, we first took a little boat trip down the Thames (yes, it was called a 'walking tour') and passed the entry to the Traitors' Gate which was part of the Tower. We had seen most of the sights along the Thames, but we got a different perspective seeing them from a boat. After getting off near St. Paul's Cathedral, we continued with our historical walk. We were the only Indians on this tour and the rest kept gasping each time I answered correctly to a query from our guide or asked a knowledgeable question about a British monarch. The point I'm making is that most of the British themselves did not know their own history – as many of us Indians know so little about our own!

Our children had shown us a fantastic time in England and we also thoroughly enjoyed the trips to Gibraltar and Holland. This was my second experience of an English winter and though it was hot when we returned to Mumbai on 20 April, it felt good to thaw out and sweat off those extra pounds we had gained.

Chapter Nineteen

2007
UNTAMED AFRICA
"Live free and beauty surrounds you, the world still astounds you... Born free to follow your heart"

Jambo, Jambo Bwana, Habari gani, mzuri sana, Wageni, mwakaribishwa, Kenya yetu, Hakuna matata ...' the Swahili welcome song which says 'Hello, hello sir, How are you? Very fine? Foreigners, you're welcome, in Kenya (or any where in Africa I would think), there is no problem ...'. I quite liked that song and its catchy tune. We kept hearing it often while on our visit to Africa, so I bought a cassette and quickly learnt to sing it, which delighted the locals. Yes, we had reached the dark and mysterious shores of Africa at last. When the opportunity to visit Africa with two others came up, we jumped at it. Like this, the costs of travel by car could be shared four ways.

Joe and I left on 13 June and travelled on Kenya Airways from Mumbai to Nairobi, and by Precision Air from Nairobi to Arusha. This cost us Rs.31,370 x 2 for our return tickets. Travel to Africa meant we had to ensure that we took the Typhoid, Rabies, Hepatitis and Anti-tetanus vaccines as also the malaria tablets. The Yellow Fever injections posed a bit of a problem as we could only take them from a government recognized centre which was in town. There was always a big queue for this and only a fixed number were injected each day so one had to queue up really early in the morning to ensure you were included. We solved this by asking our office boy to wait in line for us. All these injections, vaccines and tablets, plus insurance, set us back another Rs.14,632.

We paid for our visa on arrival in Tanzania, which was US$100 for the two of us. From Nairobi to Arusha our plane passed close to Mount Kilimanjaro and it was a spectacular sight from the aircraft as it was a real close up view. We spent two nights at Camp Masai in tiny pokey rooms for which we were charged US$10 per person per night. Somehow one associated Africa with heat so we were totally unprepared for the cold that night, and all the other nights of our stay. Fortunately, we had some handy liquid refreshment that helped ward off the chill!

One of our group had organised a car and driver for us, so early on the morning of 15 June, we set off for Mombasa via Moshi. We stopped at Marangu to see the Kinukamori Waterfalls. At the very edge of it was the statue of a young maiden, Makinuka, and a little distance away, was one of a crouching panther. Legend has it that Makinuka was with child, and since she had disgraced her family, she was sent to the Falls to await the panther that lurked there. As Makinuka saw the panther approach and crouch ready to pounce on her, she chose instead to jump to her death from the Falls. The story could well have been true and it was so sad.

The 'guide', who adopted us from the moment we drove in, stuck with us until the end. I don't know when he had bathed last, but there was an aroma of over-ripe fruit hanging heavily around him. He not only came with us to the Falls but also recommended a place where we could spend the night. This was located very far away and we had to drive down steep slopes and up again, winding through narrow paths amidst dense foliage until we reached our destination. Fortunately, the place was clean and set in peaceful and quiet surroundings. The home was run by Jasper and Helen under the name 'Amins Cottages & Campsite', Moonjo Waterfalls, Marangu, Kili, so for those interested, you can get on the net and contact them. They continue to keep in touch with us and ask us to recommend our friends to them.

Once we reached the border of Tanzania the next morning, there was a no-man's land of about two kms till the Kenyan border, and driving on that stretch was a real boneshaker. After filling out the usual forms, we had to pay for fresh visas for Kenya so that was another US$100. It was a very long drive to Mombasa, and sometimes we would see the road stretch ahead for miles and miles like a straight but undulating brown ribbon. The roads were untarred for the most part, and so it was a pretty bumpy ride we had without sight of another human being for hours. Just as well we did not have any car trouble or I hate to think what could have happened to us on those desolate stretches. We finally reached Mombasa in the evening but then we had a time searching for the Royal Reserve Safari and Beach Club, our time-share resort, where we spent a lazy luxurious week in sheer paradise. I made full use of the gym facilities and the sauna and steam rooms daily.

One morning we drove into the old city of Mombasa, which is very Muslim Arab-dominated. Joe and I chose to visit Fort Jesus which had a rich history. This Fort was built by the Portuguese at the end of the 16th century to secure their position on the east coast of Africa which was being threatened on one side by the Turks in the Indian Ocean and on the other by the persistent hostility of the Swahili town of Mombasa. What makes this Fort special is that it takes its shape from its namesake. It is built in the form of a crucified Jesus with arms outstretched. Unfortunately, it was not maintained well. Our week in Mombasa went by quickly with daily interesting evening entertainment organized by the resort. We left on the morning of 23 June to return to Arusha, and managed the long drive back in a day. We had one scary moment when we stopped to take a picture of a Baobab tree on a deserted stretch. Out of nowhere and within no time, streams of Masai women and children began to make a beeline for us from different directions. Some of the women had huge open sores on their heads and hordes of flies surrounding them. We just about managed to make our escape in time but that encounter left us a bit shaken.

After two more nights at Camp Masai we left on 25 June morning for our 13-day safari. This was the most expensive part of the trip, which was US$1950 per head, and was considered an extremely good rate. We heard that others paid as much as US$5000. Our first stop was the Arusha National Park in the north of Tanzania which covers an area of 137 sq. kms. I remember how excited we got when we spotted our first giraffes loping off into the distance on our arrival. Later we saw many more and one old guy who was busy munching on some juicy leaves by himself took time to look at us briefly before continuing with more important matters. Another time we saw both parents with their baby who was not obediently following them. When he found he had an audience, he decided to stay back and sat down with his back to us even while his parents were trying to coax him to move away. Besides giraffe, zebra, a few other animals and the black and white colobus monkey troops, we did not see much else at this park, but it was our first park and we enjoyed the thrill.

Dinner and overnight stay was at the Kiboko tented camp. The tented camps are literally canvas tents over a raised wooden floor. They contain two beds with mosquito nets and space for little else. A bath and toilet adjoined the tent at the rear. A veranda in the front is nice for sitting out if you can battle the mosquitoes. It was quite cosy and comfortable, but we did have to struggle a bit with our luggage. On our first night there was no electricity so we had to cope with candles and kerosene lamps. In spite of a generator, the man in charge said it was not working but promised that we would have lights the next day. We were based at this camp for three nights as we also visited nearby Lake Manyara, but we got lights only on one night – till 10 pm! At this camp they also had a problem getting milk and I asked why they couldn't just keep a cow. Apparently they had one but the Masai tribe who believe only they are entitled to keep cattle, came and took it away.

Besides Arusha National Park and Lake Manyara Park, we went to the Ngorongoro Crater, the sprawling Serengeti, and Tarangire. When we heard from others how they strained their eyes for days to catch even a glimpse of the Big Five, we realized that we were exceptionally lucky to have so many close-up sightings. Yes, we saw plenty of zebras, giraffes, wildebeest, the fierce wild buffaloes with their horns looking like wigs stuck on, spotted hyenas, warthogs, impala, hartebeest, Thompson gazelles, Grant's gazelles, Waterbuck, Topi, many species of monkeys and baboons, hyrax, klipspringer, dik-dik, crocodiles, and the like, not to mention ostriches and many of the 520-plus species of colourful birds … Joe ended up with over 1200 snapshots! However, what was most memorable was our first live encounter with the big cats and the elephants.

We had seen many elephants, sometimes in groups, sometimes alone. On our second day at Lake Manyara Park, we tried to follow a couple of elephants trundling along the roadway, hoping to get a close shot, but we were blocked by two jeeps which stopped bang in front of us. We were disappointed – but suddenly a huge mammoth emerged from the jungle on our left and stood looking at us. We remained transfixed at the sight of him, just 3 mts away, and after some time, very tentatively starting clicking photos. Then he walked right up to our jeep. It was evident that he wanted to cross the road, but we were bumper-to-bumper with the other jeep. Scary is not the word for what we felt. One flick of his trunk could have overturned our vehicle, but we remained stock still. He shook his head in confusion and his huge tusks scraped our vehicle. Then he gracefully retreated back into the thicket he had come from, and in seconds he was soundlessly lost to sight in the thick foliage. It was truly an awesome moment for all of us.

Our driver-cum-guide, Issa, had eyes as sharp as an eagle and he would spot animals from a great distance. We could scarcely contain our excitement when he called 'Simba' and pointed; then we had to hang on for dear life as he drove full speed to where he thought they would cross the road. We held our breath as two lionesses walked past coolly without even glancing at us, and disappeared behind a rocky outcrop. Several vehicles drove off. We waited quite a while and were rewarded when three lionesses and two tawny males emerged. And then one pregnant lioness, seeking respite from the sun came straight towards us and lay down in the shade of the vehicle behind ours. That was the first of 10 sightings we had of lions, far and close, walking, sleeping, stretching out on kopjes, and even, what is most rare, mating. After mating, the lioness, like most of the big cats, flips over on her back and stretches languidly in a very contented manner while flicking her tail at her mate. We were told that the pair remains together for a full week, during which time they neither hunt nor eat, and the male seems to follow the female's signals. We saw for ourselves that when she stood up the male stood up, when she sat down, he sat. I wonder did man get his cue from the animals?

The leopard is known to be very shy, and so difficult to spot. When we finally saw one, it was draped on the upper branches of a tree with all four paws dangling in a very relaxed manner, almost like a child, with its head resting on the branch. It seemed to be sleeping, but every now and then opened watchful eyes, glancing at the half eaten impala hidden in the foliage above him. On this occasion though we waited and watched for a long time, the leopard did not budge. He would continue to guard his trophy till he had consumed every bit of it.

Our repeated bursts of excitement scarcely seemed to touch our guide Issa; he would be gratified, but very rarely excited. At one of these rare moments Issa actually started jumping in the driver's seat – he had spotted cheetahs. He pointed. All we could see was tall grass. Issa drove up silently to where they were hiding but they immediately dashed off. (Drivers are not allowed to steer off the paths – they can be fined US$100 if caught – and nobody is allowed to alight from vehicles in the parks, except in designated areas.) Issa gave chase and managed to get really close to a bush where they had crouched. This time they (mother and two grown cubs) stayed put and watched us. Issa explained that they were full from a recent meal. We had seen vultures and hyenas picking at the remains of the animal as we drove past. We inched even closer. At first they just peeked out of the grass, but soon the mother came to inspect us. She circled our jeep, decided we were no danger to them, lolled on the grass close to us and turned on her back to show the cubs that all was safe, but they remained where they were, just periodically poking their heads up to peer at us. We felt lucky to spend over an hour in their company and get such great photos.

The Seronera Lodge and the Lobo Wildlife Lodge in the Serengeti, and the Sopa Lodge at Tarangire, were located in the middle of the parks. They were built literally into the kopjes incorporating those very huge boulders (some as big as houses) in the décor with great imagination and aesthetics so that the overall effect was very charming, and blended with the environment. I was fascinated by these kopjes and how they are formed so let me add a little more about them. The word means 'little heads' in Dutch, but the heads we saw

278

were certainly not little. I learned that five hundred million years ago, movements in the earth's surface forced up low hills and over millions of years, weather eroded them leaving behind harder crystalline kopje rocks. Clusters of these can be seen every once in a while as you pass through the Serengeti, where they shelter animals such as agama lizards, bats, snakes, porcupines, owls and other birds. Closer to the woodlands they support colonies of hyraxes as well. Troops of baboons sleep safely on high rocks, but the big cats like the lion, leopard and cheetah often use kopjes for dens, resting places, and viewpoints, so I guess they all have to watch out for themselves.

The extensiveness of the Serengeti also amazed me. The word 'Serengeti' comes from 'siring it' meaning 'land of endless space'. Nothing could be truer. We drove for mile after endless mile without encountering anyone or seeing any form of life. During the last five million years, the nine Ngorongoro volcanoes erupted and their ashes blew west blanketing the ancient landscape and forming a cement-like layer which formed the Serengeti plains. Most of the soil on the plains is shallow and tree roots cannot penetrate through the cement-like layer beneath, hence it has such a desolate look. One wonders how it sustains any life at all and yet there are thousands of creatures living there.

There was no stepping beyond the walls of the lodges after dark as wild animals were not infrequent visitors. In fact, on our first night at the Seronera Lodge, which was next to the Seronera River, we were amazed when we looked out of our room and saw this huge three-ton hippo with her half-ton baby walking around the garden below us, neatly 'mowing' the lawn. She paused for a moment to look up at us when the flash of the camera hit her. The next morning a large family of mongoose was on the lawn playing and fighting, while hordes of rock hyrax and tree hyrax (they look like a cross between rabbits and rats) roamed harmlessly all over the lodge. The monkeys were thorough pests and one frightened the life out of me when he followed us in the hope of grabbing the bag from my hand. Despite trying to scare him away, he refused to give up and instead tried to intimidate us. We finally had to run till we reached the reception area.

We were fortunate to catch the spectacular migration of the wildebeest. Between June and October over a million of them journey from the south to the northwest in search of grass and water. It is quite something to see them spreading over miles and miles of the Serengeti, literally covering the horizon from one end to the other (even satellites miles away in space are able to capture this phenomenon as a moving black mass!) They are known as the clowns of the savannah not only because of the way they scatter in different directions when attacked by a lion. Often you can see them comically walking one behind the other in single file or in pairs, and at other times milling around in big groups. When one turns and runs in the opposite direction from where they are heading, others follow blindly till they finally join another group going in the right direction again. I wondered how often they make these aimless detours. Even their body structure adds to their comical look: like young horses with heavy frontal shoulders and chests and slender posteriors, it's a wonder their slim legs can support their disproportionate body frame. To add to this, they have a very sad, woebegone and lethargic look. The only time I saw them animated was when they were fighting or charging full speed across the road. They are always accompanied by groups of zebras who not only seem to guide them but also alert them to the presence of the big cats. Although over 250,000 of them die each year during migration because of predators, stampedes, drowning and crocodiles that wait for them at the river crossings, their numbers are replenished each year between February and March, when over 400,000 calves are born, many becoming easy prey for the cats.

One afternoon we passed by hundreds of zebras taking an afternoon nap. The manner they did this was most interesting, and we still regret not stopping to take a photograph of them. Each rested its head over another's back and four of them formed a kind of swastika. The only animal we missed seeing was the black rhino – these have been poached almost to extinction – but all our other sightings more than made up for this.

Before we went to the Ngorongoro Crater we changed our programme for another experience. We drove to Lake Eyasi over very rough patches that were called roads though the route was more like an obstacle course. I don't know how Issa drove over these rocks and stones without toppling the jeep. Joe and I spent two nights in a tent in the open air, virtually in the middle of nowhere. What a great first-time experience that was. For company there were the birds and monkeys. We were not sure we were hearing right when we heard the locals calling these 'blue ball monkeys'. A closer look revealed the reason. And the photos provide proof!

While at Lake Eyasi we visited the Ajabe bushmen encampment. We went hunting with them, saw how they made fire without matches and learnt how to use their bows and arrows. The men (and even the young boys) looked very spaced out, sitting around a fire and smoking from a single pipe, and their eyes showed they were addicted to something. The topless women sat separately with their children in a shelter made of the Manyara plants. Later we met some of the Toga tribe where the men have several wives all living under one roof in their own little compartments. We also went round a 'boma' of the colourful Masai warriors and checked out the Oldupai Gorge where the oldest 'human' footprints were uncovered.

From the luxurious Sopa Lodge where we stayed when we went to visit the Ngorongoro Crater, we saw some magnificent sunsets which were said to be the best in the world. And there was always someone to accompany us to our rooms at night after dinner because they said it was possible to encounter wild buffalo on the way. We never saw any but I suppose it was a nice way of earning a tip! Our fascinating safari had given us a taste of tented rooms, open air tents and luxurious 5-star Lodges – and a fantastic experience of the wild. We had covered over 2600 kms while on safari, and did another 4000 kms or more, driving around to various places in Tanzania and Kenya. We left for Dar-es-Salaam (Dar) on 8 July and stayed at a place called Slipway with Zul Masani, a kind gentleman who put his house completely at our disposal.

When our tickets were booked for us in India, it was Mumbai-Nairobi-Arusha-Nairobi-Mumbai. Having made that long journey by road from Arusha to Dar, there was no way we would even think of going back to Arusha just to get our flight to Nairobi. So while in Dar, we went to the Kenya Airways office to change our tickets. I forget how much Joe and I were charged for this change but I do know that the other two in our party were charged much less when they went the following day to the same office to also have the same change made in their tickets. There had to be some mistake somewhere; I recall that the girl attending to us seemed to be rather inefficient and had to keep consulting a senior every few minutes. Well, we did not argue the matter there but when we got back to Mumbai we took up the matter with Kenya Airways, submitting all the details of our ticket bookings. A prolonged correspondence followed while the facts were verified and, in the end, we were finally refunded the excess we had paid, which amounted to over Rs.10,000!

We were looking forward to buying some nice handicrafts while in Dar but the few we saw were highly priced and we were disappointed that there was not much of a choice. While strolling along the main streets Joe suddenly found someone's hand deep down in one of his pockets. He closed his own over the intruder's but far from being discomfited or embarrassed, the guy just said 'Sorry' very politely and walked away, as if he was just doing his duty! From our base in Dar we made trips to various places. One was to Bagamoyo, located about 60 kms from Dar. It was the port city where the slave trade was said to have started as early as the mid-tenth century between East Africa and the Gulf Coast, which was one of the main markets. Slave trading in Africa reached its peak in the 19th century, with Bagamoyo being the busiest of all ports handling slaves in this region. The Catholic Cathedral in Bagamoyo that we visited, has a museum in its premises with a fine collection of documents and other memorabilia connected to the slave trade. The dubious prominence of this place owes much to the slave and ivory trade as also to its proximity to Zanzibar, which was the hub of commerce in the western Indian Ocean at the time.

After lunch at a wayside restaurant we drove a little further where we found a few roadside stalls selling handicrafts. This was not really along the tourist route so not many people passed that way. We bought most of our carved ebony handicrafts from one stall and were thrilled with them. In spite of a steely resolve, we could not resist buying these though we had no idea where we would put them. We realised we could have got them cheaper had we bargained but we also knew it would not have been fair to the man. I guess our joy was in buying them. The people are really so poor and when they wanted to quote a price, they would write it in the mud with a stick. At the end, when we asked the man if he was happy, his reply, translated to us was, 'Tonight, my family will eat'. To hear that was heart-wrenching.

On 14 July, we booked tickets to travel to Zanzibar by boat. It was a two-hour journey at full speed that made us nauseous even though Joe and I were sitting below deck where it was less 'bumpy'. Arrangements had been made for our stay and the next day we visited the famous Stone City and also a museum that showed us where slaves were kept huddled together awaiting deportation. The cramped miserable quarters were pathetic and not fit for even animals. We wandered round the shopping areas, bought some colourful sarongs and souvenirs, as also some spices and dates for which the place is famous. Being predominantly muslim, Zanzibar was filled with mosques at every turn. That evening, we went to the Foradhani gardens, which are famed for its seafood stalls. It was filled with people, among them many westerners, who sat in groups guzzling beer and gorging on seafood. The atmosphere was that of a mela and every single stall was full. We found a rickety table and bench where we sat and feasted on huge crabs and prawns with a kind of paratha. Joe and I went back again the next night for repeat platters before we left on the 17th to return to Dar.

After resting a day in Dar, Joe and I left by coach for Dodoma where Fr. Wilfred D'Souza welcomed us to Don Bosco's. There was nothing much to see or do in Dodoma but the weather was beautiful and the atmosphere very serene. We conducted two seminars, one for the students and another for the teachers. We returned to Dar on 22 July but left for the last and final time on 24 July for Nairobi.

If you think Bombay has bad traffic jams, wait till you reach Nairobi and leave the airport! Fr. Tom Kunnel was waiting to meet us and was most patient during the two hours of crawling we did from the airport to the Shrine of Mary Help of Christians. He did worry that we would be late for the torchlight procession and rosary that was scheduled for that evening, but we just about made it. After dinner we were driven to the Don Bosco Youth Education Centre where we remained for the duration of our stay in Nairobi.

We were scheduled to return to India some time in August but as we decided to cut short our very long visit, we went into the city to change our return dates. We were very pleased to know that Kenya Airways doubles your luggage allowance from 20 to 40 kgs when leaving the country – to encourage you to buy their handicrafts; we certainly had collected some heavyweights along the way. Later that day we went to visit the Resurrection Garden in Karen. I must make special mention here of our visit to a shrine in this garden that was dedicated to the late Cardinal Maurice Michael Otunga whose cause was up for beatification. At that time, our daughter Vanessa had mentioned to us that the father of their friend had just been diagnosed with cancer and it was pretty bad. For some reason he came to mind while we were in the cardinal's shrine and I asked for healing for him. When we got back and enquired after him, his family said they could not imagine the sudden change in his condition.

Fr. Tom took us to the Nairobi Safari Walk one evening. It has been designed very nicely with walkways that allow you to view the animals without disturbing them. The keeper was known to Fr. Tom so he asked if we wanted to enter the cheetahs' enclosure. I thought he was joking but he really did take us in and then called to the cheetahs that were named Milo and Mr. Nice. We were petrified as they walked up to us gracefully and were told to sit. Then we were asked to pet them and I was just too scared wondering if they'd turn and snap our hands off but they sat obediently and it was a great feeling to touch them. Only after the photo shoot were they taken away to be fed. Years later I read the story of a similar incident to ours that did not end so well, and I certainly would not have agreed to go in so easily had I known it was mealtime for Milo and Mr. Nice!

Visiting Nairobi was not on our agenda, but we are glad we decided to spend a week there. We not only conducted two more seminars here (one on Christian Meditation for priests and religious at Don Bosco, Utume) but Joe also recorded several of his seminar stories while I recorded several inspirational songs at the very hi-tech Don Bosco studio. They said they would try and set these to African music. I cannot close the chapter on Africa without mentioning the celebration of mass. We attended three masses in Kenya - one in Kikambala, another in Makuyu, and the third in Nairobi, and they were truly 'Celebrations'. The entire congregation, including the priest, participates fully and with gusto – they sing, dance and clap in a spontaneous manner and the beat is so pulsating that you cannot help but join in. What a joyful experience and end to our long African holiday!

BORDERLINE CROSSINGS
"See the stars in the skies above they'll shine wherever I may roam…"

My concern about travelling to Europe in November was the winter cold, and thinking about London I expected Gibraltar to also be cold. I had not stopped to think that because of its location, Gibraltar would have a more temperate Mediterranean climate, so I was happy that we could enjoy beautiful weather all through our three-week stay there. We had to travel via London as there is no direct flight to Gibraltar. Our tickets Mumbai-London-Mumbai on Emirates Airlines cost Rs.34,016 each, while the London-Gibraltar-London tickets were bought for us and paid for by Sanjay and Vanessa.

This time we took care to obtain one-year multiple entry visas for the UK which automatically permitted entry into Gibraltar. However,

Gibraltar does not allow visitors to stay for longer than four or five days at a stretch. Fortunately we could hop across to Spain, have our passports stamped and come back into Gibraltar. In my earlier narrative on Gibraltar I mentioned that it is a small land extension of Spain and people from both countries cross over daily to work. These regulars do not get their passports stamped everyday – they just hold them up as they pass the authorities.

Reaching Gibraltar on 4 November, we had to wait for Vanessa and Sanjay at the airport as they were probably held up when the road closed for our flight to land. Finally settled into a taxi we drove to their modern apartment at Rock Gardens, which was located partly up the Rock and opposite the Alameda Botanic Gardens. Joe and I were very impressed with their swanky apartment, more so for its spectacular view of the entire Bay of Gibraltar. We could watch the cruise liners arriving as also the planes coming in to land, and of course, the amazing sunsets. On some days we could see dark storm clouds rolling in from a distance and they looked very forbidding, blocking out the sunlight totally when they massed together, but often they dispersed as quickly as they gathered.

Most often, we travelled around Gibraltar by taxi, especially when we had to do grocery shopping or go some distance away from home. Even when out shopping, we had to phone for a taxi to return home. But we got our exercise when we went walking down Main Street. I enjoyed the walks though it was a bit of a climb back to the house. We were shocked to find that Vanessa often left her front door unlocked when we left to go out and said it was okay. There was no security guard in the building but I guess they were confident of the security aspect.

Sanjay often enticed us to join him on his early morning walks and we tried it a couple of times. It was difficult going for me, up those slopes but it did feel good at the end of it. One day we decided to walk to Europa Point, which is the absolute southern tip of Gibraltar and was quite a long walk. We passed by some lovely old houses and cosy little beaches. Gibraltar has two coasts – the east side has the settlements of Sandy Bay and Catalan Bay and the west side is where the vast majority of the population lives. Walking along the interior of the west side was like seeing a side of Gibraltar that few people would see or find time for. A big group of early morning cyclists passed us, some panting heavily from the climb as we went through a tunnel before coming out onto a flat area, which had a playing field, a few buildings, a lighthouse, a mosque and a catholic shrine. This was known as Europa Point. We did not stay here long that first day but decided to come back another time.

While Sanjay was at work, Vanessa took Joe and me across the border to Spain several times. La Linea de la Concepcion is the closest Spanish town. Shopping in Spain was much cheaper than in Gibraltar so many people went there regularly to shop.

Vanessa and Sanjay had planned long weekend visits to Portugal and Spain, so five days after arriving in Gibraltar, we left for Portugal.

PORTUGUESE PATRONYMICS
"No wonder my happy heart sings"

When we did a heraldic search for the Portuguese name of 'Rodrigues', we saw it was of patronymic origin. Rodrigues would therefore signify 'son of Rodrigo' which was of Germanic origin. In medieval times, Rodrigo was also one of the most popular names of the Iberian Peninsula. 'Pereira' (my maiden name), also of Portuguese origin, is said to be one of great ancient history and derived from the locality from whence the original bearer hailed – in this instance it originally denoted a dweller near a pear tree. Well, whatever the origins and however we got our Portuguese surnames, we were happy to be visiting the 'land of our ancestors' – so to say!

After considering various options, we decided to go to Lisbon in Portugal. Another reason for picking Lisbon was that our friend, Livia Lobo (I have mentioned her earlier in the chapter on The Netherlands) was also going to be in this city on an official visit, so we arranged to meet up there at the same time. On 9 November, Sanjay, Vanessa, Joe and I took a taxi to the border and crossed into Spain. From there we took another taxi to Malaga. It took us two hours driving along the Andalusian coast past some beautiful little villages and towns. At Malaga airport, we took the Iberia Airlines flight to Lisbon and booked into Hotel Le Meridien, located right next to The Ritz on Rua Castilho. Livia was also booked at the same hotel.

After settling in, we went down to the restaurant for a late lunch. It was little wonder that the food was so much like our own cooking, down to the fish curry and rice that Sanjay ordered, because most of our recipes have come to us through the Portuguese. Livia joined us in the restaurant where we caught up on our news and did some planning for the next few days.

After freshening up, the five of us trooped out to explore the city before it turned dark. From our hotel, we walked down the incline of the Rua Joaquim Antonio de Aguiar towards Lisbon Central Square known as Marques de Pombal. The marquis was the prime minister who was responsible for rebuilding Lisbon following the Great Earthquake in 1755 that destroyed most of Lisbon. The square is actually a very wide roundabout with a large monument to the marquis in its centre. He is shown standing on a tall column with his hand on a lion. Surrounding this monument are beautiful paving stones decorated with Lisbon's coat of arms. We walked down the broad and spacious Avenida da Liberdade (Liberty Avenue), which connects the Marques de Pombal Square with downtown Lisbon. It felt like we were walking down the Champs-Elysee! Shops, hotels, cafes, theatres, universities, offices, well-known fashion houses and more, line both sides of the Avenue. The shops were very inviting and my eye was immediately attracted to one of the stores selling Portugal's traditional mascot, the cock. The store had a variety of them in different sizes and colours and I bought one immediately. It fittingly adorns our house in Goa, where you will find the roofs of many houses also decorated with this symbol. Some of the pavements we walked on, especially in the centre of the avenue, have beautiful mosaic tiling that is so much part of the country. Most of the town squares had the typical Portuguese cobblestones.

At the end of the Avenue, we came to the Restauradores Square, a large, busy central square that commemorates Portugal's liberation in 1640, from 60 years of Spanish rule. From here to Rossio Square, which is the heart of the city, was but a few steps. It had started to get dark, but we continued walking. The Rossio area had a very festive air and was full of many shoppers patronizing the elegant stores.

We had done quite some walking from our hotel to the waterfront and were all a little tired. Instead of going out for dinner as we had earlier planned, we decided to go back to the hotel after buying a few necessities. Not being very familiar with the place, we had a time searching for a wine store and finally found one in the Restauradores Square. We bought two bottles of wine, some food from one of the Rossia cafes, and then met in one of the rooms after freshening up with showers. It turned out to be a jolly evening and I know that the wine was not the main contributor to this. There was sparkling wit and conversation and a general catching up of the old days.

We woke up fairly early the next morning, despite the late night, and after breakfast in the hotel, we went to the Marques de Pombal Square to book a tour of the city that covered quite a few places. Our first stop was the Belém Tower on the estuary of the River Tagus, which was built in the Age of Discoveries at a time when defending the city, was considered of prime importance. This impressive monument built between 1515 and 1521 was also a ceremonial gateway to commemorate Vasco da Gama's expedition to India in 1497. With the city acquiring more modern defences, the Belem Tower eventually lost its effectiveness as a defence bastion.

A short distance from the Belem Tower is the Prince Henry Monument to the Discoveries, which was inaugurated in 1960. Designed in the shape of a caravel, it shows Henry at the prow holding a small caravel. Behind him are many heroes of Portuguese maritime history, including Vasco da Gama and many others. In front of this impressive 50-metres monument is a huge mariners' compass cut into the paving stone. It shows the routes of the various discoverers during the 15th and 16th centuries. As we loitered in the vicinity we were entertained by a strange sight. The sides of the Tagus riverbank have a cemented wall sloping at an almost 45-degree angle towards the river. Imagine our shock to see a cyclist pedalling along this wall at a fast pace, sitting very confidently on his bike. We could not understand how gravity did not carry him to the river or how he managed to remain so steady on his cycle. He had to be a professional like those motorcyclists in the Well of Death!

For the first time we saw a Museum of Coaches. This is also located in the Belem district in what was once part of the former Belem Palace. The museum was started in 1905 by Queen Amelia to house an extensive collection of carriages belonging to the Portuguese royal family and nobility. The carriages and coaches range from the ornate to the pompous and slightly ridiculous, and illustrate the ostentation and staggering wealth of the Portuguese elite. The coach-makers went to extraordinary lengths to call attention to their work and they decorated them with paintings, large gilt woodwork cherubs, and partly nude figures. It was like carrying a huge float at the back of the vehicle.

The amazing Jeronimos Monastery is located a little away from the Museum of Coaches. This monastery is considered one of the most magnificent and well-known monuments in Lisbon and, like the Belem Tower, it has been classified as a World Heritage site by UNESCO. Vasco da Gama and his men spent the night in prayer here before they departed for India in 1497; his tomb is also located close to the western portal. The ornate main entrance is 32 mts high and 12 mts wide and extends up to the height of two storeys. After this our guide took us on a walking tour of narrow side streets and quaint cobbled lanes, where we saw many building façades decorated with lovely patterned Portuguese tiles.

When we were back in the city, we found a nice restaurant and had a long lazy lunch with a bottle (or two?) of red wine. Then after a rest and refreshing shower, we took a taxi to somewhere near the waterfront. Our hotel had booked a table for us at a restaurant where we could experience the Portuguese Fado. Our taxi stopped at quite a deserted place and we wondered what kind of a seedy joint we were going to. The street was almost deserted. Would we be mugged? We made a few enquiries and found our way up a dark street, turned off it and entered a large gate. I was still very apprehensive, wondering if we were taken to the wrong place. We entered a kind of dark hall and were asked to wait. Then a young lady escorted us inside to a table and we were relieved to see many other diners and tourists already seated at candlelit tables. We would never have guessed there was a restaurant located here but, apparently, it was a very popular place.

For the uninitiated, like me, an explanation of the fado is called for, and I took the trouble to find out more. It is a form of music characterized by mournful tunes, and lyrics about the sea or the life of the poor or about suchlike, but it has to follow a certain structure. The music of the fado can be traced from the 1820s in Portugal but probably had much earlier origins. Some claim that the roots are a mixture of African slave rhythms with the traditional music of

Portuguese sailors and also Arabic influence. The fado is sung at night, almost in the dark, in city squares or streets, and sometimes used to serenade outside the window of the woman being courted. Now we were getting the picture of dark city streets!

The music is usually linked to the Portuguese word '*saudade*'. This does not have an English equivalent but the closest is 'nostalgia' or 'pining for someone'. There are two main varieties of fado, namely those of the cities of Lisbon and Coimbra. The Lisbon style is the most popular, while Coimbra's is more refined. According to tradition, to applaud fado in Lisbon you clap your hands, while in Coimbra one coughs as if clearing one's throat.

We were pleased that we were given a table right next to the performers. It started with two guitarists and a young but plump lady singer. True to the fado tradition, she wailed and moaned and we clapped for her. She was followed by at least six others during the rest of the evening, all of them dressed in black with long tasseled scarves draped around their shoulders, hanging down almost to the floor. Most of the time their eyes were kept shut while singing with heads raised high (I wonder if it is my Portuguese ancestry that makes me do the same when I sing), and the guitarists also closed their eyes in moments of ecstasy. In between performances, we continued to dine, sip wine and clap politely for each performer. At the risk of scandalizing some, I have to admit that the fado did nothing to stir my blood. Still, we had a great evening together and managed to get taxis back to our hotel.

OUR LADY OF FATIMA HAIL
"Immaculate Mother of Grace"

We had arranged to visit the famous Shrine of Our Lady of Fatima on 11 November, which was a Sunday. There is a choice of travelling by bus, train or car to Fatima. The bus takes about 90 minutes to reach Batalha and from there another bus takes you to Fatima in 40 minutes. The train journey takes two and a half hours from Lisbon to Caxarias, which is the train station closest to Fatima, but about 10 kms outside the town of Fatima. By car from Lisbon airport, you can reach Fatima in one hour and 15 minutes. It worked out more economical for us (since we were five) to hire a car, which the hotel organized for us. Our driver-cum-guide was a pleasant lady who drove a Mercedes van and we could chat comfortably with her all along.

Most people have heard about the Shrine of Fatima and the miracles that occurred there. For those who have not, I am recounting the story in brief. Like Lourdes in France, Fatima has one of the biggest catholic shrines in the world. It is said that the Virgin Mary appeared to three shepherd children in a place called Cova de Iria, as they were tending their sheep. Lucia de Jesus, a 10-year-old girl, Francisco Marto, a 9-year-old boy and his sister Jacinta Marto, 7, received a mysterious message from the Virgin Mary. This same vision occurred on the 13th of every month from May to October in 1937. At the last visitation on 13 October, a crowd of 70,000 people, including reporters from anti-religious newspapers, had gathered at the site in a torrential rainstorm and witnessed an inexplicable spectacle that became known as the 'Miracle of the Sun'. Around noon, many of the observers testified they saw wondrous things in the heavens: the rain clouds parted, the 'sky opened up' and the sun seemed to spin in the sky, change colours, or go completely dark for several minutes, before appearing to plunge towards the earth. This phenomenon led millions to believe in the children's story, which at first had been greeted with much scepticism. Even the government had accused the church of fabricating the story, while the church was afraid to acknowledge the event, fearing it was a hoax.

The children were arrested and interrogated, but refused to change their story. They stated that the Virgin revealed three secrets. The first described a horrific vision of Hell. The second foretold the end of World War I and the beginning of World War II and called for the 'Consecration of Russia to the Immaculate Heart of Mary'. (Many believe that Pope John Paul II fulfilled this request in 1984 by giving a blessing over the world, including Russia, shortly before the collapse of the Soviet Union and the Berlin Wall.) The third secret was only told to the Pope, and was finally revealed in May 2000 by Pope John Paul II. The officially released text of this secret was unspecific in nature, leaving it open to speculation that the Vatican did not release its entire contents. The church's interpretation is that it predicted the assassination attempt on Pope John Paul II on 13 May 1981 (another 13). The Pope himself credited Our Lady of Fatima with saving his life, saying he saw her intervening to deflect the gunman's arm, and he maintained consciousness on the ride to the hospital by keeping his mind focused on her.

We thought it rather strange that the famous christian town of Fatima had a Muslim name of Arab origin. According to the legend, the town of Ourem, which is 10 kms northeast of Fatima, owes its name to a love story. During the re-conquest of Portugal, a Spanish crusader, Gonzalo Hermingues, captured the daughter of a powerful Muslim lord from Alacer do Sol. The ravishingly beautiful girl was called Fatima, after the daughter of Prophet Mohammed. Gonzalo Hermingues and his captive soon fell in love, and they married with the king's permission, on condition Fatima became a Catholic. She was baptised with the first name Ouranea, meaning 'the Golden one'. The king's wedding gift to Gonzalo and Fatima was the village of Abdegas, which name was then changed to Oureana and later shortened to Ourem. It is not known how, but Fatima died in her prime not too many months after the wedding. This left Gonzalo Hermingues inconsolable and he became a monk at the Cistercian abbey of Alcobaça, founded by Saint Bernard. The abbey had a small priory in the neighbouring mountain, where Brother Hermingues was sent. He quickly had the remains of his beloved Fatima transferred there. As a town with her Christian name, Ourem, already existed, this place took her former name, Fatima.

The large open plaza in front of the basilica, which is capable of holding a million people, is twice the size of St. Peter's Square in Rome. It was packed, but not to capacity, with pilgrims attending the service. The tombs of the three visionaries, including that of Lucia, were located inside the neoclassical basilica. Lucia had lived to the age of 97 in a Carmelite convent in Coimbra until her death on 13 February 2005 (another 13!).

By the time we walked across the huge plaza to the tall monumental cross at the other end and taken all the photos we wanted, we realised that we had spent so many hours in this one spot that it would be too late to cover all the other places we had scheduled to visit. Our guide was still patient and smiling despite the heat.

SCINTILLATING SINTRA
"Sweet dreams that leave all worries behind you"

Sintra is considered one of the most delightful places to be found in Portugal and is a popular tourist destination. In ancient times, it was known as Mons Lunae (the Hills of the Moon) because of its strong traditions of astral cults, and we believe that signs are still visible in the region's many monuments and archaeological remains. The town retains its essentially medieval layout, with narrow and labyrinthine streets, steps and arcades. Our main objective here was to see the National Palace, which is located in the very heart of this historic town. First built as a residence for the Moorish governors of Lisbon, it became the property and residence of the kings of Portugal. The palace was used by the nobility for hunting expeditions and also as a refuge from the unbearable summer heat in Lisbon, which was regularly devastated by outbreaks of plague.

The National Palace is the only surviving royal palace from the Middle Ages, and its two white monumental conical kitchen chimneys are a landmark of Sintra and an outstanding feature of the town's landscape. If one thinks back to the conical headwear that women wore in the Middle Ages, with a veil coming from its top, one will get the picture. Only, these chimneys were gigantic. The palace kitchen was built at a safe distance from the other rooms and, 600 years later, is still in use for occasional official banquets at the palace. We walked through the corridors, staircases, galleries and courtyards and through the many fabulous rooms, which were added to the Palace by various kings who redecorated parts of it. The majestic Swans' Room had a beautiful painted ceiling and was the venue for royal marriages. We marvelled at the medieval legends painted in the Magpie (or Reading) Room, and admired the fantastic Armoury Room with its ceiling decorated with the coats of arms of 72 families of the Portuguese nobility. We were happy to find the Pereira and Lobo coats of arms but could not locate that of the Rodrigues family, though I am sure it must have been among the 72 which were too high up to read. The most amazing feature of all the rooms we saw were the Mudejar azulejos (Moorish ceramics), said to be the largest and richest collection in the entire Iberian Peninsula or, for that matter, in the whole world. These tiles covered the walls of many rooms and some floors too were paved with them. It was obvious that Moorish artistic traditions continued even during the christian Middle Ages.

After our tour of the National Palace, our guide advised us to get the famous cheesecakes known as '*queijadas*' for which Sintra was known to be famous. We had to walk up a narrow alley to a tiny pokey shop where we found hordes of tourists trying to buy these cakes. Vanessa and Sanjay managed to get to the counter and bought a few. After all the hype about them, we were disappointed to find that they were no different from the little *Irani* cakes we were used to in Mumbai.

The Serra de Sintra is a 10-km long granite mountain range that twists and turns, projecting into the Atlantic Ocean to form Cabo da Roca, the headland that marks the westernmost point of continental Europe. At the top of the Serra stands the 19th century Palacio da Pena, which was built on the ruins of a 16th century monastery and looks almost like a fairy tale castle. Unfortunately, we did not have time to go up and see it. We stopped briefly at Cabo da Roca, which is also a popular tourist destination. A lighthouse, which was built in 1772, sits on top of the cliff, 144 mts above the Cape. We watched surfers enjoying themselves on the beach below while we waited to see the sunset. The haze covering it made it look as if someone had lit a giant bonfire in the sky.

Our tour also included Cascais, a coastal suburb of Lisbon and one of the richest municipalities in Portugal. However, the many extra hours we spent at Fatima now made a more detailed visit impossible as we had a long drive back to Lisbon. But we did drive through the centre square; it had a wave-like mosaic pattern, and the little church with its bell tower outlined against the sky, gave the place a charming old-world look. Cascais became home to many exiled royal families from Spain, Italy and Bulgaria due to Portugal's neutrality in World War II, and also because of its royal past. It was dark by the time we reached Estoril. We drove around the casino, which was all lit up with bright lights, and then drove directly back to Lisbon.

By any account we should have been exhausted when we got back to our hotel, but Livia wanted to go to a particular shopping mall she had heard about. With the exception of Sanjay who would have preferred to rest in the hotel, we all decided to go along, so he gave in gracefully and came along with us. I think we went to the shopping district called Saldanha. I know we took the tube and when we alighted, we stepped almost directly into this huge shopping mall. Vanessa and Livia were the main shoppers so after walking around with them for some time, Joe and I went looking for a restaurant to have dinner. We found a Mexican place that was quite charming, so we sat there and waited for the others to join us. We had a pitcher of Sangria with our meal before heading back to our hotel.

On our last morning in Portugal, we found we had time to go up to Castello de San Jorge, which is located on the highest hill of Lisbon and is one of the main historical tourist sites of the city. The castle has a history going back to 1147, when Lisbon was under the control of the Moors. One can either walk up the hill, take a cable car, a tram, or a taxi. We left early and, to save time, took a taxi going up. There is a tiny and partially restored ancient neighbourhood in the Castle area called Santa Cruz do Castelo. It is one of the most picturesque parts of Lisbon and has more old than young residents. There are many luxury hotels located here, but also some delightful cafes with outdoor seating, run by families. We stopped to have breakfast at one such place and the fare was very good. The locals do not gawk at tourists and generally mind their own business.

Vasco da Gama was felicitated in this very castle after he discovered the sea route to India. The rewards he received for this seemed unending! The castle started losing its importance when a new royal palace was built near the Tagus River in the early 16th century. From being downgraded to army barracks and then prison, it finally emerged as the big tourist attraction it is today, particularly for the spectacular views of Lisbon that it offers from every side. We wandered through the castle and its medieval corridors and tried to imagine what it must have been like in the days when it was occupied by so many different people. When we left the castle, we walked down the hill for part of the way and then decided to take a tram ride down to the city centre. At every twist and turn downhill, we saw a different vista of the city. We could have walked back to our hotel but we did not want to chance being late for our flights so we hopped into taxis, picked up our luggage and left for the airport. Here we parted ways – Livia took her flight to Amsterdam and ours was a little later to Malaga. From Malaga, we took a taxi back to the Spanish-Gibraltar border, crossed over and took another taxi back home.

It was gratifying that we managed to see and do so much in the few days we spent in Portugal. From the moment we landed there, we felt so comfortable and we all marvelled at how familiar we found things to be. The people too were so much like us and we did not stand out like sore thumbs. Perhaps our familiarity with Portuguese traditions, architecture and history, and also the ancestors from whom we inherited our names, features, customs and food habits, made us feel so much at home.

DISCOVERING THE LAND OF CHRISTOPHER COLUMBUS
"Oh this year I'm off to sunny …."

Like London, Gibraltar served as a good base for travel to European destinations. Four days after returning from Portugal, Vanessa, Sanjay, Joe and I left again on 16 November, this time for Seville in Spain. After crossing over from Gibraltar to Spain, we travelled by coach from La Linea de la Concepcion through several picturesque towns till we reached Seville, which is in the heart of Spain. Sanjay had booked us rooms at Hotel Occidental, which was close to the Santa Justa railway station.

Soon after getting into Seville, we took a taxi to the City Centre and walked around a while before deciding where we should start. As we were near the Plaza de Espana we decided to explore that first. Walking towards it, we heard some sweet music and thought it was a recording. When we came closer to the plaza we saw three musicians dressed in full Red Indian gear, large feather headdress and all, and they were actually playing instruments that made such wonderful music. We stopped to watch and listen and chat with them for some time. Unfortunately, we forgot to buy one of their CDs that they were selling, thinking we'd pick up one on our way out.

The Plaza de Espana is a huge semi-circular building that was built in 1929 on the occasion of the Latin American Fair. It has a diameter of 200 mts with twin towers at each end of the semi-circle, and a moat surrounding it. There is also a large fountain before the two picturesque bridges that take you across the moat. The place had such a feeling of space. What made it more interesting were the large ceramic friezes depicting the different provinces of Spain. Even the two bridges over the moat have this beautiful ceramic work.

It was not too far to walk from the Plaza de Espana to the Torre Del Oro (The Golden Tower). The Tower was built in the 13th century towards the end of the Muslim period and has 12 sides. Its Arabic name Bury Al Dahab, means the Golden Tower because the upper part, which may have once been a dome, was covered with golden tiles, which reflected the sun's rays. Another more romantic version of how the Tower got its name says it is because of the colour of the hair of the beautiful damsel who was kept locked up in the Tower by King Pedro the Cruel, while the damsel's husband was away at war. Today the Tower is a naval museum. We climbed to the top from where we had a spectacular view of the surroundings. Later, as we walked down, we inspected the various engravings, letters, various models of ships and the antique navigational instruments and historical documents in the museum, which is spread over several floors.

Seville has a long and interesting history spanning centuries and civilizations. This is reflected in the variety of architectural styles with Islamic, Mudejar, Gothic, Renaissance, Baroque and Roman influences. I was fascinated from the very first by the abundance of orange trees everywhere. They were planted on footpaths, in courtyards and gardens, and added such a lovely touch to the city. I love seeing fruit on trees and for me this was a memorable visual delight. I did not try plucking or eating any and felt they were there for the decoration; they certainly were a great feast for the eyes.

As we still had time before dinner, we walked up to the Plaza de Toros de la Real Maestranza, which is said to be Spain's oldest bullring. The place has a spanking clean look. The exterior, painted in white with golden yellow trim, is in late Baroque style and looks beautiful from outside as well as within. Construction of this impressive building was begun in 1761 and finished in 1881, more than a century later, with various architects adding to it over the years. The bullring is huge and slightly oval shaped with tiered seating and stalls all around. The centre of the ring is slightly raised and slopes towards the stalls. There is good reason for this because it provides a little relief when someone has to run towards protective shelter, whereas the animal has to brake when it does the same. It was not the bullfighting season, but even so, I would not have liked to attend one of these 'bloody' events.

After returning to our hotel, we dressed and left to have dinner at the famous Hotel Alphonso XIII, which was once a palace. Sanjay was keen to visit this hotel as he had heard much about it. It was known to be very exclusive and one of the most expensive hotels, and we would never think of booking a room there. However, Sanjay was still keen to experience having a meal there. One look at the menu confirmed what we had heard. We dined in a kind of internal courtyard of the hotel and the place filled up quite fast. It was still a bit chill so we asked for a table close to one of the heaters. The meal was very good and served in elegant style. With two bottles of choice wine to accompany the meal, we were soon warm enough.

On Sunday morning we decided to go to the famous Cathedral of Seville for Mass. It is the largest Gothic cathedral in the world and the third largest christian cathedral after St. Peter's in Rome and St. Paul's in London. It was huge and had so many entrances that by the time we found a door we could enter, we had walked almost around the cathedral. At that time, they were allowing entry only to those wanting to attend mass.

The cathedral was built over the main Almohad mosque, which was built between 1184 and 1198 using bricks, but all that remained of the mosque was the square minaret, known as La Giralda, and the Patio de los Naranjos (the orange gardens), but I'll come to this later.

Work on a christian church began under the reign of King Ferdinand III of Castille, but not many changes were made from the original mosque, and in 1248 this converted mosque was consecrated as a cathedral. Construction work on a new Gothic cathedral was begun in 1434 from the western side, and this time, stone was used in its construction. The intricate carving work done on the stone is amazing in its detail (especially at the main entrance) as the total surface area of the building is 23,500 sq. mts! The construction work was finally completed in 1517. The Cathedral is 126 mts long, 83 mts wide and has a height of 37 mts in the centre transept. When the decision was taken by the Chapter to build it, they said 'Let us construct such a big building that those who see it finished will think we are mad!' After seeing the cathedral, I would agree that they must have been mad. The most striking feature is the 18-metre high main altar. This has scenes of the Old and New Testaments with more than a thousand sculptures carved by Spanish and Flemish sculptors between 1482 and 1564. And what was most amazing was that the entire altar was covered with 2400 kgs of gold brought from 'the new lands' in Mexico and Peru! This main altar is surrounded by an iron grille, and with good reason.

To the right of the main altar is a mausoleum containing the mortal remains of the Italian navigator, Christopher Columbus. The texts next to his mausoleum state that his remains were brought here from the cathedral of Havana when Cuba became independent. Four heralds representing the four Spanish kingdoms of Castille, Leon, Aragon and Navarre hold aloft the coffin on their shoulders. Spanish royalty truly esteemed this man who discovered America in their name.

Seville is proud of its Cathedral and more so of its tower, La Giralda, so I must share these details. The Tower, which was built as a square minaret by the order of the Emperor of Morocco, was 76 mts high, had four golden orbs at the four corners, and could be seen from as far as 40 kms away. Its foundations go down 15 mts. La Giralda, with its intricate motifs, sculpted bricks and lobe-shaped windows, was a much admired building. When the moslems surrendered the city they asked for permission to destroy the tower. Prince Don Alfonso replied that if even one brick was removed from the tower, all the moslems would be stabbed to death. There are actually two towers built one inside the other. Between these two towers there are 35 sections of ramps (instead of steps) from the base to the top. Two explanations were given for this – one was so that the muezzin who called the people to prayer could climb to the top on his horse; the other says that it was the Sultan who used to go up on his horse to admire the view from the top, but both could be true.

As the city became wealthy with gold brought from America, the church authorities decided to augment to the tower. Accordingly, a

Renaissance style belfry was added to the Islamic structure and this took the height of the tower to 98 mts. The final addition to this tower was a statue representing Faith in the form of a woman carrying a shield in one hand and a palm leaf in the other. As the statue is actually a rotating weather vane, the tower and the statue were named 'Giralda' from the Spanish word 'girar' which is 'to turn'. Now the bell tower is referred to as the 'Giralda' and the weather vane as the 'Giraldillo'.

We had to exit the cathedral through the beautiful orange gardens, which have survived for almost 10 centuries, and I felt sure that if they could speak, they would tell a thousand stories and speak of many intrigues. After that very inspiring visit we strolled around, watched some very interesting road shows, and shopped for some souvenirs. As Joe was fond of antiques he bought a typical short sword used in bull fights and an old style flintlock gun with a nicely decorated handle. Who guessed at the time what adventures these purchases would lead to! We then went off and found a nice place to have breakfast. Only when taking off my jacket did I realize that I did not have my bag with me – it contained our passports and quite a bit of money. I realised that I must have laid it down when we were in the shop buying the sword and gun and then forgot all about it. My heart almost stood still when I realized what I had done. Sanjay quickly dashed off back to the shop, while we prayed to St. Anthony, who always answers our pleas, because we saw Sanjay returning with my bag in hand. The shopkeeper had kept it safe for us. I cannot imagine how I was so careless and distracted.

Our hotel booked us tickets to see authentic flamenco dancing at a famous and much advertised place called El Arenal. We had a choice of seeing only the show (€35), or the show with tapas (€53) or the show with dinner (€69). We chose the tapas. We had kept this for our last night in Spain and were happy when we found that we were seated right in front of the stage.

The art of flamenco dancing is traced to the gypsies from Andalusia in the south of Spain. It is commonly believed that gypsies came from Sind in North India (now in Pakistan) and their arrival in Spain dates back to 1447. In the earliest forms of flamenco, the only instruments used to make music were the hands, which would clap in a particular rhythm, and a voice to sing. The guitar was added later and the tapping of the feet was introduced only in the last century. A prominent singer and dancer was a woman dressed in white, who had a husky, throaty voice. She started the performance and sang to the accompaniment to a solo guitarist. As the evening progressed I realized that this woman was considered a virtuoso. She had such power in those hands that clapped resoundingly. I tried doing this later and within seconds my hands hurt. This lady kept at it for hours. In fact, she is featured in the El Arenal ads I saw in a magazine.

I lost track of the number of performers that came on in a continuous stream. One slim, beautiful girl looked very much like our Malaika Arora Khan, and she kept casting provocative glances and smiles at Joe. Women seem attracted by him and his Indian outfits, despite his white beard, or maybe because of it! Sometimes there were five girls dancing together and sometimes just two. With whirling large frilly skirts and stamping feet they made you want to get up and dance with them. Several more guitarists came on. Some of the dancers were older veterans. There was just a single male dancer who looked like the actor Adrien Brody and also reminded us of Joe's cousin, Neil Creado. He came on almost towards the end and did a solo with such passion and abandon that he was dripping with sweat within minutes. Later he was joined by four women and they all used castanets while they gyrated and danced in a frenzy. We truly enjoyed the show but could not say the same about the tapas.

We were scheduled to leave the next afternoon so we spent the morning walking around a few more interesting monuments and even went to a street bazaar. The stuff being sold there were antiques, stamps, old jewellery and the like, all quite expensive. While walking around, I noticed a man who thought he was being discreet while he was trying to photograph Joe in his Indian outfit and 'Alladin' *mojiris*. Somehow I instinctively sense when someone is following or dogging our footsteps and I noticed him trying to merge with the crowd every time we turned in his direction. I wonder if he eventually got a shot with all those people milling around.

Our coach journey back was very comfortable and the surrounding countryside was scenic. Once again we passed the Costa del Sol, where there were many luxury hotels and beautiful bungalows and villas, and we saw many people enjoying the sun and sand on the long stretches of beaches. We reached La Linea by evening, walked across the border into Gibraltar and took a taxi back to Rock Gardens, where we had another 10 days of our vacation to enjoy.

GOOSE BUMPS IN GIBRALTAR
"Faith can move mountains"

In the days before we left Gibraltar, we made time to go around and inspect it in more detail. Apart from visiting The Rock a second time, we also went to Europa Point once more. This time we took the local bus on which I was keen to travel. Like this, we got to see more of the beautiful old residential areas of Gibraltar along the way.

From Europa Point, looking across the Strait of Gibraltar on a clear day, you can see a part of North Africa and the Rif Mountains of Morocco. Stretching out on the right is the Bay of Gibraltar with Spanish towns along its shores. Europa Point was formerly linked with the eastern side of the Rock by a tunnel, which had to be closed in

2002 for safety reasons, after a fatal rock fall. A prominent feature that marks this point is a red and white lighthouse, which was built between 1838 and 1841. It is 49 mts above sea level and has a range of 27 kms. I was rather surprised to also see a large modern mosque there. Known as Ibrahim-al-Ibrahim Mosque, it was also called King Fahd bin Abdulaziz al-Saud Mosque. The building was a gift from King Fahd of Saudi Arabia and was built at a cost of £5 million. The mosque complex contains a school, a library, and a lecture hall and serves over 2000 Muslims who live in Gibraltar.

When the Spaniards recaptured Gibraltar from the Moors, during the 15th century, they found a little mosque at Europa Point and converted it into a christian shrine in honour of Our Lady, as Patroness of Europe. A large chapel was built at right angles to the mosque's east wall and this area became known as the Shrine of Our Lady of Europe. It flourished for over two centuries but must have fallen into disuse later. In 1979 when Pope John Paul II officially approved the title of Our Lady of Europe as Patroness of Gibraltar, the shrine was once again restored.

We had planned to go across to Spain to have dinner on at least two occasions but just thinking of crossing two check points when going and returning even for a short visit was enough to deter us. Instead, we generally ended up having luxurious dinners at waterfront cafes or in the town square that had many restaurants for fine dining. Sampling a variety of choice red and white wines was also getting to be too much of a good habit! Some hotel owners or cooks from the waterfront cafes would leave a fishing line tied to the harbour railing. When they needed a fresh fish for the table they would go out and pull one in. We saw them do this regularly and the fish were quite large too.

We picked up some unusual facts about Gibraltar. For one, the number of cars far exceeded the number of residents. Not much wonder, as this was a millionaires' paradise and a tax haven. From the number of luxurious yachts parked in the various bays, we could deduce that for ourselves. Another thing was that resident visitors to the country could not just stay where they pleased. The place of residence one was permitted to rent depended on one's income and status. The address you directed a taxi driver to take you to gave him a clear indication of status and of the size of tip to be expected. We made the most of our time in Gibraltar because we were unlikely to come back. Sanjay and Vanessa once again generously gifted us the entire holiday, including our visits to Portugal and Spain, 5-star hotel stays and airfares.

We had our last adventure at Gibraltar airport and I can tell you it was not funny in the least. Vanessa was returning with us to India as she had to raise the toast at her friend's wedding. We had our bags checked and cleared and were just getting ready to board the flight when my name was called and I was asked to report to a counter. I was then asked to open one of the suitcases, which we had to wrap securely with masking tape as the locks were threatening to open up. Since Joe had the keys, I sent him to deal with the officials. More than 15 minutes had passed and he did not return. By then, everyone had boarded the plane and only the three of us were left. The staff kept telling us that the flight would take off if we did not board. Vanessa told me to go on and she would follow with Joe. I hesitated but went. I boarded amidst total silence and some dirty looks from my co-passengers. My mouth had turned very dry and I kept praying non-stop, but from my window seat, I could still see no sign of Vanessa or Joe. I guessed that there might be something seriously wrong but could not think what or why.

In the meantime, the captain announced that we were ready for take off (and again my heart stood still) and went on to say that they were just waiting for two passengers who were about to board. Looking out of the window, I was relieved to see Joe and Vanessa walking across the tarmac. They too boarded amidst an almost hostile silence and we had no time to talk or discuss what had happened until after take off.

In my account on Spain, I have narrated how we bought two typical Spanish souvenirs – a small sword used in bullfights and an old flintlock gun with a decorative handle. Both these were packed into our checked-in luggage and the gun did not have any ammunition or gunpowder. Yet they turned out to be the cause of all the trouble and delay. Joe was asked to open up the suitcase and made to remove every article piece by piece, and each was checked, even the shirts and other clothing. When they finally came to the two items under question (which was what they were looking for to start with) they behaved as though they had caught a terrorist red-handed. Joe was surrounded by gun-toting officials and grilled about his origins, age, passport, stay, etc. He explained where and how he bought the souvenirs but they said he had committed a crime by bringing them into the airport. They even told him that the flight was taking off without him. He fortunately remained calm and cool and asked what they wanted him to do. Joe had the feeling they were waiting for him to say something incriminating, and when he remained silent, they looked at each other as if not knowing what to do next. Finally, they made a note of his passport details and told him they were confiscating the two items; he shrugged, packed up and rushed to get the flight.

When we talked to Sanjay later, he was very surprised to hear all this and asked if he should take up the matter with a legal notice in Gibraltar as he had his high level contacts through his office. However, after thinking about it, we decided against it. Everyone else who heard about this matter was really very surprised. The people of Gibraltar said that so little ever happens at the airport that is exciting, that this incident would give them something to talk and think about for a long time! I personally had forgotten about this incident until I sat down to write this account. I now wonder if it was the fact that the items were from Spain that rubbed the airport officials the wrong way!

The timing of the Gibraltar-London flight was such that we had no option but to spend a night in London to get our flight to Mumbai the next morning. Although we had many friends and family living in London, travelling back and forth just for that one night was not worth it. Anyway, since Vanessa (who was accustomed to the Gibraltar-London-Mumbai run) was accompanying us back to Mumbai from Gibraltar, she organized our stay at the Hilton Hotel which was attached to the airport, but we had to walk quite a distance within the airport complex to reach it.

That evening we dined in the hotel and the next morning we had breakfast in the airport restaurant. There was a family at a nearby table with a two-year child, who kept looking at Joe and tried to draw the attention of her parents, but they kept shushing her. Finally, when we were leaving to get our flight, the little girl once again started shouting and pointing to Joe and this time everyone in the restaurant heard her, 'Look mummy, Santa Claus is going!' loud and clear. The parents were embarrassed but we were amused because it was not the first time something like this had happened. Joe then went up to her, and told her that she was very clever to recognise him while others did not. Then shaking her hand, he slipped into it a large Toblerone he had concealed in his sleeve when he heard her earlier remarks. (After all, you get gifts only if you believe in Santa!) The little girl was delighted beyond words, and this more than made up for the ordeal we had while leaving Gibraltar.

Chapter Twenty

2008
MALAYSIA – TRULY ASIA!
"I got the sun in the morning and the moon at night"

Malaysia was not one of the places on our travel radar but since Joe had to attend a conference in Bali in April, he tried persuading me to accompany him. We decided to use our time-share there and contacted our friends, Jen and Rod Serrell, who now lived on the island of Langkawi. They agreed to join us in Bali, but when we discovered that Joe was not going to be with us for all that time, we changed plans and I dropped out of the Bali trip. Instead, Jen and Rod invited us to visit them in Langkawi, and I agreed to meet Joe in Kuala Lumpur after his conference.

We both travelled on Malaysian Airlines. Joe's ticket Mumbai-KL-Bali-KL-Mumbai cost Rs.34,664, plus a further Rs.1,289 for changing his ticket dates, and another Rs.8,699 for his ticket KL-Langkawi-KL. My ticket Mumbai-KL-Langkawi-KL-Mumbai cost Rs.26,757. Here too, we paid for visas on arrival, but I believe this facility was withdrawn immediately after our trip. Joe's Indonesian visa cost US$10 and our Malaysian ones cost RM100 each.

I didn't know what to expect but I know I did not expect what I actually saw. The airport itself was magnificent and declared the best in the world, with good reason. Malaysia achieved independence in August 1957, ten years after India, but the amazing strides this country has made in a much shorter time, leaves one wondering why India could not have achieved even half as much, at least by way of cleanliness. My first view of Malaysia proper was on the 55-km stretch from the airport to the hotel and I have to say that I was extremely impressed with the wide spaces, lush greenery and the neatly manicured parks we passed.

Joe's stay in Indonesia was taken care of by the XL Foundation, and in Kuala Lumpur we stayed at the Swiss Garden Hotel which we found on the net for a very good rate. Not having slept the previous night, I was extremely tired on arrival and just had to sleep for a few hours before we set out to explore the city. Joe had found a taxi driver and guide – rather he found Joe – who drove us around KL. One of the first places we went to was the ashram founded by Swami Satyananda. Joe was very keen to visit this ashram because of its close association with John Main, the founder of Christian Meditation. Before becoming a Benedictine monk, while in the British Colonial Service, John Main had gone to the ashram on a routine matter in 1954. There he got into a discussion with the swami, whose calm wisdom and aura of peace impressed him. Their conversation touched on meditation and John Main requested Swami Satyananda to teach him his mantra meditation. They meditated together for 18 months. This experience led John Main, through many changing pathways to uncover the ancient Christian tradition of mantra meditation as taught by St. John Cassian, a fourth century ascetic, one of the Desert Fathers and also a Christian theologian known for his writings.

We were privileged to meet the swami's successor, a lady, and be shown around the complex, even though it was closed to visitors at that time. The place had a very serene and peaceful feel. A memorial to the Swami had these words on an open marble book: 'The more the ego is eliminated the nearer man goes to the source of his life'. The Swami had worked closely with Dr. Hans Kung and The Malaysian Inter-Faith Network and I found these words on a poster very meaningful, especially for the India we live in now:

> *No peace among the nations*
> *without peace among the religions*
> *No peace among the religions*
> *without dialogue between the religions*
> *No dialogue between the religions*
> *without global ethical standards*
> *No survival of our globe without a global ethic.*
>
> - Hans Kung

Malaysia is a predominantly Muslim country but KL, like Mumbai, has a mixture of culture and races. Fancy skyscrapers are juxtaposed with beautiful pre-war heritage buildings that range from Moorish to Tudor to modern, all well maintained. The Petronas Twin Towers at a height of 451.9 mts in the city centre dominate the skyline; this is often used as a symbol of Malaysia. Though we saw and experienced a lot in the few days we spent in KL, I'm commenting on just a few.

Istana Negara, the official residence of the King of Malaysia, is a stately mansion set amidst a beautifully landscaped garden. I was fascinated to learn that the Constitution of Malaysia stipulates that a supreme ruler be elected to reign as a Constitutional Monarch for a term of five years. He is referred to as His Majesty the Yang Dipertuan Agong. The Malay Sultanate has existed for more than five centuries and is the nucleus of the system of government. We were in time for the changing of the guards who sit on horses at the two side entrances. When fresh guards arrive on horses, the old ones leave and the new ones enter from each side, cross inside the gates and come to their posts facing outwards. It's amazing how the horses stay perfectly still for hours till it's time for the next change of guards. Unlike Buckingham Palace, where photography with the guards is not encouraged, we could take as many photos as we wanted with guard and horse.

Masjid Negara is the most famous mosque in KL. Instead of the usual round domes this one has a star-shaped dome which represents the 13 States of Malaysia and the five pillars of Islam. It also has a 73-mt high minaret that looks like a needle pointing skywards. The grounds are well landscaped with pools and fountains and there was a nice eating place on a lower level where the Muslims generally eat after their prayers. We had our lunch here before going around to a few more places.

The next day we drove to Malacca (called Melaka in ancient times). It was a two-hour drive from KL. This historical city traces its origins to 1400 when it was founded by an exiled prince from Sumatra and gained fame under the Malacca Sultanate. It's strange how the Portuguese, Dutch and English fought savage wars to capture and control this powerful and prosperous trading post which today is little more than a big tourist attraction.

The main entrance of St. Peter's Roman Catholic Church, which was built in 1710, was shut, but we entered through a side chapel to view the interior. From there we came upon a group of buildings in the town square, which were all painted a bright, *gulabi*, cake pink; included the Anglican Christ Church built in 1753. The cycle trishaws are everywhere and what makes them different is the profusion of coloured artificial flowers which decorate them, as well as the blaring transistor radio music they provide for the passengers. As we walked towards China Street, we passed what looked like a canal in Holland with boats on it, but this did not have as clean a look. In this quarter of the city we also found some very old and quaint buildings right out of the pages of ancient history. We were very tempted to buy a large amethyst grotto from a Chinese shop, but the weight deterred us. Instead we bought a large jade tree which we got at a good price.

On our last day in KL we roamed around the city once more and were fascinated with the rows and rows of palm trees with eye-catching red Barks. We also noticed the different designs of lampposts on the streets. Some even had Malaysia's national flower (hibiscus) on them, and some were delicately curved like the necks of swans. They were a joy to see and they added to the charm of the streets. We also made a quick dash to Putrajaya, a half hour drive from the city. This is the new administrative capital which is famed for its innovative modern building designs. Besides the offices of the Prime Minister, Deputy Prime Minister, the Convention Centre (which looks like an alien spacecraft perched on a hillock) Customs, Income-tax and other offices, the Prime Minister also has his official residence here. This modern city is amazing for its architecture and planning – the buildings all look impressive and are spread out with a spacious feel. All in all, we were happy to have had the opportunity of exploring Kuala Lumpur and its interesting sights and now we were looking forward to more adventures.

LAID-BACK LANKAWI AND MORE
"Oh what a beautiful morning, oh what a beautiful day"

Thailand in the north and Singapore in the south are easily accessible from Malaysia by road, boat or air but we had no plans to visit either of these countries on this trip. Instead, we were about to visit one of the 99 islands that make up the Malay Archipelago. Our flight was in the evening and lasted 55 minutes. We had never heard of Langkawi and we would never have come to visit had it not been for Jenny and Rod who once lived on Chorao Island in Goa, where we too have a home. When they left Chorao they chose to live in Malaysia. They were at the airport when we arrived and drove us to their home in the Perdana Beach Resort, which was a short distance away. Before I forget I must remark on how casual I found the airport. It had a few duty free shops where you could just walk in and buy whatever you wanted, including alcohol (even if you were not travelling out of the island) and when you were travelling, you could check in your baggage, then go home and return in time for your flight.

The legend of Langkawi Island has it that a young woman, Mahsuri, was accused of committing adultery, and though she pleaded innocence, she was publicly executed. As she was dying, she cursed the island with seven generations of bad luck. Well, those seven generations were long since passed and we have no idea whether Langkawi did suffer any bad luck. All we know is that today it is a popular travel destination. In an effort to lure more tourists, Langkawi was also declared a duty free island in 1987 and this sleepy backwater became a bustling tourist destination almost overnight. Hotels sprung up by the dozens, and also plenty of beach resorts, where all kinds of water sports are available. The island also offers many nature-linked activities in delightful locations and again, the prices of liquor, tobacco and chocolate confectionary made shopping on the island more attractive when compared to the mainland.

Rod drove us around the island on our first day, to give us a feel of the place. Thereafter, we made side trips to the island of Rebak (which seems to have been completely taken over by the Rebak Marina Resort) where we spent the day. We also visited the Seven Wells waterfalls, drove across the island to Kuah Town where we shopped at the Billionaire Duty Free shop, and we sampled the fare of many restaurants in the vicinity – in fact, we were amazed to see so many of them on one road alone; these were not small but huge sprawling establishments. We wondered how they survived and whether they attracted sufficient customers to warrant keeping their business running. Jen told me that after our visit, even more have opened shop.

We had scheduled 10 days for our Langkawi visit and during that time, all four of us decided to visit the island of Penang which is located along the west coast of Malaysia and is known to have a rich cultural and historic heritage. Joe and I paid RM502 (about Rs.6,526) for our return flights. On landing, we decided to take a taxi direct to Georgetown, the bustling city of Penang, and for RM108 (Rs.1,416) a night we got very decent accommodation at Hotel Malaysia on Jalan Penang where we stayed two nights. Penang has had many names starting with Tanjung Penaga (from the betel nut trees that grew on the promontory). Sea rovers referred to it as Pulau Ka Satu and this name was retained till the British arrived and changed it to Pulau Pinang or Isle of Betel Nut, though 'Pearl of the Orient' and 'Prince of Wales Island' were the other alternatives.

The story goes that Penang was 'discovered' quite by accident in 1786 by Captain Francis Light who purchased it from the Sultan of Kedah and secured it for the British East India Company (EIC). In return, the Sultan asked for protection from marauding Siamese and Burmese armies. Because of Penang's location on the straits of Malacca, the EIC used it as a strategic base to keep an eye on the Dutch. When Captain Light landed at Fort Cornwallis, it was surrounded by ironwood trees and forested swamps. His short-cut method for clearing up the area was to fire coins out of a cannon into the forest, thus encouraging the local inhabitants who chopped down the vegetation in search of the coins. Now that's what I would call cheap labour!

Georgetown soon developed into a flourishing and busy metropolis and attracted shipping and trading from all over the world. The Chinese from South China were among the first settlers while those from the sub-continent of India were dominated by the Tamils of South India. These were mostly merchants, traders, money lenders or plantation labourers and civil clerks, and even today Penang is noted for its many ethnic minorities and diverse communities. There are Arabs, Achenese, Armenians, Buginese, Burmese, Japanese, Javanese, Minangkabaus, Siamese, Sinhalese, Europeans and Eurasians of mixed ancestries of Portuguese, Dutch, English, Irish, Scottish, French, Italian and German on one hand and Malay, Chinese, Indian, Siamese and Burmese on the other. All of these have co-existed in harmony for generations and all have their own places of worship. However, the city follows distinct Malay and Chinese traditions. After the Second World War and the trauma of the Japanese invasion things were never the same and the shipping trade too slowly dried up. The island began to flourish once again only in the late 1970s with rapid expansion and industrialization.

Tourists are advised to view the historic core of Georgetown on foot or by trishaw to fully appreciate details that are likely to be missed if on a bus tour. We had heard a lot about the Cheong Fatt Tze Mansion-cum-

Museum and since there were fixed times for viewing it, we decided to go there first. It was conveniently located just behind our hotel. In fact, it also functions as a hotel with a limited number of rooms. We tried booking a room on the net, but being popular and much in demand, none were available. The magnificent Chinese courtyard mansion constructed in the 1880s was built with a mix of European architectural elements but otherwise in keeping with traditional Chinese feng shui planning and design. It looked distinguished even from the outside with its indigo blue lime-wash, and was dubbed 'La Maison Bleu'. We had a knowledgeable girl guide to show us around and she explained everything in great fascinating detail. The author of this famous building was an early Chinese immigrant named Cheong Fatt Tze, who typified the rags to riches story. From being penniless at the age of 16, he became the most powerful overseas Chinese merchant and industrialist of his time. He was so famous that when he died in 1916, the British and Dutch authorities ordered that flags be flown at half mast throughout their colonies. This mansion featured in the Oscar-winning movie 'Indo-Chine' starring Catherine Deneuve.

As we were happy with our guide we asked her to show us some other places of interest in Penang the next day, but since some of these were rather far apart, she organized a car to take us around. Apart from touring briefly round Fort Cornwallis, State Assembly Buildings, City Hall, Town Hall and other important places of interest in Georgetown, we asked our guide if she could take us to see the Kek Lok Si Temple that was situated some distance away. This temple is reputed to be the biggest Buddhist temple complex in South-east Asia and was built in 1886. It is located on a hill in a place called Air Itam and contains a 30-metre, seven-storey tall pagoda known as the Pagoda of Ten Thousand Buddhas. What makes this pagoda unique is its blend of Chinese, Burmese and Thai architecture. The temples are spread over several levels and all are dedicated to the Buddha.

I had no idea that Penang was regarded as the food capital of Malaysia, but having been a cultural melting pot for over 200 years, the local cuisine is heavily influenced by Malay, Chinese, Indian and Thai flavours. Jen and Rod had enjoyed Indian food in India so for their sakes we opted to go to a restaurant named 'Little India' which was run by Tamilians. Throughout our stay in Malaysia we had sampled only western food and tried Malay food just once in Langkawi; I found it very spicy and difficult to get through. As Joe and I are not 'foodies' I have not focused on food during our travels.

Back in Langkawi we took a boat ride around the island. It was really exhilarating, especially when we speeded out into the open sea, in what the boatman told us were Bangkok waters. Once when it appeared as if we would crash into a bank of rocks at high speed, he turned to smile at us after giving us a scare and then neatly manoeuvred the boat through a hidden space in the rocks. At another he managed to take the boat into a low cave, which was a feat in itself as the top of our boat just about scraped the ceiling of the cave.

While driving around Langkawi, you could sometimes believe you were in the countryside of Goa with its laid-back lifestyle and extensive open stretches. The one constant about the Malay climate was its consistently hot daytime temperatures that made me a little uncomfortable, though living in Mumbai should have acclimatized us to the heat. We had most of our meals at the many restaurants in Langkawi, and on our last night we dined at one on the Perdana Quay. It reminded us so much of Gibraltar as it was located near the waterside and had a lovely ambience.

Our packed fortnight in Malaysia was finally at an end. Jen and Rod had exchanged one island paradise of Chorao for another on Langkawi and they were happy there and we were happy for them.

NEW YORK, NEW YORK!
"I want to be a part of it …"

With both daughters living abroad and away from us, it is natural that we made more visits to the countries where they resided, and hence the repeated trips to New York and London. Visiting either of the daughters is like transferring from one home to another so somehow we don't think of doing too many 'touristy' things and just go with the flow. Come to think of it, we have not seen all the interesting sights of Mumbai as yet! It is only when we have friends coming from abroad that it becomes an occasion for us to also visit some of these places. If I'm not much mistaken I think this is the case for most other people too. I mean, how many take the time or trouble to see the places of interest in their own home towns?

In June we were back in America for the sixth time. We had bought tickets to travel on British Airways, and our two Mumbai-New York-London-Mumbai tickets cost us a whopping Rs.1,21,244 this time. I left on 9 June while Joe followed two weeks later, and we had 'full house' when Vanessa and Sanjay also completed the family circle on their way to and from San Francisco where Sanjay's work took him. Plans to go to Mexico, Arizona and Florida were tossed around, but in the end, only Joe went off to Los Angeles for a few days while I stayed put in NY devoting some time to the various family trees that I was working on, but the biggest time waster was the TV.

When in Mumbai I complain of our busy lifestyle which leaves little time to relax. Now that I was on the other side of the fence, I missed my busy bustle and was waiting to come back! Of course, I was happy to be with family but sitting idle without doing anything useful, '*dolce far niente*', is just not my cup of tea. There were breaks for beach outings, trips to Manhattan and Times Square, a visit to a posh seniors' home to meet with my friend Joan O'Donnell, occasional get-togethers, and the new experience of going to a street party. One of the challenges there was to hold your mouth under a slab of ice while someone poured whisky over the ice and let it slide down directly into your mouth. I was cheered for trying it out and was also gifted a bottle opener!

Every time I was in the States, Kerman had tried to get me tickets for an Engelbert Humperdinck concert, but somehow my visits just did not coincide with Englebert's concert dates. To make up, Kerman booked tickets for Joe and me to a Tom Jones concert in Atlantic City, and all five of us made the long drive there one evening. Our seats were not up front but somewhere in the middle. It felt a little claustrophobic being clustered together with others so tightly. Although they were not planning to be at the concert, once it began, Kerman managed to get three more tickets at a much discounted price and so they phoned and told us to join them. Their seats were at the back but on a higher level where the view was much better. Besides the singing sensation, we were treated to even more entertainment. I've heard about people in audiences screaming and going crazy over the singers, but now we were experiencing it for the first time. It was more the older women who were making a spectacle of themselves dancing and singing in the aisles. Some younger ones made bold to climb onto the stage and had to be taken off by security. The shocking part for me was the way they kept slinging various undergarments at Tom Jones which he pretended not to notice. One of the women sitting right next to us with someone, who must have been her husband or boyfriend, calmly got up and went down the aisle. I watched her as she walked right up to the stage and flung something onto it; it had to be an undergarment because those were the only 'bouquets' being flung at the singer. Whatever happened to decency and good manners?

We love going to Broadway shows but the price of even the cheapest seats is over US$60, and so we have to ration this entertainment. This time we decided on 'Mama Mia', though I wasn't sure how good it would be. It turned out very entertaining and I'm so glad we went to see the play. What terrific acting and fantastic singing, especially by the main star. She got a spontaneous standing ovation after she had sung 'The Winner Takes it All', which had my hair standing on edge when she held that last high note. We also loved 'Mama Mia', the movie with Meryl Streep, which we keep watching over again, but I'd still say that the play won hands down.

During our stay in New York, Melissa joined Jet Airways their corporate office, which was located in New Jersey. The long commute and job were stressful and tiring but she learnt to adjust and was soon able to enjoy her work. However, we saw much less of her after that as she often returned quite late at night. I had stayed in New York for almost two months making the most of my lazy time there. Joe enjoyed his rambles visiting places to find interesting gadgets that he was unlikely to find in India.   On 4 August we both left for London. Having already met up with Vanessa and Sanjay in New York, we set aside only three weeks to spend with them.

SHORT AND SWEET
"Memories, light the corners of my mind ..."

Vanessa and Sanjay had moved from their lovely old Victorian house in Ealing to a beautiful and fancy apartment in Richmond (all their homes were fancy – and I'm not saying this to show off ... okay, I am, just a little!). Richmond was the obvious choice as Sanjay's office was also located there, close to the Thames promenade, which we had visited in 2006. Their home was close to another bend in the Thames, and Sanjay took to cycling to work along the tow path. We too often went for long walks along this shady path that was much used by cyclists, joggers and dog-walkers.

Soon after arriving in London we met up with Horace and Joan Rodricks and their daughter, Dawn. Dawn had seen Vanessa on Facebook and wrote to say that since they were both 'Rodrigues' (though the spelling was different) she wondered if they might be related. Vanessa then wrote to me to check if she featured in the Rodrigues family tree that she knew I had been compiling. When I confirmed this, Dawn was thrilled, also because she and Vanessa were about the same age and they were both living in London. I then made contact with Dawn on Facebook, and she promptly invited us over for dinner – this, without even consulting her parents, who later told us they were quite aghast at what she had done because they had no idea who we were. I am not going into the detailed history of how we are related except to mention that the common ancestor was Braz Rodrigues, who was the grandfather of Horace, and Joe's great grandfather. Somewhere along the line, one of Horace's ancestors had changed the spelling of the name to 'Rodricks' while another branch had changed it to 'Rodericks' (this being more English than the original Portuguese spelling).

It was a long and expensive taxi ride from Richmond to Farnborough. I had brought along some copies of the preliminary incomplete tables I had compiled on the Rodrigues family tree to give to Horace and family. Naturally the talk went back to the old days and our common ancestors, and we ended up having a lovely time. Horace and Joan have a beautiful home and were very gracious hosts. We felt at home right away and it did not seem like we had met for the first time. Horace is the man with the green thumb and we were very impressed with his well-maintained neat garden and lawn in which he takes great pride, while Joan served up a delicious and fancy meal we all thoroughly enjoyed. That was the first of many meetings in the years that followed.

Although we had just three weeks in England, Sanjay and Vanessa still made time to take us to Berlin over a long weekend.

CLEAR ACROSS THE BERLIN WALL
"I'm off to see the world …
there's such a lot of world to see"

The very name 'Berlin' brought to mind World War II, Hitler, the Berlin Wall and the sufferings and deaths of millions of people. But we had also heard about all the beautiful places in Germany and hoped one day to visit some of those hamlets. We left on 14 August and took the KLM flight via Amsterdam. After a 30-minute taxi ride from Tegel International Airport, we reached the Hilton Berlin Hotel where we had booked rooms. This was located in the historic Gendarmenmarkt area. The name 'Gendarmenmarkt' dates back to the Napoleonic occupation of the city and was once part of East Germany. In the neoclassical square opposite our hotel, there were two similarly designed buildings, the French and German cathedrals, one on either side of the Square, with the Konzerthaus (Concert Hall), home of the Berlin Symphony Orchestra, between the two. This was a favourite tourist spot.

The next morning we booked ourselves on the Stadtrundfahrten Sightseeing bus tour of Berlin City. There were 15 stops along the route and ear phones on each seat that allowed you to follow what you were seeing. You could stay on the bus for the entire tour or hop on and off when you wanted to stop longer at any particular place. It was difficult to spell or pronounce some names so I didn't try too hard to remember all the places we passed. Of course we were most interested in the infamous Berlin Wall, so we alighted at Checkpoint Charlie, which is one of the great tourist attractions. This name was given by the Western Allies to the point of crossing between East and West Berlin during the Cold War. There were other sector crossing points between the East and West, but Checkpoint Charlie was the only crossing point for foreigners and members of the Allied forces by foot or car. The East Germans looked upon Checkpoint Charlie as a gateway to freedom, and many movies on the war and about spies featured this section.

We had heard and read about many daring escape stories from East to West Berlin after the Wall was constructed. In the early days when the Russians had not thought of many factors, escape was easier, but they made it practically impossible later. In November 1989 when the wall was finally opened up, Checkpoint Charlie remained the official crossing for foreigners and diplomats. It was only in October 1990, at the time East and West Germany were reunited that the guardhouse was removed. As Checkpoint Charlie continues to be a great tourist attraction, a replica of the guardhouse was re-erected at the same spot together with sandbags stacked in front of it and visitors love to pose there with the guards.

Close to the guard house at Checkpoint Charlie is a private museum, which was opened in 1963. It portrayed the desperation of the people who were ready to try any means to escape from their tyrannical rulers. Because of Hitler and his atrocities the world directed their hatred against Germany but there were many innocent Germans who needlessly suffered in the process. After the war, their sufferings continued under the Soviets who were supposed to be their liberators. There is an open-air exhibition of art painted directly on the last existing portions of the Berlin Wall, known as the East Side Gallery. It is the largest remaining evidence of Berlin's division. Throughout the city you will see a double brick line which now marks the course of the former wall, and we kept crossing it often. We got back on the bus to complete the tour before we finally stepped off at Kurfurstendamm to have lunch. After that we strolled around, window shopping on this grand boulevard which is flanked by fashionable shops, sidewalk cafes, theatres, hotels and night clubs, and Europe's largest department store, KaDeWe.

The next morning we were booked on a trip to Potsdam, which became popular when it was chosen as the hunting residence of Frederick William I in 1660. Later it was chosen as the residence of the Prussian royal family and remained the residence of the Prussian kings till 1918. Located on the River Havel, it is 25 kms southwest from the centre of Berlin city, about a 30-minute drive away. The first sight that greeted us as we got off the coach was a large windmill located in the immediate vicinity of the Sans Souci Palace. Legend has it that King Frederick I was annoyed by the noise the windmill made and tried everything in his power to shut it down. He first offered to buy the mill but when the miller refused, the king told him that he had the power to take it without paying for it. The miller is said to have responded, 'With all due respect, your majesty, you would have that power if it weren't for the Supreme Court in Berlin.' Thus, because of a newly introduced balance of power, the miller was the first commoner in German history to win a case against royalty. But stories often get twisted in the telling. An account does exist of a miller and the king going to Court, but it was the other way round; it was the miller who sued the king, complaining that the palace blocked the wind for the mill. The king had to buy a new mill elsewhere for the miller in 1787. The king then decided that he liked the mill and said it added a certain rural ambience to the place, so it remained as a historic monument. Unfortunately, at the end of World War II, it was hit by a Russian bazooka and burned down. So the one we saw was the one built and completed in 1991, which now forms part of the Park and Palace of the Sans Souci World Heritage Site.

I read somewhere that Potsdam is to Germany what Windsor is to England, but this comparison is not about size.   I have seen the enormous Windsor Castle in London from inside and out, and Sans Souci Palace is nowhere near its size.   However, the grounds (consisting of parks and many palaces) of Sans Souci are the largest World Heritage site. These vast grounds contain other royal residences like the Neues Palais, the Orangery, the Chinese Tea House and more, and are so vast that between Sans Souci and the New Palace, it was a 2-km walk on a beautiful tree-lined pathway, interspersed with fountains and many marble sculptures.

Although the work of landscaping the royal grounds of Potsdam began in the 17th century by Frederick I, it was his son, Frederick II (known as Frederick the Great), who built all the majestic royal residences.   We concentrated on visiting the famous Sans Souci Palace.   The French words 'sans souci' mean 'without cares or worries', and Frederick so named it because here he could leave behind the pomp and protocol of the royal court in Berlin and have time for his hobbies: music and philosophy. He made it clear that this was his place of relaxation and not a seat of power.   The palace has 12 beautifully decorated Rococo-style rooms. Though based on the style of the French Baroque Versailles Palace, this large single-storey, elongated structure is more like a villa.   It has floor-to ceiling windows that look out on one side towards a semi-circular colonnade, beyond which, in the distance, is a hill with artificial Roman ruins. On the other side, a grand terraced vineyard takes up an area several times the size of the palace itself, descending towards a central road which connects the various palaces in the park.

Frederick's childhood and growing-up years were very sad with a strict authoritarian, ill-tempered father who was known to strike men in the face with his cane and kick women in the street, justifying this as religious righteousness.   His mother was well-mannered and well-educated and belonged to the family from which England's present royal family are descended. Many marriage alliances were proposed for Frederick, who was finally persuaded to marry a relative of the Habsburgs. However, he saw his wife just once a year, preferring to hide himself at Potsdam with a group of intimate friends, including Voltaire. It is said there were violent and public quarrels with these friends; in fact, he even encouraged rumours of his homosexuality. As soon as he became king in 1740, he prevented his wife from visiting his court there, but despite his treatment of her, she remained devoted to him.

Frederick desired to be buried at his favourite Potsdam palace and wanted a burial at night, without pomp, on one of the terraces. But that was not to be for a long time. First interred in the garrison church in Potsdam, his body was moved to many different locations over many years. His remains were finally returned to Potsdam in 1991 when the reunification of Germany took place. After an official lying in state at the Court of Honour of Sans Souci palace, he was finally laid to rest, alongside his favourite greyhounds, on his beloved terrace overlooking the gardens he had created. The palace became a tourist attraction after World War II. For a king who was called 'the Great', he had a very simple grave and the only inscription on the square slab of light brown stone reads 'Friedrich Der Grosse.' It had a single rose on it together with a few potatoes. We were surprised to hear that Frederick was referred to as the 'Potato King'. This was because of his efforts to introduce widespread potato farming in Germany, which helped to avoid famine after the Seven Years War. At first, the people were suspicious of the tuber so Frederick used the psychology of planting a royal field of potatoes, which he kept under armed guard. Assuming that anything worth guarding is worth stealing, the local peasants found ways to sneak in and take the plants for their own gardens – thus beginning the popularity of potatoes in Germany. Visitors now regularly leave flowers and potatoes on his grave.

On Sunday we attended mass at St. Hedwig's Cathedral and then walked towards the Unter den Linden that led to the famous Brandenburg Gate. The Brandenberg Tor (as it is called in German), is one of the main symbols of Berlin and Germany, even appearing on their coins. It was installed in 1793 and was formerly one of the city gates. Its design is based on the gateway to the Acropolis in Athens and consists of 12 Doric columns, six on each side, to form five passageways. Gracing the top is the Quadriga, a chariot drawn by four horses driven by Victoria, the Roman goddess of victory. When the Nazis came to power they used the Gate as a party symbol. The Gate was one of the few structures that survived World War II, but after the construction of the Berlin Wall, it formed part of East Germany. It was through this Gate that Helmut Kohl, the West German Chancellor walked and was greeted by the East German prime minister. Today the Gate stands as a symbol of the reunification of the two sides of this city.

In Goa there is a road named '18 June Road'. In Berlin there is one named 'Strasse des 17 Juni' or '17 June Road', which commemorates the uprisings in East Berlin of 17 June 1953. I wonder if one day there'll be a road somewhere named '11 June Road' for me! The 17 June Road is a continuation of the Unter den Linden and runs through the Tiergarten, a large forest park west of the city centre. In the last weeks of World War II, when Berlin's airports were unusable, this road served as a landing strip for the Nazis. Most of Berlin's historic landmarks are clustered around the Potsdammer Platz and the Brandenberg Gate. The Reichstag is the largest of these. It housed the German parliament and was the last stand for the German Army who fought on literally retreating from one room to the next. As a result, the building is scarred with bullet holes. The German soldiers were unaware that Hitler had already committed suicide in his bunker, which was just a few hundred meters away. Over 2000 Russian soldiers lost their lives trying to take over this building. We would have loved to enter and see the place in detail but the clouds were gathering and it had begun to rain. We darted into a shop selling touristy stuff and thought we would wait out the rain but in the end we hopped into a taxi and went back to our hotel where we freshened up, picked up our luggage and left for the airport to catch our flight back to London.

With my limited knowledge of East and West Germany, I had always imagined the East side to be poor and decrepit, and so it was found to be when the Wall was brought down. The East German government had taken care to maintain only the big and famous monuments while neglecting the rest of the city. After reunification it was an uphill task to bring the East up to the standard of the West. Some say it will never be the same or as classy as the West, but frankly, I did not find much of a difference. The destruction of that infamous Wall not only brought freedom to the people of the East but also gave the world an opportunity to see sights that were kept hidden for years.

IT'S ALWAYS A RAINY DAY!
"Lucky, lucky, lucky me ..."

Back in London, Sanjay and Vanessa treated us to three plays. We finally saw 'The Lion King'. Having seen the movie I wondered how the play would be enacted, thinking it would be meant more for children, but we found it totally amazing. Every character performed beautifully – having to not only sing and dance, but also keep on acting, sometimes in a crouched position, while holding a mask. I really cannot describe this fantastic musical, except to say, if you get a chance, go see it. Now we realized why it was running for such a long time on Broadway, and here too at the West End.

When we had booked tickets to see George Bernard Shaw's 'Pygmalion' at the Old Vic, a very old world theatre, we expected it to be entertaining but we were disappointed with the acting. The main character playing Henry Higgins overdid his part and walked almost with a slouch, while the girl playing Eliza Doolittle did not have even a bit of the spark of Audrey Hepburn and behaved more like a school marm. In fact, it was almost like watching a school play. The third play we saw was at Trafalgar Studios, called 'Fat Pig'. This was a modern drama with, yes, a fat girl who falls in love with a handsome guy. The relationship works for some time, till his friends intervene to make fun and he is embarrassed, especially when they are spending a day at the beach. Not a 'happy ending' drama but a change from the other plays we had seen.

On our last night in England we went to Whitechapel. This was not considered a nice area to be in late at night (wasn't this place made famous by Jack the Ripper?) but we were going to have dinner at the famous Tayab's restaurant. It was a small place run by Pakistanis and full of whites lapping up the kebabs, chicken tikkas and curries. Like in Udipi restaurants in India, the tables were all crowded together and one could hardly move between them. We had literally to wait in line to be seated and could not linger over the meal as there were others waiting to take our place. We were more fortunate to get seating in an inner, less crowded room. It was a great meal, but not spectacular for us since we could have our fill of these delicacies back home at any time.

We left London on 23 August and were back in India at midnight. I count myself fortunate to have had opportunities of visiting so many people and places and enjoying the hospitality of our many friends and family. I'll adapt that well-known saying, 'It is better to have loved and lost than never to have loved at all', to suit my thought: 'It is better to have used our money well, than saving it for a rainy day that may never come'. I'm an adventurer – who knows what the future holds for us!

Chapter Twenty-one

2009
JOYS AND SORROWS UNLIMITED
"But there's one thing I know
the blues they send to meet me won't defeat me,
it won't be long till happiness steps up to greet me"

I had decided to put 'finis' to this travelogue which I had begun so many years earlier, with the events of 2008, but as we continued to travel so much, there was scarcely time to attend to the editing and the publishing aspects. Still with just one trip to the Northeast planned for April this year, I had great hopes of wrapping it all up by the end of 2009.

In January, however, we started major home renovations that turned our lives upside down. In fact with the dust, the exertions and mainly the stresses, I fell ill and had to be hospitalized. Then there was a scramble to make at least one part of the house habitable for both our daughters and our granddaughter who said they would be landing up here at the end of February. Work could be resumed only after they left, and continued for several weeks. Then just when we were settling down to devote the coming months solely to the travelogue, our daughter in England announced that she was expecting – and wanted us to be there for the birth of their first baby!

We had already re-scheduled our visit to the Northeast for July, and now we pushed it further back to October. On our last visit to Mirik (West Bengal) in 2005, we had promised to return, but though three years had passed, we had not made good on our promise. Now Fr. Mathew Pulingathil was delighted to hear that we had included Mirik in our itinerary for 2009 as he was keen to show us the new constructions and other remarkable changes in their institution. For us, the main reason was to meet our good friend, the inimitable Fr. Luigi Jellici.

Before leaving for London at the end of July, I made the travel arrangements for all our internal journeys in October. The baby was due in early August but we wanted to give ourselves at least a week to settle in before the great event. At short notice, Melissa, who was by then working in the Corporate Office of Jet Airways in New Jersey, arranged for complimentary tickets, and would not even let us pay the taxes. Our two UK visas cost Rs.11,600, and overseas insurance for 63 days worked out to another Rs.12,282 for both.

On 7 August, well before dawn, Vanessa checked into St. Mary's Hospital in Paddington, while Joe and I stayed home in Richmond, keeping in constant touch with Sanjay by phone. Vanessa was fortunate to have her gynaecologist and obstetrician, the noted Harley Street Consultant, Mr. Charles Wright, in attendance. I thought he looked a lot like Kenny Rogers. The hours passed and it appeared almost certain that she would need a C-section but the doctor decided on one last attempt at natural childbirth. On hearing this we redoubled our prayers. In the labour room, music selected by Vanessa and Sanjay was playing and it was precisely when the Gayatri Mantra started that our little grandchild made her appearance, which is one reason she is called 'Gayatri' (Gaia for short).

We could not get to Paddington fast enough. What a delight it was to hold that little bundle of curiosity and watch her expressions! She was already so alert and kept bobbing her head back and forth as those beautiful eyes seemed to take in everything around her while we had to hold on tightly to make sure she did not squirm out of our arms. I don't know whether it is due to evolution of the human race or some other factors, but babies today seem to be quite different. When we were young we saw other babies who remained still, with eyes tightly shut and slept for 22 hours; they only woke for feeds or nappy changes. It would scarcely surprise me if, in some future generation, the newborn enters the world already speaking its first words!

When we were leaving the hospital a few days later, one of the matrons asked if we knew which room Vanessa had been assigned. We were surprised to hear that it was the very room Princess Diana had occupied when she delivered Prince William and later Prince Harry. Well, that was some royal connection for our little princess!

Four days after the happy event, we got the sad news that Fr. Luigi Jellici had passed away peacefully on 11 August. I wept at his demise as I recalled that wonderful, good-humoured and holy man. He and his family had become close to us and I felt very sad when I realized that we would not be seeing him again. He often joked about how he prayed to God that he would 'die young, but not for a long time'! He surely got his wish for he remained irrepressibly young at heart till his passing at the age of 94!

The arrival of Melissa and Kerissa from New York helped to take our minds off the sad event. We were now house-full and baby Gayatri got more than her share of fuss and attention. While the New Yorkers were there, Joe and I decided to make a quick dash to Scotland, mainly to pay our respects at the grave of our other dear friend, Fr. Gerry Prior. We left on 17 August taking the National Express coach from Victoria to Edinburgh. Jim Fraser came to pick us up from the coach station and drove us back to their charming farmhouse in Pencaitland. It was a joyful reunion with Fr. Gerry's sister, Lynn. Their daughter, Cissy, was in bed so we met her only the next morning. She was a friendly, happy-go-lucky child and I never once heard her whine or cry needlessly. She shared a great companionship with their large dog, Jess, and also with their neighbour, Emily, who was older than her.

Fr. Gerry's parish was in West Lothian, and Pencaitland was in East Lothian, which was about 12 miles southeast of Edinburgh city. Lynn and Jim's house was once part of a large farm and a little isolated from the rest of the village, with just one close neighbour. Jim made time to drive us around the village and I was thrilled to find a few 'goodwill' stores which always attracted me. I know that many people who live in England (and even America) are mortified to be seen walking into one of them. Joe and I found them treasure troves and we enjoyed foraging in them. In fact, these shops are the best places today for the old porcelain dolls that I was collecting, and I picked up two very beautiful ones in Pencaitland for just £6 each. They were brand new. You might also find some fantastic books at these shops. Items people do not want or have no use for, end up being donated to such charity shops. We once bought a brand new baby book and going through it at home, we found a cheque for quite a large sum evidently meant for the new baby. Without even being flipped open, the book had been given away, cheque and all! Of course the cheque was many years old and no good to anyone.

Agnes Prior, Gerry's mother, came to meet us in Pencaitland and she took us to the Mount Vernon Catholic Cemetery where Gerry had been laid to rest. We could not help shedding tears as we remembered our friend's bubbly and fun-loving nature, mulling over the cruel fate that had snatched him away at such an early age. Lynn, who was as devastated as her parents by her brother's death, had kept a little sailboat on his grave, a mute reminder of the promise Gerry had made to take her sailing one day, but did not live to do so. Later, we sent two marble candlesticks to be placed on the grave. Lynn told us that when Gerry announced one Christmas that he had bought a cemetery plot for his parents, they were over the moon with delight. To many of us it may seem very strange that someone would be thrilled to get a grave as a Christmas gift but these plots are actually very expensive and not easy to purchase. The irony was that Gerry was the first to be interred there, and his father, Owen Prior, followed a few years later. We also missed meeting Owen on this trip and listening to his warm and oft repeated welcomes. Agnes insisted on treating us to lunch and then she took us home for a cup of tea, after which she spontaneously gave us a picture frame with Gerry's photo. Today, the only two pictures in our home that are not of our immediate family are of Fr. Gerry and Fr. Luigi.

We were back in Richmond by 20 August and we enjoyed the remaining 10 days with the whole family together except for Kerman. Melissa and Kerissa returned to New York by the end of August, but Melissa could not resist coming back for a second quick visit in September, taking advantage of her free flights and a long weekend. And since she was around to help out, Joe and I once again took the opportunity of dashing over to Southampton to meet our friends Bash and Asha. This time too we travelled by the National Express Coach, setting out in the morning and returning by evening. We could spend only a few hours with them but it was worth the effort to renew old ties and especially to see how their two little boys had grown into tall young men!

The autumn trees were ablaze with colour and Nature was orchestrating a glorious display for us to enjoy before slowly closing shop to take her long winter nap. The weather was already getting cooler, but with Gaia to dote over, the days passed quickly. Before we knew it, September drew to a close and we flew back to Mumbai with sweet memories of the delightful new addition to our family.

Chapter Twenty-two

2009-2011
THE TIMES THEY ARE A-CHANGING
"I'm going back someday, come what may to ..."

Two weeks after getting back from London in 2009, we were on our way again to the Northeast. I'm keeping to a very few details in this chapter. We had been to Nagaland several times, but so far we had never been to Sechu-Zubza, a village that lies between Dimapur and Kohima in the foothills of the Himalayas. It was named for the nearby river Zubza, (the anglicized corruption of the native 'Dzuza'). Adding the prefix 'Sechu' was part of the cost of expanding the village by acquiring land from the neighbouring village of Sechu. The village does not differ much from other villages in Nagaland but a fairly large army base is located there. I found it strange that despite this army presence, the road that led to their quarters was in a deplorable condition. Possibly the force of the rain water gushing down the mountains was responsible for the large exposed boulders, which made it quite a feat to manoeuvre any vehicle. The stretch from the army HQ to the Don Bosco novitiate, which is located higher up the mountain, was in an even worse condition and it felt like we were on a roller coaster! But the view from the novitiate made the bone-rattling ascent worthwhile. The short time we were in Sechu-Zubza was spent in conducting an intensive seminar for the novices of the Salesians and FMA societies. It was very fulfilling to work with such simple and sincere persons who were able to grasp the most profound truths without getting entangled in sophisticated intellectualizing. At the close they presented us with two beautiful traditional shawls and a set of embroidered table covers.

On the one free day we had, Fr. MP took us on a long rambling drive to Khonoma and a few other surrounding villages for short visits. Khonoma is a 400-year old village which is endowed with rich forest cover and is known as the 'Green Village' in Nagaland. Located 20 kms from Kohima, Khonoma was once a Naga stronghold, and when the British infiltrated the Naga Hills in 1879, the Naga warriors fought back valiantly. The imposing Naga structure at the entrance to the village commemorates their last stand. It is said that the soil here is of a unique variety. That, combined with the elevation of the land, has resulted in 20 types of rice being grown here on extensive terraces carved out of the hill slopes.

Sechu-Zubza was new to us and we were enchanted by its serenity and peaceful isolation. We were already thinking of accepting the invitation to return the next year! When we left this quaint village, it was in the company of Fr. MP as we went on to our next destination – another first for us, the Kaziranga Wildlife Sanctuary, where we met up with Fr. Joseph Thelekkatt and Sanjay Aggarwal, who arrived from Guwahati that same evening. Sanjay was an ex-student of Don Bosco's, Guwahati, and was always there to lend a helping hand. Fr. Joseph told us that Sanjay had arranged for our overnight stay at the Sanctuary. We all checked into a nice fancy lodge with comfortable rooms and had a pleasant evening together.

Early the next morning, we set off in a safari jeep and were surprised to find that we had to drive a great distance from our lodge, which was part of the National Park, to the actual safari locale. The Kaziranga Sanctuary stretches for 40 kms from east to west and 13 kms from north to south, covering an area of approximately 629 sq. kms. This vast expanse of tall elephant grass, marshlands and moist tropical forests is crisscrossed by four major rivers, including the Brahmaputra. Two-thirds of the world's great one-horned rhinos are to be found here as also the largest number of tigers in a protected area, not to mention large populations of elephant, wild water buffalo, swamp deer and varieties of birds. This prior information gave us so much to expect that our excitement peaked at the thought that we were finally and actually in Kaziranga, but we were doomed to disappointment. Except for a couple of rhinos in the very far distance, and a few deer, we did not catch sight of any other creature. From the fresh dung we saw in various spots, we knew that the animals were there all right, but as the tall grasses had not yet been cut they all remained very well camouflaged. Joe and I were consoled that we had had marvellous sightings during our African safari (2007). After returning to our lodge, we had a substantial breakfast and left for Guwahati, sad to say good-bye to Fr. MP, who returned to Sechu-Zubza. Ironically, on the drive to Guwahati, from the highway we spotted many rhinos and elephants quite close to the boundaries.

LEGACIES OF LOVE
"So it's the laughter we will remember,
whenever we remember, the way we were"

On 26 October we boarded the Rajdhani at Guwahati and were on our way to Mirik once more. Fr. Mathew Pulingathil timed his arrival perfectly and walked onto the platform just as our train had pulled in. The transformation that had taken place in Mirik since our last visit was a very pleasant surprise. There was a spanking new residential section, a well designed chapel and a very elite school in place of the old dilapidated building. But more about this later.

The next day we left early and drove for two and a half hours to Sonada to visit the grave of Fr. Luigi and pay him our respects. Then after breakfast at the college, we drove to Darjeeling, which took another hour because of bad roads. And when I write 'bad', I mean really very bad! We were told that this was a direct fallout of political wrangling and indulging in blame games. I won't judge whether this was true or false. All we could see for sure was that the common man suffered the consequences. Darjeeling is now so overpopulated and noisy and full of shops and wayside stalls burgeoning onto the roads that we have vowed never to go back. After lunch at Darjeeling's iconic Glenary's we drove another two and a half hours to Dhajea on winding roads that were also bad. Dhajea was a favourite haunt of Fr. Luigi and he often wrote to me saying that when he retired (as if he ever would!) he would do so in Dhajea.

The next day was more restful. We went on a detailed tour, first of the new house, and then of the school. We could see that a lot of care and planning had gone into the designing and construction. It looked imposing from the outside, and the interiors were no less remarkable, with spacious offices, meeting rooms and comfortable guest rooms. The new chapel too was a welcoming place of prayer. The school was a totally new construction with every modern amenity. There were computer rooms, labs, an all-faiths prayer room, a beautiful large auditorium, large basketball courts and playing fields, and just about everything one could hope to have in a high class school. Fr. V.C. Jose, the Principal, was the brain behind most of this, backed of course by the funds brought in by Fr. Luigi's unstinting efforts on his various 'begging' trips to Italy, while Fr. Mathew stood behind the entire project wholeheartedly. At one time not many people aspired to have their children study at the simple Don Bosco School in Mirik and preferred the other more elite ones in the area. Now there was a clamour to get admission in the new school, but we were thrilled to hear that the criterion for admission was that the child had to come from a poor family. And to ensure that nobody cheated, the priests actually trudged the long distances to their homes to check the economic status of each child's family.

The long awaited Letter of Recognition of the School by the West Bengal Education Department had arrived just about the time the new House and School were being blessed. It was the crowning joy of all those who had worked long and hard on the project. The House has been dedicated to the memory of Fr. Luigi Jellici, who unfortunately passed away before the work was completed. However, he did have the satisfaction of seeing it take shape and also seeing two other legacies of his love – beautiful churches built for the villagers of Gopaldhara and Busty.

He was indeed resting in peace.

TEA FOR TWO AND FOUR FOR TEA
"Oh give me a home where the 'elephants' roam"

Visiting the Northeast of India and going to more exotic places each time is getting to be a good habit!   In 2011 we paid Rs.16,472 for both our return tickets Mumbai-Guwahati-Mumbai, which we took care to book early on the internet. We had first planned to be out for only two weeks in the first half of October as we were scheduled to leave for Dublin and New York soon after.   However, when Fr. Joseph Thelekkatt heard that we were coming again, he organized a string of seminars that he wanted us to conduct so we agreed and instead delayed our departure for Dublin.

As a special treat, Fr. Joseph had arranged with Sanjay Aggarwal, whom I have mentioned earlier, to take us for an overnight stay to the Badlapara Tea Estate and Gardens, and we were looking forward to this. Joe and I arrived in Guwahati on 30 September and the very next afternoon Sanjay drove us and Fr. Joseph through a long-winded, often dusty route, through many villages and towns. We stopped for lunch on the way and later enjoyed the hospitality of the Don Bosco School at Dimakuchi. Sanjay then drove a little off course just to show us a special tree, the branches and leaves of which had spread so far out that they were said to cover an area of almost one acre.   It was amazing to look at. Under it were gathered hordes, of mainly women with very colourful attire. Apparently they were tea pickers and were there to collect their weekly wages which were being dispensed under this huge tree. The scene reminded me so much of R.K. Narayan's 'The Financial Expert', a story I really enjoyed.

We reached the Tea Estate by evening, before the manager, Mr. Koushik Paul, had returned from work. He had left instructions with his many servants, and of course Sanjay was also a regular visitor there, so we were shown up to our rooms to freshen up. The size of this house, the wide verandas and the sprawling grounds brought to mind the days of colonial grandeur. In fact, it was a Scotsman, the then manager of the place, who had constructed this mansion for himself, probably in the 19th century, and even at that time, it had cost a fortune as he had imported a lot of material from England and Scotland. By the time his superiors realized the extent of his extravagance it was too late so they recalled him and then probably sacked him. I presume it is from the time the Badlapara Tea Company bought the estate, that the Senior Manager has since been allotted this house for himself and his family. We were led up a wide carpeted wooden staircase to an air-conditioned bedroom on the first floor. In size it rivalled the carpet area of an entire large one-bedroom flat in Mumbai. The bed itself was in a room-within-a-room, with floor-to-ceiling 'walls' of mosquito netting. The rest of the room had comfortable sofas, a TV, a writing desk, and more space than an average Mumbaite could ever hope to have in a 'bedroom'. The bathroom was separate from the dressing room, which were both large rooms in themselves.

Koushik's wife, Nazima, who belonged to the Karbi Anglong tribe, had gone to Delhi to visit one of their two daughters who was studying there. The other girl was in a school in Guwahati. Though she could not be home during our visit, she had taken great care to provide for our stay, keeping everything she thought we would need, from soap to creams, shampoos to oil, shaving kit to perfumes, etc. The extent of her graciousness could be seen throughout the house that was tastefully decorated with interesting do-dads and artifacts, and so well maintained. With Koushik's arrival, we all got together in the vast high-ceilinged living room while the servants wheeled in a trolley laden with a tea service, cookies and Indian sweets, which they automatically brought to me, the only lady around, to dispense as is the custom. Later they wheeled in another trolley with drinks and more snacks. We had a lovely evening together conversing on various topics till dinner was served, again in a huge dining room. It was agreed that we would go round the tea gardens the next morning so we were off to bed soon after.

The next morning, we strolled around the gardens for some time. Nazima was a great connoisseur of plants and flowers, having won many prizes for her exotic blooms. The gardens and innumerable pots around the veranda were evidence of this. She had even cultivated a large vegetable garden that produced enough for their table. The elephants that roam around the tea gardens frequented them often. Instead of angrily chasing them away as most people did, Koushik told us that his wife would call to them to leave some for her family – and they always did – walking calmly away when they were done, and never destroying the gardens as they would in other places. Pity we missed seeing them that morning.

While a large breakfast was being prepared for us, we all set off by jeep traversing through miles and miles of eye-soothing tea gardens, with Koushik giving us explanations about them as we drove along. Sanjay too owned 30 acres of these gardens in that region and he was keen to show them to us. We walked through part of these lush gardens and spent over an hour outdoors. We were told that Bhutan was on the other side of the mountains we could see not too far away. We returned to the house with huge appetites and enjoyed the breakfast that had been so painstakingly prepared for us. Nazima, meanwhile, had kept phoning to check that we were all well taken care of and lacked for nothing.

We decided to leave soon after breakfast as Sanjay wanted to take us to the tea factory and show us the entire process of how tea was made, right from the time the tender leaves are plucked and kept in special units on a bed of meshing under which heat is dispersed till the leaves are dried and ready to move on to be crushed. Then on through a long complicated process in different machines till the final product is packed in huge crates or sacks, ready for dispatch to the auction houses. When we were leaving the manager at the factory presented us with huge packets of tea to take with us.

During our tour of the tea gardens I had begun to wonder how there were so many workers from various tribes that did not ethnically belong to that region. My enquiry led me to uncover some interesting details not only of the tea plantation workers but also the story of the tea plant, which I would like to share here.

The Bodo tribe has been credited with having first brought tea into Assam. The word 'Bodo' has been derived from 'Bod' which means Tibet, and it is thought that they entered Assam through the Bhutan passes. There are at least 10 different names by which they are known, depending on where they lived. For instance, those that lived below the Himalayan Range were called Cachari but those living in West Bengal and Nepal are known as Mech or Meche. In Tripura they are called Borok. It is fascinating to trace their origins and make the connections. The use of the tea plant had been restricted to their tribe till a Scottish adventurer, Robert Bruce, 'discovered' it in 1823 while trading in the region. He had noticed that the local tribesmen were brewing tea from the leaves of the bush. He planned to have these leaves and seeds scientifically examined and so he arranged to get samples from the local tribal chiefs. However, as Robert died shortly after this, it was his brother Charles who sent the seeds of this plant to the botanical gardens in Calcutta for proper classification in the early 1830s, mentioning that it was growing wild in Assam. The plant was finally identified as a variety of tea and the British Government in Calcutta lost no time in having the tea assessed in London.

It was not long before the British East India Company followed up on the positive feedback they received from London, and the infamous 'Wasteland Acts' then allowed the dispossession of agricultural and forest lands, all of which were transformed into tea plantations. The British learnt the method of tea production from the Chinese and crossed the local variety with the Chinese one, which eventually gave rise to the present Assam tea. Before the British arrived, there were few people living in the region, but once they took charge of the district, cheap labour was imported from Bihar and Orissa, and the people who then settled there came to be known as Assamese. Today there are more than 850 tea estates and more than 2500 tea gardens in Assam alone. With huge baskets on their back in which the tea leaves are collected, the workers slog through rain and sun for daily or weekly wages that are a mere pittance.

On our way back to Guwahati we travelled by a different route as Sanjay had to stop and meet some of his business contacts in Tangla, his hometown. There was a Don Bosco church in Tangla, painted a bright pink and green which reminded us of those creamy iced cakes one would find in *Irani* restaurants in the old days. We stopped by for a visit and the good hospitable fathers in charge specially organized some chilled beer for us to quench the heat of the noonday sun; they also insisted that we have lunch with them but we were still stuffed with the large late breakfast. We reached Guwahati by the evening of 2 October with tantalizing memories of gracious living, tea and elephants.

From Guwahati we went on to Nagaland (Sechu-Zubza and then Chumukedima for two seminars) and back again to Guwahati where we conducted several sets of seminars for teachers and students before leaving on 22 October for Siloam and Shillong.

FINDING YOURSELF IN SILOAM
"Knock, and the door will open, Seek, and you will find, Ask, and you'll be given the key to ..."

F r. Joseph Thelekkatt had often spoken to us about Siloam but we had not made time to break journey there on our many visits to Shillong. It was 80 kms from Guwahati and just 15 to 20 kms short of Shillong. We let Fr. Joseph make the arrangements for us to spend two days in that idyllic setting. For those who do not know the story mentioned in the bible, it is the place where Jesus told a blind man to go and wash at the Pool of Siloam and after doing this, the blind man received his sight. The translation of the Hebrew word Siloam means 'sent' and the English equivalent is 'apostle'. Catholics believe that Jesus was the Messiah 'sent' from heaven. During our tour of the Holy Land, we saw what we were told, were the ruins of this place. That it existed is a fact, according to a 6th century pilgrim who described it thus:

> *'You descend by many steps to Siloam, and above Siloam is a hanging basilica beneath which the water of Siloam rises. Siloam has two basins constructed of marble, which are separated from each other by a screen. Men were in one and women in the other to gain a blessing. In these waters miracles take place, and lepers are cleansed. In front of the court is a large man-made pool and people are continually washing there; for at regular intervals the spring sends a great deal of water into the basins, which goes on down the valley of Gethsemane (which they also call Jehosaphat) as far as the River Jordan.'*

(Translated from Hebrew by J. Wilkinson)

So it was based on this place of healing that the Salesians of Don Bosco opened their Institution in 2006. Headed by Fr. George Palamattathil, who is the Director, various programmes are conducted with the main focus on counselling skill, training for clergy, religious, teachers, parents and youth leaders. Siloam also promotes what they call 'The Siloam Experience'. The large 5.6 hectares property is spread out at an altitude of 1066 mtrs above sea level over a slope that goes down to the Umiam lake-reservoir. The main building at Siloam is set in the midst of pine forests, almost hidden from sight from the outside. The 11 cottages dotting the lakeside all have beautiful views of the serene lake. Every cottage has been named after a great saint in the hope that if one dares to walk the journeys with these saints they would discover the same fulfilment and happiness as the saints. This is part of what was referred to as 'The Siloam Experience'.

From Siloam it was but an hour's drive up to Shillong. The occasion this time was the wedding of Nola and Dr. Sandi's son, Gideon, on 25 October. We were booked to stay at the Pinewoods Hotel, which was reminiscent of the British Raj days with its typical hill cottages and traces of decadence over the years. The temperatures had dropped drastically when the sun went down and I ended up with an awful cold that night. This had happened to me before and I began to wonder if I was allergic to Shillong! Fortunately I was well next morning when we left to attend the wedding. I have never seen such an array of rich, colourful *jainsems*, one prettier than the other, and I felt like a poor country cousin in the simple one I was wearing. The wedding service took a little over an hour and when we streamed out everyone's cameras were busy clicking for a long time with the bridal couple posing under the floral entrance arch. The cake cutting ceremony was to take place immediately, so we went back to Pinewoods Hotel which was also the venue for the reception. The reception was very well attended and till the time we left to return to our rooms, there were people still streaming in. We had experienced a Scottish wedding, an

Italian wedding and now we had our taste of our first *Khasi* wedding. I wonder what comes next!

We took a taxi back to Guwahati the day after the wedding and we completed the last seminar on 28 and 29 October. Then we had one day to visit a few shops in Guwahati where we bought beautiful Assam silk stoles and were back in Mumbai on 31 October. And with this chapter, I definitely close my writings on the Northeast ... till the next time, of course!

Chapter Twenty-three

2010
HELLOS AND GOODBYES
"Far across the distance and spaces between us …"

The year 2010 was kept aside to be spent completely in India working to get my book published. But after Melissa was laid off from her job with Jet Airways due to the economic meltdown, she insisted we use up the tickets she was entitled to. Though we scheduled our New York visit for mid-April, our decision to postpone it by a week led to a stream of more delays – from the Iceland volcano, to the vacation rush, to the unexpected illness of my brother, who then passed away on 17 May, a week after I had finally left for the States and on the very day Joe had just reached New York.

We had taken overseas insurance for 72 days, which worked out to Rs.15,266 for the two of us but out of those 72 days, Joe spent just 21 days abroad, and I about 30 days! Melissa and family did their best to entertain us, and though they even celebrated my birthday in June, we were quite off mood. From the start, we had been given enough indications that this trip to the States was really not meant to be. A pity we did not go by the signs and our instincts.

The trip to New York had left us with a feeling of incompletion. Now back in Mumbai, we found ourselves having to handle many jobs, including tax matters, before we could leave the country again. So much for our decision not to travel abroad in 2010! We were now getting ready to leave for London and we had just one month to complete all the jobs on hand. Somehow everything got done in record time with relentless hard work that saw us burning the midnight oil on most nights. Getting visas for England was not a problem and we collected them within a couple of days after shelling out Rs.9,700 for both visas. Overseas insurance for the two of us for 44 days was another Rs.6,430.

Exactly one month to the day after I returned from New York, Joe and I flew to London. Still sub-load passengers, we were lucky to both get on the flight at our first attempt. We were in London for two reasons – the wedding of Dawn Rodricks and Adrian Mendez, which was scheduled for 31 July, and for our grandchild Gaia's first birthday on 7 August.

Dawn's parents, Horace and Joan, had visited us in Goa the previous year and Dawn had ordered their wedding rings to be made in Goa. The primary and more urgent reason for making the trip to England was to deliver the rings in time. However, Horace managed to have these collected, so we thought of cancelling or delaying our visit, but there was no arguing with daughters. Melissa insisted we utilize the last of the free tickets she had for us, and Vanessa said that we should be there for Gaia's first birthday, so we finally agreed to be present for both the wedding and the birthday.

Dawn is the only child of Horace and Joan and so they had a very grand and lavish celebration. We were also very happy to meet up with many of the relatives who featured in the Rodrigues Family Tree – people we only had names for before, but could now put faces to them. The champagne, wine and spirits were flowing at the reception and the dinner that followed. Horace, as father of the bride, surprised us with the eloquent and humorous toast he raised, and so did Dawn. You could see the happiness on the faces of the young couple who were bubbling and, as Dawn put it in her 'Thank You' note to us, 'Our wedding was the best day we could ask for – it's a shame we can't do it all over again!'

Prior to Gaia's birthday I had started to sing 'Happy Birthday' to her and teach her to shake hands when she was wished, and she learnt this soon enough. I enjoyed teaching her a lot more, including how to hug and kiss and she soon started to practise this on her dolls and other toys. Sometimes she even tried to join me in singing which I did all the time.

Vanessa and Sanjay had planned a big party for her and this was held on 8 August at a pub called 'Revolution', which was right on the Thames, next to Sanjay's office. One might think this was rather an unconventional venue for a child's party, but there was a separate area for such functions. I do think children hardly enjoy their own parties when they are so young, so it is mainly the adults who have a good time, and we all did. The day after the party Joe and I left for Spain.

IN THE CATALAN CRADLE
"Here is the rainbow I've been prayin' for"

When Joe's cousin, Audry Rodericks, heard that we would be in England in 2010, he once again invited us to see his mountain retreat in Girona. He had invited us the previous year too but we could not make it then. Everyone we talked to told us that getting a visa from Spain would prove to be very difficult. We just applied through our travel agent, giving all the relevant documents and Rs.10,000 (which included the agent's fee) for both of us. The many stamps in our double passports made our traveller status evident. Not once have we ever been refused a visa for any country, nor have we ever had to apply twice; a refusal now would not have bothered us but it would have surprised us. We were scheduled to leave for England on the night of 14/15 July, and till the 13th, there was no sign of our passports being returned from the Spanish Embassy. I told our travel agent to get these back even if the visas were not granted as we did not want to delay our departure for England. On the 14th morning our passports were returned to us – with the visas!

When our friends, Clare and Johnny Arago, heard that we were coming to Spain, they invited us to spend some days with them in Barcelona. Accordingly we changed our return dates from 13 to 17 August. So here we were on the morning of the 9th taking the Heathrow Express to Gatwick airport, from where we were to fly to Girona. We travelled by Ryan Air and had booked early believing we would get cheaper fares. This was supposed to be a no-frills airline but whether it was really economical is a question we had to ask ourselves. A fee of £1 was charged for every phone call they made to us or SMS they sent us, we had to pay £50 for just one checked-in bag (meant for both of us) that could not weigh more than 15 kgs. If it exceeded 15 kgs a huge fine could be levied. If carry-on bags did not meet specifications, you were once again charged a big fine, and for changing our ticket date we were charged another £50. We were therefore rather scared and took great care to make sure we were within all the limits. So, when you really thought about it, you ended up paying a lot more than you would on a regular airline, except that we had no option because I think that is the only airline that flies to Girona.

Our plane reached Girona just before midnight. We were surprised to see what a tiny airport it was and Joe and I were even more surprised at the immigration check which was the fastest we have ever experienced. It was quicker than a ticket check at a railway platform. I'm wondering if the official even bothered to look at our passports properly or if he was just thinking of getting home to his warm bed. Audry, and his Spanish wife, Isabella (known as Bel) were waiting for us outside, and we apologized for making them come to the airport at such a late hour to pick us up. They very kindly said it was no trouble and that they lived close by. The 'close by' turned out to require over an hour's fast driving on empty roads. We forgot to tell them that we had eaten on the way so we had a second meal which they had prepared, and insisted we have. Audry also opened a bottle of wine, which we enjoyed. It was past 2 am by the time we went to bed. We had to be quiet because their daughter Sandra, her partner Albert, and their twin children were asleep in the rooms next to us.

With the morning light we could finally see the house in more detail and we also met Sandra, Albert, Jana and Teo. Jana and Teo were twins (not identical); they were both very cute and their grandparents doted on them. Audry's younger daughter, Ruth, was an architect and she had designed and planned their beautiful home. It was located in the mountains in several acres of farm land, and the surrounding scenery was awesome. But how they discovered that place is an interesting story.

Audry told us that when his brother, the late Bishop Joey Rodericks of Jamshedpur, went to visit them in Barcelona, the family took him for a hot air balloon ride. Unfortunately, they ran into some problems and their balloon got stuck in a tree on the mountains in Girona. Apparently this was not a common occurrence, but rather a freak accident – scripted by destiny. Even so, I could imagine how scary this must have been for them. By the time the rescue team arrived, they had a chance to survey their surroundings and that's when Audry spotted the plot he would end up choosing for their holiday home. There was an old dilapidated little farm cottage still standing on the property. When they were safely on terra firma once more, they made enquiries, bought the place and soon started construction. From being just a holiday home for the family, it finally became their regular home, away from the busy city life of Barcelona. Besides their house, there were just two other habitations, one a little further up the mountain and the other lower down. To reach these three places from the city one had to cross a river with a narrow flat concrete bridge fording it. But when the river was in spate, especially after very heavy showers, this only access to their homes was cut off. So if they were on the other side, they could spend the night at a hotel in town till the waters abated, and the government footed the bill!

Though it may not have been necessary, a security system was installed. There were many trees already on the property when they bought it, but Audry planted more fruit trees like yellow and red plums (we enjoyed eating the sweet plums that fell when you shook the tree) apples, peaches and others. There were also two walnut trees, and they also cultivated fresh vegetables and large potatoes which lasted them throughout the year. The huge pods of garlic they grew were strung and hung up in the kitchen. Some distance from the house was a pen, which housed a huge male sheep and his two wives. The male glared at us and stood protectively at attention when we went to have a look at them. On a lower level of the grounds were several hens that provided fresh eggs for the table. Living on a farm looks and sounds like a lot of fun but there's a tremendous amount of hard work involved, especially during winter. However, Audry and Bel were coping well with a little outside help for the heavier work, and they seemed to be thriving in this unadulterated atmosphere.

On our first day in Girona, Audry drove us to the nearby town of Besalu. The most significant feature of Besalu is its 12th century Roman bridge, built over the Fluvia River. At the mid-point of this bridge is a gateway that leads to the quaint old-world town with its arcaded narrow medieval streets and squares. At one time there was quite a large Jewish community in Girona but most of them were expelled from Catalonia in 1492 by the catholic kings. Jews later settled in Besalu at the beginning of the Middle Ages, where they co-existed peacefully with Christians and their descendents continue to live there to this day. It felt good to walk through those narrow streets where the tops of the buildings seemed almost to meet, and at certain angles the walls seemed to be sloping inward or outward. The ground floors of most buildings had been converted into souvenir shops and I could not resist buying a cute ceramic burrito, which had two side panniers for potted plants. We left this in England for Vanessa.

While driving back from Besalu to Girona we stopped at a small village where we thought we'd get a cool drink. However, every single place was shut and the entire village seemed to be taking its afternoon siesta very seriously. We walked down the main street for a while, admiring the balconies covered with vines loaded with clusters of grapes, drank water from a wayside fountain and then went back home for lunch.

When we were still in England, Audry had e-mailed to ask if we would like to also go to Lourdes, which was just a four-hour drive away from Girona. Would we? Of course we would, and we jumped at the offer! We had been to Lourdes very briefly in 1996 but then I did not get a chance to bathe in the waters and always regretted the lost opportunity.

CITY OF MIRACLES – AND TOURISTS!
"I Say a Little Prayer for you"

The town of Lourdes is located in the foothills of the Pyrenees in the southwest of France and hence, just north of Spain. We left in the morning after breakfast, and with Audry's expert driving, we were across the Pyrenees and in Lourdes in time for lunch. It was a glorious day with the sun shining, very unlike the usual weather in Lourdes. Our first priority was to get to a hotel and dump our bags. After Paris, Lourdes has the greatest number of hotels per square kilometre in France. There are reported to be about 270 of them, but we did not have to go hunting for one. Audry always stayed at Hotel Atlantic as he knew the owners well, so we went directly there, checked in and left soon after to find a place close to our hotel where we could lunch.

After a satisfying lunch with a carafe of wine, we returned to our rooms for a rest.

In the evening, when the sun was sinking, we went to the Shrine that we remembered so well. At the Information counter we checked the timings for the baths, and then we walked to the grotto to pray the rosary. We then walked back to the Pius X Underground Basilica for the healing service which was scheduled for 5.30 pm. The sanctuary is located in the centre on a raised platform and from there the ground slopes gently upwards thus affording a view of the main altar from any part of the large oval nave. It can accommodate up to 25,000 worshipers but with no natural lighting, it has a gloomy interior. It was almost empty when we went in, but soon we saw streams of handicapped children and adults being wheeled in by their families or volunteers who were caring for them. These were lined up in front of the altar and a touching ceremony followed, but we did not witness any apparent miracles.

The significance of the water of Lourdes is inscribed above the place where the taps are located: 'Wash Your Face and ask God to Purify Your Hearts'. After filling our bottles with the miraculous waters we returned to our hotel for another short rest. We were back in the night for the torchlight procession. It's a beautiful sight to see thousands of people from all parts of the globe walking in procession with lit candles, reciting the rosary, each decade of which was said in a different language. We noticed that there was a strong presence of Tamilians from Sri Lanka in Lourdes so one decade was also recited – rather sung – by a small child, in Tamil. It sounded very nice.

As the baths were opening at 7.30 am, we decided to go early the next morning. I thought I would be one of the first so was surprised to see that the lines were already fairly long. The weather that morning was dull with no sun shining. In fact, it began to drizzle while I was waiting in the queue. Surprisingly, there were quite a few people who, on one pretext or another, pushed ahead of their place without an apology. I was lucky that I could finally move to the sheltered part before it began raining more heavily because I did not have an umbrella with me. In the leaflet we picked up en route, I read: 'You can have a wonderful pilgrimage without going to the baths. Bernadette only washed her face (the mirror of the soul) and drank 'a little water'.' Even so, I was keen to experience the baths now that I was actually nearing the end of the queue.

Joe had described the procedure for me when he had the opportunity to dip in the waters in 1996. I experienced the same routine when it was my turn at the baths, which were manned totally by volunteers who were schooled to work with prayerful detachment. At that time, the waiting period to be called upon for volunteer service was five years. When I reached the inner rooms, a volunteer sheltered me with a towel while I stripped completely and hung my clothes on a peg. (There were at least five other ladies in each room going through this process with me, but only one at a time went to the inner baths.) I was wrapped in this towel and led to the inner screened-off enclosure which had the baths. Two other ladies there asked if this was my first time and what language I spoke. They then held my arms, one on each side, and asked me to pray the Hail Mary with them, as they led me down a couple of steps into a deep cemented pool. The shocking cold of the water made me shiver, tremble and gasp and they asked if I wanted some water to drink. After having the water, I kissed the statue at the edge of the pool and prayed for everyone I could think of, starting with our families. Then they told me to kneel in the water and immerse myself. I asked for various healings, not just of the body but also of the mind and spirit and I did feel so cleansed. When I got out of the water, I thanked the ladies and once again I was screened by the towel while I changed back into my clothes. I was amazed to discover that my body was absolutely dry even without having to wipe it and that in itself is a miracle that all experience.

Joe had already finished his bath much before me (somehow the lines for the men are always shorter than those for the women) and was waiting in the rain for me to come out. Audry told us that the dreary wet weather we were experiencing that day was the actual Lourdes weather and was one reason that Bernadette Soubirous was always sick and asthmatic. I'm not going into any more details of this visit since I covered some of them in the 1996 chapter. While countless miracles have been recorded at Lourdes, not everyone comes away with one. However, I do believe that we can create our miracles with our faith and belief, but one needs to experience this for oneself.

We left Lourdes soon after breakfast, amidst a heavy downpour, but made good time and actually got back much quicker than we anticipated. While nearing Girona, instead of driving directly home, Audry thought we should stop for lunch. He had heard of a special restaurant in the vicinity but his family had not made time to go and check it out so he thought he'd do that now while we were in the area. After leaving the town of Olot we branched off at Lake Banyoles, and after asking around a bit, we finally found the Restaurant 'Can Roca D'Esponella'. The Roca family have been running this restaurant since 1910 and the family members personally do the cooking and serving. We left Audry to do the ordering of the gourmet meal which included escargots, which he and Joe thoroughly relished. I am not an epicure. We were so stuffed after that grand meal that we skipped dinner.

We saw the most spectacular rainbows we've ever seen that last evening in Girona. There were two of them one below the other and the colours were vivid and rich. The rainbows, as seen from the balcony of the house, spanned the entire width of sky and lasted for over half an hour. What a colourful end to our packed three days in Girona. We left on 13 August with Albert driving first to Barcelona airport to drop off Audry and Bel who were leaving for their vacation, and then he took us to the Arago residence on Salvador da Mundi, an upmarket residential area in Barcelona. We had thoroughly enjoyed our visit to Girona and Lourdes, and what was even more remarkable, was the warm and lavish hospitality shown us by Audry and Bel.

THE ALL-EMBRACING BARCELONA
"Hasta Manana 'til we meet again,
don't know where, don't know when"

Joe had been to Barcelona once before but this was my first time. Clare's brother, Eustace Fernandes, used to work with Joe in Advertising and Sales Promotion Co., and so our association with their family went back to the early 1970s. When Clare married Johnny Arago, she moved to Spain and had often extended to us an invitation to visit them. Clare and I both lost our brothers to cancer that same year and we spent that first day mainly catching up with news.

We were ready to explore next morning and Johnny took us to the metro where he helped us purchase coupons to travel. Though he insisted on coming with us to show us the way, we told him we'd manage on our own. And we did – till we reached Catalunya and exited onto the huge Plaza Catalunya that had several roads leading off it. We were supposed to walk down the famous La Rambla but we did not know which road to follow since there were no signboards in English and few people spoke English anyway. After two wrong starts, we were finally pointed in the right direction. La Rambla is a popular destination for tourists and locals. This pedestrian mall extends for over one kilometre along a tree-lined street and connects Plaza Catalunya with the tall Christopher Columbus monument at Port Vell, with shops on both sides. In the wide central walking area, there are many side shows with people posing as statues or dressed in different costumes. One man was even dressed as Marilyn Monroe in her famous role in the 'Seven-Year Itch', and though he had painted his face a chalky white and wore a blond wig to resemble the actress, I thought he looked hideous, but he still drew crowds.

Several streets branch off from the main avenue that lead to interesting shopping and other tourist attractions. We took one of these side streets to try and find the Cathedral of Barcelona. We had almost given up, when we came upon it suddenly at the end of a turning in the Gothic Quarter of Barcelona. The actual name is The Cathedral of the Holy Cross and Saint Eulalia, but it is commonly known as the Cathedral of Barcelona. St. Eulalia, to whom the cathedral is dedicated, was a 13-year old virgin who was said to have suffered martyrdom at the hands of the Romans. One of the stories told is that she was exposed naked in the public square but a miraculous snowfall in mid-spring covered her nudity. Later she was put into a barrel into which knives were stuck and then it was rolled down a street that is now named after her. The saint's body is entombed in the Cathedral's crypt. The other interesting story connected to the cathedral concerns the side chapel of Christ of Lepanto, which has a crucifix from a ship that fought in the Battle of Lepanto. The body of Christ on this cross hangs towards the right. True or not, Catalan legend has it that during the battle, the corpus on the cross suddenly and miraculously shifted to the right to avoid being hit by a cannonball. They took this as a sign from God that the Ottomans would be defeated which, I presume, they were.

We returned to the main thoroughfare of La Rambla and continued walking along, stopping every now and then to watch the side shows. I was happy that I could finally visit Barcelona – the second largest city in Spain after Madrid, the twelfth most visited city in the world, and the fourth most visited in Europe after London, Paris and Rome. It was also renowned for the architectural works of their famous artist Antoni Gaudi. Like in Girona, the people here speak Catalan and not Spanish, and are proud to be known as Catalonians or Catalans.

Clare and Johnny had told us to be sure to see the Aquarium and they also warned us about pickpockets in the area. With more tourists than locals around, this was now a favourite haunt of theirs. We walked towards the Maremagnum, a sort of continuation of La Rambla, on a wooden walkway that extended into the harbour called Rambla de Mar. The aquarium was located right at the end of this. We bought our quite expensive tickets and made our way to the entrance. On the way there were some photographers taking snaps of people posing in front of the open jaws of a monster shark of everyone going to the aquarium. Since there was no obligation to buy the photo, we too posed and I must say the photograph turned out so good that we willingly ended up paying the €8 for it on our way out.

The aquarium itself was very good but not significantly different from the underworld aquariums we had already seen in Scotland, New York and San Francisco. We were quite tired by now and I went to sit on the steps while Joe lagged behind. He finally came to tell me that he had lost his camera. There were only two places he could have left it – one was the gift shop we went into briefly, and the other when we stopped to collect the photo. After checking the gift shop and coming up with a blank, we took permission from the girl at the exit of the aquarium and, Joe went back to look, but there was no sign of the camera. As we were leaving the girl told us to check at the Information counter, and right enough, someone had found it and deposited it there. What a relief that was. We might never have thought of doing this on our own.

The following day we decided to go to Tibidabo. Audry, Clare and Johnny all said we must see it and could not leave Barcelona without going there. Tibidabo is a 512 metre high mountain which can be reached by bus, funicular railway and by car. We took the local bus and when we asked the driver and the people at the bus stop whether it was going to Tibidabo they all nodded vigorously but we found ourselves at the terminus at Plaza Catalunya instead. We took the next bus going in the opposite direction and this time we managed to get off at the John F. Kennedy Plaza where we changed to another bus that climbed up the mountain. There is also a tram service which most tourists like to take, but it is much slower and also more expensive. The Funicular railway took us up to the top, along an almost vertical incline.

The name 'Tibidabo' (Latin: I will give you) refers to the temptation of Jesus by the devil, recounted in the Gospel of St. Luke (4:6) where it is said that the devil took Jesus up to the top of a high mountain and offered Him all the kingdoms of the world if He would fall down and worship Satan. Most catholics and christians believe that this took place in the Holy Land, but the Catalans believe that this was staged at Monte de Tibidabo and they take great pride in this. The author James Michener has an explanation for this belief of the Catalans in his travelogue on 'Iberia'. He says, 'the way the Catalans see it, there would not be much of an effort for Jesus to stand on top of some arid mountain in Palestine and reject a swathe of miserable, dusty desert. But if He stood on top of the Sierra de Collserola with a spectacular view of the lush green hillsides, vineyards, and fields, the beautiful port city, and shining Mediterranean Sea all below, and could reject THAT, then He truly was Divine.' There is no doubt that Barcelona is indeed a unique city in that it occupies a vast plain that is surrounded by hills and mountains (the Sierra de Collserola) and thus forms a sort of natural giant amphitheatre.

At the pinnacle of Tibidabo is the Church of the Sacred Heart, now a minor Basilica. In the interior of the Church is a mosaic of St. John Bosco being handed over the deeds to the land. Some years prior to Don Bosco's arrival in Barcelona in 1886, a group of pious landowners had purchased the peak of Tibidabo and some of the land around it to preserve it for a christian shrine. When they learned that Don Bosco was in Barcelona to collect funds to build a shrine to the Sacred Heart of Jesus in Rome they decided that the perfect way to use the Tibidabo site would be to have a similar shrine in Barcelona.

Don Bosco was stunned when these men approached him with their offer, because he himself was contemplating building another shrine there when his project in Rome was completed. Carting materials up to that high point posed a lot of problems. The church took 60 years to construct and was completed only in 1951, but the bell towers took another 10 years to erect.

The place was filled with tourists when we got there. We walked up some steps of the church and then took the lift (for a fee) to the first level from where we had a spectacular view of the city. From the second level you get a sweeping view of Barcelona and its coastline. Joe climbed the steps up to the third level which was at the base of the 7-metre golden bronze statue of Christ the King which is mounted at the very top of the church. This statue that is visible from most parts of the city has its arms outstretched, seeming to embrace all of Barcelona and the world. I always marvel at how these shrines are constructed at such heights. Joe came down feeling rather dizzy so I'm glad I did not attempt the last climb.

When we got back to the JFK Plaza, we took the local bus, but once again it was a bus going in the wrong direction, so when we discovered our mistake we jumped off in between terminals, crossed the road and took another bus going in the opposite direction. Again we could not recognize the stop where we had to get off and ended up going to the terminus at the other end! It took us over an hour of walking in the hot sun to get back to Salvador da Mundi. What should have been just a half day's excursion turned into a full day's adventure and, in the process, we had used up all our coupons on wasted trips!

After that, Johnny did not risk sending us out alone so he came with us when we went to see Antoni Gaudi's famous work – the unfinished Church of the Sagrada Familia (Church of the Holy Family). We were put off on seeing the long queue at the ticket counter and were ready to go elsewhere, but Johnny enquired and found we would have less than a 20-minute wait. We're glad we stayed. Antoni Gaudi was a Spanish architect and his works are unique and highly individualistic with a wealth of symbolism. Most of his designs are based on Nature and natural phenomena, and are instantly recognizable throughout Barcelona. He began work on the Church of the Sagrada Familia in 1882, and this is not expected to be completed till the year 2026. Gaudi devoted 43 years of his life to this project, and work continued after his death in 1926. The ongoing construction of the church is as much a part of its attraction as the church itself as many tourists come to admire the artists and the construction workers.

The first view I had of the Church of the Sagrada Familia from the outside was not very inspiring, perhaps because of the scaffolding on some sections. Of course the spindle-shaped spires are its most striking aspect. There are eighteen spires in all, in ascending order of height. These represent the twelve Apostles, the four evangelists and the Virgin Mary, the tallest of all at 170 mts, representing Jesus Christ. There is much more to write about this church but I have to necessarily condense my description, hence this limited version.

The church has three grand façades. The Nativity façade faces the rising sun in the east (symbol for the birth of Christ). He wanted this façade to be the most attractive and accessible to the public, which indeed it was. The Passion Façade facing the setting sun in the west is a symbol of the suffering and death of Christ. It has spare, gaunt, tormented characters that are almost skeletal. It was intended to portray the sins of man, and Gaudi wanted this façade to strike fear in those who gazed at it. The Glory façade faces south and will be the largest of all the facades offering access to the central nave. It represents the road to God: Death, Final Judgment, and Glory. All three façades are truly striking and you can feel the passion that went into sculpting them. The inside of the church is in the shape of a Latin cross with five aisles. The pillars and columns are a unique Gaudi design. They not only support the roof but look like trees with an intersection of various geometric forms. They start with a square base, evolve into an octagon and then further up, into a sixteen-sided form and finally a circle. There is so much symbolism in all of Gaudi's work, which was explained beautifully in the museum attached to the Church. Now I could finally understand why this was considered to be one of the top tourist attractions in Barcelona.

After exiting the Church we took a taxi to Park Guell, a garden complex, which was also executed by Gaudi. The two buildings flanking the entrance look almost like cake houses, reminiscent of the Hansel and Gretel fairy tale. The roofs look like icing and have unusual pinnacles. The main terrace of the Park has a long bench in the form of a sea serpent and Gaudi used the imprint of buttocks left by a naked workman sitting in wet clay to design the curvature of the bench. Looking at the Park today with its lush vegetation and many trees one could hardly believe that it was once just a sparse rocky hill. In addition to the many pigeons and sparrows, we saw hordes of monk parakeets that made one hell of a racket, engrossed as they were in socializing and building their huge community nests in the tall palm trees. Despite the many noisy tourists milling around (there is no entrance fee) the park induces a feeling of peace. We did not venture going up to the higher terraces which offered more spectacular views of Barcelona as we were happy with our vantage point.

In Barcelona, I found one of the nicest fruits I've ever eaten. They are the San Lucar Paraguayos, known simply as '*paraguayos*'. They are like squashed flat peaches to look at, but their taste is unique and I loved them. Spain has the perfect climatic conditions for growing them so we may never hope to see them in India. I thought they were a bit expensive but that did not stop me from having my fill of them and we even bought some to take back with us to England.

When we left Barcelona on 17 August we took a taxi to the Estacio d'Autobusos Barcelona Nord, the main bus terminal, and bought our tickets to the Girona-Costa Brava airport. While waiting for our coach to leave I wandered around the few shops and bought a Gaudi doll for my collection. The coach journey took about an hour, and from the Girona bus terminal to the airport it was another 15-minute bus ride away. Airport formalities over, we got talking to a Kashmiri Indian guy who worked for Ryan Air and chatted with him for quite some time before saying goodbye. When Joe suddenly remembered that he had forgotten to request for a Priority boarding ticket for me we went back to attend to this. With free seating on the aircraft, there was generally a rush to grab seats so for a fee of £2 or £4 (I forget) you are escorted in before the others. When our new friend heard that we did not have Priority boarding he immediately issued these cards for both of us – at no charge whatsoever! We were very touched by this gesture and Joe spontaneously removed the brass kada he had on his wrist and gave it to him. He would not accept it at first and was also very touched by our small gesture. He told us that if we ever returned to Girona we should contact him but, unfortunately, we don't even remember his name. It was a lovely ending to a wonderful, packed week in Spain.

THANK GOD FOR FAMILY AND FRIENDS
"I'm leaving on a Jet Plane"

When we were back in Richmond, we received a really warm welcome from little Gaia, who suddenly discovered that she had missed us a lot and was so happy to see us that she even refused to go to her mother but clung to Joe and me. We were really pleased with the extra affection we received subsequently.

Another 10 days in England passed by quickly, during which we packed our bags and were surprised to find how much stuff we had collected in one month even though we had planned not to do any shopping. Gaia kept climbing into our suitcases when they were open and we wished we could have brought her back with us. We tried getting the Jet evening flight on 26 August, and though we waited at the airport till the very last, the flight went absolutely full, with some fare-paying passengers walking in when the counter had almost closed. We had no option but to go back home, leaving our main luggage in the left luggage section. In a way, I was glad of that good night's rest which I needed, and woke up early the next morning feeling very refreshed. We made the 9.30 am flight without any difficulty. The airport staff told us that the night flights were always heavily booked and we wished we had thought of this to start with. It would have saved a lot of money (taxis and left luggage charges) and unnecessary tensions.

I have now realized the value and importance of keeping records of all our travel dates and expenses rather than having to fish for these details every time we have to apply for visas or supply details for tax returns. This practice has saved me great amounts of time and also helps me in my writing. After this trip, we found that we had spent less than Rs.1.25 lakhs for the two of us, and that included our UK and Schengen visas, overseas insurance, credit card payments and foreign exchange! Thank God for family and good friends!!

Chapter Twenty-four

2010-2011
OVER THE MOON DOWN UNDER
"Memories, pressed between the pages of my mind, memories, sweetened through the ages just like wine"

In 1974, Joe and I had almost emigrated to Australia. Mr. L.K. Ratna, my then boss in A.F. Ferguson & Co., had written a letter of recommendation to Price Waterhouse & Co. in Perth and so a job for me was practically in the bag. Joe too had enough to show for his work in pharmaceutical sales promotion to find quick placement. But fate was to have it otherwise. Deferring to Joe's mother's plea that we stay to look after family matters, we remained rooted in India – a decision we have never regretted. Strangely enough, about 40 years earlier, Joe's father, who had been awarded a scholarship to study Life Insurance in America, could not bear it when, just two days before he was due to depart, his father started weeping with grief. He promptly cancelled his trip.

When we could afford to gratify our urge to travel, our journeys invariably took us westwards, never east. With one daughter settled in the USA and the other living in the UK, those two countries automatically became our main destinations. Our first visit east was in 1997, to Thailand; later, in 2005 we went to China and in 2008, to Malaysia. Somehow we had never made it to Australia, in spite of the warm, annually-repeated invitations from Melissa D'Silva (nee Hancock). Our friendship with Melissa, Mark and Michael Hancock, who had all married and settled in Perth, went back to the 1980s. Those were days of partying, barbecues, picnics, card sessions and lots of fun. It all gradually came to a stop when the Hancocks migrated and the others in the group married and moved from Bandra to more distant suburbs.

Melissa Hancock married Joslyn D'Silva and they have two boys, Evan and Jason. After surviving the initial difficult years while adjusting to life in a new country and changing homes a couple of times, they finally built their own beautiful and large home in Kiara, an eastern suburb of Perth. Over the years, all three Hancocks had made several visits to India, but we had not attempted even a single visit to Perth. When our daughter Vanessa told us that she would not be visiting us for Christmas in 2010, we finally made up our minds to spend the festive season in Perth, and informed Melissa and Joslyn that we had definitely decided to 'jump' across to Australia. All this transpired in May 2010 when we were just about to leave for New York. To save on fares which were sure to be much higher around Christmas time we immediately booked our tickets to Perth – seven months in advance! Melissa informed her brothers, and Michael and his wife, Andrea, immediately wrote to tell us that they were making time to take us around.

Who would have thought we'd be making three trips abroad in 2010 – New York in May/June, London in July/August and Australia in Dec.'10/Jan.2011! Luckily, for the first two trips we had free tickets on Jet Airways, courtesy of our daughter Melissa, so we had to pay air fare only for the last, which set us back Rs.39,843 each. Visas with the agent's fee was another Rs.11,400 and overseas insurance another Rs.4,170 for both of us. We travelled by Malaysian Airlines on the night of 15 December, changed aircraft at Kuala Lumpur and were in Perth by the 16th afternoon.

Hearing how strict the authorities were in Australia, we were a little wary as we collected our luggage and walked towards Customs. A lady official asked if we were carrying any foodstuffs, and handed us a card with some sort of code. After waiting our turn in a fairly long queue, another gentleman checked the card and directed us to join the longer of two bifurcated queues. We noticed that each passenger's bags were opened and checked thoroughly and some items were even discarded. After that, the bags had to be hefted onto machines for further screening. When it came to our turn, we had a young girl to check our baggage. She appreciated the fact that we had made a comprehensive list of food items in which Joe had included even the rudraksh beads in the necklace he was wearing (as we were told we had to declare any seeds, even those contained in jewellery). We had packed all the foodstuffs in one suitcase. Imagine our chagrin when, on opening it, the first thing that greeted us was leakage from a pouch of pickle! This had never happened to us before but I guess rough handling of the luggage had caused the mishap. I had packed the three pickle packets inside a plastic container just for this type of eventuality. We thought we would then have to scan our luggage as all the others before us had to but, after giving us tissues to clean up, she told us we could leave. Apparently, the Australians value honesty and I guess they were convinced of ours.

Melissa and Joslyn D'Silva were at the airport to meet us and they were so pleased that we were finally in Perth. There was so much of laughter and chatter and trying to catch up with the missing years all at once, that we went on talking till late into the night. Michael and Andrea who were also to have met us at the airport could not be there as Michael, a Detective Sergeant with the Australian Police, was called out on a job at the last moment; but they did drive over to Melissa's house for a short visit later in the day. Subsequently we met up with Mark and Beaullah when they invited us over to their lakeside house for lunch. There we met their three children, Celeste, Alicia and little Lucas, a late arrival to the family, who was much fussed over. Beaullah was getting ready to leave for India so it was the only time we could meet her. Joslyn's brother, Jeffrey, was leaving for India the same night we arrived, but he still dashed over to greet us. Joe and I were truly touched with the warm welcome we received from all of them.

One of our first outings was to the Margaret River Chocolate Factory in the Swan Valley where we helped ourselves to free samples, drooled over the varieties of chocolates and truffles on sale, watched through viewing windows how chocolate was made and finally sat at the outdoor café to enjoy coffee and ice-cream, while we caught up on some more of each other's news. From there we drove to the Swan Valley vineyards. The rich loamy soil of this valley makes it ideal for producing a vast range of both whites and reds. Most of these vineyards offer free tastings and some even have alfresco dining and restaurants with an inviting ambience. We obviously could not visit all, so we selected three.

Lancaster Wines was on a sprawling estate, which boasted of some of the oldest vines in the Swan Valley. Besides us, there were many others sipping the different wines complemented by a selection of cheeses, and we too tried to look like connoisseurs, but I don't think we fooled anyone, so after sampling about four or five wines and some cheese, we scooted to the next place. Sandalford Winery, located on the banks of the Swan River in the heart of the Swan Valley, dates back to 1840. It is known to be one of Australia's oldest, largest and most prestigious privately-owned wineries and has won several West Australian Tourism Awards. Here we not only tasted some of the wines, but also bought a bottle to take back with us. The Pinelli Cellar Door Winery was our third and definitely last stop. So far none of us was tipsy but one could never say when the 'tipsing' point would come! This winery produces around 150,000 litres of wine every year, and they claim that their wines are drinkable even without prolonged ageing. Here we bought not bottles but flagons of wine at fairly reasonable prices and we even carried one back to India with us!

Melissa had saved up her leave and so had made time to take us round to the places of major interest. One of the highlights of our visit was when she took us to the Perth Mint. On the way we stopped for a short while at her office in the Ministry of Conservation and Land Management. A short walk down from the cathedral brought us to the

Perth Mint, one of the world's oldest mints, which still operates from its original premises on Hay Street, East Perth. We were lucky to have a young and knowledgeable guide to take us round the Mint. We were shown the world's largest collection of pure gold bars and we could even handle AU$400,000 worth of gold bullion by putting one hand through an opening to try and lift the bar – which I couldn't. The Normandy Nugget, the second largest in the world, was also on display. It was found in a dry stream bed near Kalgoorlie, WA, as recently as 1995, and weighed an astonishing 25.5 kgs! On the way to the melting house, we stopped to weigh ourselves and discover the value of our weight in gold. I was worth AU$2,223,456 and Joe AU$2,531,104, but we didn't need those certificates to tell us how priceless we are in the eyes of our Maker.

When we entered the melting house, we felt a blast of intense heat but when we sat on the tiered seats for the demonstration, there seemed to be a cool draft of air flowing over us so it was not uncomfortable. I don't want to think of what the guide had to endure. Though he wore special clothing and thick padded gloves, he had to stand next to the heating pit, exposed to those high temperatures while he demonstrated the pouring of 5670 gms of molten gold to form a solid bar of pure gleaming gold. As for the 19th century brick walls of the melting house, it is said that they are literally embedded with particles of gold that have accumulated over many decades of continuous processing.

At the gift shop, Melissa ordered a special gold-plated silver medallion with a personalized message for us, a souvenir of our visit to the Mint and Australia. While we were waiting for this to be struck and engraved, through a viewing window we could see coins of various denominations being minted and stacked neatly. While returning from the Mint, we hopped into a CAT (Central Area Transit) bus which operates in central Perth. There are Red, Blue and Yellow CAT buses covering various city sectors and the rides are for free. I thought that was pretty cool and so helpful to be able to just jump on and off the bus without having to fish around for change each time. We alighted close to the picturesque Hay Street Mall.

Hay Street Mall reminded me a bit of Covent Garden in England, with several artistes performing and entertaining the public in the streets. London Court, an open-to-sky arcade, was known to be a big tourist attraction with a distinctive mock Tudor/Elizabethan façade. Complementing the Tudor look were gargoyles, masks, shields, crests and wrought iron signs and brackets, gabled roofs and weather cocks, and a flooring of terracotta tiles. The large clock at the entrance to this arcade is fitted with a clever mechanism. When it chimes, which is every quarter hour, four knights appear from a castle and move in a semi-circle, appearing to joust with each other. At the other end of the arcade another clock in a window shows Saint George battling the dragon. All the original residences had been converted to commercial establishments with many shops and cafes on the ground floor level. Here Joe bought a striking T-shirt with aboriginal art which he likes so much.

Michael and Andrea took time off from work to take us to Fremantle. Michael accompanied us on the boat from Perth to the mouth of the Swan River in Fremantle while Andrea (who works for the Commissioner of Police in Perth) dropped us off at the dock and went back to the office. Later she drove the 19 kms from Perth to Fremantle so that we would have transport to roam around in the city. The captain steering the boat was lively and amusing; he not only pointed out places of interest on both sides of the river as we passed but also kept us entertained with his non-stop patter and anecdotes.

Fremantle was once an important city in West Australia and many migrants first set foot in Australia at the Fremantle Wharf. A young Swan River colony was established here in 1929 but this growing community soon realized that they had a serious shortage of labour, so in 1849 the farmers petitioned the colonial authority to request that skilled convicts be sent from England. The town was unprepared when the first ship with 75 prisoners aboard arrived and temporary accommodation was arranged at the harbour master's warehouse till a prison was constructed for them – using convict labour. Penal transportation to Western Australia was discontinued in 1868 and the number of convict inmates gradually declined. In 1991 the Fremantle Prison was closed permanently and reopened as a historic site and public museum. It is now one of the biggest tourist attractions for visitors from all over the world.

Michael booked us on a tour that took a little over an hour. Spread over 6 hectares the site houses the prison proper, gatehouse, perimeter walls, cottages, tunnels, solitary cells and gallows. Here too we had a very experienced guide who also kept us entertained with many anecdotes about prisoners and guards. Our guide gave us a graphic account of the prison riot that erupted on 4 January 1988 when the recorded temperature inside the prison reached 52.2 degrees C! The unbearable heat must have driven those 70 convicts crazy; it triggered a rampage during which they took 15 officers hostage and caused a conflagration which resulted in extensive damage to the tune of AU$1.8 million. However, through all the chaos not a single inmate managed to escape.

The main prison block housed the solitary confinement cells, the gallows and two chapels. The gallows room had an eerie feel to it, as if the ghosts of those who had been executed there were still 'hanging' around. Of the two chapels in the prison, one Protestant and one Catholic, we were taken to the Anglican chapel which had a painted representation of the Ten Commandments. The guide drew our attention to the sixth commandment where the standard wording, 'Thou Shalt not Kill' had been altered to, 'Thou Shalt do no Murder'. The original version would have been a glaring condemnation of the official 'killing' of prisoners at the gallows.

I had been vaguely puzzled about the 'sixth' commandment bit as, in the 'Catechism of the Catholic Church' it is not the sixth, but the fifth commandment that forbids killing. (The sixth commandment forbids adultery.) However, I just let it pass, but the discrepancy did not escape the eagle eye of our friend, Fr. Cyril deSouza, when he received our Christmas 2011 newsletter detailing our Australia visit. Fr. Cyril is a tenured professor in the Faculty of the Educational Sciences, in the Salesian Pontifical University in Rome. A little 'googling' showed Fr. Cyril that what I had reported about the wording of the 'sixth' commandment in that prison chapel was correct. Probing further, and after examining the commandments one by one, he realised that other Christian Churches follow a different order. Most have split the first commandment into two; thus the Roman Catholic fifth becomes their sixth commandment! Then to maintain the original total of 10 commandments, they combined the catholic ninth and tenth, into a single tenth. (I have added this explanation in case the same question arose for other readers.)

On our return from Fremantle, we drove to the Pinnaroo Valley Memorial Park which is actually a cemetery where cremated remains are memorialized. The reason Michael and Andrea took us there was not to visit the dead – but to get our first glimpse of the kangaroo! Like some first-time visitors to India who expect to see elephants walking the streets, or people living in tree houses, we too thought we would see plenty of kangaroos everywhere in Australia. What we saw in the park were small specimens, some so tame that you could walk right up to them. A few had joeys in their pouches and all-in-all they looked a sorry lazy bunch that did not have to work for their food .

King's Park can definitely be called the crowning glory of Perth. It is a sprawling 405 hectares of bushland, parkland and botanical garden atop and along the slopes of Mount Eliza on the western edge of the city. We made two visits to this historic, magnificent park, once at night to marvel at the spectacular overview of a spangled tapestry of twinkling lights beneath a starlit sky, and once during the day to enjoy the sweeping panorama of the entire city spread out in all directions, skirted by the placidly flowing Swan River. We were impressed to hear that this park is larger than New York's Central Park and is open 24x7x365. It is one of the most popular visitor destinations in Western Australia.

I would like to touch upon the original inhabitants of Australia, the Aboriginals and the Torres Strait Islanders. It is believed that they arrived in Australia in migratory waves from south-east Asia between 40,000 and 150,000 years ago. Aboriginal laws and customs evolved from the myths that grew from their beliefs that their ancestors created the land and were 'great spirits of the dreaming' who controlled the movements of the planets and stars, the seasons and the tides. They also believed that the ritual telling of these myths, whether in dance, song or painting, enabled them to draw on the power and influence of their ancestral spirits. They have no written language but their distinctive art form which has evolved over millennia and records the beliefs and stories which are being passed on to successive generations shows a deep connection with the land and the environment. With the arrival of European settlers, these people were dispossessed of their lands, and their traditional lifestyles and cultures were totally disrupted. As a result, they face innumerable problems relating to livelihood, health, education, employment, and opportunity in general. For those who have survived, it is a losing battle in still trying to maintain their traditional way of life. Today they make up only 1.5 per cent of Australia's total population and are among the most disadvantaged groups in Australian society.

Our stay in Perth was at the height of their summer. Everyone we visited had their homes air conditioned. While we found the mornings and evenings quite cool and pleasant, walking outdoors in the heat of the sun at midday felt like a blowtorch was trained on your skin! Fortunately, we didn't have to walk out too often.

Before we realised it, we found ourselves on the eve of Christmas. We took a break from our sightseeing to get ready for 'Midnight' Mass, which we attended at the Good Shepherd Church at 8 pm. Melissa and Joslyn were hosting Christmas lunch the next day for family and a few friends and everyone contributed by bringing along a dish. I must say I was impressed with Melissa's efficiency in the kitchen. In a seemingly effortless manner she completed the day's cooking and even made traditional Christmas sweets – all this before we even woke up!

We had one pre- and one post-Christmas party with some of Joe's cousins, Sandra and Frank Lawlor, Ashley and Monica Pereira and Arden and Dierdre Pereira, who had settled in Perth years ago. It was good to finally meet up with them on their turf and also catch up with their families.

Post-Christmas, the lunches and dinners continued well into the New Year, but we took a break to visit Whiteman Park, which covers an area of more than 4200 hectares. It has many picnic spots and is a popular place for Sunday family outings. Within Whiteman Park is located the Caversham Wildlife Park, a family owned and managed park that has one of largest private collections of native Australian animals like koalas, kangaroos, wombats, quokkas, emus, camels, dingoes, echidnas and more. Our first stop was at Molly's Farm where a handsome guy explained to us how trained dogs mustered the sheep, and he went on to demonstrate the shearing process. He made it look quite simple but I'm sure that besides skill, it needed a lot of strength to hold the large sheep still while quickly shearing it with an electric razor. The whip cracking demonstration also looked easy but the first volunteer to try it did not succeed. We were rather surprised when a Sri Lankan chit of a boy volunteered and actually succeeded in doing it not once but several times. Then we saw how they made billy tea by swinging the can in wide circles overhead without letting a single drop spill, and we watched in amusement the lamb feeding and cow milking. When I saw a huge black and white dappled cow being led in I could not help remarking to Melissa that it made me think of her brother, Michael, because when he was younger his sometimes brooding sulky look made someone nickname him 'cow'. But when the cow was 'introduced', the audience was asked if anyone would like to milk 'Brenda!'

New Year's Eve was party time again. We all went to the dance organised at the Goan Club and I surprised myself by dancing almost non-stop. I thought that because of my bad ankle I would have to sit out for most of the evening, but fortunately it did not trouble me that night or the next morning. It was a fun night and I even sang with the band who later invited me to join them at another venue, which of course I had to decline. After my name was announced, many came forward to meet us and we were happy to exchange greetings with long lost acquaintances from India, some of whom had migrated to Perth over 30 years ago. We rested for most of New Year's Day but in the evening Mark insisted on taking us to see the Burswood Casino. The place was quite packed when we got there and practically every coin operated game machine had an ardent and engrossed male or female glued to it. After strolling around the casino Joe and I finally decided to stay and watch the live band performing, while Mark went to try his luck at his favourite tables. Except for the singer, the band members were elderly but played with gusto. In addition to the music, we had bonus entertainment watching a lady, who was a little the worse for drink, dancing by herself, while two buxom gals, well past their prime, were doing their best to catch the eye of the singer – who in turn was eyeing the younger, prettier gals.

On our last day with Melissa, Joslyn and family, they drove us to see a few more local sites and to Tranby House in Maylands. This historic English cottage-style farmhouse was one of the oldest surviving buildings from the early settlement of the Swan River Colony who arrived in Western Australia from Yorkshire, England, on the ship

'Tranby' in 1830. Unfortunately, we were unable to view the interior of this cottage as we reached after visiting hours. Several oak, olive and mulberry trees that surrounded the house were also believed to have been planted by the original inhabitants. We spent some time in this very peaceful setting almost wishing we could have joined some of the people quietly fishing on the riverbank.

Mel, Jos and family were soon to leave on their annual vacation, so on 4 January, we packed our bags and got ready to move to Michael and Andrea's place. We also said goodbye to Buddy, their Border collie. It had been an unending delight to watch him play football and cricket with such focused attention. No matter how we tried to misdirect him when kicking or throwing the ball, he always managed to intercept it. I think he found great playing companions in Joe and me and became fairly attached to us, especially when Joe started taking him for walks. Melissa told us that after we left, on several occasions she found Buddy in the room we had occupied, where he had gone to check for us. She was rather surprised at this, because that part of the house was off limits to Buddy who had been trained not to cross the line drawn between the living room and the bedrooms.

On the day we returned from our visit to Fremantle Michael and Andrea had given us a quick tour of their impressive beach-front house with swimming pool, in Hillary's Harbour. Hillary's Harbour is a northern coastal suburb of Perth in the city of Joondalup and gets its name from Bertram John Hillary who was blinded in one eye during World War I while fighting in Gallipoli. During the Great Depression he came to this area with his brother Harry. They built a boatshed on the beach in 1930 and earned their livelihood by fishing. For years, the family were the only residents of that isolated spot, with the nearest store a 5-km. walk away. During the Second World War, the Australian Army labelled the area 'Hillary's Beach' on their maps, and the name stuck.

Knowing that Joe was interested in fishing, Michael had arranged to take us on a fishing trip the following day. He drove us to the house of his friend, John Williams, and there we transferred to John's vehicle to which he had hitched a trailer on which his boat was loaded. After reaching the harbour, John, with Michael ably assisting him, launched the boat into the water very expertly. After we all got in John zoomed off in a sweeping curve, taking us fairly far out to sea very soon. The day had started out sunny, but soon black clouds began massing and in a vindication of the weather forecast, it began to pour. There was no real shelter on the boat so we quickly donned raincoats which gave us some protection. John, Michael and Joe baited hooks and cast off; I too held a line but soon gave up as I caught nothing. The others kept getting bites, but invariably, the catch was a puffer fish which was immediately thrown back. Then John caught a 'good' fish. We were surprised to see him measure it on a foot-scale and then throw it overboard. There was a strict rule that fish below a certain size had to be returned to the sea. To make up for the weather playing spoilsport, we had a very special treat. A great big dolphin came out of nowhere and began to frolic with us. Leaning over the gunwale, we even touched him. We were happy that he stayed with us, circling around and under the boat for quite a long time before he decided to go find someone who would feed him. That alone made the trip worthwhile.

On 6 January Michael and Andrea took us to Yanchep National Park, which was 26 miles north of Perth. For thousands of years prior to the arrival of the Europeans, these were the hunting grounds of the aboriginals. Joe lost the race with Andrea who rushed to buy us the entrance tickets for a guided tour of the Crystal Caves. These underground limestone caves are home to tiny amphipods, shrimp-like crustaceans that live in the streams of the caves. On one occasion the caves were vandalized and several stalagmites and stalactites were broken and carried off. Word was put out, and the culprits were eventually caught when a passer-by found the stumps used for decorating a garden. The Park is also noted for its koala colonies and we enjoyed walking along a boardwalk and studying the koalas sleeping, eating or staring at us lazily. Most had a drugged look!

On our last-but-one day in Perth, Michael drove the 245 kms to Nambung National Park, home to the Pinnacles Desert. The Park was named after the winding Nambung (meaning 'crooked' in the Aboriginal language) River. Practically unknown to the general public till the late 1960s, this desert is now a popular tourist destination. The 'pinnacles' were a unique geological phenomenon and presented an almost surreal landscape of eerie limestone protuberances erupting as it were out of a vast stark desert of yellow rippled sand dunes. Like most deserts, this place too teemed with wildlife, mostly nocturnal, so we did not catch sight of any. At first glance I was reminded of the Guilin landscape in China, except that these were more like pillars that ranged in size from dwarfs to giants 4 mts tall. Michael asked me to pose with one, pressing my lips against it, saying it was traditional for visitors to be photographed this way, but I unfortunately neglected to ask why. I complied without thinking, but when he started laughing I looked back and realized that the pillar was a perfect phallic shape! Well, after that 'cow' story at the Caversham Park, he certainly got his own back at me.

On our last evening in Perth, we thought we should make at least one visit to the beach area. Unfortunately, the beach at Hillarys is difficult to access because of large sand dunes and vegetation. Instead we walked on the Sorrento Quay, a large marina which also has a retail complex on the site. We enjoyed walking the length of the boardwalk, delighting in the beautiful items on display in the windows.

The next afternoon Michael and Andrea saw us off at the airport. Before we left Perth we spoke to Melissa, Joslyn and family who were already enjoying their vacation. Our friends had spared no effort to ensure we had a thoroughly good time. Joe and I both found Perth a delightful place and became quite enamoured of the wide open spaces, the broad roads, the low spreading cottages, and the friendly people who didn't need a reason to start up a conversation. We realised that we would have enjoyed settling in such a place had we decided to follow through on our decision to emigrate in 1974. Now it was much too late and, in any case, we are content to live in our own country.

Chapter Twenty-five

2011-2012
WHEN IRISH EYES ARE SMILING
"In Dublin's fair city, where the girls are so pretty…"

Like my belief about Edinburgh in Scotland being a distant dream, Ireland was another place I felt I would never see. And with all the fighting that went on there between the Catholics and Protestants, it felt like a dreary place to visit. Thank goodness I didn't hold on to this belief because when Vanessa and Sanjay moved to Dublin in mid-2011, they thought it was the most natural thing to extend an invitation to us. We first planned to spend Christmas with them and asked Melissa and family to also join us from New York. This did not work out as Kerissa's Christmas vacation would last a short time and Kerman could not get leave. It was then decided that we would all travel from Dublin to New York to spend the festive season together for the first time. To avoid the Christmas rush, Joe booked our tickets early via the internet. Each Mumbai-Dublin-NY-Mumbai ticket cost us Rs.60,878 and was cheaper than what most other airlines were charging. The routing to Dublin added to the cost of our tickets and we travelled by thrcc different airlines.

Winter had already set in when we arrived in Dublin on 24 November. With Sanjay at work and little Gaia at nursery, Vanessa met us at the airport and we took a taxi to Sandy Mount, which is a coastal seaside suburb in Dublin, located about 5 kms from the city. Their beautiful apartment on Claremont Road was large, airy and had lovely views, not to mention the high security and special access lifts. Joe and I soon made ourselves familiar with the village, the few shops, restaurants and cafes (which we visited during the course of our stay) located around the triangular park known as Sandymount Green.

Though there are buses and trains that connect to the city, Vanessa ended up taking taxis which took about 20 minutes as compared to using public transport which required three to four changes and took about an hour. Also, not having a car made it difficult to do short runs. Our first ride was to fetch 2-year old Gaia from nursery that evening. She had been speaking about our visit for months before we arrived but when she first saw us, she stared for some time and then greeted us with a coy shy smile and willingly took hold of my hand after giving us a hug and a kiss. She had agreed to give us her bedroom while she moved to a smaller room but we enjoyed the many forays she made daily to check on us, her toys and her large collection of books.

One of the first things that Vanessa did was to march us off to Grafton Street and make sure we bought warm (and expensive!) boots which she insisted on paying for. Many know what a colourful character and philanderer King Charles II of England was, and I discovered that Grafton Street was named after one of the many illegitimate sons (Henry FitzRoy, First Duke of Grafton) of this English king who did not produce a single legitimate offspring. This was one of the main shopping areas in Dublin; in 2008 it was the fifth most expensive main shopping street in the world! Now I believed what Vanessa told us about Dublin being even more expensive than London! Like many big cities that have pedestrianised shopping areas, Grafton Street too, for the most part, is free of traffic. At a junction of the short stretch that has traffic, is a life-size bronze statue of Molly Malone, a very colourful Irish character. But whether she was a real person or not, the legend of 'Molly Malone' selling her 'Cockles and Mussels' in 'Dublin's Fair City' became immortalised in the different titles of that famous Irish song that is almost an unofficial anthem of Dublin. While taking a tour of the city, our very jovial coach driver, who also acted as a guide, remarked that this beautiful fishmonger plied her trade by day but at night she sold other wares. A 20th century legend claimed that a real Molly, who was a hawker by day and a part-time prostitute by night, existed in the 17th century and is supposed to have died of a fever at a young age. However, there is no evidence that the song is based on a real woman. There were many Molly Malones born in Dublin over the centuries, but the one commemorated died on 13 June 1699, which is now declared as 'Molly Malone Day' (there we go again with another June day!).

Ireland has many celebrities and Oscar Wilde was one of the most famous of them. While on the bus tour of the city and also while travelling by taxi, we often passed by the statue of him in Merrion Square where he used to live. What a sad end for such a great man who lived in an age when homosexuality was considered a crime and punishable by being imprisoned. He died in Paris and was buried there, but his remains were brought to Dublin and interred in a special tomb in 1909. The design, in relief, on his tomb was a modernist angel which was originally complete with male genitalia but this was vandalised. Then in 2000 a multimedia artist installed a silver prosthesis to replace them. The epitaph on his tomb is a verse from 'The Ballad of Reading Gaol':

> *And alien tears will fill for him*
> *Pity's long-broken urn,*
> *For his mourners will be outcast men,*
> *And outcasts always mourn.*

We were very happy to meet one of Sanjay's colleagues from work: Mari Hurley very sweetly made time to drive us around the beautiful Irish countryside one Sunday. One of the places she took us to was Powerscourt House, where a 13th century medieval castle that belonged to the Le Power Family once stood . Powerful Irish families had battled for possession of the castle and lands for 800 centuries. In the 18th century, Powerscourt House was built around the medieval castle but a fire destroyed it in 1974. Once again the castle was restored and re-opened in 1996 and that is what we saw. This tourist site draws many visitors not just for the beautiful Irish gifts, clothes and furniture sold there, but also for the range of food at the exotic Terrace Café (where we had a heavy lunch) and the palatial and extensive terraced grounds through which we strolled after that. Gaia went rushing through this park and climbed fairly steep grassy slopes on her own and it was a job keeping up with her. It reminded us of the time her mother at the same age, rushed into the sea regardless of whether we were following or not. If one had the time, and the weather was more clement, it would have been an ideal place to spend the day, but evening temperatures were dropping fast and forced us to return indoors.

On our drive back, Mari asked if we would like to visit a very famous pub. We hesitated only because we were worried whether Gaia would be up to extending our day a little longer but she was in her element there (yes, everyone is welcome, even children). 'Johhnie Fox's' pub started in 1798 and is located on top of the Dublin mountains at a place called Glencullen. No wonder it is called the highest pub in the country. It is also one of the oldest in Ireland. The patrons of this pub include a long list of Royalty, World Presidents, Prime Ministers, World Ambassadors, Political figures, and many famous Film, TV and Musical Celebrities. We were fascinated with the ancient bric-a-brac filling every available space indoors and outside as well. They seemed to have a little, and sometimes a lot, of almost everything from the past many centuries. A three-piece band was playing and singing with gusto when we entered. The music was feet-stomping and made one want to get up and dance spontaneously. Gaia did just that. I don't think anything other than traditional Irish music and songs are featured here and the patrons just love it; they sing along or dance as they feel. Though it was a detour on our route home, we all agreed that it was well worth the visit.

On another day, Mari arranged for us to visit the Houses of Parliament and got us special passes for this. We were quite awed with Leinster House, the stately building that houses the national Parliament. This was originally the palace of the Duke of Leinster and the grand interior, carpeted staircases and corridors still retained the feeling of a palace. More modern buildings have been added on since 1922 and we were given a tour of the place together with a group of school children who were also visiting at the same time. All the officials we met were very kind and went out of their way to be helpful and share information. Since Parliament had adjourned when we arrived, we were shown to the café where we had some refreshments before we once more made our way to the Visitors' Gallery from where we could watch the proceedings of the House. The debate that afternoon was on Education (which accounted for the presence of the school children) and while a member of the ruling party gave a long speech, he also heckled the Opposition where only two members were present. The speaker also addressed some issues related to the school children. Frankly, I could not follow much of the proceedings and, anyway, we had to leave soon after as Gaia became restless and was drawing attention with her chatter. None of us could deny that visiting the Irish Houses of Parliament was indeed a special treat and privilege.

Ireland may not be as affluent as England economically, but one thing the Irish are never in short supply of, is good humour. And they are not afraid to talk to you or say 'Good Morning', which is why I guess their eyes are always smiling.

THE GODS ARE NOT CRAZY
"Bolo-Tara-ra…"

The Irish are fiercely patriotic and now, as in days gone by, one can see evidence of this. Before our visit to Ireland, we really had no idea

387

about the country or its rich history and its many ancient monuments. The interest grew when we went on a special tour to the Hill of Tara and then on to Newgrange in the Boyne Valley.   I listened more closely to our very knowledgeable lady guide who rattled off dates and events without a pause. However, there was one instance where we could enlighten her about a fact of which she was unaware – that Bombay was given as a dowry to King Charles II when he married Catherine of Braganza from Portugal. It was then that she could make the connection of the British in India and she acknowledged us for this information when she brought in the topic during her narration.

When I saw the movie 'Gone with the Wind', I had wondered why the big family house of the O'Haras was named 'Tara', which I took to be an Indian name. Visiting the Hill of Tara in County Meath, Leinster, which is located near the River Boyne, I realised how and why so much feeling went into Scarlett O'Hara's attachment to the family house.   Down the ages, the Hill of Tara continued to draw archaeologists and historians who have been trying to unravel the deep mysteries attached to it, but all they could come up with was that the place was the political and spiritual capital of the island. Even at the turn of the 20th century, there were some Jewish people in Britain who excavated the Hill when they thought that the Irish were part of the lost tribes of Israel and that the Hill of Tara contained the Ark of the Covenant. (Maybe they should think of visiting the village of Chui in Mon, Nagaland!) Earliest records show that high kings were inaugurated here. They had to drink ale and symbolically marry the goddess Maeve in order to acquire the high kingship. Another reason it acquired prominence is that The Hill afforded a view of the surroundings for miles in every direction and that also made it a strategic place to be warned of the enemy approaching.   Actually, when we got to the Hill, we were not very impressed and felt there was not much to see but our guide explained a lot to us. She wisely remained seated in the coach while we all ventured out to examine the Hill more closely, but most of us beat a hasty retreat back to the warm coach since the exposed hill made it very uncomfortable to remain there too long.

Tara and Newgrange (which I will get to in a while) go back in time to the first known settlements in Ireland, around 8000 BC when Mesolithic hunter-gatherers migrated from continental Europe. A few traces of this group have been unearthed by archaeologists but it was their descendants and later Neolithic arrivals, mainly from the Iberian Peninsula, who were responsible for these two major Neolithic sites. Of course there are others scattered all over Ireland but I'm writing about just the two we inspected. As a hill and as a capital Tara seemed to have had political and religious influence on the people, but this diminished after the arrival of St. Patrick and other christian missionaries in the early to mid-5th century. Over the next 600 years, the indigenous Celtic religions were gradually overtaken by christianity. While it is generally believed that it was St. Patrick who first brought christianity to Ireland, other sources say that there were missionaries active in southern Ireland long before St. Patrick. Palladius, a contemporary chronicler had been sent by the Pope in 431 as the first bishop to 'the Irish believing in Christ' in the Leinster and Meath kingdoms. St. Patrick was said to have arrived in Ireland in 432 (though some sources say it was as late as 461) but his main mission was to convert the pagan Irish in the more remote kingdoms in Ulster and Connacht. Well, whatever and whoever was first, the new faith was to have the most profound effect on the Irish.

In the centuries that followed, there were invasions by the Vikings and Normans, and after several generations, a group of mixed Irish and Norse ethnic backgrounds emerged. They were known as the Gall-Gaels (Gall being the old Irish word for 'foreign'). Today Gaelic is still spoken and written in Ireland and it was very difficult for us to even pronounce some of the street signs. Gaia has already picked up quite a bit of it in nursery, though she still retains the British accent she acquired in England.

In my quest to understand how the bitter Catholic-Protestant divide came about in Ireland and continues to this day, I have necessarily to recount a very condensed part of this history. Pope Alexander III, wanted to eradicate pagan Irish customs that conflicted with the teaching of the catholic church and he 'gave' Ireland to Henry II, King of England. (England had catholic monarchs at that time.) It was this papal declaration in 1172 that led to the English conquest of Ireland. The English continued to be in control in Ireland for more than 700 years (and British involvement continued in Ireland even after). However, it was not until the time of Henry VIII's rejection of papal authority over the Church of England and the English Reformation (which was not accepted in Ireland) that things changed. When the English and Scottish protestant settlers arrived by the thousands (that explains the many common surnames in Scotland and Ireland), the catholic landholders were displaced and their lands given to the protestant settlers. Thus with the military and political defeat of Gaelic Ireland in the early 17th century, religion became a new divisive element in Ireland and sectarian conflict in Irish history was here to stay. It took seven and a half centuries for the Irish to regain their freedom, and hats off to them that they did.

From the Hill of Tara it was a long drive to *Bru na Boinne* or Palace of the Boyne, a name given to one of the world's most important archaeological landscapes in the county of Meath. After getting off the bus at the Visitor Centre, we were shown a short film in an auditorium. Then after shopping a bit for souvenirs, we lunched in the adjoining café and left sufficient time to walk across the small bridge spanning the River Boyne and get the shuttle bus on the other side – we had to be there at a fixed time. This is the only visitor access to Newgrange, and a five-minute ride brought us to our destination.

The first sight of this large kidney-shaped mound (which looked more circular from some angles) that covered an area of over one acre was awesome. We had to wait for some time till a new guide took over.

She led us up to the entrance but before she could take us in, she stopped to give us a long explanation about Newgrange, the significance of the famous Entrance Stone and the Roof Box. Standing on that exposed mound with no shelter from the cold winds, we could barely pay attention as we were freezing despite our warm coats and hats. I kept willing her to move on but I think we stood there for a good 15 minutes or more.

The *Bru na Boinne* World Heritage site condenses 9000 years of history and is one of the largest prehistoric megalithic sites in Europe. The entire area covers 780 hectares and contains around 40 passage graves and other prehistoric sites. Newgrange, Knowth and Dowth are the three largest and most spectacular of these. We were going to be seeing only Newgrange, which was said to have been constructed over 5000 years ago, around 3200 BC. This predates Stonehenge in England and the Great Pyramid of Giza in Egypt, and I can't believe how few people have heard of it! The outside base of the mound had 97 kerb stones, some with richly decorated megalithic art, but the huge entrance stone was indeed most impressive. We entered through a 19-metre long inner passage and had to stoop a bit in some places, till we reached a cross chamber. We were so impressed by the interior, constructed as it was without any visual supports, with slabs interlocking.

Though archaeologists had first classified Newgrange as a passage tomb, it is now recognised to be much more. The people who built it had a great knowledge of science and astronomy, and while we were in the chamber, the presence of the Roof Box was once again explained. This box was discovered only at the time of excavations between 1962 and 1975. At that time, this small square opening above the entrance baffled the experts who were later thrilled to discover its purpose. We too were given a demonstration of how the dark passage and chamber are illumined by the winter solstice sun through the roof box. From 19 to 23 December, a narrow beam of light starts penetrating the roof box at dawn and reaches the floor of the chamber, gradually extending to the rear of the chamber. As the sun rises higher, the beam widens within the chamber so that the whole room becomes dramatically illuminated. This lasts for 17 minutes from 9 am onwards. The builders probably constructed this to mark the new year, though some feel it served as a powerful symbol of victory of life over death. It was fascinating and just too amazing! The accuracy is remarkable. Till today there are many who make the journey just to witness this phenomenon, but only a lucky few get picked via a free annual lottery. And even then you need more luck to have a clear sky with the sun shining to witness the event, but if Irish weather is anything to go by, one will indeed need the gods on your side!

WALKING IN A WINTER WONDERLAND
"We hear the Christmas angels the great glad tidings tell, O come to us, abide with us Our Lord Emmanuel"

Christmas 2011 was scheduled to be special as our family was going to celebrate all together for the first time. Vanessa, Sanjay, Gaia, Joe and I all travelled together on 15 December. Gaia is in her element when travelling by air and particularly likes to frolic in airports. She continued to entertain and enchant the flight crew throughout the journey with her chatter, occasionally making trips to visit 'grandma and grandpa' as we did not all get seats together.

Those first days we relaxed a bit and then got into the Christmas shopping mode as we had not yet completed our gift buying. Everyone helped a bit to decorate the tree, especially Gaia, who thoroughly enjoyed being indulged by everyone. Joe took charge of decorating the house; I was designated official gift-wrapper and ended up packing all the gifts – except those meant for me! When we were more settled, we made many forays into Manhattan which was gaily lit up with Christmas lights, the famous FAO Schwartz shop and the many shopping malls that offered tempting bargains. Of course, there were invitations from friends to many parties. While Kerman was at work, Melissa drove us around, mainly to shopping malls where Vanessa indulged herself after the expensive malls of Dublin. Though Sanjay was supposed to be on vacation, he continued to work from home and was on many conference calls with Dublin and London, some early in the morning, because of time differences.

Instead of a Broadway play, Joe and I were treated to something different this time. Just before Christmas Kerman was given two tickets to the Annual Christmas Spectacular, and he very kindly gave them to us. This Christmas stage musical has been a New York tradition since 1933 and features The Rockettes, a women's precision dance team. So on 23 December, Kerman dropped us off at Radio City Hall in Rockefeller Centre while the others went off to roam around Manhattan. The décor, lighting and plush splendour of Radio City Hall was a sight to behold, and we even had excellent seats. The 2011 show was titled 'The Rockettes Magical Journey' and featured over 140 performers, lavish sets and costumes and an original music score. The Rockettes are best known for their eye-high leg kick performed in perfect unison in a chorus line in every performance. A new addition was a 3D live scene so we were given special 3D specs to use for this. Of the many different performances, the best of all were the Parade of the Wooden Soldiers and the Living Nativity. This last was no song and dance routine but conveyed so much more in the movements and the way the actors walked, especially the three Magi who had come to worship the Christ and offer him gifts which were carried by an array of servants who followed them as they walked majestically across the stage. The show lasted 90 minutes and combined singing, dancing and humour. We enjoyed the show very much and I was really happy that we got the opportunity to see it just before Christmas. Like the name said, it was indeed spectacular!

We spent Christmas morning opening up piles of gifts with Gaia being the chief opener for everyone. It was a laid back day with a late brunch till we left in the evening for a Christmas dinner at Sophie and Lileesh's house. Our friend Fr. Joby Mathew, who was in New York for further studies, said a special mass for us. It was almost midnight by the time the party broke up and we left to go home.

A New Year's party was organised in Long Island and soon after that Vanessa, Sanjay and Gaia left on 3 January to return to Dublin. Gaia was very sad to leave her 'New York home' as she called it. Having stayed with them before coming to New York, she had presumed that Joe and I would be returning with them and was upset that 'grandma and grandpa' were not accompanying them back to Dublin. After getting home she pestered her parents daily to bring her back to her 'New York home'. The noisy house had suddenly turned quiet and Joe and I also began to think of returning home earlier than scheduled, but Mel, Kerman and Kerissa would have none of it. They insisted that we remain to celebrate Kerissa's 16th birthday on 19 February. Our thoughts were on all the work waiting for us at home but in the end we relented. To stave off the boredom that comes from doing nothing around the house I kept busy for part of the day editing the chapters of this book and spent the rest of the time in front of the idiot box watching my favourite game shows. Mel had also enrolled Joe at her gym but I joined only in the last month to work off the extra weight we had put on eating and drinking indiscriminately.

On 5 February we attended the Carmina Burana Choral Project at Carnegie Hall, the famous concert venue located on Seventh Avenue in Midtown Manhattan. Kerman bought good tickets for us all as the occasion was special. We were there to listen to Kerissa sing with her school choir and the choirs of two other schools in the beautiful Isaac Stern Auditorium. Carnegie Hall was built by Andrew Carnegie, the US President, in 1891 and today it is one of the most prestigious venues in the world for both classical and popular music, so it was no wonder that Kerissa was thrilled to have her name on the Playbill. The performances were all stunning and very enjoyable, and we were happy to meet up with one of the young composers, Anthony Constantino, after the performance. He was pleased to hear that Kerissa had sung one of his compositions and he happily signed her Playbill.

Kerissa's 16th birthday was celebrated in style at Nirvana, an Indian restaurant in Manhattan. Joe had been preparing some trendy decorations for days in advance and they certainly made the place look festive. Kerissa was thrilled that almost all the friends she had invited turned up to celebrate with her. Of course, half the guests comprised friends of Mel and Kerman and we were close to a hundred. Some of the Americans tasted Indian food for the first time and liked it. As the restaurant owner happened to know Mel he put on a great buffet; the snacks too were plentiful and excellent so all had a great time. The celebrations continued at home with some of Kerissa's friends coming over to chat and laugh till midnight, and open up her gifts together. I guess this will remain a memorable birthday for our eldest granddaughter.

Four days after the celebrations, we were ready to leave. Joe and I had been careful about shopping even in Dublin because we had three months to go and we knew how even a few small things at a time accumulate into uncontrollable baggage. In New York too, we went easy on the shopping expeditions – till the last month, when I also fell prey to the bargains in every shop. I had planned not to buy even a single item of clothing for myself but ended up with more than I needed, including a lovely evening dress for whenever the occasion arises.

OUR GREAT BIG WONDERFUL WORLD
"He's got the whole world in His hands"

Although by now we had made many visits to the Big Apple, we had spent little time going to 'touristy' places. This trip we made up for it, thanks to Hira Daruvala, whom I have mentioned in an earlier chapter. Actually, we did not think we'd be meeting her at all because when we arrived in New York Hira left for India to take care of her mum during her surgery. When she returned in February she was happy to find us still in New York and then went out of her way to take us to places we had never even heard existed in New York.

Our first expedition was to The Cloisters Museum and Gardens, located on Margaret Corbin Drive, near the northern tip of Manhattan's Fort Tryon Park. It was difficult to believe that we were still in New York City when we got there because the ambience is so old world. The admission rates were pretty steep but Hira insisted on doing the honours and said that since she was a Member of the Metropolitan Museum of Art (the Cloisters is a branch of the Met) she gets discounted tickets. In any case, she did not give us the option. Spread over 1.6 hectares, The Cloisters is a recreation of medieval Europe as it incorporates parts from five French cloistered abbeys. We learnt that the buildings were disassembled brick by brick – or rather, stone by stone – and then shipped to New York where they were reassembled between 1934 and 1938. If that wasn't amazing enough, even the landscaped gardens were planted according to horticultural information obtained from old manuscripts, and include many medieval-style cloistered herb gardens.

There are about five thousand works of art which date from the year 800, with particular emphasis on pieces dating from the 12th through the 15th centuries. The huge Flemish Unicorn Tapestries from the Middle Ages are among the best known works of art. The Merode Room containing the 15th century altarpiece, the Gothic Chapel with its rich stained-glass windows from the 14th century and The Treasury Gallery are worth a special mention. The last had an array of many precious objects in gold, silver, ivory and silk from medieval churches and also a set of 15th century playing cards. Not only the land on which The Cloisters is located, but all the works of art, stained-glass, treasures and the very architecture have been painstaking collected from France, Spain, Germany, Austria and Italy and donated by John D. Rockefeller, Jr. The George Grey Barnard collection which forms the nucleus of the Cloisters collection was also acquired by Rockefeller. Barnard was an American sculptor who travelled extensively in France and there he purchased these old sculptures and architectural elements, mainly from descendants of citizens who had appropriated objects abandoned during the French Revolution. This explained a lot to me because I was puzzled when I first saw so much of European architecture in New York. Some might argue that these treasures should never have been moved from their original locations but I think Rockefeller and Barnard were responsible for salvaging great works of art that might have otherwise been lost forever. For instance, the column supports of The Chapter House in the Museum were being used to tether farm animals and would have found their natural way to a graveyard of obscurity.

We really enjoyed going around this museum and the fantastic views of the Hudson River from there but, like all museums, it can get tiring walking around for a long time. We would have enjoyed the guided tour which was scheduled for a little after we completed our rounds, and we even considered waiting for it, but then decided against a second round of walking. Instead, we drove the short distance to the New Leaf Restaurant and Bar for a late lunch which we enjoyed in each other's company.

From here we drove to Hira and Toos' plush 14th floor three-bedoom Manhattan apartment with a gorgeous view of the Hudson River on one side and an array of the New York skyline on the other. After freshening up, we went for a walk past the Juillard School to the Lincoln Centre for the Performing Arts, which is located on the Upper West side of Broadway. As we stood outside the Metropolitan Opera, we visualised Nicolas Cage waiting for his date with Cher in the movie 'Moonstruck'. How grand it looked in the movie and how pleased we were that we could enter and see parts of the building. Now I don't pretend to be a great classical music buff nor do I understand too much of it, but Opera is Opera and something everyone should experience at least once in their lifetime. Hira too was very keen that we should attend one so we checked out the announcements of the different shows. The following day a new production 'Anna Bolena' was being staged, with the famous Anna Netrebko in the lead role. Yes, it dramatised the story of Anne Boleyn, second wife of Henry VIII. The hitch was that tickets were priced at $100 and more, and tickets were sold out well in advance. Hira was insistent that we try for it and she told us how we could still get tickets at affordable rates. Though we were sceptical, we decided to go for it, which meant coming back again the next day.

The next morning, Hira came and picked us up from Forest Hills, and after dropping me off at the Met to save me the walk back, she and Joe went to park her car at the apartment. That's because parking charges anywhere in Manhattan cost an arm and a leg!

Now I have to explain about the affordable tickets we were going to try for and I have to begin with Agnes Varis, a Pharma Mogul who had made a fortune producing generic drugs. The daughter of Greek immigrants, Agnes was the only one of eight children to go to college. Her father scraped by as a greengrocer in Brooklyn while her mother was illiterate. Perhaps because of that background she had a soft spot for old people and poor people and decided to spread happiness by using her vast wealth. From 2007 she decided to underwrite cheap orchestra seats and made a huge donation to the Met for this very purpose. She also ensured that seniors would not have to wait in line.

They were allowed to phone in and book their seats starting at 10 am for the same day's show. Alternatively, they could do this online. Our enquiries from the various attendants at the Met warned us that it was extremely difficult to get through so Joe and I worked together that morning – while he remained online and logged into the booking site, I got through on the phone on the dot of 10 am. We were both kept waiting for a few minutes and then informed that all seats for seniors were sold out. Yes, that's how fast they are snapped up!

When we told Hira about this, her spirits were not dampened like ours. She had told us – and the attendants confirmed it – that two hours before the show, about 200 tickets are released, courtesy of Agnes Varis. We thought of coming back at 5 pm to stand in the queue but the attendant laughed and told us that the lines start queuing up from midday! It was already past 1 pm when we went down to check the line that had already grown quite long. Hira still did not give up but started counting the people to ensure that we would not be wasting our time till 5.30 pm. Joe was not at all keen to wait, but since there was still hope for us, Hira said that she would wait in line while Joe and I could roam around. With my bad ankle, walking did not appeal to me so I volunteered to wait while Hira went out to get us a bite to eat and Joe went off on his wanderings. Like the others waiting, some with their portable chairs and their packed lunch, I too spread my coat on the cold floor and opened my book of crossword puzzles. The time passed fairly quickly after Hira returned with lots of goodies and Joe too joined us. By 5 pm we were asked to move up to the floor above and at 5.30 pm sharp the booking began. By then, Hira and Toos had decided to join us for the show and not only did we each get 2 tickets but they were excellent orchestra seats at just $20 each! I've written all this so that music lovers visiting New York will know what to do if they are keen to attend the opera and cannot afford the price of regular tickets. Needless to say, the experience of the opera was great, with Anna Netrebko giving a stunning performance in a poignant role, especially at the time of her beheading. We got a different perspective of history in that performance.

Since it was rather late to return to Forest Hills, Hira and Toos graciously asked us to spend the night at their place and dropped us back the following morning. On Hira's next free day she once again picked us up, and this time, after driving around Manhattan and pointing out some unusual aspects of the city, we decided to visit the American Museum of Natural History (AMNH), located on the upper west side of Manhattan, across the street from Central Park. To save me the trouble of that long walk from her apartment to the museum, she ended up paying a fortune for parking her car at the closest car park. Once inside, Joe bought the tickets and we found that a guided tour was scheduled to begin shortly. However, the very aged lady guide was planning to do a tour of the Asian section which had a lot to do with India, so after listening politely for some time, we took our leave and made our way to the more exotic sections.

The AMNH is one of the largest and most famous museums in the world and has 25 interconnected buildings with exhibition halls, research laboratories, a large library, and over 200 scientific staff. Most fascinating for me was the Hayden Planetarium, which was part of the Earth and Space Centre, and we spent most of our time in this section. The stunning show takes you through time and space to experience the start of the Universe with the Big Bang theory. Walking down the spiral pathway after the show, we stopped to look at the exhibits of the planets around the spherical planetarium and read various explanations along the way. One of the museum's personnel came up to us to ask if he could be of any help with explanations; we got talking and had a very interesting dialogue with Richard Edelstein – that was his name. I suspect he was a little surprised about our interest in astronomy and was pleased to know that Hira was a doctor. The Hall of the Universe on the level below was also very interesting and we spent quite a long time here. There were several areas on the floor where we could check how much we would weigh on different planets.

As we were by then a bit tired and also very hungry, we stopped to have a very filling lunch of soup and a sandwich with salad at the Museum Café. Next stop was the Hall of Human Origins which covered 7 million years of human evolution. We saw a replica of the famous first set of hominid footprints discovered in Laetoli, Tanzania, to which I had made reference in my 2007 chapter on Africa. Then on to the Hall of Meteorites which had the most amazing specimens. A huge section of the Cape York meteorite found in Greenland was on display among the many others. The columns that support it extend through the floor and into the bedrock below the museum! I wonder how they managed to transport it.

The Hall of Minerals and Gems had a really big collection of gems and stones and this section also took a lot of time before we completed the Hall of Ocean Life with the wonderful marine specimens. As anyone who has gone to a museum knows, it is physically impossible to cover everything in a day, but we had yet to see the dinosaur section and it was almost closing time so that's where we rushed and managed to walk through those huge exhibits before we were asked to make our way to the exits.

Joe and I have visited so many museums in different parts of the world and in each we learn something new. At the AMNH we had the humbling experience of learning just how insignificant our Earth is in the grand scheme of the Universe. When Voyager I took a photograph of the Earth from four billion miles away, the Earth showed up only as a 'Pale Blue Dot' in a sea of stars and dust! As for the place of human beings, I think I would not be far wrong in believing that even a billionth of a grain of sand would still be larger. And yet man struts about on the earth immersed in his own little world never once considering the immensity of the jungle that surrounds us. And if this image still does not depress us, let me quote from the book Carl Sagan was inspired to write after he saw the photograph of the 'Pale Blue Dot':

> *"We succeeded in taking that picture (from deep space), and, if you look at it, you see a dot. That's here. That's home. That's us. On it everyone you know, everyone you love, everyone you've ever heard of, every human being who ever was, lived out their lives. The aggregate of all our joys and sufferings, thousands of confident religions, ideologies and economic doctrines. Every hunter and forager, every hero and coward, every creator and destroyer of civilizations, every king and peasant, every young couple in love, every hopeful child, every mother and father, every inventor and explorer, every teacher of morals, every corrupt politician, every superstar, every supreme leader, every saint and sinner in the history of our species, lived there – on a mote of dust suspended in a sunbeam".*

Chapter Twenty-six

THIS IS OUR ISLAND IN THE SUN
"All my days I will sing in praise of your forest, waters, your shining sun"

It was in the year 2003 that we started hunting for a second home in Goa. This harebrained scheme (we just did not have the funds to buy a place) was in keeping with other crazy things we've done. Still, we went full steam ahead with our go-Goa plan. That's one way of 'creating' what you want in life. We had narrowed down our choice of location to Dona Paula and Porvorim, believing them to be ideal. We put the matter in the hands of a broker and we inspected many places on three different trips to Goa for work or conventions, but none of the places we saw appealed to us.

Then one Sunday afternoon Joe called attention to an ad in the 'The Examiner' (a catholic weekly) offering furnished and unfurnished villas, apartments and studios for sale on an island in Goa. It had a name we had never heard of, but Joe suggested I call up the number given in the ad and get more details. I dislike making telephone calls and it was afternoon, certainly a bad time to call. But that phone call to Mr. Subhash Agnelo Coutinho resulted in quick action. He suggested that I come and see the place for myself and promised to send a car to pick me up from wherever I would be staying in Goa. I told him I would be there in four days' time. Joe was unable to accompany me because of his work, but I was fortunate that our friend, Mayrose Fernandes, agreed to come with me. Besides, she had a house in Khorlim, a village just off Mapusa where we could stay. We reached Khorlim on a sunny May morning and that same day we drove to Pomburpa, crossed by the ferry and soon found ourselves at the main gate of the Chorao Island Resort. We entered and drove down an avenue which had a profusion of colourful bougainvillea lining it. On our left were several villas and we stopped at the last one, where Mr. Coutinho was waiting for us.

Our first, very positive impression of the place was reinforced as Mr. Coutinho did the honour of escorting us around. He started with the villas and the duplex apartments and then showed us the one-bedroom cottages. Next we admired the one- and two-bedroom flats and peeped into several studio apartments. Each unit was well designed and elegantly furnished, down to picture frames and aesthetically chosen artefacts. More than I, it was Mayrose who was totally enamoured of all she saw. Added attractions of the complex were a large swimming pool and an ayurvedic and yoga centre. After satisfying my curiosity by asking a lot of questions while enjoying the cool and refreshing coconut water we were served, we left, promising to get in touch after returning to Mumbai.

Back in Khorlim, we could not stop talking about the resort, with Mayrose squirming with excitement, as she told me how she longed to be able to buy one of the small cottages for herself. The next morning we decided to return for a second visit. The Resort was deserted except for the security guard, as Subhash Coutinho and his family had left for Mumbai. Once again we went around looking and dreaming of what we could own. After a couple of days in Goa, we returned to Mumbai. I gave Joe all the details and said I liked the place very much and that he should come and take a look at it too, but he said he did not have the time and if I liked it I should go ahead and make a booking. But now came the tough part – we did not have the money for a down payment! As if that stopped us!! We had been thinking of selling our Breakthrough office in Bandra, so Joe and I went and spoke to Mr. Coutinho, telling him that we would put our office up for sale, and once that money came in, we could pay him – but in the meanwhile, could he please reserve a two-bedroom apartment fronted by a 28 mts lawn for us? To start with we offered a down-payment of the handsome sum of Rs.10,000! That he accepted us and our proposal at face value will tell you much about the man. Also, though he said he would charge us interest on the balance to be paid, he generously never did. That day a bond was forged that has grown stronger through the years.

It took several months before we managed to sell our office and make full payment for the apartment. Once again, it was off to Goa, alone, to sign the documents and complete registration formalities – and nobody in my family had as yet even seen the place! But I'm happy to say that when Joe and Vanessa finally made a trip to Goa, they were delighted with my choice. Though I had been attracted by the villas, I did not really care for their location near the main gate, so I finally opted for the apartment which was near the swimming pool and also centrally located. The price too was irresistible especially compared to the crazy Mumbai property rates. Subhash Coutinho had named all the residences after birds which were found on the island, which, incidentally, is a bird sanctuary. Our fully furnished two-bedroom apartment was named 'Flamingo' (but I have yet to see one of these birds on the island!) Of course we made some changes and additions to suit our needs and personalities and to make it feel like 'home' for us. We spent three wonderful years in 'Flamingo' and enjoyed every one of them with plenty of house guests and lots of entertainment.

Since many who heard about our place in Chorao were curious to know more about the resort and how we came to hear of it, I've included some details.

Subhash, a son of the soil, had spent a good part of his life on the island. He grew up roaming the land, swimming in the numerous inlets and in the pools created by the monsoon rains, fishing in the river with his father and catching enough fish for the table and more. Hearing what Subhash had to say about his father, Jose Balduinho Coutinho, I wished I had known him when he was alive. From the little we heard of him, he seemed an enterprising person. He had started a restaurant with a partner in Colaba, Bombay, and when the Navy acquired their property under the Land Acquisition Act, they returned to Goa feeling dejected – but not for long. The partners then decided to buy and run a bus in Panjim. In those days, the buses were made of brass and wood and while the partner drove the bus, Jose acted as conductor. When the bus ran off the road one day it literally broke into pieces, and once again they found themselves stranded by the wayside. They went on to open another eatery, this time in Goa. When a friend sounded Jose out about joining a ship, his interest was aroused as he was keen to see the world. However, he decided that he would work only on cruise liners. This he did, and when he returned to his native village of Ambarim in Chorao, it was in a canoe from Panjim, laden with gifts for the entire village. Every man woman and child turned up to help ferry the packages from the jetty to his house.

Over the years, Jose rose to become the Chief of the Indian crew aboard the P&O cruise liners, which earned him a seat at the Captain's table on every occasion. That's how he found himself sitting at the same table with H.M. Queen Elizabeth II. Jose was an accomplished ballroom dancer of exceptional finesse, a gold medallist from the Victor Silvester Academy of Ballroom Dancing in London, no less. As he glided across the floor dancing with the purser's wife, the queen watched avidly. The next thing he knew, Her Majesty had requested the Captain to inform Jose Balduinho Coutinho that she would like him to dance with her! And he did. I could not resist adding this snippet in my narrative as I was very impressed.

When Subhash married his college sweetheart Bina, who belonged to the Punjabi community, both families were outraged and disowned them so they had to struggle on their own to make ends meet. At times they did not even have enough money to buy their baby girl a tin of milk powder. However, as the years passed Subhash made a success of the business venture he had started in Mumbai, and of his life. Because of his innate love for his native land, Chorao, I think one of the first things he did when he had saved some money was to purchase the four and a half acres that was on sale in the village of Belbhat. He says his original intention was to have a farm and build two houses for himself and his brother. But when a school friend of his got wind of this, he put a sum of money in Subhash's hands and insisted he build him a place too. Clearing and landscaping the plot, which was almost barren, was no small job. Somewhere along the way Subhash got the idea of constructing a few more cottages for sale in order to recover some of his investment in the property. One prospective buyer, a known film-maker, who saw it at that stage, was put off by the arid look and sparse vegetation. When this same person visited the resort years later, he could not believe his eyes. Subhash had transformed rocky fields into a veritable oasis with luxuriant trees and beautiful flowering plants.

The resort has kept undergoing changes. The green cover has improved, the entrance avenue now has almond and palm trees lining both sides, forming a shady canopy, the ayurvedic and yoga centres have been closed for various reasons, and almost every residence in the complex got sold. An astrologer had told Joe before he married me that I had 'lucky feet' and would bring prosperity with me wherever I walked! When I told Subhash that I had brought him the luck when we booked a place in his resort, he never let on whether he believed that or not.

The building which housed the ayurvedic and yoga centre was remodelled into four apartments. The two on the first floor, which each had an open-to-air extension to the living room plus an overhead terrace, and commanded a spectacular river view, were snapped up immediately. Two ground floor apartments were still available. We had by this time realized that there were too many distractions around our centrally located 'Flamingo', and here was an opportunity to make a change for the better. That's how we moved to 'Osprey', also a 2-bedroom apartment but much larger, airier and brighter than

'Flamingo', and certainly more secluded and 'private'. Actually, what sealed our decision to buy it was the entrance porch, which I fell in love with. Silly reason, some might say, but we've often done 'silly' things before and they brought great results!

Those who have visited 'Osprey' or seen pictures of it asked why we would ever want to return to the concrete jungle of Mumbai. We asked ourselves the same question, and the balance weighed heavily in favour of our retreat in Chorao, where we can enjoy such peace and quiet. I have been doing most of my writing here in undisturbed solitude. Joe and I have also taken to having our breakfast and evening tea on the balcony which has a sweeping and panoramic view of paddy fields, a sliver of river, and rolling hillsides covered with lush vegetation in various shades of green, all so soothing to the eye (especially during and just after the monsoons). The white-painted Mae de Deus Church in Pomburpa (all Churches and chapels in Goa are painted white in traditional Portuguese style) stands out starkly in the middle of the green hillside directly opposite, and seems to send a benediction to us across the river. Twice a day it reminds us to pray the Angelus, which we faithfully do. Could one ask for more?!

Most people opting for a second home in Goa pick places near the beach. Not us. If we, or our guests want to visit the beach, we make a day of it and then return to the enfolding peace of our island. We prefer to live insulated from the noisy touristy spots or the crowded residential areas, even if they are considered elite. The Resort is one of the very few places on the island that can be labelled 'modern' and yet, because of its secluded location and greenery, it retains a natural rustic charm. For the same reason, many residents on the Island are not in favour of the proposal to construct a bridge connecting Chorao with the mainland. Yes, the bridge will give easy access to and from the Island, but once that happens, Chorao will become just another suburb of Panjim, and the influx of larger numbers will pose a greater threat to security.

At first we thought that Chorao was little more than a scattered spread of simple villages. As we began spending more time there and conversed with new-made friends, we were amazed to learn that Chorao had a glorious past. This led me to research the island in greater detail. Many, even from Goa, have not heard of Chorao (pronounced 'show-rao'). It is an island about 5 kms from Panjim, held in the embrace of the Mapusa River flowing in from the north and the Mandovi River from the south. To get there, one could take the ferry from Ribandar which is on the road from Panjim to Old Goa. The boat ride takes about 20 minutes. Across the island, to the west, is another ferry crossing that links Chorao to Pomburpa and takes about five minutes. A third approach to the island is from Bicholim over a short-spanned bridge across a rivulet. This is the route we use when we arrive by train at Thivim.

There's a romantic legend about how the island got its name: Yashoda, mother of Krishna, threw seven diamonds into the Mandovi River. The biggest one she called 'chudamani', meaning 'stunning precious stone' in Sanskrit. This became 'Chodan' or 'Chodna' as it is still called by many. The Portuguese changed the name to 'Chorao'. Of the 17 islands of Goa, Chorao, spread over 21 sq. kms is the largest and most diverse of all, with a wide variety of flora and fauna.

Vasco da Gama found the sea route to India and arrived in Calicut in 1498, but it was Alphonse de Albuquerque who first made it to Goa around 1510. It is said that the island of Chorao was one of the first places to be captured by the Portuguese but I am unable to say how far this is true. The earliest known settlers on this island were 10 families of the Goud Saraswat Brahmins. However, with the arrival of the Portuguese, there were forced conversions and eventually the Jesuits Christianized large tracts of the islands of Chorao and Divar and also Salcette. There were three villages that mainly figured in the saga of Christianization in Chorao: Maddel, Orando and the village Horta. By 1552, 10 per cent of Chorao's population of 3,000 was Christian,

409

but by 1560 there appears to have been mass conversions to catholicism, and the upper caste Hindus chose to leave and settle elsewhere.

In his zeal to bring Christ to the natives as quickly as he could, St. Francis Xavier is said to have petitioned the king of Portugal to order an Inquisition in Goa. King John III, reputed to be a bigoted fanatic, favoured a policy of enforced mass conversions and instituted the Inquisition in Goa in 1560 (which was eight years after St. Francis died). I have necessarily had to condense this conquest of Goa by the Portuguese and the often brutal methods they used to convert the natives. It makes me feel ashamed to think of how terribly the Hindus were made to suffer at the hands of religious fanatics who believed they were doing God's work. (Is it poetic justice that today the tables have been turned?) Many ancient Hindu temples were destroyed by the Portuguese, and those who refused to convert had their lands and valuables confiscated and handed over to the Jesuits. The Hindu Brahmins managed to smuggle some of their deities to Naroa and Marcel where they are still worshipped. There are at least three big Hindu temples on Chorao as well as some smaller shrines, which demonstrate how Hindus and Christians now co-exist peacefully on this island.

Overlooking the entire island, from its highest point 93 mts above sea level is a shrine dedicated to Christ the King. From here you get a panoramic view of Bardez and Panjim and also parts of Old Goa with its many convents and churches. Unfortunately, the dense and unkempt vegetation all around obstructs some of the spectacular views. The first church on the island was the Church of Nossa Senhora da Graca (Our Lady of Grace) erected in 1551. On feast days, large fairs would be held there; these attracted foreign merchants who came to trade horses, camels and textiles. A second church of Our Lady of Grace was built facing east, not too far from the first one, at some time between the years 1598 and 1648. Construction of the third church which is now in existence in Maddel was begun in 1855 at a very different location from the first two. It was blessed and opened for public worship in 1860, closed again to erect a new roof, and re-opened for worship in 1903. This church faces north and is about one kilometre from the Maddel ferry.

The first church in the village of Querem, erected in 1569 by the Jesuits was known as the church of the Infant Jesus. Later it became the Church of St. Bartholomew. It is said to have been rebuilt and expanded in 1649. Set on a small hill that virtually separates east from west, this church faces west towards the Arabian Sea and is now the oldest church on the island. St. Bartholomew is said to be the disciple, Nathaniel, whom Jesus saw sitting under a fig tree and of whom He said, 'Here is a true Israelite in whom there is nothing false'. A chapel on the other side of the hill facing east is named *Nossa Senhora De Saude*. This was in Boctavaddo now referred to as '*Saude*'. It is said to be the oldest monument on the Island, but this is not entirely correct because though the original façade of the first chapel was retained, the chapel itself was re-built in 1940.

The Plague that struck Goa in the late 16th century triggered a general exodus from the capital city of Old Goa, fuelled by the imminent danger of an enemy attack (probably by the Dutch). Together with the commoners, the Portuguese noblemen, known as *fidalgos*, also moved to the islands of Divar and Chorao and had sprawling mansions surrounded by gardens and palm groves. Instead of glass, the window 'panes' in many houses consisted of thin polished oyster-shells set in lattice work – one may still come across these in old bungalows in Goa. Chorao came to be referred to as *Ilha dos fidalgos*, or Island of noblemen. Some of these were proud and arrogant. It seems that persons who failed to remove their hats or head-coverings while passing by the opulent fidalgo mansions on the main road were pelted with stones – which were even collected and kept on the verandas as ready ammunition. In effect, people had to keep their heads uncovered from the ferry of Orando (which was located on the West of the island near Our Lady of Grace Church) till the border of the village of Santetim. And when the *fidalgos* went to church for Mass, a special place was reserved to stack their fancy umbrellas of red damask. The affluence of the people of the island attracted merchants who came even from foreign lands bringing merchandise of luxury items.

Few traces remain of the fancy fidalgo mansions. They were built mainly of compacted mud and stone, and disintegrated due to lack of maintenance. If you experience the intensity of the monsoons in Goa and see the havoc they can cause, especially to a house that has been shut up and left neglected for even a few years, not to mention the devastation that termites can wreak in a short span, you will realize how the lordly villas and so many houses crumbled into heaps of rubble, leaving not a trace of the splendour of bygone days. A walk around the island will reveal quite a few of these ruins.

As for the poorer inhabitants of the island, they spread out and settled in pockets around Chorao, but most preferred the areas around the church of Graca, as it was close to the ferry from where they could easily commute to the mainland for work. This explains why an area of just 4 sq. kms of the large island was so densely populated. When the plague broke out in Chorao in June 1775, the first to be affected were the people living in this area and the village of Querem. Entire families were wiped out while others left the island and settled elsewhere. Only a handful, not wishing to leave the land of their ancestors, remained.

I was truly impressed to find out that Chorao once boasted of a University which taught Sanskrit and Ancient Literature and was affiliated to the University of Benares. In 1761, a Seminary called *Real Colegio de Educcacao de Chorao* took its place. A woodcut in the book, 'The island of Chorao', by Monsignor Gomes Catao shows that the Seminary was located on a level directly below the Chapel of St. Jerome in the village of Horta. The chapel was formerly known as the Chapel of the Celestial School. ('Celestial' because it belonged to the Seminary where spiritual subjects were taught.) It was polygonal in shape, had an elegant dome which rested on Grecian style columns and had perfect acoustics. Nobody knows how the rumour started that treasures lay concealed within the walls of this chapel. As a result there were indiscriminate excavations of the walls which were stripped bare. Strangely, the chapel still stands despite being abandoned for centuries and being exposed to the elements on the top of a hill. There's no doubt that this monument survived only because it was maintained and re-built by different people from time to time. The vicar of the Church of Graca had it repaired in 1900. He cleared the vast grove of trees that blocked the view of the building and re-opened it to the public on 17 August 1901. It was further extensively renovated in 1959 by the Department of Public Works. Recently a local tried to take over the land by breaking the steps leading up to the chapel, but a public official who was invited to a function organized at that location, took note and ensured that the steps were restored and the property protected as a Heritage site. The cupola of St. Jerome's Chapel can be seen from the Maddel ferry if you look towards the north of the island. The feast of St. Jerome is celebrated with a mass in this chapel once a year. As for the seminary, all traces of it have disappeared, though one can still catch glimpses of sections of the boundary wall, now shrouded in foliage, which runs alongside the main road.

Coming to present day Chorao ... When approaching the island from the Ribandar side, you see little except dense mangroves. These cloak the Dr. Salim Ali Bird Sanctuary, which covers an area of just 1.8 sq. kms but nurtures over 400 species of local and migratory birds, and also some animals. To name some of the birds one could hope to see, there are kingfishers, mynas, parrots and parakeets, bee-eaters, blue-throated barbets, pheasants, jungle fowl, quail, shrikes, white-breasted water hens, orioles, drongos, cuckoos, bulbuls, owls, babblers, flycatchers, tailor and weaver birds, magpies, robins, wagtails, house sparrows, egrets, eagles and vultures, and even exotic peacocks.

When our relatives from London, Horace and Joan Rodricks, stayed with us in February 2011, we visited the sanctuary for the very first time. Waking up early one morning, we drove to the Orando ferry near Maddel where we were met by the guide. I was appalled when I saw the canoe in which we were to travel but it was too late to turn back and so we gingerly climbed in one at a time and sat on dirty upturned soda crates. Each move tilted the canoe and I was petrified that it might overturn and land us all in the river. I was shocked also when the outboard motor was switched on and felt sure that any birds in the vicinity would scatter at our approach. However the boatman-guide, who seemed knowledgeable, cut the motor once we entered the inland waterways and paddled around silently. Apart from many egrets, herons, sandpipers, cormorants and a large Adjutant stork which took off quickly as we came into sight, we saw little else and we all found the expedition quite disappointing. The person who booked us on this trip told us that we should go at high tide, whereas the guide said that we would have seen much more at low tide. Who is right I'll never know because I don't intend to risk another canoe ride in order to find out.

Having been to the sanctuary, I can now say for a fact that we see many more birds inside our resort than we did within the sanctuary. We have spent most of the summer and monsoon months (while editing this book in 2011) on Chorao, and the bird activity here is something amazing. Swallows have built their mud nest under our balcony and they keep busily flying in and out all day, a pair of hornbills came several times in search of a suitable nesting place, the 'seven sisters' birds continue their daily noisy family squabbles, the magpies enjoy frisking in the bird bath we put out, the many sunbirds and finches (some, scarcely bigger than one's thumb) flit playfully in the bushes around us, the peacocks are in the thicket outside the compound but keep wandering into the Resort (their call is like a cat meowing with a hoarse throat), and of course the bulbuls, with the sweetest of whistles. One pays us a daily visit at around 5.30 pm (I call him my 5.30 bulbul) and we have a whistling duet for quite some time. The huge black-brown koels are shy creatures and scoot off when you approach. Several owls doze peacefully during the day under the eaves of one of the cottages, tired out from their nightly prowls. Occasionally, I heard a sound that scared me no end at first – it's like someone giving you the heavy breathing treatment at the other end of the phone line! I have not been able to find out from which rara avis this comes. And as I edit this, several finches are building a community nest in the frangipani tree in our side garden.

There were never many (if any) crows on the island but recently they have begun to make a bit of a nuisance of themselves and seem to be bringing in more of their kind. We're afraid that these noisy and territorial birds may frighten off the beautiful island birds we have enjoyed watching in quiet solitude. Sitting on the balcony one evening, we saw one of them leading about five others and giving them loud cawing instructions as they flew swiftly and very determinedly towards some unknown destination on the island. On another day, while I was returning on the ferry, I noticed one perched on the roof and cawing continuously and loudly. I also noticed two large beautiful fish eagles perched on a nearby coconut tree and when one of them flew gracefully down to the water, the crow immediately went after it to attack and chase it away; I was surprised that the larger bird did not turn and fight back. Perhaps the eagle was just better mannered!

The fauna include animals like crocodiles, otters, mongoose, jackals, flying squirrel, foxes, wild boar, monitor lizards, chameleons, snakes (a high population of which helps to keep the rodent numbers in check,) and many species of colourful frogs. Some say that the foxes have been hunted to extinction by the peacocks that have proliferated on the island. They used to be confined mainly to the hills but recently they seem to be spreading out even in the plains. We can tell from their calls when they are quite close to us and when they enter our complex. In fact, once when we returned to Goa after a long absence, we found a few peacock feathers in the garden and were told by the staff that there was a fight between a peacock and a snake. In the process, both were killed, but considering the peacock is our national bird, they buried it, while the poor snake was unceremoniously flung over the wall. Crocodiles have been seen sunning themselves on the banks of a few inland waterways nearer Aldona, and 'crocodile spotting' trips can be booked. Recently some friends told us that they had seen large otters near the Pomburpa ferry, but I have not yet had any such luck. With so many rivers and waterways, estuaries and lagoons, there is an abundance of a variety of fish. The mangrove ecosystem acts as a habitat for smaller fish and insects, and are rich feeding grounds for the birds. In addition, there are lobsters, shrimp and oysters and a species of black crab which is considered a great delicacy. A common daily sight is locals fishing at various spots, and often they get a good catch. As for the flora, apart from the dense mangroves around the water's edge, there are the ubiquitous coconut and cashew trees (Goa is well known for its coconut *feni* and cashew *feni*), deciduous vegetation like teak, varieties of bamboo cane, chillar, Maratha, bhirand, and fruits like mango, jackfruit, pineapple and blackberries.

The ferries are Chorao's lifeline. During the Portuguese occupation of Goa, before the present-day ferry service, there were Gasoline Motor Boats. The first class section was located within the sheltered portion inside the boat, while the second class passengers had to remain outside in all weathers. The boats plied from the Lovell Jetty in Chorao to Panjim on the mainland, stopping on the way at Divar Island and Maddel. Another service operated from Aldona to Panjim, stopping at Ambarim and Pomburpa. After the Portuguese left Goa, these jetties were left to deteriorate. I have visited the Lovell and Ambarim jetties which are now in very bad shape but still have a lovely ambience, the latter especially is an out-of-the-world venue for a twilight party (though mosquito protection is essential). Once vehicles started to use ferries, new ones had to be built for the crossings from Maddel and from Pomburpa. Today pedestrians and two-wheelers travel free, four-wheelers pay Rs.7 at Pomburpa and Rs.10 at Ribandar. The ferries shut down at night – but if you honk your car horn and flash your lights you can wake the operators to take you across on a 'special' for Rs.55.

When I used an excerpt from this chapter as part of my 2010 Christmas newsletter, I mentioned that I would be interested in getting hold of a CD of the film 'Sea Wolves', because it was shot in Chorao in 1980, at the Lovell Jetty, situated directly behind the large family house belonging to Dr. Chico and the late Dr. Neela Vaz. Our son-in-law, Kerman, told me that he had managed to get hold of a copy for me and even managed to send it to me from New York, but unfortunately, I have not yet had time to view it as I have been caught up in one job or another since then. Though the movie did not get such good reviews I was fascinated to know that the big star cast of Gregory Peck, Roger Moore, David Niven and others were actually on Chorao. I believe they would often stroll down the road to have a drink or a meal at the small family-run Lafayette Bar, which is still in business, but has never capitalized on the fact that it was the watering hole of celebrity guests. The film was based on the book 'Boarding Party' by James Leasor. During World War II, British intelligence based in India established that information was being passed to the U-Boats by a radio transmitter hidden on board one of the three German merchant ships that were docked in Mormugao. As a result, German submarines sank thousands of tons of British shipping. Because of Portugal's neutrality, the German ships could not be attacked by the regular forces, so a territorial unit of ageing British expatriates was

417

co-opted to carry out the mission. 'Boarding Party' dramatized the covert attack carried out by the Calcutta Light Horse regiment. During the first 11 days of March 1943, the U-boats had sunk 12 Allied ships in the Indian Ocean but after the Light Horse raid on 9 March 1943, only one ship was lost for the remainder of that month.

I'm sure there will be more interesting facts on Chorao that will come to light in future, but for now I am happy to be ending my travelogue with this chapter. It's a fitting and peaceful 'Alleluia' to roads well travelled and lives fully lived.

EPILOGUE

"I've lived a life that's full
I've travelled each and every highway
And more, much more than this I did it my way."

I chose to end this travelogue with my chapter on Goa, and Chorao in particular. We had hoped to spend the rest of our days in that island paradise, but several factors and events in 2011 have led us to think more seriously of our 'old age'. We still hope, like Fr. Luigi Jellici, 'to die young, but not for a long time'. With that in mind, we are moving to a more senior-friendly place, still in Goa, but no longer on our beautiful island.

At the risk of seeming to show off, I wish to correct any impression readers may have formed that our travels took us only to the foreign lands covered in this travelogue and, likewise, the Northeast of India. Joe and I both consider ourselves very fortunate in having been able to visit so very many places in this incredibly diverse country of ours. Compiling the list below gave me a thrill, which was all the more as we just did not have the means to think of travel even for our honeymoon in Goa we first had to open up the envelopes of cash gifts received at our wedding.

So here are some of the names I can recall of other places visited by both or one of us, on one or more occasion, for short or longer stays, for seminars, or holidays, on work, or pilgrimage. Starting with Maharashtra: Panvel, Alibaug, Lonavla, Khandala, Nigdi, Pune, Mahableshwar, Deolali, Nashik, Ratnagiri, Kolhapur, Sholapur, Aurangabad, Nagpur; Dalhousie in Himachal Pradesh; Amritsar, Jalandar and Chandigarh in Punjab; Parvanoo in Haryana, and of course New Delhi; Agra, Kanpur, Allahabad, Lucknow and Varanasi in Uttar Pradesh; Jodhpur, Jaipur and Udaipur in Rajasthan; Indore, Ujjain, Bhopal and Mhow in Madhya Pradesh; Patna and Ranchi in

419

Bihar; Ahmedabad and Baroda in Gujarat; Mangalore, Bangalore, Mysore and Malkhed in Karnataka; Hyderabad and Vishakhapatnam in Andhra Pradesh; Chennai, Coimbatore, Madurai, Ooty, Kanyakumari in Tamilnadu; Ernakulam, Kochi, Thodupuzha, Thekkady, Munnar, Thiruvanthapuram, Barananganam and more in Kerala... We cannot leave out Goa, which is now our second home. Our one regret is that we have not yet been to beautiful Kashmir, but hopefully that can still be remedied; it's not too late.

It would take a chapter and more to explain how we do it, but even if I spelled it out, most would still remain rooted in disbelief, refusing to believe that we did not have fat bank balances to start with. On the contrary! My ability to 'create' and visualise what I want in life, and allow it to manifest itself in the physical world, has also helped me reach my potential in many spheres and achieve all I set out to do. This in turn has shaped my destiny. So instead of focusing on, 'How much money do I need to collect in order to make this trip?', think, see, feel, 'WOW! This is the kind of trip I really want to make'.

It truly works. Pack your bags. Bon Voyage!